Lecture Notes in Computer Science   1681

Edited by G. Goos, J. Hartmanis and J. van Leeuwen

W0050925

Springer

Berlin
Heidelberg
New York
Barcelona
Hong Kong
London
Milan
Paris
Singapore
Tokyo

David A. Forsyth   Joseph L. Mundy
Vito di Gesú   Roberto Cipolla (Eds.)

Shape, Contour and Grouping in Computer Vision

Springer

Series Editors

Gerhard Goos, Karlsruhe University, Germany
Juris Hartmanis, Cornell University, NY, USA
Jan van Leeuwen, Utrecht University, The Netherlands

Volume Editors

David A. Forsyth
University of California at Berkeley, Computer Science Division
Berkeley, CA 94720, USA
E-mail: daf@cs.berkeley.edu

Joseph L. Mundy
G.E. Corporate Research and Development
1 Research Circle, Niskayuna, NY 12309, USA
E-mail: mundy@crd.ge.com

Vito di Gesú
Palermo University, C.I.T.C.
Palermo, Sicily, Italy
E-mail: digesu@dipmat.math.unipa.it

Roberto Cipolla
University of Cambridge, Department of Engineering
Cambridge CB2 1PZ, UK
E-mail: cipolla@eng.cam.ac.uk

Cataloging-in-Publication data applied for
Die Deutsche Bibliothek - CIP-Einheitsaufnahme

Shape, contour and grouping in computer vision / David A.
Forsyth ... (ed.). - Berlin ; Heidelberg ; New York ; Barcelona ; Hong
Kong ; London ; Milan ; Paris ; Singapore ; Tokyo : Springer, 1999
  (Lecture notes in computer science ; Vol. 1681)
  ISBN 3-540-66722-9

CR Subject Classification (1998): I.4, I.3, I.5, I.2.10

ISSN 0302-9743
ISBN 3-540-66722-9 Springer-Verlag Berlin Heidelberg New York

Typesetting: Camera-ready by author
SPIN: 10704339   06/3142 – 5 4 3 2 1 0   Printed on acid-free paper

Preface

Computer vision has been successful in several important applications recently. Vision techniques can now be used to build very good models of buildings from pictures quickly and easily, to overlay operation planning data on a neurosurgeon's view of a patient, and to recognise some of the gestures a user makes to a computer. Object recognition remains a very difficult problem, however. The key questions to understand in recognition seem to be: (1) how objects should be represented and (2) how to manage the line of reasoning that stretches from image data to object identity.

An important part of the process of recognition – perhaps, almost all of it – involves assembling bits of image information into helpful groups. There is a wide variety of possible criteria by which these groups could be established – a set of edge points that has a symmetry could be one useful group; others might be a collection of pixels shaded in a particular way, or a set of pixels with coherent colour or texture. Discussing this process of grouping requires a detailed understanding of the relationship between what is seen in the image and what is actually out there in the world.

The international workshop on shape, contour and grouping in computer vision collected a set of invited participants from the US and the EC to exchange research ideas. This volume consists of expanded versions of papers delivered at that workshop. The volume contains an extensive introduction consisting of three articles: one sketches out common cause on what is understood in recognition, and the other two indicate different possible agendas for future research in the area. The editors have encouraged authors to produce papers with a strong survey aspect, and this volume contains broad surveys of shape representation, model selection, and shading models as well as discursive papers on learning in character recognition and probabilistic methods in grouping. These papers are accompanied by more focussed research papers that give a good picture of the current state of the art in research on shape, contour and grouping in computer vision.

It remains for the editors to thank the participants, the sponsoring institutions (which are listed separately), the management and staff of the Hotel Torre Artale, and Professor and Mrs. di Gésu who, with help from Roberto Cipolla, handled local arrangements admirably.

August 1999   David Forsyth

Organization

The international workshop on shape, contour and grouping was organised jointly by David Forsyth (U.C. Berkeley), Joe Mundy (GE Center for Research and Development), Vito Di Gesú (Palermo University) and Roberto Cipolla (Cambridge University).

Sponsoring Institutions

The National Science Foundation, 1601 Wilson Blvd, Arlington, VA22230, USA under grant IIS-9712426

GE Center For Research and Development, 1 Research Circle, Niskayuna, NY 12309

The Centro Interdipartimentale Tecnologie della Conoscenza (C.I.T.C.), Palermo University, Palermo, Sicily

Table of Contents

V   Representation and Recognition

VI   Statistics, Learning, and Recognition

Part I

Introduction

Introduction

David Forsyth and Joe Mundy

Computer Science Division, U.C. Berkeley, Berkeley, CA 94720, USA
daf@cs.berkeley.edu,
http://www.cs.berkeley.edu/~daf

Abstract. Our understanding of object recognition can address the needs of only the most stylised applications. There is no prospect of the automated motorcars of Dickmanns *et al.* knowing what is in front of them anytime soon; searchers for pictures of the pope kissing a baby must search on a combination of text, guesswork and patience; current vision based HCI research relies on highly structured backgrounds; and we may safely guess that the intelligence community is unlikely to be able to dispense with image analysts anytime soon. This volume contains a series of contributions that attack important problems in recognition.

1 What We Do Well

We can solve some problems rather well. Unfortunately, these problems seem to be connected only rather tenuously with potential applications of object recognition. This is because all current algorithms for object recognition all model recognition as direct exploration of correspondence. Each belongs to a small number of types, each with characteristic individual misbehaviours. Much of this material is (or should be!) common cause, and will be reviewed only very briefly.

1.1 Geometric Detail for Point-like Primitives

Point-like primitives project like points; points project to points, lines to lines, conics to conics, etc., with no more complex geometric behaviour than occlusion. This means that, though objects can look different from different views, these changes are highly structured. For point-like primitives, correspondences between image and object features can be searched in various ways for detailed geometric models (a fair sample of this literature includes [2, 3, 4, 6, 7, 9, 10, 11, 18, 19, 23, 24, 25]; there are hundreds of papers dealing with variant algorithms or specific technical issues). Typical algorithms of this class can usually find instances drawn from a small number of object models (sometimes from parametric families) against a background of moderate clutter and despite the effects of occlusion. Problems include: the restriction to exact geometry; the limited number of primitives; the difficulty of building sufficient appropriate models; the general unreliability of verification and segmentation; and the restriction to a small number of models.

D.A. Forsyth et al. (Eds.): Shape, Contour ..., LNCS 1681, pp. 3–8, 1999.

1.2   Some Cases of Curved Primitives

The difficulty with curved surfaces is that, though the change of outline with viewpoint is highly structured, this structure is generally complicated — so complicated that a detailed record is basically unmanageable. A great deal is known about particular cases, none particularly practical at present; all this information tends to suggest that *given a geometric class*, outline is a powerful constraint on geometry and viewpoint. There appear to be class-specific constraints on outlines for all cases, though only very few useful cases are known. This picture is complicated by the absence of any kind of covariant approximation theorem. We know no useful geometric theorems about the outlines of surfaces that "almost" belong to a particular class, and all indications are that such theorems are difficult to get.

1.3   Template Matching

Template matching works rather well on some kinds of recognition problem (finding frontal faces is a good example; while some details are being worked out, the problem is quite well understood [1, 8, 14, 20, 21, 16]). Crude template matching behaves poorly under change of aspect and of illumination, but this can be resolved by adopting parametric families of templates (e.g. [12, 13, 15]). This approach requires objects to appear on their own, and becomes unwieldy for all but a few degrees of freedom. For more complex cases, models can consist of composites of primitives, which are themselves from parametric families of templates (e.g. [1, 5, 8, 14, 17, 22]).

2   What This Volume Describes

The authors of this piece see two quite different agendas for future research on object recognition. These agendas have been sketched in the next two papers. In the first, Forsyth argues that the main current difficulty in building acceptable recognition systems is the poor management of uncertainty within those systems; some sort of Bayesian reform is long overdue. He takes the position that many difficult issues — for example, what is an appropriate representation for a particular set of objects? or how should distinct cues be used to come up with a single recognition strategy? — are essentially empirical and statistical in nature, and that the community should be attempting to master and apply various statistical methods. In the second, Mundy argues that empirical methods can offer no fundamental breakthrough, but that better understanding of appropriate physical and formal models — for example, an understanding of the relationship between the geometry of objects, their surface properties and their image appearance — might. The rest of this volume consists of contributions from leading researchers, dealing with shape, shading, grouping, cue integration and recognition. Each section contains both research papers and papers with review and introductory material.

2.1   Shape

For the vast majority of recognition problems, shape is an important cue. In *"Shape models and object recognition,"* Jean Ponce and colleagues describe the current state of the art in shape modelling. The paper demonstrates a variety of representations for recognition, including their reworking of the idea of a generalised cylinder. They describe representations in terms of "parts", and show one way to get a canonical decomposition of an object into parts from an image. Finally, the paper discusses how the effects of viewing direction are themselves affected by image scale.

The relationship between image measurements and object shape is complicated. This relationship has combinatorial, as well as geometric, aspects as Stefan Carlson shows in *"Order structure, correspondence and shape based categories."* The order structure of groups of points does not change arbitrarily as the groups are projected to an image; this fact can be used to reason about the object in view.

Plane curves are often subject to some form of group action before they are seen in an image. A standard mechanism for discounting this group action is to represent a curve by a plot of invariant properties against an invariant parameter. This approach usually requires that one be able to measure an inconvenient number of derivatives. In *"Quasi-invariant parametrisations and their applications in computer vision"*, Sato and Cipolla show how to use a quasi-invariant parametrisation for representing curves. This has the advantage that fewer derivatives need be measured if one is willing to accept some variation in the representation.

2.2   Shading

Illumination is an important source of the variation in object appearance. In *"Representations for recognition under variable illumination,"* Kriegman, Belhumeur and Georghiades describe a device called the *illumination cone*, which records the appearance of an object under all possible illuminants. They show that this convex cone can be used to recognise faces, despite substantial shading variations which confound the usual strategies. This theory does not treat shadows, which are dealt with in *"Shadows, shading, and projective ambiguity,"* by Belhumeur, Kriegman and Yuille. Objects that give the same shadow pattern in a fixed view are geometrically equivalent up to a *generalised* bas-relief *ambiguity*; furthermore, objects can be reconstructed up to this ambiguity from multiple images under multiple, unknown light sources.

2.3   Grouping

Grouping is the process of assembling image components that appear to belong together. There are a variety of reasons that components may belong together — in *"Grouping in the normalized cut framework"* Malik and colleagues describe a mechanism that segments an image into components that satisfy a global goodness criterion. Their mechanism is attractive because (as they show) it can be used for a variety of different grouping cues, including intensity, texture, motion and contour.

Another reason that image components may belong together is that they lie on the same plane in the world. In *"Geometric grouping of repeated elements within images,"* Schaffalitzky and Zisserman show how to determine when a pattern consists of plane elements, repeated according to a variety of rules. They determine the basic element of the pattern, and can then reconstruct the pattern because repetition rules on the plane lead to repetition rules in the image in a well defined way.

In satellite image applications, both the pose of the ground plane and the calibration of the camera are usually known. This means that one can tell whether objects lying on the ground plane appear to have a symmetry, as Curwen and Mundy demonstrate in *"Constrained symmetry for change detection."* This cue makes it possible to group together interesting edge fragments, which are likely to have come from, for example, human artifacts.

In *"Grouping based on coupled diffusion maps,"* Proesmans and Van Gool describe the use of anisotropic diffusion processes for grouping. In this approach, pixels are connected by a diffusion process that is modified to prevent smoothing over large gradients. They show examples where this process is used for segmentation, for detecting symmetries, for stereoscopic reconstruction and for motion reconstruction.

2.4   Representation and Recognition

In *"Integrating geometric and photometric information for image retrieval,"* Schmid, Zisserman and Mohr describe a local representation of images in terms of *interest points.* These interest points are defined using photometric information; collections of interest points yield a representation that incorporates information about shape and about photometry. This representation can be used to match query images against an image database. They show how the representation can be extended to 3D curves, using the osculating plane of the curve, to obtain a matching process that can match 3D curves between small baseline stereo pairs.

Mundy and Saxena describe another approach for integrating photometric and geometric information in *"Towards the integration of geometric and appearance-based object recognition."* They propose using facet models of surface brightness to index object identity, and compare renderings using the Oren-Nayar model of surface reflectance to real data. This approach is extended to colour images in *"Recognising objects using color annotated adjacency graphs,"* by Tu, Saxena and Hartley. In this paper, objects are represented by adjacency graphs of coloured faces, which are matched using a graph matcher. Their approach uses a method from linear algebra for computing graph compatibilities that is somewhat reminiscent of the method of Malik *et al.*.

In *"A cooperating strategy for object recognition,"* Chella, Di Gesù, Infantino, Intravaia and Valenti describe a complete recognition system. Objects are represented using either interest points or a discrete symmetry transform; their system uses cooperating agents to mediate the crucially important relationship between top-down and bottom-up information flow.

2.5 Statistics, Learning, and Recognition

Methods from statistics and from statistical learning theory are starting to have a substantial impact on the practice of computer vision. A classical statistical problem that turns up in many different vision applications is *model selection* — from which of several models was the data set obtained? This issue must be dealt with in recognition, where it is often known as *verification* — the issue is *do the pixels in this region come from an object or the background?* — in structure from motion (*what kind of camera produced this scene?*), and in a variety of other areas of vision. Torr reviews this topic in *"Model selection for two view geometry: a review."*

Forsyth, Haddon and Ioffe describe probabilistic algorithms for object recognition in *"Finding objects by grouping primitives."* These algorithms are structured around the use of simple primitives: firstly, people and animals are represented as cylinders, and can then be found by a grouping process that assembles cylinders that together "look like" a person; secondly, folds in cloth are found using a classifier that recognizes their appearance, and then the Markov chain Monte Carlo method is used to group them into assemblies that look like buckle patterns in clothing. It is usually difficult to know what to use as a primitive in this sort of work; the paper argues that the criteria are statistical in nature, and that primitives could be learned from data.

A more detailed committment to learning appears in in *"Object Recognition with Gradient-Based Learning."* by LeCun, Haffner, Bottou and Bengio. Images of hand-written characters are filtered by a sequence of filters at various scales, and the filter outputs passed to a neural net classifier. Not only the classifier, but the filters themselves are learned from example data, using a procedure known as *gradient based learning*. Convolutional neural networks are then rigged together, to yield a *space displacement network*, that can read a sequence of handwritten characters. Information about the probabilistic structure of handwritten numbers is incorporated using a *graph transformer network*.

References

[1] M.C. Burl, T.K. Leung, and P. Perona. Face localisation via shape statistics. In *Int. Workshop on Automatic Face and Gesture Recognition*, 1995.

[2] O.D. Faugeras and M. Hebert. The representation, recognition, and locating of 3-D objects. *International Journal of Robotics Research*, 5(3):27–52, Fall 1986.

[3] D.A. Forsyth, J.L. Mundy, A.P. Zisserman, C. Coelho, A. Heller, and C.A. Rothwell. Invariant descriptors for 3d object recognition and pose. *PAMI*, 13(10):971–991, 1991.

[4] W.E.L. Grimson and T. Lozano-Pérez. Localizing overlapping parts by searching the interpretation tree. *IEEE Trans. Patt. Anal. Mach. Intell.*, 9(4):469–482, 1987.

[5] C-Y. Huang, O.T. Camps, and T. Kanungo. Object recognition using appearance-based parts and relations. In *IEEE Conf. on Computer Vision and Pattern Recognition*, pages 877–83, 1997.

[6] D.P. Huttenlocher and S. Ullman. Object recognition using alignment. In *Proc. Int. Conf. Comp. Vision*, pages 102–111, London, U.K., June 1987.

[7] D.J. Kriegman and J. Ponce. On recognizing and positioning curved 3D objects from image contours. *IEEE Trans. Patt. Anal. Mach. Intell.*, 12(12):1127–1137, December 1990.

[8] T.K. Leung, M.C. Burl, and P. Perona. Finding faces in cluttered scenes using random labelled graph matching. In *Int. Conf. on Computer Vision*, 1995.

[9] D. Lowe. Three-dimensional object recognition from single two-dimensional images. *Artificial Intelligence*, 31(3):355–395, 1987.

[10] J.L. Mundy and A. Zisserman. *Geometric Invariance in Computer Vision*. MIT Press, Cambridge, Mass., 1992.

[11] J.L. Mundy, A. Zisserman, and D. Forsyth. *Applications of Invariance in Computer Vision*, volume 825 of *Lecture Notes in Computer Science*. Springer-Verlag, 1994.

[12] H. Murase and S. Nayar. Visual learning and recognition of 3D objects from appearance. *Int. J. of Comp. Vision*, 14(1):5–24, 1995.

[13] S.K. Nayar, S.A. Nene, and H. Murase. Real time 100 object recognition system. In *Int. Conf. on Robotics and Automation*, pages 2321–5, 1996.

[14] M. Oren, C. Papageorgiou, P. Sinha, and E. Osuna. Pedestrian detection using wavelet templates. In *IEEE Conf. on Computer Vision and Pattern Recognition*, pages 193–9, 1997.

[15] H. Plantinga and C. Dyer. Visibility, occlusion, and the aspect graph. *Int. J. of Comp. Vision*, 5(2):137–160, 1990.

[16] T. Poggio and Kah-Kay Sung. Finding human faces with a gaussian mixture distribution-based face model. In *Asian Conf. on Computer Vision*, pages 435–440, 1995.

[17] A.R. Pope and D.G. Lowe. Learning object recognition models from images. In *Int. Conf. on Computer Vision*, pages 296–301, 1993.

[18] L.G. Roberts. Machine perception of three-dimensional solids. In J.T. Tippett et al., editor, *Optical and Electro-Optical Information Processing*, pages 159–197. MIT Press, Cambridge, 1965.

[19] K. Rohr. Incremental recognition of pedestrians from image sequences. In *IEEE Conf. on Computer Vision and Pattern Recognition*, pages 9–13, 1993.

[20] H.A. Rowley, S. Baluja, and T. Kanade. Human face detection in visual scenes. In D.S. Touretzky, M.C. Mozer, and M.E. Hasselmo, editors, *Advances in Neural Information Processing 8*, pages 875–881, 1996.

[21] H.A. Rowley, S. Baluja, and T. Kanade. Neural network-based face detection. In *IEEE Conf. on Computer Vision and Pattern Recognition*, pages 203–8, 1996.

[22] C. Schmid and R. Mohr. Local grayvalue invariants for image retrieval. IEEE *Transactions on Pattern Analysis and Machine Intelligence*, 19(5):530–534, May 1997.

[23] D.W. Thompson and J.L. Mundy. Three-dimensional model matching from an unconstrained viewpoint. In *IEEE Int. Conf. on Robotics and Automation*, pages 208–220, Raleigh, NC, April 1987.

[24] S. Ullman. *High-level Vision: Object Recognition and Visual Cognition*. MIT Press, 1996.

[25] S. Ullman and R. Basri. Recognition by linear combination of models. *IEEE Trans. Patt. Anal. Mach. Intell.*, 13(10):992–1006, 1991.

An Empirical-Statistical Agenda for Recognition

David Forsyth

Computer Science Division, U.C. Berkeley, Berkeley, CA 94720, USA
daf@cs.berkeley.edu,
http://www.cs.berkeley.edu/~daf

This piece first describes what I see as the significant weaknesses in current understanding of object recognition. We lack good schemes for: using unreliable information — like radiometric measurements — effectively; integrating potentially contradictory cues; revising hypotheses in the presence of new information; determining potential representations from data; and suppressing individual differences to obtain abstract classes. The problems are difficult, but none are unapproachable, given a change of emphasis in our research.

All the important problems have a statistical flavour to them. Most involve a change of emphasis from the detailed study of specific cues to an investigation of techniques for turning cues into integrated representations. In particular, all have a statistical flavour, and can be thought of as inference problems. I show an example that suggests that methods of Bayesian inference can be used to attack these difficulties.

We have largely mapped out the the geometrical methods we need. Similarly, all the radiometric information that conceivably could be useful already exists. I believe that the next flowering of useful vision theories will occur when we engage in an aggressive study of statistics and probabilistic modelling, particularly methods of Bayesian inference.

1 What We Do Badly

The weaknesses in current understanding of object recogntion all appear to come from our conception of an object model as a passive, unstructured repository of detailed geometric information.

1.1 Managing Information

The literature is rich with individual cues to object identity, from surface colour to geometric primitives. It is unusual to have these cues agree on anything; the resulting embarrassment is avoided by not comparing the cues, or by ignoring such effete measures as colour or texture. This is a serious mistake. It is quite clear that it is generally better to have more cues, even if some are more reliable than others.

Our use of colour and shading information is still uncomfortably weak, probably because we don't have models that handle (or ignore) the nasty physical effects of interreflections or colour bleeding. I'm not aware of the use of texture

D.A. Forsyth et al. (Eds.): Shape, Contour ..., LNCS 1681, pp. 9–21, 1999.

in recognition, except in template matching approaches. Texture doesn't really lend itself to direct template matching — not every tiger has every stripe in the same place — but it can be described and these descriptions contain information. We ignore this information, probably because we don't have mechanisms for integrating it with other cues, and because we haven't properly formulated models that cope with individual variations (abstraction again!).

1.2   Abstraction

Performing recognition at a properly abstract level (where the "fish", "person" or "bicycle" decision is made before the species, height or manufacturer are known) is something we know nothing about. We know from computer science that hierarchies are the proper way to access large numbers of objects efficiently, and there is some evidence [20, 21] that people make different kinds of decision about object identity ("category-level" and "instance-level" discrimination), suggesting the presence of a hierarchy. In turn, this suggests that abstraction may help with efficiency.

All current recognition algorithms perform recognition at the level of individual instances in a flat modelbase; any category-level recognition is performed later. This leads to the characteristic ludicrously inefficient search through models. Implicitizing this search by using geometric invariants simply creates clogged hash tables; it does not solve the problem because it does not scale.

1.3   Segmentation

There is a suspicious profusion of white objects on black backgrounds in the current recognition literature (significant variants include multihued objects on green backgrounds, and black objects on white backgrounds). This is a product of the view that segmentation and recognition are distinct problems, and that when the early vision community gets round to solving segmentation, everything will be ok. The view is pernicious, and the practices it encourages are dubious. A recognition system that operated at a sensible level of abstraction would draw broad, generic distinctions between objects at first; a knowledge of these kinds of distinctions is precisely what the starting stages of segmentation needs. In other words, objects are segmented in wholes because they are objects; we should rig the segmentation process to find the kind of evidence that leads to the objects we are looking for.

This view of segmentation is usual in practice — this is what interest operators, lines and conics are all about — but exploring the full power of the view hasn't been easy because we have only the vaguest notion of what the evidence should be. The old-fashioned view is that objects should be modelled as composites of primitives — the term "part" is often used — and that finding image evidence of the presence of these primitives is what segmentation is about [2]. These primitives might be shapes (hence the GC/SHGC/Geon/etc. debate), but they might also be characteristic shading or colour events. The strength of this view is that one can see, dimly, how to build sensible recognition systems like this: one builds repeated segmentation processes that find very general, widely used primitives first and then assemble these primitives into larger and larger regions of image evidence. The segmentation is practicable, because *at each stage, we know what we're looking for.* Again, this is old news, but basically sensible news — for example, now the fuss about appearance based recognition has died down, that community is moving very quickly in this direction [9], precisely because it is the only way to deal with segmentation and complex model bases. The weakness is that we don't know what the primitives are, what the models look like, or how to build the models.

1.4   Learning

It would be a good thing if our recognition systems could recognise many objects, and if the recognition process did not require substantial reengineering each time a new object was encountered. Ideally, models of new objects could be obtained by showing the system various instances in various views. This is not necessarily an argument for *statistical* learning theory; these properties are have been built into geometric reasoning systems [22], although doing so generally requires some form of implicit statistical reasoning.

The selection of measurements, broadly interpreted, is poorly understood. Typical current recognition systems will use some set of geometrical measurements to determine whether an object is present; of course, there will be alternative sets of measurements that could be used. Which one should we use, and why? This is a narrow version of the problem of primitives — which primitives should we use in recognition, and why? Both problems appear, in abstract, to be model selection problems.

1.5   Nagging Issues

The state of verification is a disgrace; either we shouldn't do it (which could be preferred on the grounds that we're only doing it because we haven't assembled much of the available evidence for our hypothesis before testing it), or we should do it properly. The current practice of counting edge points and crossing fingers simply isn't good enough. The problem is one of hypothesis testing (or of discrete model selection) — to what degree does the image evidence in this region support the following object hypothesis? This is a fairly straightforward problem with relatively straightforward statistical solutions — model selection, again.

2   A Brief Sketch of Bayesian Inference

Probability provides a mechanism for comparing instances with a collective of previous examples; this mechanism makes it possible to combine evidence from various sources. The process of comparison is through a probabilistic model of the measurements produced given the state of the world. For example, we might take a large number of pictures of sunsets and estimate

$$P(\text{big red blob}|\text{picture is a sunset})$$

by a frequency estimate. This number could be interpreted either as a statement of expected frequencies, or as a "degree of belief" that a big red blob will appear in a picture of a sunset. It gives the probability of measurements, given the state of the world; this term is often referred to as the *conditional*, or *likelihood*.

The main use for a probabilistic model in recognition is inference. Generally, we expect to have a probabilistic model of the state of the world before we measured it. This is the prior — in the example, the probability that a picture taken from our collection is a picture of a sunset, or

$$P(\text{picture is a sunset})$$

The Bayesian philosophy says that all our knowledge of the state of the world is encapsulated in the *posterior* — the probability of a world state given observations. The posterior accounts for the effect of observations on the probability that (in our example) a picture taken from our collection is a picture of a sunset. By Bayes' rule, the posterior is proportional to the product of the prior and the likelihood, so we have

$$P(\text{picture is a sunset}|\text{big red blob}) \propto P(\text{big red blob}|\text{picture is a sunset})$$
$$\times P(\text{picture is a sunset})$$

Most computer vision researchers have seen this expression many times without any great delight. Its great importance is that *generative* models — which give the way that data is produced, given the state of the world — can be turned into recognition models just by multiplying by the prior. One common objection — that priors can be arbitrary — is, I think, empty; all but the silliest choices of prior are overwhelmed by data in the kinds of problem we wish to solve. The real problem is that we need to be able to compute with the resulting posterior, and that is where difficulties arise.

2.1   How Probabilistic Models Can Address Our Problems

The simple relationship between generative models and inference is the attraction of Bayesian models. If one accepts the basic hypothesis of the Bayesian philosophy — that the posterior encapsulates our knowledge of the world — information integration is simple. One just forms the posterior corresponding to the measurements available. No additional complications appear, because the generative model (or likelihood — which describes the process that leads to the measurements) is usually easy to obtain.

In the following piece, Joe Mundy makes the case that there is no canonical structure of class abstraction and so no basis for dealing with the world at any level other than that of instances. This may well be sound philosophy, but it is impractical system architecture. The advantage of class abstraction is, basically, that one kind of measurement can do multiple duty. Thus, it is worth finding extended regions with near parallel sides, because there are an awful lot of things that look rather like cylinders. Class hierarchies appear to offer efficient representations by making relatively small numbers of decisions to identify relatively large numbers of objects. If this promise can be realised, the fact that the hierarchy is artificial is irrelevant.

Probabilistic models simplify constructing class hierarchies because they can encode explicitly the variation between instances of a class. This yields an immediate solution to an old problem with geometric primitives: it is hard to prove anything useful about objects that are not *exactly* instances of the primitive class, but vary only slightly from instances. The solution is to build a likelihood model around the measurement. Thus, for example, if we are looking for human limbs we can benefit from the fact that the outlines are not only *not* straight and parallel, but the way that they differ from being straight and parallel is structured.

Probabilistic models may also help to determine appropriate primitives. I do not agree with Mundy's argument that a primitive decomposition is — or even should be — canonical. It seems more constructive to view a decomposition into parts, or primitives, as a convenience for representational efficiency. In this view, the distinctive properties of primitives are that they occur on many objects in similar forms; that their presence is a useful guide to the presence of an object; and that their presence leads to distinctive image properties to guide inference. These appear to me to be statistical criteria.

All these comments offer some hope for a rational theory of segmentation, *if we can extract information from posteriors easily.*

2.2   Using Posteriors

The attraction of the Bayesian view is that (given a decent generative model) all problems with integrating information disappear. Of course, the tricky bit is extracting information from the posterior, and this has tended to be the problem in the past. It is very easy to set up problems where the priors and the likelihoods all appear simple, and yet the posterior is very hard to handle (the colour constancy example given below is of this kind). Vision problems are too big and too disorderly to use conjugate distributions (an old-fashioned dodge of using models where the prior, likelihood and posterior all turn out to have an "easy" form). We might decide to choose a world model that maximises the posterior, but how do we get this maximum? Bayesian segmentation using Markov random fields foundered on this point.

The currently fashionable view in the statistical community says that information can be extracted from the posterior by drawing a large number of samples from that distribution. Thus, for example, if we wanted to decide whether to blow something up or not based on image evidence, we would form the posterior, draw samples from this, compute an expected utility for blowing it up and for not blowing it up by averaging the utilities for these samples, and choose the option with the larger expected utility[1].

Drawing samples from a posterior is not at all easy. Markov chain Monte Carlo methods appear to be the answer. A typical algorithm is the Metropolis-Hastings algorithm, which would produce in this case a sequence of hypotheses, by taking an hypothesis T_i and proposing a revised version, T_i'. The new hypothesis T_{i+1} is either T_i or T_i', depending (randomly) on how much better the posterior associated with T_i' is. Once sufficient iterations have completed, all subsequent T_i are samples drawn from the posterior; the number of iterations required to achieve this is often called the *burn in* time. These samples may or may not be correlated; if this correlation is low, the method is said to *mix* well. It is known how to apply this algorithm to chains whose domain of support is complicated (for example, the number of hypotheses may not be known *a priori*) [7].

Metropolis-Hastings algorithms should be viewed as a kind of souped up hypothesize and test process. We propose a representation of the world and accept or reject it based on the posterior; our representation of the *posterior* then consists of a large set of accepted proposals. This view justifies using current vision algorithms as a source of proposals. The crucial improvement is that we can use different, incompatible algorithms as distinct sources of proposals, and the samples we obtain represent the posterior incorporating all available measurements. The example in section 3 illustrates this approach in greater detail.

There are some serious algorithmic problems: it is not possible to tell reliably whether a chain has burnt in by looking at the samples the chain produces; chains can mix extremely slowly, and often do if not very carefully designed [10]; and the difference between a successful algorithm and a catastrophic failure rests on the proposal process. Exact sampling, or coupling from the past, is a (not terribly practical) method for dealing with the first problem [19, 17]; the other two are not going away anytime soon. The advantages of representing ambiguity and error explicitly appear to outweigh these difficulties.

3   An Example: Colour Constancy by Sampling

Colour constancy is a good simple example that has some of the flavour of recognition, in the sense that we are using a model to make inferences from image observations. In the simplest version, we are in a world of flat frontal surfaces whose diffuse reflectances belong to a low dimensional linear family, illuminated by a coloured source. We do not know the colour of the source, and wish to determine surface colour, whatever the source colour. The problem can seldom, if ever be solved exactly.

There are many different mechanisms, each of which gives a different estimate. It is usual to assume that the illuminant changes slowly over space; cues

---

[1] Right now, it would have to be a fairly slow target; but computers get faster.

include an assumption of constant average surface colour [3, 8, 11], the subspace
of receptor space to which the surfaces map [15], the presence of sharp changes
in image brightness [13], the fact that specularities typically take the source
colour [12, 14], and physical constraints on reflectance and/or illuminant [5, 4].
All of these cues are basically valid and all should be used. Let us go back to
the case of colour constancy. We would like to use the following constraints:

- Illuminants vary only slowly over space.
- Specularities yield cues to surface colour.
- Illuminants and reflectances are drawn from finite dimensional linear fami-
  lies.
- Reflectances are everywhere above 0.012 and below 0.96 in value (this gives
  an 80:1 dynamic range at each wavelength, consistent with other methods
  and physical evidence
- Illuminants are everywhere positive.

We ignore average reflectances, as they will be covered by the prior.

3.1   The Generative Model

We model surface reflectances as a sum of basis functions $\phi_j(\lambda)$, and assume
that reflectances are piecewise constant:

$$s(x, y, \lambda) = \sum_{j=0}^{n_s} \sigma_j(x, y) \phi_j(\lambda)$$

Here $\sigma_j(x, y)$ are a set of coefficients that vary over space according to some
model; in the example we describe, they are constant in a grid of boxes, where
the grid edges are not known in advance.

Similarly, we model illuminants as a sum of (possibly different) basis functions
ψ_i and assume that the spatial variation is given by the presence of a single point
source positioned at $\mathbf{p}$. The diffuse component due to the source is:

$$e_d(x, y, \lambda, \mathbf{p}) = d(x, y, \mathbf{p}) \sum_{i=0}^{n_e} \epsilon_i \psi_i(\lambda)$$

where ϵ_i are the coefficients of each basis function and $d(x, y, \mathbf{p})$ is a gain term
that represents the change in brightness of the source over the area viewed. The
specular component due to the source is:

$$e_m(x, y, \lambda, \mathbf{p}) = m(x, y, \mathbf{p}) \sum_{i=0}^{n_e} \epsilon_i \psi_i(\lambda)$$

where $m(x, y, \mathbf{p})$ is a gain term that represents the change in specular component
over the area viewed.

Standard considerations yield a model of the k'th receptor response as:

$$p_k(x, y) = \int s(x, y, \lambda)(e_d(x, y, \lambda, \mathbf{p}) + e_m(x, y, \lambda, \mathbf{p}))\rho_k(\lambda)d\lambda$$

$$= d(x, y, \mathbf{p}) \sum_{i,j} g_{ijk}\epsilon_i\sigma_j(x, y) + m(x, y, \mathbf{p}) \sum_i h_{ik}\epsilon_i$$

where $g_{ijk} = \int \rho_k(\lambda)\psi_i(\lambda)\phi_j(\lambda)d\lambda$ and $h_{ik} = \int \rho_k(\lambda)\psi_i(\lambda)d\lambda$. In this case, $\sigma_j(x, y)$ is piecewise constant with some spatial model — in what follows, we assume that it is piecewise constant on a grid, *but we do not know what the grid edges are.* The spatial model for the illuminant follows from the point source model, where $\mathbf{p}$ is the position of the source and $m(x, y, \mathbf{p})$ is obtained using Phong's model of specularities.

We choose a uniform prior for reflectance coefficients. We expect illuminants to have no chromatic bias, and so use a Gaussian prior, whose mean is white; we allow a fairly substantial standard deviation, to allow for illuminants that are coloured.

Thus, the generative model is:

- sample the number of reflectance steps in x and in y (k_x and k_y respectively);
- now sample the position of the steps ($\mathbf{e}_x$ and $\mathbf{e}_y$ respectively);
- for each tile, sample the reflectance for that interval from the prior (σ_j^m for the m'th tile;
- sample the illuminant coefficients ϵ_i from the prior;
- sample the illuminant position $\mathbf{p}$ from the prior;
- and render the image, adding Gaussian noise.

So we have a likelihood,

$$P(\text{image}|k_x, k_y, \mathbf{e}_x, \mathbf{e}_y, \sigma_j^m, \epsilon_i, \mathbf{p})$$

The posterior is proportional to:

$$P(\text{image}|k_x, k_y, \mathbf{e}_x, \mathbf{e}_y, \sigma_j^m, \epsilon_i, \mathbf{p}) \times Prior(kv_x)Prior(kv_y)$$
$$\times Prior(\mathbf{s}_x)Prior(\mathbf{s}_y)$$
$$\times \prod_{m \in \text{tiles}} Prior(\sigma_j^m)$$
$$\times Prior(\epsilon_i)Prior(\mathbf{p})$$

and all we have to do is draw samples from this.

3.2   The Sampling Process

The sampling process is straightforward MCMC. Proposal moves are of four types:

- **Birth of a step:** the details are as in example 1 of [7], with the exception that we derive a proposal distribution for the position of the step from the image gradient, so that we are more likely to propose a step where the gradient is high.
- **Death of a step:** as in example 1 of [7].
- **Change position of a step:** as in example 1 of [7].
- **Change reflectance and illumination:** this has some subtle pitfalls. It is tempting to fix illumination and change reflectance, then fix reflectance and change illumination, because both steps will involve sampling a Gaussian, which is easy. This, it turns out, is a bad idea, because the chain moves extremely slowly if we do this. The explanation is quite simple; given a reflectance/illumination pairing that is quite good, small changes lead to huge increases in the error. Thus, the process will lead to a reflectance that works well with the current illuminant or an illuminant that works well with the current reflectance and will move extremely slowly. Instead, we use a method due to Neal [18] that suppresses random walk by adjoining momentum variables and then modelling the state as the position of a particle in an energy field; typically, the state moves to positions of large posterior value quickly, at which point we throw away the momentum variables.

3.3   Experimental Examples

I show some results obtained using a real dataset from [5]. This data was photographed with a CCD camera, then displayed on a CRT, photographed from that screen with a film camera, subjected to unknown printing processes and then scanned from the published paper; I used such battered data deliberately, to illustrate the potential power of the process. There are no specular components in this dataset, making the specular reasoning simple. I obtained a basis using the mechanisms of Marimont and Wandell [16]. Constraints on coefficients were estimated using a graphical method.

In each case, the spatial model placed edges at the right points; this is hardly surprising, as each column and row edge has some high contrast points. Figure 1 shows a scatter plot of reflectance samples estimated for various corresponding tiles for images obtained under different coloured illuminants, under the assumption that each image was completely independent. Since the samples lie in reasonably close groups compared with the receptor response groups, the algorithm is displaying constancy. These samples contain not only estimates of reflectance, but also *information about a reasonable range of solutions*. This is crucial, and powerful.

Current colour constancy algorithms cannot deal with prior knowledge about the world. This algorithm can. For example, consider the effect of knowing that tile i in an image under white light is "the same" as tile j in an image obtained under purple light. It is quite plausible to want to know this — knowing that an object is a bus can and should affect our reports on its colour. In our representation, we can perform this calculation by *resampling* the set of samples. We sample pairs of representations — one obtained under the white light, the other

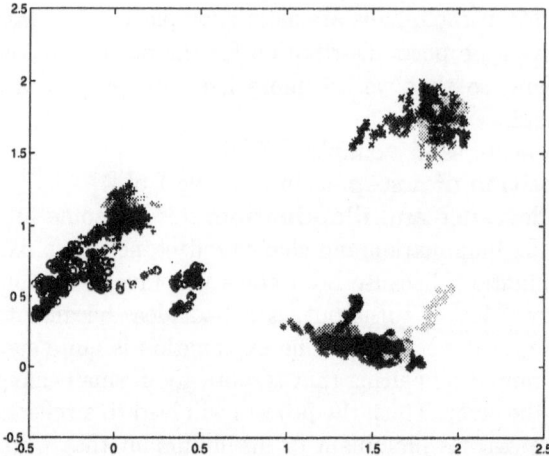

Fig. 1. *The first two components of surface reflectance samples, plotted on the same axes for four different surfaces. Each sample is colour keyed to the image from which it was obtained; red samples for the red image, etc, with black corresponding to the white image. The circles show samples of the reflectance coefficients for the blue surface at the top left corner of the Mondriaan; the stars for the yellow surface in the second row; the plusses show samples for the orange surface in the top row of the Mondriaan and the crosses for the red surface in the bottom row. Notice that the smear of samples corresponding to a particular surface in one image intersects, but is not the same as, the smear corresponding to that surface in another. This means that the representation envisages the possibility of their being the same, but does not commit to it.*

under the purple light — so that pairs where the two reflectances are similar are represented more often (this can all be made formal). Figure 2 shows the effect on results; this added information has reduced uncertainty. Further details appear in [6].

4   How Inference Methods Can Help Address Our Problems

Probabilistic models are difficult to use and to set up and there are no reliable algorithms for handling probabilistic models on the scale that vision will require. The paradigm is the right one; we learned to use geometric models well, and we should now be directing our efforts toward using probabilistic models well.

4.1   Information Integration

While sampling algorithms are currently slow and difficult to build well, the advantages that compensate for this are:

- We get a good representation of all the conclusions that can reasonably be drawn from the data (i.e. the posterior).

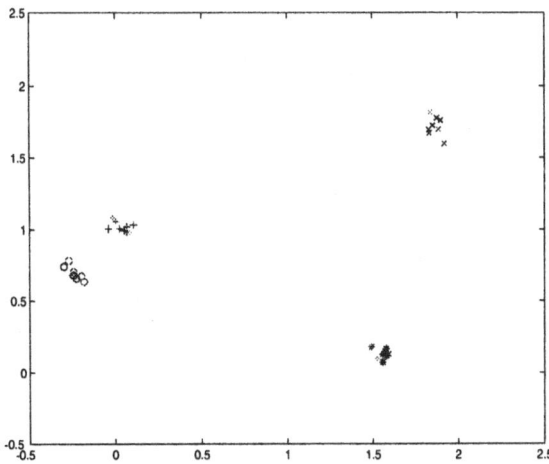

Fig. 2. *The first two components of surface reflectance samples, plotted on the same axes for four different surfaces. These come from the samples of figure 1, resampled under the assumption that the blue surface in the top left hand corner of the Mondriaan is the same for each image. We use the same representation and axes as in that figure. Notice that this single piece of information hugely reduces the ambiguity in the representation.*

- It is easy to see how to include other forms of information in the reasoning process; rewrite the likelihood, add more proposal mechanisms and proceed. If a form of conditional independence applies (which it does in useful cases), we can resample an existing set of samples.
- We do not need to abandon current algorithms to achieve this; instead, we can cloak them in probability and use them as a proposal process (as with the use of the gradient to propose step positions).

4.2   Segmentation

The colour constancy algorithm described above had a segmenter built into it with very little fuss — this is the spatial model of reflectances being piecewise constant in tiles. This illustrates a strength and a weakness of sampling methods.

The strength is that the relationship between segmentation and recognition is built in; the image is segmented into regions that are given by the model, and we are not required to perform generic segmentation. The weakness is that the model "hides" segmentation in the proposal processes; if we have good proposal processes, the problem of segmentation largely disappears, but if they are bad, we may never see a sensible interpretation. The good news is that there is some general information about what makes a good proposal process (e.g. [18]), and that it is easy to obtain proposal processes from current knowledge of vision.

4.3 Learning, Representation, and Primitives

The mechanisms for learning likelihoods ($P(measurement|model)$) from data exist. We expect that a modelbase would be represented by a complicated likelihood function, that would have a hierarchical structure and intermediate representations of one form or another. For example, a model for recognising clothed people is likely to manipulate a representation of what clothing looks like at one stage, and what arms look like at another. The ideal is to lay out efficient and accurate models automatically from pictures. We need to determine what primitives to use. Geometric reasoning has been very little help here in the past. The difficulty comes from obvious sources: a useful geometric primitive will have a characteristic appearance in an image that is informative about its 3D structure, and must also be useful for many objects and unlikely to arise from non-objects. These criteria are statistical, rather than geometric in nature. Amit and Geman have constructed some promising algorithms for automatically determining simple image primitives [1], but there is a long way to go.

4.4 Feature Selection

Feature selection has received embarassingly little attention in the recognition community. The question is simple; which measurements should be used to recognise an object? It appears in all current algorithms, in both the indexing and the verification phase. The answer can only be statistical.

The main difficulty with statistical work on feature selection is the absence of a notion of computational or measurement cost. The Bayesian answer to feature selection is to use all measurements, appropriately weighted to take account of their reliability. This is all very well, but it misses the fact that measurements may be difficult or expensive to make and that there is a limited amount of computation available. It is quite surprising that this question, which is obviously central in object recognition, has received so little attention in the literature.

5 Summary

Probabilistic models can be used to address the greatest weaknesses in our understanding of object recognition: integration, abstraction, segmentation and feature selection. The great power of probabilistic models is that they can encapsulate sources of variation whose origins are too complex to bear investigation — for example, the variations in the outline of each person's limb due to different muscle bulk. Sampling methods are good enough to produce attractive solutions to simple vision problems. There are substantial challenges in building efficient computational implementations, but these difficulties are worth addressing. Geometry and radiometry are simply not our most important areas of ignorance. In fact, we can currently predict the appearance of objects rather well — i.e. we can build quite good likelihood models. We should now be studying modelling and inference instead, because these are the theories on which a systematic view of the overall process of recognition will be based.

References

[1] Y. Amit, D. Geman, and K. Wilder. Joint induction of shape features and tree classifiers. *IEEE T. Pattern Analysis and Machine Intelligence*, 19(11):1300–1305, 1997.

[2] T.O. Binford. Visual perception by computer. In *Proc. IEEE Conference on Systems and Control*, 1971.

[3] G. Buchsbaum. A spatial processor model for object colour perception. *J. Franklin Inst.*, 310:1–26, 1980.

[4] G. Finlayson. Colour in perspective. *IEEE T. Pattern Analysis and Machine Intelligence*, 18:1034–1038, 1996.

[5] D.A. Forsyth. A novel algorithm for colour constancy. *Int. J. Computer Vision*, 5:5–36, 1990.

[6] D.A. Forsyth Sampling, Resampling and Colour Constancy. *Proc. IEEE Conf. on Computer Vision and Pattern Recognition*, 1991.

[7] P.J. Green. Reversible jump markov chain monte carlo computation and bayesian model determination. *Biometrika*, 82(4):711–732, 1995.

[8] H. Helson. Some factors and implications of colour constancy. *J. Opt. Soc. America*, 48:555–567, 1934.

[9] C-Y. Huang, O.T. Camps, and T. Kanungo. Object recognition using appearance-based parts and relations. In *IEEE Conf. on Computer Vision and Pattern Recognition*, pages 877–83, 1997.

[10] Mark Jerrum and Alistair Sinclair. The markov chain monte carlo method: an approach to approximate counting and integration. In D.S.Hochbaum, editor, *Approximation Algorithms for NP-hard Problems*. PWS Publishing, Boston, 1996.

[11] D.B. Judd. Hue, saturation and lightness of surface colors with chromatic illumination. *J. Opt. Soc. America*, 30:2–32, 1940.

[12] G.J. Klinker, S.A. Shafer, and T. Kanade. A physical approach to color image understanding. *Int. J. Computer Vision*, 4(1):7–38, 199.

[13] E.H. Land and J.J. McCann. Lightness and retinex theory. *J. Opt. Soc. Am.*, 61(1):1–11, 1971.

[14] H.C. Lee. Method for computing the scene-illuminant chromaticity from specular highlights. *J. Opt. Soc. Am.-A*, 3:1694–1699, 1986.

[15] L.T. Maloney and B.A. Wandell. A computational model of color constancy. *J. Opt. Soc. Am*, 1:29–33, 1986.

[16] D.H. Marimont and B.A. Wandell. Linear models of surface and illuminant spectra. *J. Opt. Soc. Am.-A*, 9:1905–1913, 1992.

[17] D. J. Murdoch and P. J. Green. Exact sampling from a continuous state space. *To appear in the Scandinavian Journal of Statistics*, 1908.

[18] R.M. Neal. Probabilistic inference using markov chain monte carlo methods. Computer science tech report crg-tr-93-1, University of Toronto, 1993.

[19] James G. Propp and David B. Wilson. Exact sampling with coupled markov chains and applications to statistical mechanics. *Random Structures and Algorithms*, 9:223–252, 1996.

[20] E. Rosch and C.B. Mervis. Family resemblances: Studies in the internal structure of categories. *Cognitive Psychology*, 7:573–605, 1975.

[21] E. Rosch, C.B. Mervis, W.E. Gray, D.M. Johnson, and P. Boyes-Braim. Basic objects in natural categories. *Cognitive Psychology*, 8:382–439, 1976.

[22] A. Zisserman, D.A. Forsyth, J.L. Mundy, C.A. Rothwell, and J.S. Liu. 3d object recognition using invariance. *Artificial Intelligence*, 78:239–288, 1995.

A Formal-Physical Agenda for Recognition

Joe Mundy

GE Corporate Research and Development,
1 River Road, Schenectady, NY12345, USA
mundy@crd.ge.com

1   Overview

1.1   The Recognition Task

The central task for computer vision is to extract a description of the world based on images. An important element of a description is the assertion that a specific individual object has been previously observed or that an object is similar to a set of objects seen in the past. This process of *recognition*, literally to RE-cognize, permits an aggregation of experience and the evolution of relationships between objects based on a series of observations.

The ability to recognize objects in a cluttered scene with complex illumination and shadows has proven to be one of the most difficult challenges for computer vision. This assertion is in complete agreement with the main thrust of the companion article by Dave Forsyth. Were we differ is what to emphasize in order to make progress.

First, it is essential to frame the problem of recognition in a bit more detail so that significant issues can be clearly identified. Indeed some of the difficulties of recognition arise from what are philosophical problems with the definition of *class* itself. The implicit assumption is that there is some *thing* in the world which can be associated with observable attributes, and that these attributes are in some sense *invariant* from one observation to the next. There is also the deeper assumption that the entity is discrete, and can be visually segmented from the background of all other material.

The assumption of class is that a number of individual observable things are in some way associated and should be treated as instances of a more general concept. This latter assumption is primarily a human imposition on reality which provides a means for controlling complexity and for reasoning about the world around us.

Centuries of philosophical debate have called into question even these apparently fundamental assumptions. We will not take space here to explore these considerations, however the problems are severe and mistakes about these issues have led to considerable wasted research effort. For example, it was popular in the 1980's to try to implement generic recognition classes such as *house* or *chair* without realizing that there was no operational class definition possible.

The philosophical state of affairs today is summarized by the following two principles:

D.A. Forsyth et al. (Eds.): Shape, Contour ..., LNCS 1681, pp. 22–27, 1999.

1. only individual objects exist;
2. a class is defined by its individual members, which resemble each other.

For our purposes, it will be assumed that two objects are the same if a sufficient number of *significant* visual attributes are *similar*. Further, the definition of object classes is based on such visual similarity and that the main purpose of classes is to enable *effective* recognition.

The definition of what is significant is centered on the processes of image segmentation and spatial organization. A significant attribute can be reliably and invariantly extracted from images of an entity. A significant attribute is also *salient* in that its variation is primarily due to differences in object class and not due to observation and differences between individuals of a class. The definition of what is similar requires some quantitative measure on object attributes, where measure is some mapping from attributes to a set of orderable values.

1.2   The Current State

We can already see from this set of definitions why recognition is intrinsically hard. While humans are quite expert at recognition, we have little formal under- standing of the attributes which might satisfy the desired properties just stated. Investigations of the physiological and behavioral bases of human vision have provided little insight as to the mathematical representation of object models suitable for recognition.

Instead, the main approach over the forty some odd years of computer vision research has been to apply formal representations and mathematically derived al- gorithms. These representations and algorithms are borrowed from diverse fields such as photogrammetry, optics, logic, linguistics, geometry, numerical analysis, statistics, etc.

These mathematical-physical disciplines have proven effective in particular problem domains and are accessible to the technically educated population who embark on computer vision research. As a consequence, computer vision research is dominated by fads where a new formal mechanism, for example graph theory, is introduced as the missing link which will unify previous approaches and provide the long-sought attributes and measures required for recognition models. While such sweeping claims are never realized, the introduction of new representational machinery is often beneficial and some progress results. However the fundamental difficulties are still with us.

The situation described in the introduction is an accurate depiction of our state of capability. We have the ability to extract intensity discontinuities from imagery and use them to bound regions of slowly varying intensity, representing the projection of surface patches into perspective imagery. The projected 2-d geometry of the occluding boundaries of a 3-d shape can be accurately predicted. So far we can say little about the geometric behavior of general shape classes.

The rather well-understood mathematical foundations of algebraic projective geometry, as a model for perspective image formation, has motivated consider- able research over the last decade to develop geometric object models. Invariant geometric descriptions for planar shapes have proved to enable effective index-ing with a much slower growth in required verification than for an exhaustive consideration of all known models[10].

However, the construction of such invariants requires accurate and almost complete boundary segmentations which cannot be achieved under complex scene conditions. Additionally, the extension of these invariant methods to 3-d shape place even greater burdens on the accuracy and completeness of seg-mentation. Further, invariants of general 3-d classes are known only for shapes which obey strict mathematical requirements. We have no theory for the effects of distortion from exact shape models, such as a solid of revolution or object with bi-lateral symmetry.

It has long been recognized that the intensity of surfaces conveys important information for recognition, but the combined effects of illumination direction and variations in surface reflectance and texture lead to almost unpredictable project image intensity values for a given object surface patch. It is not that the intensity values are random, it is that the physical situation is complex with many unknown parameters.

The state of the art of physics and geometry is such that accurate intensity simulations can be achieved when elaborate scattering models are fitted to con-trolled surface materials and when the illumination sources are known. Current object recognition practice has not made significant use of this capability be-cause of the variability of object surfaces within a class and ignorance of local illumination due to shadowing and reflections.

Faced with this situation, a new theme was initiated in face recogntion re-search about eight years ago and has become known as appearance-based recog-nition. The approach is fundamentally *pattern recognition*(e.g., [8, 4], where a set of features is defined and the statistical relationship between the features and class is establish empirically. The approach does not preclude the introduction of structure in terms of parametrized models but the work to date has emphasized purely empirical clustering.

It will be argued that this reliance on empirical methods while, apparently successful will not enable real progess in the problem of object recognition. The argument is elaborated in the following section.

2   Theory vs Empiricism

In the Forsyth article, it is argued that probability provides an effective model of the world and is a key to progress. Here, quite a different emphasis is pro-posed, that is to redouble our efforts to achieve a practical formal model of the appearance of object categories.

First, what is a formal model? By *formal* we mean that we have a logi-cal/computational definition of an object class which leads to a prediction of the image appearance of any instance of the class. We expect that the model requires specific attributes of the object instance, image sensor and illumination in order to construct appearance. We value models which have few parameters compared to the predicted appearance data.

As stated so far, the definition would not rule out statistical models. An additional requirement on the formal model is that it be capable of abstraction. For example, suppose we have an effective recognition model for the category *horse*. A key function of the formal model is to be able to express the differences between horses and elephants. The goal would be to derive a new recognition model by knowing structural differences and differences in surface material. One should be able to specify class definition in terms of a vocabulary of formal structures.

One approach to this requirement has been class description by *parts*. An object is composed of parts, perhaps described geometrically, and constraints on the geometric relationship between parts. It is true that inter-part constraints can be derived empirically for a given class[5, 2]. However the very specification of the part composition itself is not empirical, it represents a commitment to a formal definition of the class.

While this reductive structural representation clarifies the difference between formal and empirical models, the representation by parts paradigm has not been particularly sucessful for recognition. The key difficulty is recovering the parts and part relationships from imagery in complex image scenes. This difficulty has been interpreted as a failure of formal class representation and has increased the emphasis on statistical class models.

It is asserted that formalism is not to blame, but that instead we need to develop a theory of classes based on their appearance and what is recoverable from imagery under occlusion and complex illumination. So the key question is how do we effectively determine what is recoverable?

It is proposed to focus on physically derived models. It is argued that, using our limited formal representation of physical relatity and extending it is the best we can do. While this choice may limit the object classes we can implement, when we do succeed we can understand why and the general implications of succesful results.

In this approach object descriptions are based on physical models such as geometry and reflection theory. The theory of these domains is used to derive descriptive invariants which drive the definition of recoverable attributes. This is not to say that all parameters of such descriptions can be specified apriori. Instead, we expect formal analysis to reduce the dimensionality of the description to a manageable set of free parameters that characterize individual object instances.

3   Evidence for Optimism

This physical reductionist approach to object recognition has driven the field until recently with modest success. Why should it be still considered as a promising avenue? The following are a series of examples.

The Bi-directional Reflectance Distribution Function(BRDF) introduced by Koenderink[6] provides an elegant combination of theoretical and empirical models. The Koenderink BRDF accounts for the general properties of surface illumination but with free parameters that can be acquired from empirical observations of real surfaces. This concept has been reduced to practice by Dana et al[3] where over 60 different surfaces were measured and the empirical BRDFs constructed. These results give hope that complex object appearance can be modeled by attributing object surfaces with empirically derived BRDFs.

A related relevant theme is the work of of Belhumeur and Kriegman[1] who show that the space of possible images for a given 3-d surface has only three degrees of freedom. For polyhedra, this space is a faceted convex cone defined by the range of illumination directions and surface normals. Even though limited to Lambertian reflectance functions, work of this type is an important step in advancing our theoretical understanding of appearance models. Constructing similar theories based on more representative surface reflectance abstractions like the Koenderink BDRF model is a badly-needed generalization.

There have been a few attempts to directly integrate intensity and geometric information in recognition systems. Perhaps the most extensive work is that of Schmid[9] where local intensity derivative *jets* are used to construct an invariant representation of local object appearance. This representation is purely empirical but relatively immune to the occlusion and shadowing limitations of more global intensity representations as in SLAM[7]. The invariance of the local feature intensity attributes could be considerably advanced by incorporating features parametrized by reflectance models. Why not consider material properties as well as geometric properties? Some very effective BRDF's have only three parameters and could be acquired from three or more illumination/viewing conditions.

A recent thesis by Hoogs shows that even a modest introduction of formal modeling can greatly accelerate the rate of empirical learning. Hoogs uses the relationship between illumination source and sensor viewpoint with respect to object surfaces to characterize the samples empirically derived from a set of images. He shows that this characterization greatly improves the rate of learning by even crudely accounting for the systematic variations which are due to occlusion and shadowing. He shows that dramatic improvement in the reliablity of object matching can be achieved with just one image sample, using integrated empirical and formal models.

4   Summary

Statistics does have a role to play in object recognition, but mainly to account for variations we cannot or choose not to directly model. It should not be a substitute for working hard on understanding the relationship between physical properties, class and image appearance.

Probability is also a useful metric for evidence. In this regard, there is no contrast to the assertions by Forsyth. The key distinction in the thesis here is that object classification evidence takes two forms: logical truth and conditional probability. The role of conditional probability is to account for unknown variations and unknown relationships not as a substitute for working out better logical models.

References

[1] P.N. Belhumeur and D.J. Kriegman. What is the set of images of an object under all possible lighting conditions? In *IEEE Conf. on Computer Vision and Pattern Recognition*, pages 270–277, 1996.

[2] T.F. Cootes, G.J. Edwards, and C.J. Taylor. Active appearance models. In *European Conference on Computer Vision*, 1998.

[3] K.J. Dana, S.K. Nayar, B. van Ginneken, and J.J. Koenderink. Reflectance and texture of real-world surfaces. In *IEEE Conf. on Computer Vision and Pattern Recognition*, pages 151–157, 1997.

[4] R.O. Duda and P.E. Hart. *Pattern classification and scene analysis*. Wiley, 1973.

[5] D.A. Forsyth and M.M. Fleck. Body plans. In *IEEE Conf. on Computer Vision and Pattern Recognition*, 1997.

[6] J.J. Koenderink, A.J. Van Doorn, and M. Stavridi. Bidirectional reflection distribution function expressed in terms of surface scattering modes. In *European Conference on Computer Vision*, 1996.

[7] H. Murase and S. Nayar. Visual learning and recognition of 3D objects from appearance. *Int. J. of Comp. Vision*, 14(1):5–24, 1995.

[8] B.D. Ripley. *Pattern recognition and neural networks*. Cambridge University Press, 1996.

[9] C. Schmid and R. Mohr. Combining greyvalue invariants with local constraints for object recognition. In *Proceedings of the Conference on Computer Vision and Pattern Recognition, San Francisco, California, USA*, June 1996.

[10] A. Zisserman, D.A. Forsyth, J.L. Mundy, C.A. Rothwell, and J.S. Liu. 3d object recognition using invariance. *Artificial Intelligence*, 78:239–288, 1995.

Part II

Shape

Shape Models and Object Recognition

Jean Ponce, Martha Cepeda, Sung-il Pae, and Steve Sullivan*

Dept. of Computer Science and Beckman Institute
University of Illinois, Urbana, IL 61801, USA

1 Introduction

This paper discusses some problems that should be addressed by future object recognition systems.

In particular, there are things that we know how to do today, for example:

1. Computing the pose of a free-form three-dimensional object from its outline (e.g. [106]).
2. Identifying a polyhedral object from point and line features found in an image (e.g., [46, 89]).
3. Recognizing a solid of revolution from its outline (e.g., [59]).
4. Identifying a face with a fixed pose in a photograph (e.g., [10, 111]).

There are, however, things that we *do not* know how to do today, for example:

1. Assembling local evidence into global image descriptions (grouping) and using those to separate objects of interest from the background (segmentation).
2. Recognizing objects at the category level: instead of simply identifying Barney in a photograph, recognize that he is a dinosaur.

This is of course a bit of an exageration: there is a rich body of work on grouping and segmentation, ranging from classical models of these processes in human vision (e.g., [65, 116]) to the ever growing number of computer vision approaches to edge detection and linking, region merging and splitting, etc.. (see any recent textbook, e.g., [38, 73] for surveys). Likewise, almost twenty years ago, ACRONYM recognized parameterized models of planes in overhead images of airports [17], and the recent system described in [33] can retrieve pictures that contain horses from a large image database. Still, segmentation algorithms capable of supporting reliable recognition in the presence of clutter are not available today, and there is no consensus as to what constitutes a good representation/recognition scheme for object categories.

This paper examines some of these issues, concentrating on the role of shape representation in recognition. We first illustrate some of the capabilities of current approaches, then lament about their limitations, and finally discuss current work aimed at overcoming (or at least better understanding) some of these limitations.

---

* This work was partially supported by the National Science Foundation under grant IRI-9634312 and by the Beckman Institute at the University of Illinois at Urbana-Champaign. M. Cepeda is now with Qualcomm, Inc. and S. Sullivan is now with Industrial Light and Magic.

D.A. Forsyth et al. (Eds.): Shape, Contour ..., LNCS 1681, pp. 31–57, 1999.
© Springer-Verlag Berlin Heidelberg 1999

2   The State of the Art and Its Limitations

Let us start with an example drawn from our own work to illustrate the capabilities and limitations of today's recognition technology. While it can certainly be argued that more powerful approaches already exist (and we will indeed discuss alternatives in a little while), this will help us articulate some of the issues mentioned in the introduction.

2.1   An Example of What Can Be Done Today

Here we demonstrate that the pose of a free-form surface can be reliably estimated from its outline in a photograph. Two obvious challenges in this task are (1) constructing a model of the free-form surface that is appropriate for pose estimation and (2) computing the six pose parameters of the object despite the absence of any three-dimensional information.

We have developed a method for constructing polynomial spline models of solid shapes with unknown topology from the silhouette information contained in a few registered photographs [106]. Our approach does not require special-purpose hardware. Instead, the modeled object is set in front of a calibration chart and photographed from various viewpoints. The pictures are registered using classical calibration methods [110], and the intersection of the visual cones associated with the photographs [9] is used to construct a G^1-continuous triangular spline [22, 30, 60, 100] that captures the topology and rough shape of the modeled object. This approximation is then refined by deforming the spline to minimize the true distance to the rays bounding the visual cones [108]. Figure 1(a)-(b) illustrates this process with an example.

The same optimization procedure allows us to estimate the pose of a modeled object from its silhouette extracted from a single image. This time, the shape parameters are held constant, while the camera position and orientation are modified until the average distance between the visual rays associated with the image silhouette and the spline model is minimized. In fact, the residual distance at convergence can be used to discriminate between competing object models in recognition tasks. Figure 1(c)-(d) shows some examples. But..

2.2   Is This Really Recognition?

Of course not: we have relied on an oracle to tell us which pieces of contours belong to which object, since the spline representation does not provide any support for top-down grouping (as shown by Fig. 1(d), occlusion is not the problem). Although it is possible that some bottom-up process (e.g., edge detection and linking, maybe followed by the elimination of small gaps and short contour pieces and the detection of corners and T-junctions) would yield appropriate contour segments, this is not very likely in the presence of textured surfaces and background clutter. Indeed, the contours used as input to the pose estimation algorithm in Fig. 1 were selected manually [107].

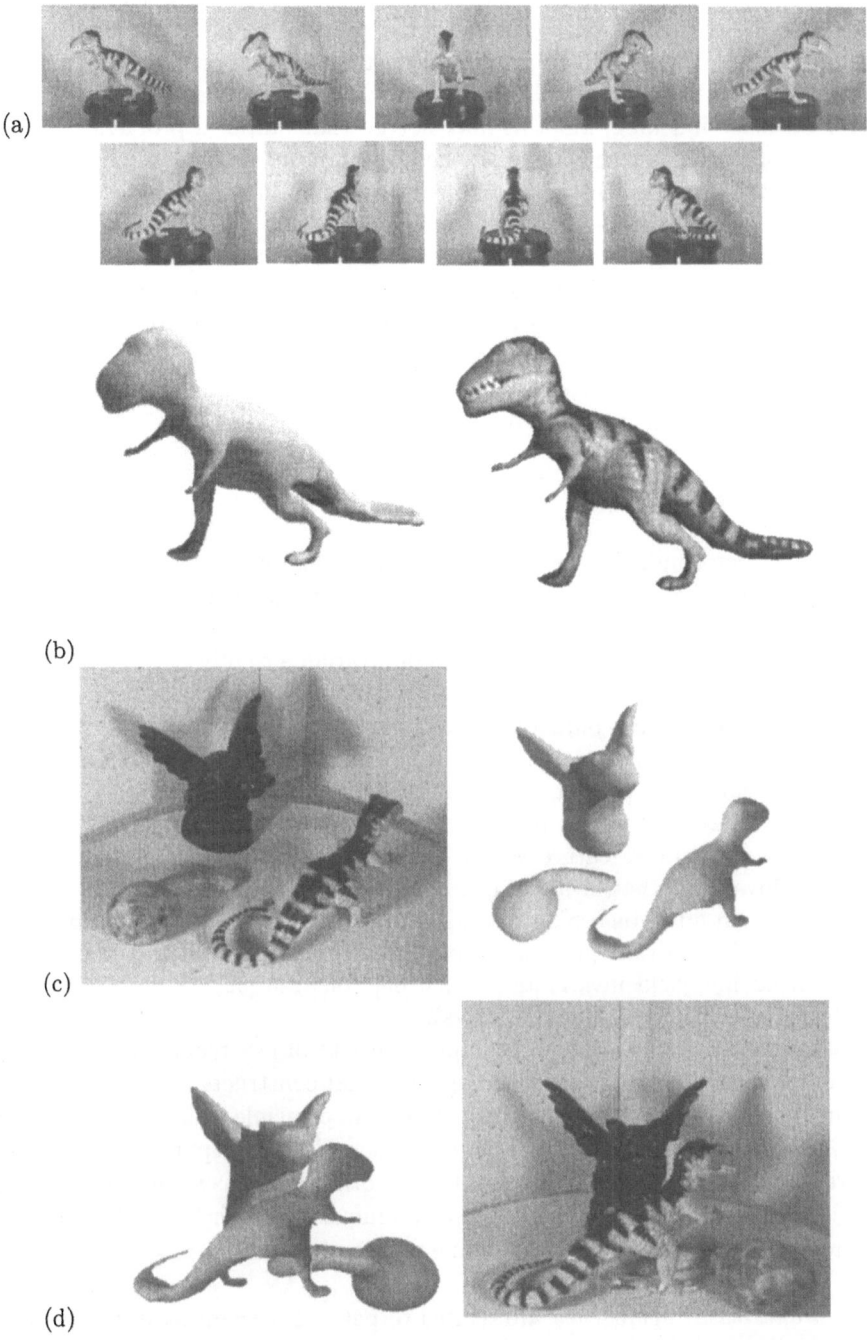

Fig. 1. Automated modeling and pose estimation: (a) nine views of a (toy) dinosaur; (b) the corresponding spline model, Gouraud-shaded and texture-mapped; (c) and (d) results of pose estimation.

The Barney (or maybe T. Rex in this case) vs. generic dinosaur problem mentioned earlier is also apparent here: the spline is a purely numerical object description, and it is hard to imagine how it would support the recognition of object classes. Another possible objection to this approach is the lack of support for modelbase indexing, but this may not be that bad of a problem: after all, the cost of matching every model to the given contour data is only linear in the size m of the database (in our example, $m = 3$, a rather small value).

All this does not mean that the spline models of Fig. 1 are not useful in practice: indeed, they provide a low-cost alternative to using, say, a Cyberware rangefinder to construct detailed graphical models of three-dimensional objects. Likewise, pose estimates could be used in pick-and-place robotic manipulation of isolated[1] objects presented on a dark background. However, it is pretty clear that this approach does not hold the key to constructing the recognition systems of the future. The next section discusses alternatives.

2.3   What Else Then?

Numerical/combinatorial methods use geometric filters to identify a sufficient number of matches between image and model features. They include alignment techniques (e.g., [46, 62, 89, 112]) and affine and projective invariants (see, for example, [26, 115] for early applications of invariants to object recognition, and [69, 70] for recent collections of papers). In the former case, matching proceeds as a tree search, whose potentially exponential cost is controlled by using the fact that very few point matches are in fact sufficient to completely determine the object pose and predict the image positions of any further matches (see [4, 31, 36] for related work). In the latter case, small groups of points are used to directly compute a feature vector independent of the viewpoint (hence the name of invariant) that, in turn, can be used for indexing a hash table storing all models. An advantage of invariants is that indexing can be achieved in sublinear time. A disadvantage is that groups of three-dimensional points in general position do not yield invariants [20, 23, 68] (but see [32, 59, 120] for certain object classes that do admit invariants).

Alignment- and invariant-based approaches to object recognition do not require (in principle) a separate grouping stage that constructs a *global* description of the image and/or its features: instead, it is in principle sufficient to construct a reliable *local* feature detector (a *much* easier task), since spurious features will be rejected by the matching process. On the other hand, as in the case of spline models, it is not clear at all how these techniques, with their purely numerical characterization of shape, would handle object categories.

Appearance-based approaches are related to pattern recognition methods. They record a description of all images of each object, and they have been successfully used in face identification [10, 111] and three-dimensional object recognition

---

[1] But possibly quite complex (at least by computer vision standards): have another look at the gargoyle and the dinosaur in Fig. 1.

[71]. Their main virtue is that, unlike purely geometric approaches to recognition, they exploit the great discriminant power of image intensity information. However, it is not clear how they would generalize to category-level recognition (see, however, [8] for preliminary efforts in that direction), and they normally require (due to their essentially global nature) a separate segmentation step that distinguishes the objects of interest from the image background. For example, the three-dimensional object recognition system described in [71] uses images where isolated objects lie in front of a dark background. Despite its very impressive performance (real-time recognition of complex free-form, textured objects from a single photograph), it is unlikely that this system would perform as well with occlusion and background clutter.

It should be noted that the recognition method proposed in [94] combines the advantages of invariant- and appearance-based techniques: it uses *quasi-invariant* properties [15] of the projection process to faithfully represent all images of an object by a small set of views, and relies on local descriptions (*jets*, see [54]) of the brightness pattern at interest points [40] for efficient indexing. Explicit segmentation is avoided, and the results are excellent (e.g., a dinosaur (again!) is easily recognized in a picture that contains a very cluttered forest background). Like other appearance-based techniques (e.g., [111]), this one is sensitive to illumination changes, although recent advances in color analysis [41, 102] suggest that combining the jets used in the current version of the system with local illumination invariants may solve the problem. Again, this approach does not address the problem of representing object classes.

Structural representations. An alternative to the techniques discussed so far is to describe objects by part-whole networks of stylized primitives, such as generalized cylinders [13] or superquadrics [5, 77]. This approach has several (potential) advantages: first, it offers a natural representation for object classes (similar objects will hopefully have similar part-whole decompositions). Second, and maybe not quite as obviously, appropriate primitives may prove useful in guiding top-down grouping and segmentation: e.g., to look for cylinder-like structures in an image, look for pairs of curves that are more or less straight and parallel to each other [63]. There are also some known difficulties: for example, the images of a particular class of primitive shapes may not have simple properties that can readily be exploited by a top-down segmentation process. Another very difficult problem is to precisely and operationally define what constitutes an object part.

A different type of structural representation is what might be called a *weak modeling* scheme, i.e., an approach where only very general assumptions are made about the world, and general mathematical results valid under these assumptions are used to parse images. Aspect graphs [52, 53] are an example of this approach: they exploit the fact that both the structure of image contours and the manner in which it changes with viewpoint are mathematically well understood. Hopefully, similar objects will have similar aspect graphs, and the understanding of image structure may serve as a guide to image segmentation. In practice however, aspect graphs have not fullfilled their promise, partly because of the great difficulty of reliably extracting contour features such as terminations and T-junctions from real images, and partly because of the fact that even relatively simple objects may have extremely complicated aspect graphs (e.g., a polyhedron with n faces has an orthographic aspect graph with $O(n^6)$ cells [35]; the situation gets even worse when perspective projection [105] and curved objects [78] are considered).

Still, at this point we believe that structural approaches to recognition offer the best hope of tackling the segmentation and class representation problems, so we will revisit in the next two sections both generalized cylinders and aspect graphs (the latter in the context of evolving shape), and discuss some new twists that we are currently exploring. Before that, let us stress that we do not claim that generalized cylinders or aspect graphs are the way to go. Nor do we claim that the results presented in the next two sections are particularly impressive or an improvement over existing recognition technology. Rather, we believe that it is important to assess what these representation schemes really have to offer since we do not know of viable alternatives at this time.

3 Generalized Cylinders

Binford introduced generalized cylinders (GCs) in a famous unpublished 1971 paper [13], defining them in terms of "generalized translational invariance". Roughly speaking, a GC is generated by a one-dimensional set of cross-sections that smoothly deform into one another. Binford noted that a space curve forming the spine of the representation may be defined (but not always uniquely, e.g., a cylinder), and that "in general, we don't expect to have analytic descriptions of the cross-section valued function, or the space curve called the spine" [13].

Such a definition is very general and quite appealing, but it is also very difficult to operationalize: in other words, although a great many objects (the fingers of my left hand for example) can certainly be described by sweeping smoothly-deforming cross-sections along some space curve, it is not clear at all how to construct the description of a given shape in a principled way.

Most of the early attempts at extracting GC descriptions from images focused on range data [1, 74, 103]. Among those, the work of Nevatia and Binford [74] is particularly noteworthy since it does implement a version of generalized translational invariance: their algorithm tries all possible cross-section orientations of objects such as dolls, horses, and snakes, then selects subsets of the cross-section candidates with smoothly varying parameters.

Methods for finding GC instances in video images have traditionally been based on the assumption that three-dimensional GCs will project onto two-dimensional ones, or *ribbons*: this is the approach used in the ACRONYM system of Brooks and Binford [17, 18] for example. For the limited class of GCs (circular cylinders and cones) and ribbons (trapezoids and ellipses) used by ACRONYM's geometric reasoning system,[2] there is indeed a natural correspondence between GC projections and ribbons, and the assumption is justified.

---

[2] ACRONYM employed a wider repertoire of primitives for geometric modeling, but not to draw inferences from images [17].

The situation is not as clear for more general GC and ribbon classes, and this is probably one of the reasons why, following ACRONYM, most vision systems using GCs as their primary shape representation moved toward simpler, and better understood, *parametric and globally generative* GC classes: Shafer and Kanade [97, 98] paved the way by introducing a taxonomy of generalized cylinders, of which the most commonly used today are probably straight homogeneous generalized cylinders (SHGCs, also called generalized cones [44, 66] and constructed by scaling an arbitrarily-shaped planar cross-section along a straight spine) and solids of revolution (or RCSHGCs in Shafer's and Kanade's terminology). Another example of a sub-class of GCs is formed by *geons*, a set of twenty four GC types proposed by Biederman in the context of human vision [12], which have recently found use in machine vision [11, 25, 75].

Limiting the class of GCs under consideration makes it possible to predict viewpoint-independent properties of their projections [72, 83, 81]: for example, Nalwa proved that the silhouette of a solid of revolution observed under orthographic projection is bi-laterally symmetric [72] (i.e, it is an instance of straight Brooks ribbon [90]). Ponce, Chelberg and Mann showed that, under both orthographic and perspective projection, the tangents to the silhouette of an SHGC at points corresponding to the same cross-section intersect on the image of the SHGC's axis [84]. Other important problems (e.g., whether a shape admits a unique SHGC description [80]) can also be addressed in this context.

Such analytical predictions provide a rigorous basis for finding individual GC instances in images [45, 84, 86, 93, 113, 118, 119] or recognizing GC instances based on projective invariants [59], and, indeed, very impressive results have been achieved: for example, the system implemented by Zerroug and Medioni is capable of automatically constructing a part-based description of a teapot from a real image with clutter and textured background [118].

Despite these undeniable successes, we believe that it is necessary to go beyond simple sub-classes of GCs: most objects around us are not made up of instances of solids of revolution, SHGCs, canal surfaces, etc.: we do not live in a world made of glasses, bottles, cups and teapots. Restricting the application domain is useful, but in the end we must interpret scenes that contain the familiar objects in my office, stapler, scissors, telephone and people, who may (or may not) have elongated parts, but cannot be described in terms of a small set of rigid primitives. This is our motivation for introducing a new breed of GCs in the next sections.

3.1 Approach

The notion of generalized cylinder proposed in this section is based on the intuition that the elongated parts of a shape are naturally described by sets of cross-sections whose area is as small as possible. These cross-sections correspond to *valleys* of a height function that measures the area of all possible cross-sections of the shape. The following definition of the topographic notions of *valleys* (or *ravines*) and *ridges* was given by Haralick, Watson, and Laffey [37, 39] in the context of image processing.

Definition 1. *The valley (resp. ridge) of the surface defined in $\mathbb{R}^3$ by a height function $h : U \subset \mathbb{R}^2 \to \mathbb{R}$ over a 2D domain U is the locus of the points where the gradient ∇h of h is an eigenvector of the Hessian $\mathcal{H}$, and where the eigenvalue associated with the other eigenvector of the Hessian is positive (resp. negative).*

Other definitions of ridges and valleys have been given by various researchers, including Crowley and Parker [24] and Eberly, Gardner, Morse, Pizer and Scharlach [27]. As shown by Koenderink [55], the definitions of Haralick *et al.* and Eberly *et al.* are in fact equivalent to a much earlier one proposed by de Saint-Venant in 1852 [92]. Koenderink's paper also includes a modern account of the different 1912 definition due to Rothe [91] that better captures the intuitive notion that water should flow down the valley and not cross the course of a river, but unfortunately does not afford a local criterion for detecting ridges and valleys.

We will use the definition of Haralick *et al.* since, as shown in Section 3.2, it can be used to derive a local geometric condition for a cross-section of a shape to participate in a ribbon or a generalized cylinder. It also has the advantage of having been implemented in several ridge and valley finders [34, 39]. Finally, as shown by Barraquand [6, 7] and detailed in Section 3.3, it is readily generalizable to higher dimensions, where it still yields one-dimensional valleys and ridges. This will prove particularly important for defining GCs.

3.2 Ribbons

Consider a 2D shape bounded by a curve Γ defined by $x : I \to \mathbb{R}^2$ and parameterized by arc length. The line segment joining any two points $x(s_1)$ and $x(s_2)$ on Γ defines a cross-section of the shape, with length $l(s_1, s_2) = |x(s_1) - x(s_2)|$. We can thus reduce the problem of studying the set of cross-sections of our shape to the problem of studying the topography of the surface S associated with the height function $h : I^2 \to \mathbb{R}^+$ defined by $h(s_1, s_2) = \frac{1}{2}l(s_1, s_2)^2$.

The lowest (resp. highest) points of S correspond to places where the region bounded by Γ is the narrowest (resp. the widest). More interestingly, the valleys (resp. ridges) of this surface correspond to narrow (resp. wide) subsets of the region, which leads to the following definition of ribbons.

Definition 2. *The ribbon associated with the shape bounded by some curve Γ is the set of cross-sections whose end-points correspond to ridges and valleys of the associated surface S. The narrow (resp. wide) ribbon is the subset of the ribbon corresponding to a valley (resp. ridge) of S.*

At this point, let us make a few remarks:
• The narrow ribbons are of course of primary interest for implementing two-dimensional GCs. However, we will see in the next section that wide ribbons also capture interesting shape properties, such as certain symmetries.
• The description of a given shape is uniquely defined: in particular, it is obviously independent of the choice of arc-length origin. In fact, as shown in

[37], the valleys of a surface are invariant through monotonic transformations of the height function (so replacing h by l for example would not change the ribbon associated with a shape).

- Although this representation superficially "looks like" a skeleton [95] or medial axis [16], it is fundamentally different, since a shape is described by a set of line segments instead of a set of disks. This is indeed an instance of 2D generalized cylinder [13].

- As noted earlier, using valleys and ridges to define ribbons allows us to construct the ribbon description of a given shape by constructing a discrete version of the surface S, then using some implementation of a valley/ridge-finder [34, 39] to finds its valleys and ridges.

Figure 2 shows the narrow ribbons found in synthetic and real images using two very simple valley finders that we have developed to conduct preliminary experiments. The top of the figure shows results from the first implementation with, from left to right: the ribbon of a worm-like object, the mid-points of its cross-sections (spine), another synthetic example, and the silhouette of a person and the spine of its narrow ribbons. The bottom part of the figure shows results from our second program with, from left to right: the height function associated with a bottle shape, the ribbon cross-sections, and the associated spine.

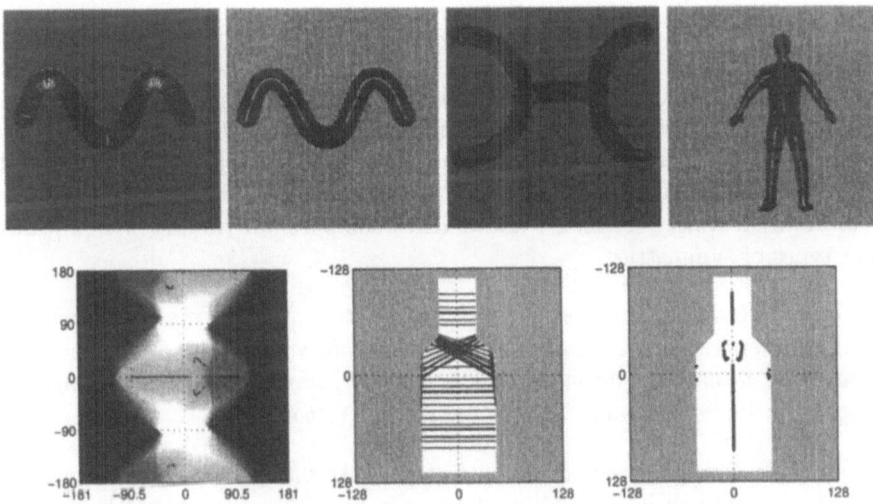

Fig. 2. The narrow ribbons extracted from synthetic and real images.

Formal properties. We first give a geometric criterion that two points must satisfy to define a ribbon pair. Let us parameterize the curve by arc-length, and define the unit vectors u, v forming an orthonormal right-handed coordinate system, such that $x_1 - x_2 = lu$ (Fig. 3). We denote by t_i and n_i the unit tangent and normals in x_i ($i = 1, 2$), and by θ_i denote the angle between the vectors u and t_i.

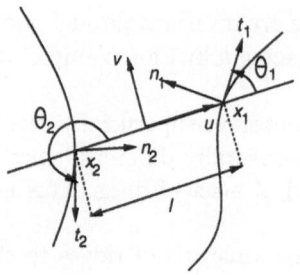

Fig. 3. Notation.

Lemma 1. *The ribbon associated with a two-dimensional shape is the set of cross-sections of this shape whose endpoints satisfy*

$$(cos^2\theta_1 - cos^2\theta_2)cos(\theta_1 - \theta_2) + l\cos\theta_1\cos\theta_2(\kappa_1\sin\theta_1 + \kappa_2\sin\theta_2) = 0. \quad (1)$$

This lemma follows from the definition of ridges and valleys and from the fact that the gradient ∇h is an eigenvector of the Hessian $\mathcal{H}$ if and only if it is a non-zero vector and

$$(\mathcal{H}\nabla h) \times \nabla h = 0, \quad (2)$$

where "$\times$" denotes the operator associating to two vectors the determinant of their coordinates. Rewriting this condition in geometric terms yields (1) after some algebraic manipulation. It should be noted that the eigenvalues of the Hessian can also be expressed geometrically in terms of the distance l, the angles θ_1, θ_2 and the curvatures κ_1, κ_2. The formula, however, is a bit complicated and not particularly illuminating, and it is omitted here.

More interestingly, Lemma 1 allows us to compare our ribbons with various other types of symmetries.

Lemma 2. *Radial symmetries, bi-lateral symmetries, and worms are ribbons. In radial symmetries, concave pairs of symmetric points form narrow ribbons, and convex pairs form wide ribbons. Concave pairs of points in bi-lateral symmetries always form narrow ribbons. Worms are narrow ribbons.*

Lemma 2 shows that ribbons include some interesting shape classes (worms are ribbons obtained by sweeping a line segment with constant width perpendicular to some generating curve). For example, an ellipse admits the following description in terms of ribbons: one narrow ribbon corresponding to its major axis of symmetry, and two wide ribbons corresponding to its minor axis of symmetry and its radial symmetry.

The lemma follows easily from (1), the formula for the Hessian's eigenvalues mentioned earlier, and the angle and curvature properties of worms and radial or bi-lateral symmetries [80]. Note that (1) also provides another method for finding ribbons: construct a discrete version of the surface S, and find the zero-crossings of (1).

Part decomposition. As mentioned earlier, parts can be defined as the pieces of an object which are well approximated by some primitive shape [77], as the pieces of an object which are separated by some prototypical discontinuities [43, 85], or as a combination of both [48, 101]. Here we follow Binford's suggestion and decompose complex shapes into ribbon parts whose cross-sections vary smoothly, so that cross-section area discontinuities delimit separate parts.

Figure 4 shows examples using real images. The cross-section discontinuities are defined as valley endpoints as well as points where the width function is discontinuous.

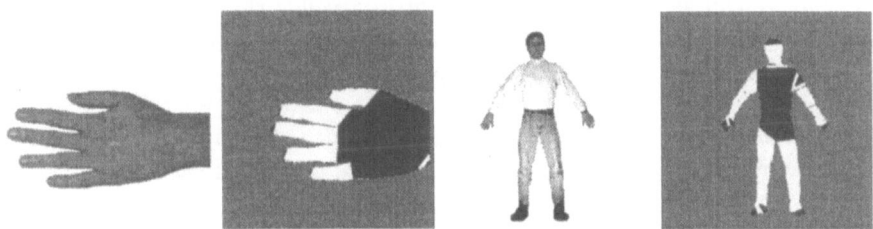

Fig. 4. Parts. From left to right: a hand, its parts, a person and his parts.

Let us stress again that we do not claim that the results shown in Figs. 2 and 4 are better than those that would have been obtained by previous methods [43, 48, 101]. Nor do we claim at this point to have a robust program for part decomposition. Rather, we believe that our preliminary results demonstrate the feasibility of the approach and pave the way toward achieving part decomposition for three-dimensional objects, as discussed in the next section.

3.3   Generalized Cylinders

Definition. The definition of valleys presented in Section 3.1 has been extended by Barraquand and his colleagues [6] to arbitrary dimensions, with applications in robotic planning [7]. The generalization is as follows: the valley (resp. ridge) of a hypersurface defined in $\mathbb{R}^{n+1}$ by a height function $h : U \subset \mathbb{R}^n \to \mathbb{R}$ over an n-dimensional domain U is the locus of the points where the gradient of h is an eigenvector of the Hessian, and where the eigenvalues associated with the other eigenvectors of the Hessian are positive (resp. negative). (Mixed eigenvalues yield topographic entities lying somewhere between valleys and ridges.)

Barraquand has shown that valleys are (in general) one-dimensional, independent of the value of n. This is intuitively obvious since the gradient ∇h is an eigenvector of the Hessian $\mathcal{H}$ when the vectors ∇h and $\mathcal{H}\nabla h$ are parallel to each other. This can be expressed by a system of $n-1$ equations in n unknowns, defining a curve in the domain U.

For example, in the case $n = 3$, the condition is again (2) where "$\times$" denotes this time the cross product. This vector condition yields two independent scalar equations in the three domain parameters, hence a curve.

We now show how the valleys of a height function defined over a three-dimensional domain can be used to define generalized cylinders. In the three-dimensional case, there is no natural parameterization of the cross-sections of a shape in terms of points on its boundary. Instead, we propose the following idea: consider a volume V and the three-parameter family of all planes $P(s_1, s_2, s_3)$ in $\mathbb{R}^3$ (we will not worry about the choice of the plane parameterization for the time being). We consider the hyper-surface S of $\mathbb{R}^4$ associated with the height function $h(s_1, s_2, s_3) = \text{Area}(V \cap P(s_1, s_2, s_3))$.

In other words, h measures the area of the slice of the volume V contained in the plane P. The set of valleys of the surface S is as before a one-dimensional set, and we can associate with each point in a valley the slice of V associated with the corresponding plane. This yields a description of V in terms of planar cross-sections swept and deformed in space.

Definition 3. *The* generalized cylinder *associated with a shape is the set of cross-sections corresponding to the valleys of the associated surface S.*

Time for a few more remarks:

• The definition of a GC given above is not quite satisfying: it depends on the choice of plane parameterization used in defining the height function h. Changing the parameterization will not merely scale the values of h like the monotonic transformations mentioned in Section 3.2: it will deform the domain over which the surface S is defined and thus change its valleys. This difficulty stems from the fact that there is no obvious natural parameterization similar to arc length in the three-dimensional case.

We propose to use a *local* parameterization of planes in the neighborhood of a given cross-section to guarantee that the GC description attached to a given shape is uniquely defined: we attach to each cross-section a reference frame whose origin is its center of mass and whose x, y axes are its inertia axes. This allows us to parameterize each plane in a neighborhood of the cross-section by the spherical coordinates of its normal and the signed distance to the origin. In turn, we can use this parameterization and the local criterion (2) to determine potential GC cross-sections of an object (of course, the sign of the eigenvalues of $\mathcal{H}$ must also be checked). The GC description of a given shape is obviously uniquely defined, independent of any global coordinate system. It is in fact easy to show that it is also independent of the particular choice of the coordinate axes in the cross-section plane. Note however that the representation (i.e., the height field and its valleys) depends on the particular local plane parameterization chosen, e.g., we could have used Cartesian coordinates instead of spherical ones for the normal. Likewise, we could have used a different origin for the coordinate frame associated to each cross-section: the only objective reason for choosing the center of mass is that it defines an origin uniquely attached to the shape. Clearly, more research is needed in this area, and we will investigate alternate plane parameterizations.

• In the three-dimensional case, we do not make the distinction between "narrow" and "wide" generalized cylinders because it is not intuitively clear what the ridges of S would correspond too. Also, remember that mixed eigenvalue signs in the three-dimensional case may give rise to intermediate topographical entities whose properties are at this point poorly understood.

- As in the two-dimensional case, the "spine" of our representation is the one-dimensional set of cross-sections, not a particular curve in three-dimensional space. If such a curve is desired, the locus of centers of mass of the cross-sections is a natural choice, *given the parameterization proposed above*. This is in agreement with Binford's remarks quoted earlier [13].

Where do we stand? We are still at a very early stage of our research for three-dimensional shapes. At this point, we have shown the following lemma.

Lemma 3. *Solids of revolution are generalized cylinders.*

The proof is given in [21]. Briefly, it computes analytically the area of the cross-section of a solid of revolution by an arbitrary plane, then goes on to show that cross-sections orthogonal to the axis direction are valley points. We plan to investigate other class of GCs such as circular tubes (three-dimensional worms), SHGCs and canal surfaces (the envelopes of one-dimensional families of spheres).

There are other properties of our GCs that we plan to investigate in the near future:

- Stability: we plan to explore both theoretically and empirically the stability of the representation. In particular, it would be desirable that the GC descriptions of two similar shapes also be similar. Characterizing the stability of any shape representation scheme is difficult (defining shape similarity is in itself a non-trivial problem). An instance of this problem is whether the GC description of a shape that can be approximated by a simple GC class (e.g., a solid of revolution) has a GC description similar to an instance of that class (in the solid of revolution example, roughly circular cross-sections swept along an almost straight line). As noted several times before, this is very important since, except in very special situations, real objects and/or their parts will *not* be exact instances of simple primitive shapes [42].

- Projective properties: do our generalized cylinders project onto ribbons? This is at present an open question, and we will try to give it a rigorous answer. Understanding the stability of the GC representation will provide partial answers (e.g., solids of revolution project to bi-lateral symmetries under weak perspective [72]). We will of course try to articulate more complete ones.

We have implememted a simple program that uses the marching cube algorithm [61] to detect valleys in a three-dimensional terrain, and Fig. 5 shows very preliminary experiments. Note that we have not implemented the local parameterization of GCs, and our program uses a global plane parameterization instead. Much more work is of course needed in this area.

Once we have developed robust algorithms for constructing GC descriptions of complex shapes, we will attack the part-decomposition problem using an approach similar to the one developed in the two-dimensional case. More generally, the ultimate goal of this project is of course to develop methods using part-whole

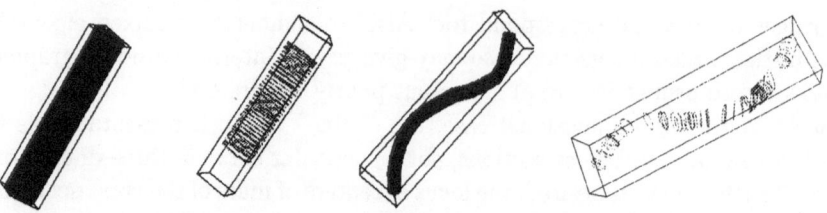

Fig. 5. Some simple shapes and their GC description.

hierarchies describing objects and object classes for efficient indexing in object recognition [14, 74].

Another interesting issue is how to introduce a notion of scale in the representation. This would allows us to maintain hierarchies of part decompositions potentially useful in coarse-to-fine matching. At this point this remains an open problem. A different application of scale-space techniques to shape representation is considered in the next section.

4   Evolving Surfaces

Imagine a smooth density function defined over a volume. The set of points where the density exceeds a given threshold defines a solid shape whose surface is a level set of the density. Blurring the density function will change its level sets and the shape it defines. When do "important" changes occur? This is the question addressed by Koenderink in the section dedicated to dynamic shape of his book [51], where he goes on to give several examples of structural changes under the name of morphological scripts. Recently, Bruce, Giblin and Tari [19] have given a complete classification of the structural changes in the parabolic set of a smooth surface undergoing a one-parameter family of deformations, as well as geometric and analytical conditions under which these transitions happen. We address in this section the problem of actually computing these transitions.

4.1   Background

The idea of capturing the significant changes in the structure of a geometric pattern as this pattern evolves under some family of deformations has a long history in computer vision. For example, Marr [65] advocated constructing the primal sketch representation of an image by keeping track of the patterns that do not change as the image is blurred at a variety of scales. The idea of recording the image changes under blurring lead to the scale-space approach to image analysis, which was first proposed by Witkin [117] in the case of inflections of a one-dimensional signal, and has since been applied to many domains, including the evolution of curvature patterns on curves [3, 58, 64] and surfaces [82], and more recently, the evolution of curves and level sets under diffusion processes [49, 96].

Koenderink's and Van Doorn's aspect graphs [52, 53] provide another example where a geometric pattern can be characterized by its significant changes. This time, the objective is to characterize the possible appearances of an object. The range of viewpoints is partitioned into maximal regions where the (qualitative) appearance of an object remains the same, separated by critical boundaries where the structure of the silhouette changes according to some visual event. The maximal regions (labeled by the object appearance at some sample point) are the nodes of the aspect graph, and the visual events separating them are its arcs. For smooth surfaces, a complete catalogue of visual events is available from singularity theory [2, 52, 53, 87], and it has been used to compute the aspect graphs of surfaces of revolution [28, 56], algebraic surfaces [79, 88], and empirical surfaces defined as the level set of volumetric density functions [76] (see [109] for related work).

In his book [51], Koenderink addressed the problem of understanding the structural changes of the latter type of surfaces as the density function undergoes a diffusion process. He focused on the evolution of certain surface attributes, namely, the parabolic curves and their images via the Gauss map, which are significant for vision applications: for example, the intersection of a parabolic curve with the occluding contour of an object yields an inflection of the silhouette [50], and the asymptotic directions along the parabolic curves form the lip and beak-to-beak events of the aspect graph [47]. Koenderink proposed to define *morphological scripts* that record the possible transformations of a given shape and use these as a language for describing dynamic shape. Bruce, Giblin and Tari [19] have used singularity theory to expand Koenderink's work and establish a complete catalogue of the singularities of the parabolic set under one-parameter families of deformations. We recall their results before presenting an approach to computing the critical events that they have identified. Once these events have been computed, we characterize the structure of the parabolic set and its Gaussian image at a sample point between each pair of critical events, which yields a data structure similar to the aspect graph but parameterized by time instead of viewpoint.

4.2 Singularities of Evolving Surfaces

This section introduces the parabolic set, its Gaussian image, and their singularities in the context of contact between planes and surfaces. It also summarizes the results of Bruce, Giblin and Tari [19].

Generic singularities. The intersection of a surface with the tangent plane at one of its points can take several forms (Fig. 6): for most points, this intersection is either reduced to the point itself (this is the case for *elliptic* points, where the surface has locally the shape of an ovoid or the inside of an egg shell, see Fig. 6(a)) or composed of two curve branches intersecting transversally (this happens at *hyperbolic* points, where the surface has locally the shape of a saddle, see Fig. 6(b)). Elsewhere, the intersection may consist of a curve that cusps at the point of interest (which is then said to be *parabolic*, see Fig. 6(c)), a unode (a double extremum of the height function measured along the surface normal, see Fig. 6(d)), or a tacnode (two smooth curve branches joining tangentially, see Fig. 6(e)). Points corresponding to the last two cases are called *godrons*, *ruffles* [51], or *cusps of the Gauss map*, because the curve traced on the Gauss sphere by the unit surface normals along the parabolic curve has a cusp at these points.

For *generic* surfaces, there are no other possibilities; elliptic and hyperbolic points form extended areas of the surface, separated by smooth curves made of parabolic points; the cusps of Gauss are isolated points on these parabolic curves.

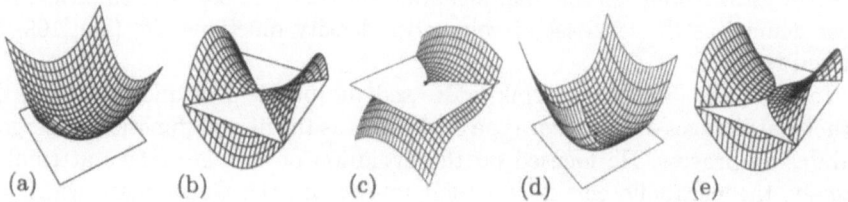

Fig. 6. Contact of a surface with its tangent plane: (a) an elliptic point, (b) a hyperbolic point, (c) a parabolic point, (d) a unode, (e) a tacnode.

Singularities of one-parameter families of surfaces. As shown in [19], there are a few more possibilities in the case of one-parameter families of deforming surfaces: indeed, three types of higher-order contact may occur at isolated values of the parameter controlling the deformation. The corresponding singularities are called A3, A4 and D4 transitions following Arnold's conventions [2], and they affect the structure of the parabolic set as well as its image under the Gauss map (Fig. 7).

There are four types of A3 transitions: in the first case, a parabolic loop disappears from the surface, and an associated loop with two cusps disappears on the Gauss sphere (this corresponds to a *lip* event in catastrophe theory jargon, see Fig. 7(a)). In the second case, two smooth parabolic branches join, then split again into two branches with a different connectivity, while two cusping branches on the Gauss sphere merge then split again into two smooth branches (this is a *beak-to-beak* event, see Fig. 7(b)). Two additional singularities are obtained by reversing these transitions.

At an A4 event, the parabolic curve remains smooth but its Gaussian image undergoes a *swallowtail* transition, i.e., it acquires a higher-order singularity that breaks off into two cusps and a crossing (Fig. 7(c)). Again, the transition may be reversed. Finally, there are four D4 transitions. In the first one (Fig. 7(d)), two branches of a parabolic curve meet then split again immediately; a similar phenomenon occurs on the Gauss sphere, with a cusp of Gauss "jumping" from one branch to the other. In the second transition (Fig. 7(e)), a parabolic loop shrinks to a point then expands again into a loop; on the Gauss sphere, a loop

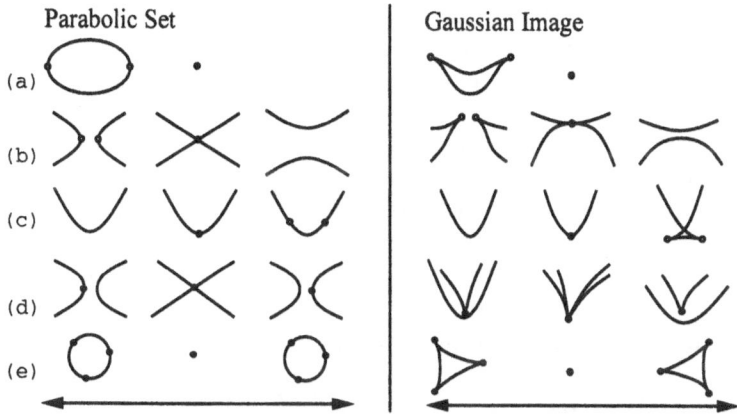

Fig. 7. The singularities of evolving surfaces. The events are shown on both the surface (left) and the Gauss sphere (right). The actual events are shown as black disks, and the (generic) cusps of Gauss are shown as white disks. See text for more details.

with three cusps shrinks to a point then reappears. The transitions can as usual be reversed.

4.3 Computing the Singularities

We now present an approach to computing the singularities of evolving algebraic surfaces. We first derive the equations defining these singularities, then propose an algorithm for solving these equations and finally present results from our implementation.

Singularity equations. Bruce, Giblin and Tari [19] give explicit equations for all the singularities in the case of a surface defined by a height function $z = f(x, y)$. Here we are interested in surfaces defined by some implicit equation $F(x, y, z) = 0$. Although it is possible to use the chain rule to rederive the corresponding equations in this case, this is a complex process [109] and we have chosen instead to first construct the equations characterizing the parabolic curves and the cusps of Gauss, which turn out to have a very simple form, then exploit the fact that the parabolic set or its image under the Gauss map are singular at critical events to characterize these events.

The normal to the surface defined by $F(x, y, z) = 0$ is of course given by the gradient $\nabla F = (F_x, F_y, F_z)^T$. As shown in [79, 109, 114], the parabolic curves are defined by $F(x, y, z) = P(x, y, z) = 0$, where where $P = \nabla F^T \mathcal{A} \nabla F$ and $\mathcal{A}$ denotes the symmetric matrix

$$
\begin{pmatrix}
F_{yy}F_{zz} - F_{yz}^2 & F_{xz}F_{yz} - F_{zz}F_{xy} & F_{xy}F_{yz} - F_{yy}F_{xz} \\
F_{xz}F_{yz} - F_{zz}F_{xy} & F_{zz}F_{xx} - F_{xz}^2 & F_{xy}F_{xz} - F_{xx}F_{yz} \\
F_{xy}F_{yz} - F_{yy}F_{xz} & F_{xy}F_{xz} - F_{xx}F_{yz} & F_{xx}F_{yy} - F_{xy}^2
\end{pmatrix}.
$$

(Note that $\mathcal{A}\mathcal{H} = |\mathcal{H}|\mathrm{Id}$, where $\mathcal{H}$ denotes the Hessian matrix associated to F.)

The cusps of Gauss are points where the asymptotic direction along the parabolic curve is tangent to this curve [51]. Let us show that the asymptotic direction at a parabolic point is $\mathbf{a} = \mathcal{A}\nabla F$. Asymptotic tangents are vectors of the tangent plane that are self-conjugate. The first condition is obviously satisfied at a parabolic point since $\mathbf{a} \cdot \nabla F = \nabla F^T \mathcal{A}\nabla F = 0$. The second condition is also obviously satisfied since $\mathbf{a}^T \mathcal{H}\mathbf{a} = |\mathcal{H}|(\mathbf{a} \cdot \nabla F) = 0$. Since the tangent to the parabolic curve is given by $\nabla P \times \nabla F$, it follows that the cusps of Gauss are given by $F = P = C = 0$, where $C = \nabla P^T \mathcal{A}\nabla F$.

Note that ∇P has a relatively simple form:

$$\nabla P = \frac{\partial}{\partial \mathbf{x}}(\nabla F^T \mathcal{A}\nabla F) = \begin{pmatrix} \nabla F^T \mathcal{A}_x \nabla F \\ \nabla F^T \mathcal{A}_y \nabla F \\ \nabla F^T \mathcal{A}_z \nabla F \end{pmatrix} + 2|\mathcal{H}|\nabla F,$$

since $(\frac{\partial}{\partial \mathbf{x}}\nabla F^T)\mathcal{A} = \mathcal{H}\mathcal{A} = \mathrm{Det}(\mathcal{H})\mathrm{Id}$. In particular, this simplifies the expression of C since the ∇F term above cancels in the dot product. Similar simplifications occur during the computation of the non-generic singularities below.

We are now ready to characterize these singularities. Note that in the case of a surface undergoing a family of deformations parameterized by some variable t, F, P and C are also functions of t. Let us first consider A3 and D4 transitions. Since they yield singular parabolic curves, they must satisfy $F = P = 0$ and

$$\nabla_{\mathbf{x}}F(x, y, z, t) \times \nabla_{\mathbf{x}}P(x, y, z, t) = 0,$$

where $\nabla_{\mathbf{x}}$ denotes the gradient operator with respect to $\mathbf{x}$, and the third equation simply states that the normals to the original surface and the "parabolic" surface defined by $P = 0$ are parallel. This is a vector equation with three scalar components, but only two of these components are linearly independent. It follows that the singularities of the parabolic set are characterized by four equations in four unknowns.

The case of A4 singularities is a little more complicated since the parabolic set is smooth there. On the other hand, the curve defined in $\mathbb{R}^4$ by the cusps of Gauss is singular, and the A4 singularities can thus be found by solving the system of equations defined by $F = P = C = 0$ and

$$|\nabla_{\mathbf{x}}F, \nabla_{\mathbf{x}}P, \nabla_{\mathbf{x}}C| = 0.$$

Solving the equations. Our objectives are to compute all the critical events and characterize the structure of the parabolic set and its Gaussian image at a sample point between each pair of critical events. This yields a data structure similar to the aspect graph but parameterized by time instead of viewpoint.

All critical events are characterized by systems of four polynomial equations in four unknowns. They can thus be found using homotopy continuation [67], a global root finder that finds all the solutions (real or complex) of square systems of polynomial equations.

Between singularities, the structure of the parabolic set does not change, and the curve tracing algorithm proposed in [57, 79] is used to determine its structure. Briefly, the algorithm traces an algebraic curve by first using homotopy continuation to find all its extremal points (including singularities) in some direction, as well as sample points on the smooth branches bounded by those extrema, then marching numerically from the samples to the adjacent extrema. See [57, 79] for details.

We have implemented this approach. All algebraic manipulations, including the computation of the result of Gaussian diffusion and linear morphing processes and the derivation of the singularity equations have been implemented in Mathematica. The singularities are computed using a parallel implementation of homotopy continuation [104] which allows the construction of the continuation paths to be distributed among a network of Unix workstations. The curve tracing algorithm described in [57, 79] has been implemented in Mathematica.

Figure 8(a) shows the results of applying Gaussian diffusion to a dimple-shaped quartic surface defined by

$$(4x^2 + 3y^2)^2 - 4x^2 - 5y^2 + 4z^2 - 1 = 0.$$

The surface and its parabolic curves are shown in the first row of the figure, and the corresponding Gaussian image is shown in the second one. As before, generic cusps of Gauss are shown as white discs. Singularities occur in the second, fourth and sixth column. There is a last singularity which is not shown in the figure, and that corresponds to the disappearance of the surface.

Figure 8(b) shows the singularities found when linearly morphing the dimple into a squash-shaped surface defined by

$$4y^4 + 3xy^2 - 5y^2 + 4z^2 + 6x^2 - 2xy + 2x + 3y - 1 = 0.$$

The evolving surface is shown in the first two rows, and its Gaussian image in the two bootom ones. As in the previous case, we have not found any A4 event.

4.4   Toward a Scale-Space Aspect Graph

We show in this section preliminary results in an effort to characterize the change in visual appearance of an object as it undergoes a diffusion process. Approaches to the construction of such a *scale-space aspect graph* can be found in [29] in the two-dimensional polygonal case and [99] in the three-dimensional polyhedral case. Here we attack the case of curved surfaces formed by the zero set of polynomial density functions, focusing on the case of solids of revolution. Equations for the visual events of solids of revolution can be found in [28, 56]. These visual events form parallels of constant latitude on the unit sphere. When the diffusion parameter is added, the events transform into curves in (σ, β) space, where β denotes the angle between the axis of the solid of revolution and the viewing direction.

Computing the singularities of these curves for a sample solid of revolution yields the scale-space aspect graph shown in Fig. 9. Note that multi-local visual

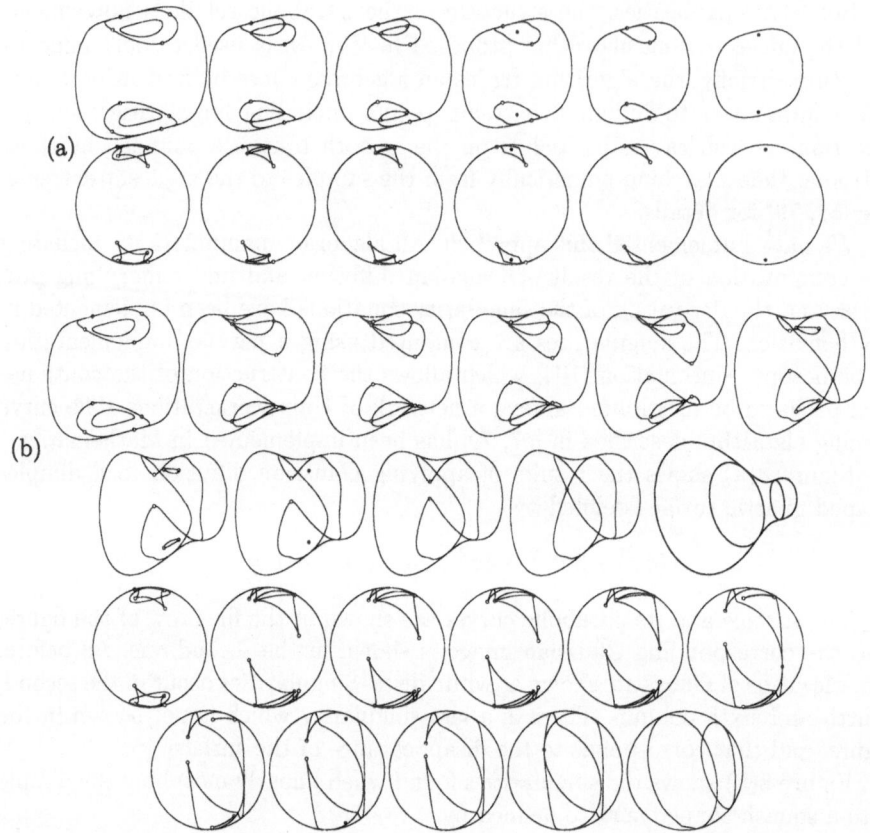

Fig. 8. Evolving shapes: (a) diffusion of a dimple; (b) morphing the dimple into a squash.

events have not been traced yet, so aspects that only differ through T-junctions are considered equivalent. Figure 9(top) shows the regions of the (σ, β) plane delimited by visual events. There are two "diffusion events" (dashed vertical lines in the figure) in this case: the first one corresponds to the surface splitting into two parts, and the second one corresponds to the disappearance of its parabolic lines. A close-up of the diagram near these two events is shown in Fig. 9(top-right).[3] Note that the visual event curve with a vertical inflection switches from beak-to-beak to lip at the inflection.

The two diffusion events separate three qualitatively different aspect graphs. The aspects and visual events corresponding to the first one are shown in Fig. 9(middle). Close-ups of the aspects and visual events associated with the second one are shown in Fig. 9(bottom). These are centered at the corresponding sin-

---

[3] There are in fact two more diffusion events that occur for larger values of σ and are not shown in the figure. They correspond to the disappearance of the two parts of the surface after splitting.

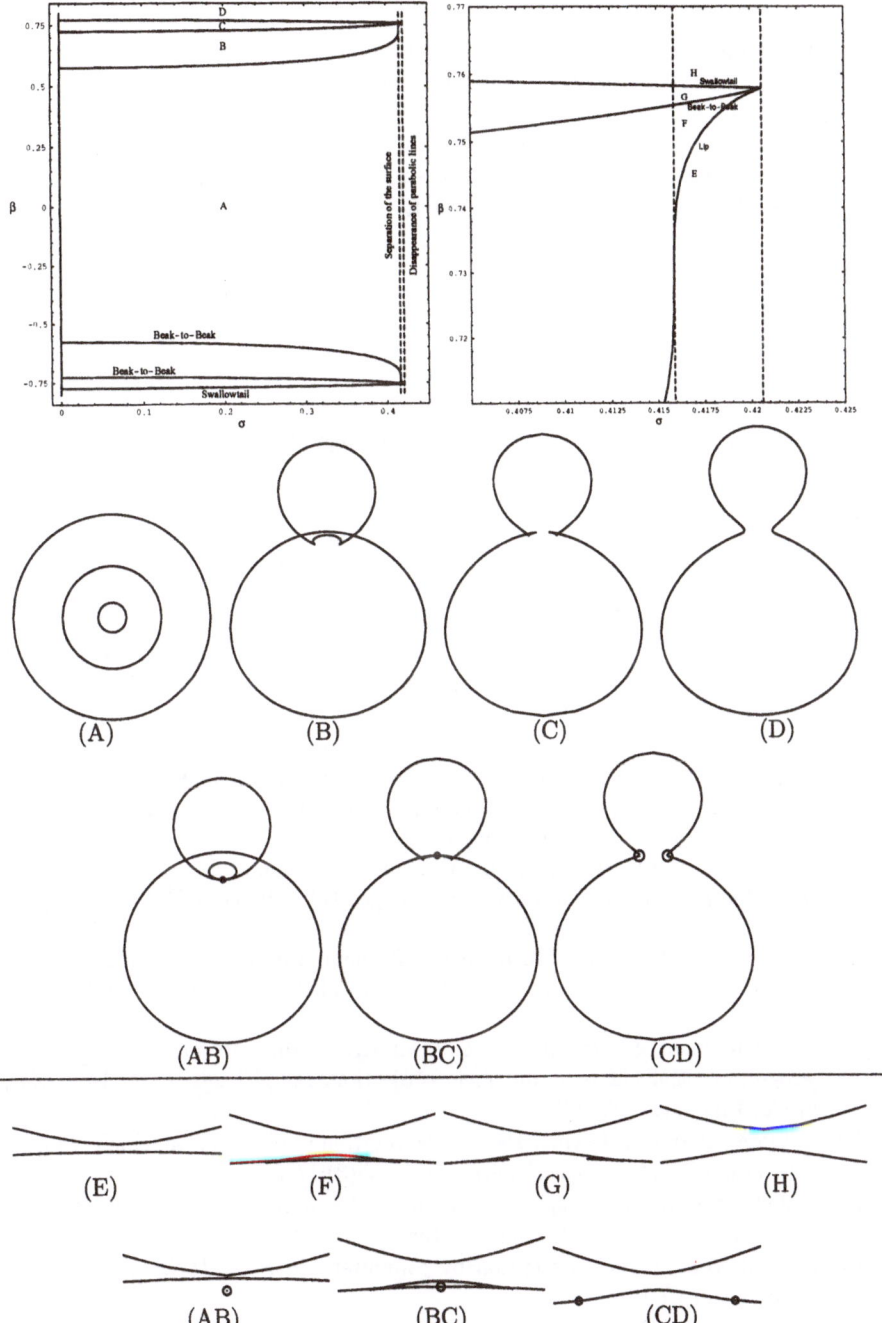

Fig. 9. Scale-space aspect graph. See text for details.

gularities for clarity. Ignoring multi-local events, there is only one aspect for the
third aspect graph, and it is not shown in the figure.

As in the case of generalized cylinders, much more work is needed here: this includes computing the multi-local visual events, generalizing our approach to algebraic surfaces that do not bound solids of revolution, and linking the changes in aspect graph structure to the singularities of evolving parabolic and flecnodal curves. An even more challenging problem is to consider the effect of diffusion processes applied to the image instead of the surface, which is a much more realistic model of optical blur. A lot is left to learn.

References

[1] G.J. Agin. *Representation and description of curved objects.* PhD thesis, Stanford University, Stanford, CA, 1972.

[2] V.I. Arnol'd. Singularities of smooth mappings. *Russian Math. Surveys,* pages 3–44, 1969.

[3] H. Asada and J.M. Brady. The curvature primal sketch. *IEEE Trans. Patt. Anal. Mach. Intell.,* 8(1):2–14, 1986.

[4] N. Ayache and O. Faugeras. Hyper: a new approach for the recognition and positioning of two-dimensional objects. *IEEE Trans. Patt. Anal. Mach. Intell.,* 8(1):44–54, January 1986.

[5] A.H. Barr. Superquadrics and angle preserving transformations. *IEEE Computer Graphics and Applications,* 1:11–23, January 1981.

[6] J. Barraquand and M. Berthod. A non-linear second order edge detector. In *International Image Week, Second Image Symposium,* Nice, France, 1986.

[7] J. Barraquand, B. Langlois, and J.C. Latombe. Robot motion planning with many degrees of freedom and dynamic constraints. In *Int. Symp. on Robotics Research,* pages 74–83, Tokyo, Japan, 1989. Preprints.

[8] R. Basri, D. Roth, and D. Jacobs. Clustering apperance of 3D objects. In *Proc. IEEE Conf. Comp. Vision Patt. Recog.,* pages 414–420, Santa Barbara, CA, June 1998.

[9] B.G. Baumgart. Geometric modeling for computer vision. Technical Report AIM-249, Stanford University, 1974. Ph.D. Thesis. Department of Computer Science.

[10] P.N. Belhumeur, J.P. Hesphanha, and D.J. Kriegman. Eigengaces vs. Fisherfaces: recognition using class-specific linear projection. *IEEE Trans. Patt. Anal. Mach. Intell.,* 19(7):711–720, 1997.

[11] R. Bergevin and M. Levine. Part decomposition of objects from single view line drawings. *CVGIP: Image Understanding,* 55(3):17–34, 1992.

[12] I. Biederman. Human image understanding: Recent research and a theory. *Comp. Vis. Graph. Im. Proc.,* 32(1):29–73, 1985.

[13] T.O. Binford. Visual perception by computer. In *Proc. IEEE Conference on Systems and Control,* 1971.

[14] T.O. Binford. Body-centered representation and recognition. In M. Hebert, J. Ponce, T.E. Boult, and A. Gross, editors, *Object Representation for Computer Vision,* number 994 in Lecture Notes in Computer Science, pages 207–215. Springer-Verlag, 1995.

[15] T.O. Binford and T.S. Levitt. Quasi-invariants: theory and applications. In *Proc. DARPA Image Understanding Workshop,* pages 819–829, 1993.

[16] H. Blum. A transformation for extracting new descriptors of shape. In W. Wathen-Dunn, editor, *Models for perception of speech and visual form*. MIT Press, Cambridge, MA, 1967.

[17] R.A. Brooks. Symbolic reasoning among 3-D models and 2-D images. *Artificial Intelligence*, 17(1-3):285–348, 1981.

[18] R.A. Brooks, R. Greiner, and T.O. Binford. Model-based three-dimensional interpretation of two-dimensional images. In *Proc. International Joint Conference on Artificial Intelligence*, pages 105–113, Tokyo, Japan, Aug. 1979.

[19] J.W. Bruce, P.J. Giblin, and F. Tari. Parabolic curves of evolving surfaces. *Int. J. of Comp. Vision*, 17(3):291–306, 1996.

[20] B. Burns, R. Weiss, and E. Riseman. The non-existence of general-case view-invariants. In *Geometric Invariance in Computer Vision*, pages 120–131. MIT Press, 1992.

[21] M. Cepeda. Generalized cylinders revisited: theoretical results and preliminary implementation. Master's thesis, Department of Computer Science, University of Illinois at Urbana-Champaign, 1998.

[22] B. Chiyokura and F. Kimura. Design of solids with free-form surfaces. *Computer Graphics*, 17(3):289–298, Nov. 1983.

[23] D.T. Clemens and D.W. Jacobs. Model group indexing for recognition. *IEEE Trans. Patt. Anal. Mach. Intell.*, 13(10):1007–1017, 1991.

[24] J.L Crowley and A.C. Parker. A representation of shape based on peaks and ridges in the difference of low-pass transform. *IEEE Trans. Patt. Anal. Mach. Intell.*, 6:156–170, 1984.

[25] S. Dickinson, A.P Pentland, and A. Rosenfeld. 3D shape recovery using distributed aspect matching. *IEEE Trans. Patt. Anal. Mach. Intell.*, 14(2):174–198, 1992.

[26] R. Duda and P. Hart. *Pattern classification and scene analysis*. Wiley, 1973.

[27] G. Eberly, R. Gardner, B. Morse, S. Pizer, and C. Scharlach. Ridges for image analysis. Technical report, Univ. of North Carolina, Dept. of Comp. Sc., 1993.

[28] D. Eggert and K. Bowyer. Computing the orthographic projection aspect graph of solids of revolution. In *Proc. IEEE Workshop on Interpretation of 3D Scenes*, pages 102–108, Austin, TX, November 1989.

[29] D. Eggert, K. Bowyer, C. Dyer, H. Christensen, and D. Goldgof. The scale space aspect graph. *IEEE Trans. Patt. Anal. Mach. Intell.*, 15(11):1114–1130, 1993.

[30] G. Farin. *Curves and Surfaces for Computer Aided Geometric Design*. Academic Press, San Diego, CA, 1993.

[31] O.D. Faugeras and M. Hebert. The representation, recognition, and locating of 3-D objects. *International Journal of Robotics Research*, 5(3):27–52, Fall 1986.

[32] D. Forsyth. Recognizing an algebraic surface from its outline. *Int. J. of Comp. Vision*, 18(1):21–40, April 1996.

[33] D.A. Forsyth and M.M. Fleck. Body plans. In *Proc. IEEE Conf. Comp. Vision Patt. Recog.*, pages 678–683, San Juan, PR, June 1997.

[34] J.M. Gauch and S.M. Pizer. Multiresolution analysis of ridges and valleys in grey-scale images. *IEEE Trans. Patt. Anal. Mach. Intell.*, 15(6), June 1993.

[35] Z. Gigus, J. Canny, and R. Seidel. Efficiently computing and representing aspect graphs of polyhedral objects. *IEEE Trans. Patt. Anal. Mach. Intell.*, 13(6), June 1991.

[36] W.E.L. Grimson and T. Lozano-Pérez. Localizing overlapping parts by searching the interpretation tree. *IEEE Trans. Patt. Anal. Mach. Intell.*, 9(4):469–482, 1987.

[37] R.M. Haralick. Ridges and valleys in digital images. *Comp. Vis. Graph. Im. Proc.*, 22:28–38, 1983.

[38] R.M. Haralick and L.G. Shapiro. *Computer and robot vision.* Addison Wesley, 1992.

[39] R.M. Haralick, L.T. Watson, and T.J. Laffey. The topographic primal sketch. *International Journal of Robotics Research*, 2:50–72, 1983.

[40] C. Harris and M. Stephens. A combined edge and corner detector. In 4th *Alvey Vision Conference*, pages 189–192, Manchester, UK, 1988.

[41] G. Healey and D. Slater. Global color constancy. *J. Opt. Soc. Am. A*, 11(11):3003–3010, 1994.

[42] M. Hebert, J. Ponce, T.E. Boult, A. Gross, and D. Forsyth. Report on the NSF/ARPA workshop on 3D object representation for computer vision. In M. Hebert, J. Ponce, T.E. Boult, and A. Gross, editors, *Object Representation for Computer Vision*, Lecture Notes in Computer Science. Springer-Verlag, 1995. Also available through the World-Wide Web at the following address: //www.ius.cs.cmu.edu/usr/users/hebert/www/workshop/report.html.

[43] D.D. Hoffman and W. Richards. Parts of recognition. *Cognition*, 18:65–96, 1984.

[44] J. Hollerbach. Hierarchical shape description of objects by selection and modification of prototypes. AI Lab. TR-346, MIT, 1975.

[45] R. Horaud and J.M. Brady. On the geometric interpretation of image contours. In *Proc. Int. Conf. Comp. Vision*, London, U.K., June 1987.

[46] D.P. Huttenlocher and S. Ullman. Object recognition using alignment. In *Proc. Int. Conf. Comp. Vision*, pages 102–111, London, U.K., June 1987.

[47] Y.L. Kergosien. La famille des projections orthogonales d'une surface et ses singularités. *C.R. Acad. Sc. Paris*, 292:929–932, 1981.

[48] B.B. Kimia, A.R. Tannenbaum, and S.W. Zucker. The shape triangle: parts, protrusions and bends. Technical Report TR-92-15, McGill University Research Center for Intelligent Machines, 1992.

[49] B.B. Kimia, A.R. Tannenbaum, and S.W. Zucker. Shapes, shocks, and deformations I: the components of shape and the reaction-diffusion space. *Int. J. of Comp. Vision*, 15:189–224, 1995.

[50] J.J. Koenderink. What does the occluding contour tell us about solid shape? *Perception*, 13:321–330, 1984.

[51] J.J. Koenderink. *Solid Shape.* MIT Press, Cambridge, MA, 1990.

[52] J.J. Koenderink and A.J. Van Doorn. The singularities of the visual mapping. *Biological Cybernetics*, 24:51–59, 1976.

[53] J.J. Koenderink and A.J. Van Doorn. The internal representation of solid shape with respect to vision. *Biological Cybernetics*, 32:211–216, 1979.

[54] J.J. Koenderink and A.J. Van Doorn. Representation of local geometry in the visual system. *Biological Cybernetics*, 55:367–375, 1987.

[55] J.J. Koenderink and A.J. Van Doorn. Local features of smooth shapes: Ridges and courses. In *Geometric Methods in Computer Vision II*, pages 2–13, 1993.

[56] D.J. Kriegman and J. Ponce. Computing exact aspect graphs of curved objects: solids of revolution. *Int. J. of Comp. Vision*, 5(2):119–135, 1990.

[57] D.J. Kriegman and J. Ponce. A new curve tracing algorithm and some applications. In P.J. Laurent, A. Le Méhauté, and L.L. Schumaker, editors, *Curves and Surfaces*, pages 267–270. Academic Press, New York, 1991.

[58] M. Leyton. A process grammar for shape. *Artificial Intelligence*, 34:213–247, 1988.

[59] J. Liu, J.L. Mundy, D. Forsyth, A. Zisserman, and C. Rothwell. Efficient recognition of rotationally symmetric surfaces and straight homogeneous generalized cylinders. In *Proc. IEEE Conf. Comp. Vision Patt. Recog.*, pages 123–128, New York City, NY, 1993.

[60] C. Loop. Smooth spline surfaces over irregular meshes. *Computer Graphics*, pages 303–310, Aug. 1994.

[61] W. Lorensen and H. Cline. Marching cubes: a high resolution 3D surface construction algorithm. *Computer Graphics*, 21:163–169, 1987.

[62] D. Lowe. The viewpoint consistency constraint. *Int. J. of Comp. Vision*, 1(1):57–72, 1987.

[63] D. Lowe and T.O. Binford. Segmentation and aggregation: An approach to figure-ground phenomena. In *Proc. DARPA Image Understanding Workshop*, pages 168–178, 1982.

[64] A. Mackworth and F. Mokhtarian. The renormalized curvature scale space and the evolution properties of planar curves. In *Proc. IEEE Conf. Comp. Vision Patt. Recog.*, pages 318–326, 1988.

[65] D. Marr. *Vision*. Freeman, San Francisco, 1982.

[66] D. Marr and K. Nishihara. Representation and recognition of the spatial organization of three-dimensional shapes. *Proc. Royal Society, London*, B-200:269–294, 1978.

[67] A.P. Morgan. *Solving Polynomial Systems using Continuation for Engineering and Scientific Problems*. Prentice Hall, Englewood Cliffs, NJ, 1987.

[68] Y. Moses and S. Ullman. Limitations of non model-based recognition schemes. In *Proc. European Conf. Comp. Vision*, pages 820–828, 1992.

[69] J.L. Mundy and A. Zisserman. *Geometric Invariance in Computer Vision*. MIT Press, Cambridge, Mass., 1992.

[70] J.L. Mundy, A. Zisserman, and D. Forsyth. *Applications of Invariance in Computer Vision*, volume 825 of *Lecture Notes in Computer Science*. Springer-Verlag, 1994.

[71] H. Murase and S. Nayar. Visual learning and recognition of 3D objects from appearance. *Int. J. of Comp. Vision*, 14(1):5–24, 1995.

[72] V.S. Nalwa. Line-drawing interpretation: bilateral symmetry. In *Proc. DARPA Image Understanding Workshop*, pages 956–967, Los Angeles, CA, February 1987.

[73] V.S. Nalwa. *A guided tour of computer vision*. Addison Wesley, 1993.

[74] R. Nevatia and T.O. Binford. Description and recognition of complex curved objects. *Artificial Intelligence*, 8:77–98, 1977.

[75] Quang-Loc Nguyen and M.D. Levine. Representing 3D objects in range images using geons. *Computer Vision and Image Understanding*, 63(1):158–168, January 1996.

[76] A. Noble, D. Wilson, and J. Ponce. On Computing Aspect Graphs of Smooth Shapes from Volumetric Data. *Computer Vision and Image Understanding: special issue on Mathematical Methods in Biomedical Image Analysis*, 66(2):179–192, 1997.

[77] A.P. Pentland. Perceptual organization and the representation of natural form. *Artificial Intelligence*, 28:293–331, 1986.

[78] S. Petitjean. *Géométrie énumérative et contacts de variétés linéaires: application aux graphes d'aspects d'objets courbes*. PhD thesis, Institut National Polytechnique de Lorraine, 1995.

[79] S. Petitjean, J. Ponce, and D.J. Kriegman. Computing exact aspect graphs of curved objects: Algebraic surfaces. *Int. J. of Comp. Vision*, 9(3):231–255, 1992.

[80] J. Ponce. On characterizing ribbons and finding skewed symmetries. *Comp. Vis. Graph. Im. Proc.*, 52:328–340, 1990.

[81] J. Ponce. Straight homogeneous generalized cylinders: differential geometry and uniqueness results. *Int. J. of Comp. Vision*, 4(1):79–100, 1990.

[82] J. Ponce and J.M. Brady. Toward a surface primal sketch. In T. Kanade, editor, *Three-dimensional machine vision*, pages 195–240. Kluwer Publishers, 1987.

[83] J. Ponce and D. Chelberg. Finding the limbs and cusps of generalized cylinders. *Int. J. of Comp. Vision*, 1(3):195–210, October 1987.

[84] J. Ponce, D. Chelberg, and W. Mann. Invariant properties of straight homogeneous generalized cylinders and their contours. *IEEE Trans. Patt. Anal. Mach. Intell.*, 11(9):951–966, September 1989.

[85] W. Richards, J.J. Koenderink, and D.D. Hoffman. Inferring 3D shapes from 2D codons. MIT AI Memo 840, MIT Artificial Intelligence Lab, 1985.

[86] M. Richetin, M. Dhome, J.T. Lapresté, and G. Rives. Inverse perspective transform from zero-curvature curve points: Application to the localization of some generalized cylinders from a single view. *IEEE Trans. Patt. Anal. Mach. Intell.*, 13(2):185–191, February 1991.

[87] J.H. Rieger. On the classification of views of piecewise-smooth objects. *Image and Vision Computing*, 5:91–97, 1987.

[88] J.H. Rieger. Global bifurcations sets and stable projections of non-singular algebraic surfaces. *Int. J. of Comp. Vision*, 7(3):171–194, 1992.

[89] L.G. Roberts. Machine perception of three-dimensional solids. In J.T. Tippett et al., editor, *Optical and Electro-Optical Information Processing*, pages 159–197. MIT Press, Cambridge, 1965.

[90] A. Rosenfeld. Axial representations of shape. *Comp. Vis. Graph. Im. Proc.*, 33:156–173, 1986.

[91] R. Rothe. Darstellende Geometrie des Geländes. 1914.

[92] De Saint-Venant. Surfaces à plus grande pente constituées sur des lignes courbes. *Bulletin de la soc. philomath. de Paris*, March 1852.

[93] H. Sato and T.O. Binford. Finding and recovering SHGC objects in an edge image. *CVGIP: Image Understanding*, 57:346–358, 1993.

[94] C. Schmid and R. Mohr. Local grayvalue invariants for image retrieval. *IEEE Trans. Patt. Anal. Mach. Intell.*, 19(5):530–535, May 1997.

[95] J. Serra. *Image Analysis and Mathematical Morphology.* Academic Press, New York, 1982.

[96] J.A. Sethian. *Level set methods: evolving interfaces in geometry, fluid mechanics, computer vision and materials sciences.* Cambridge University Press, 1996.

[97] S.A. Shafer. *Shadows and Silhouettes in Computer Vision.* Kluwer Academic Publishers, 1985.

[98] S.A. Shafer and T. Kanade. The theory of straight homogeneous generalized cylinders and a taxonomy of generalized cylinders. Technical Report CMU-CS-83-105, Carnegie-Mellon University, 1983.

[99] I. Shimshoni and J. Ponce. Finite-resolution aspect graphs of polyhedral objects. *IEEE Trans. Patt. Anal. Mach. Intell.*, 19(4):315–327, 1997.

[100] L. Shirman and C. Sequin. Local surface interpolation with Bezier patches. *CAGD*, 4:279–295, 1987.

[101] K. Siddiqi and B.B. Kimia. Parts of visual form: computational aspects. *IEEE Trans. Patt. Anal. Mach. Intell.*, 17(3):239–251, March 1995.

[102] D. Slater and G. Healey. Recognizing 3-d objects using local color invariants. *IEEE Trans. Patt. Anal. Mach. Intell.*, 18(2):206–210, 1996.

[103] B.I Soroka and R. Bajcsy. Generalized cylinders from cross-sections. In *Third Int. J. Conf. Patt. Recog.*, pages 734–735, 1976.

[104] D. Stam. Distributed homotopy continuation and its application to robotic grasping. Master's thesis, University of Illinois at Urbana-Champaign, 1992. Beckman Institute Tech. Report UIUC-BI-AI-RCV-92-03.

[105] J. Stewman and K.W. Bowyer. Creating the perspective projection aspect graph of polyhedral objects. In *Proc. Int. Conf. Comp. Vision*, pages 495–500, Tampa, FL, 1988.

[106] S. Sullivan and J. Ponce. Automatic model construction, pose estimation, and object recognition from photographs using triangular splines. In *Proc. Int. Conf. Comp. Vision*, pages 510–516, 1998.

[107] S. Sullivan and J. Ponce. Automatic model construction, pose estimation, and object recognition from photographs using triangular splines. *IEEE Trans. Patt. Anal. Mach. Intell.*, 20(10), Oct. 1998. In press.

[108] S. Sullivan, L. Sandford, and J. Ponce. Using geometric distance fits for 3D object modelling and recognition. *IEEE Trans. Patt. Anal. Mach. Intell.*, 16(12):1183–1196, December 1994.

[109] J.P. Thirion and G. Gourdon. The 3D marching lines algorithm: new results and proofs. Technical Report 1881-1, INRIA, 1993.

[110] R.Y. Tsai. A versatile camera calibration technique for high-accuracy 3D machine vision metrology using off-the-shelf TV cameras. *Journal of Robotics and Automation*, RA-3(4):323–344, 1987.

[111] M. Turk and A.P. Pentland. Face recognition using eigenfaces. *J. of Cognitive Neuroscience*, 3(1), 1991.

[112] S. Ullman and R. Basri. Recognition by linear combination of models. *IEEE Trans. Patt. Anal. Mach. Intell.*, 13(10):992–1006, 1991.

[113] F. Ulupinar and R. Nevatia. Using symmetries for analysis of shape from contour. In *Proc. Int. Conf. Comp. Vision*, pages 414–426, Tampa, FL, December 1988.

[114] C.E. Weatherburn. *Differential geometry*. Cambridge University Press, 1927.

[115] I. Weiss. Projective invariants of shapes. In *Proc. IEEE Conf. Comp. Vision Patt. Recog.*, pages 291–297, Ann Arbor, MI, 1988.

[116] M. Wertheimer. Laws of organization in perceptual forms. *Psychol. Forsch.*, 4:301–350, 1923. English translation in: W.B. Ellis, *A source book of Gestalt psychology* pages 71–88, 1973.

[117] A.P. Witkin. Scale-space filtering. In *Proc. International Joint Conference on Artificial Intelligence*, pages 1019–1022, Karlsruhe, Germany, 1983.

[118] M. Zerroug and G. Medioni. The challenge of generic object recongnition. In M. Hebert, J. Ponce, T.E. Boult, and A. Gross, editors, *Object Representation for Computer Vision*, number 994 in Lecture Notes in Computer Science, pages 217–232. Springer-Verlag, 1995.

[119] M. Zerroug and R. Nevatia. Using invariance and quasi-invariance for the segmentation and recovery of curved objects. In J.L. Mundy, A. Zisserman, and D. Forsyth, editors, *Applications of Invariance in Computer Vision*, volume 825 of *Lecture Notes in Computer Science*, pages 317–340. Springer-Verlag, 1994.

[120] A. Zisserman, D.A. Forsyth, J.L. Mundy, and C.A. Rothwell. Recognizing general curved objects efficiently. In J. Mundy and A. Zisserman, editors, *Geometric Invariance in Computer Vision*, pages 228–251. MIT Press, Cambridge, Mass., 1992.

Order Structure, Correspondence, and Shape Based Categories

Stefan Carlsson

Numerical Analysis and Computing Science, Royal Institute of Technology, (KTH),
S-100 44 Stockholm, Sweden,
stefanc@nada.kth.se, http://www.nada.kth.se/~stefanc

Abstract. We propose a general method for finding pointwise correspondence between 2-D shapes based on the concept of order structure
and using geometric hashing. The problem of finding correspondence and
the problem of establishing shape equivalence can be considered as one
and the same problem. Given shape equivalence, we can in general find
pointwise correspondence and the existence of a unambiguous correspondence mapping can be used as a rule for deciding shape equivalence. As
a measure of shape equivalence we will use the concept of *order structure*
which in principle can be defined for arbitrary geometric configurations
such as points lines and curves. The order structure equivalence of subsets of points and tangent directions of a shape is will be used to establish
pointwise correspondence. The finding of correspondence between different views of the same object and different instances of the same object
category can be used as a foundation for establishment and recognition
of visual categories.

1   Introduction

The problem of computing visual correspondence is central in many applications
in computer vision but it is notoriously difficult compared to the ease at which we
solve it perceptually when looking at images. Given two images of the same object from different viewpoints or even two different instances of the same object
category, humans are in general able to establish a point to point correspondence
between the images. In the example such as fig 1 there is no "correct" geometric
answer to the correspondence problem. This raises the question of what rules
actually govern the establishment of correspondence. One alternative would be
that the objects in the images are recognised as birds and point correspondence is established based on correspondence of part primitives such as head,
throat etc. which in general have invariant relations for the category of birds.
Another alternative however, would be to assume that correspondence is established based on some general similarity measure of image shapes, independent
of the fact that the images are recognised as birds. In that case, correspondence
can be used as a basis for recognition and categorisation instead of the other way
around. The two alternatives can easily be seen to be connected to alternative
theories of object recognition and categorisation that have been proposed over

D.A. Forsyth et al. (Eds.): Shape, Contour ..., LNCS 1681, pp. 58–71, 1999.

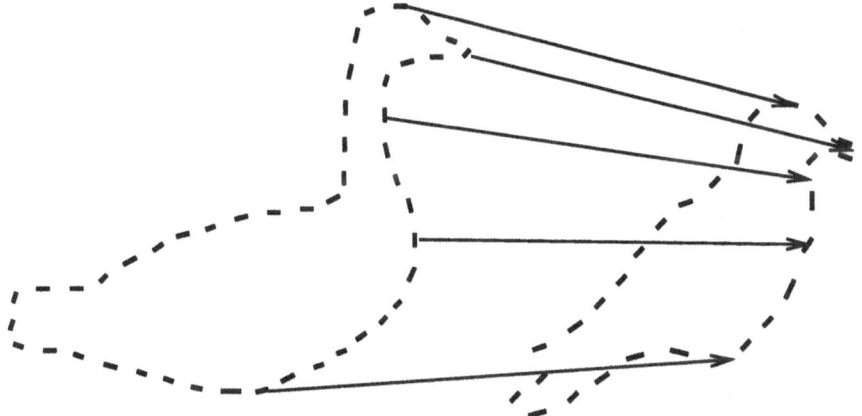

Fig. 1. By looking at pictures of instances of the same category of objects we are in general able to establish point to point correspondence

the years: 1. Recognition by components (RBC), where objects are described as composed of generic parts that are recognised in the image (Marr and Nishihara 1978, Biederman 1985) and 2. Recognition based on similarity of views (Blthoff et al. 1995, Tarr et al. 1995) which can form a basis for object categorisation (Edelman 1998). In this paper we will take the second point of view and define a general shape concept that can be used in the definition and computation of correspondence.

Historically the problem of computing correspondence between deformed shapes has been formulated as finding the minimum of a cost function defined on the two shapes, (Burr 1981, Yoshida and Sakoe 1982). For a recent review see (Basri et. al 1998). This is most often limited to the case when the shapes are described by their outlines so that the matching is a problem of curve matching. The need to a priori extract the outlines of the shapes limits the applicability of these methods. The definition of the cost function and the complexity of the matching are other problems that have to be faced.

The approach we will propose does not require any pre segmentation of shape outlines but works for arbitrary 2-D shapes. The input data to the algorithm will consist of groups of image coordinates with an associated tangent direction that can be obtained with extremely simple means. The input data structure has been simplified deliberately in order to avoid any complex perceptual grouping stage.

2   Order Structure

Order structure can be seen as the generalisation of the concept of ordering in one dimension to several dimensions. (Goodman and Pollack 1983, Bjorner et al. 1993). Order properties can be defined for point sets and other algebraically defined sets of features in arbitrary dimension. In (Carlsson 1996) the concept was used for sets of line segments in an algorithm for partial view invariant recognition of simple categories. It is also closely related to the idea used to describe qualitative difference of views in the concept of the aspect graph (Koenderink and van Doorn 1979). For computer vision problems, geometric structure can be described in a unified stratified way ranging from metric, affine and projective to that of order and incidence structure (Carlsson 1997). This can also be seen as going from quantitative detailed descriptions to qualitative and general ones which is necessary if we want to describe equivalence of instances of object categories or different viewpoints of an object.

Any structure concept defines equivalence classes of geometric shapes. Order structure seems to imply equivalence classes that are in accordance with those that are subjectively reported by humans which make it especially interesting to use for problems of visual recognition and categorisation.

2.1   Capturing Perceptual Shape Equivalence

If we look at the sequence of deformed shapes A-F in fig 2 we see that they are easily divided into two qualitatively different classes by the fact that the shape changes between C and D from a pure convex to a shape with a concavity. The concept of order structure can be used to capture the perceptual equivalence classes of shapes A-C and D-G respectively. If we sample the shapes D and F at five points and draw the tangents at those points, fig. 3, the qualitative structure of combined arrangement of points and lines can be seen to be in agreement in the sense that there is a one to one correspondence between the points of the two shapes such that the intersection of corresponding tangent lines are ordered relative to each other and to the points in exactly the same way. This relative ordering can be given a formal treatment using the concept of order structure for the arrangement of points and lines. The same order structure of points and

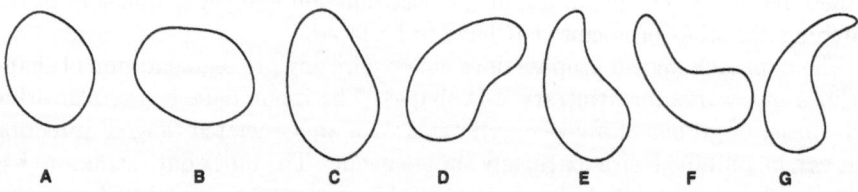

Fig. 2. Sequence of successive deformations

tangents can be obtained by sampling any of shapes D-F at five points. Note that the sampling points are in general in perceptual correspondence between different shapes. It is not possible to obtain the same order structure by sampling shaped A, B or C however, due to the fact that they are convex and lacks the

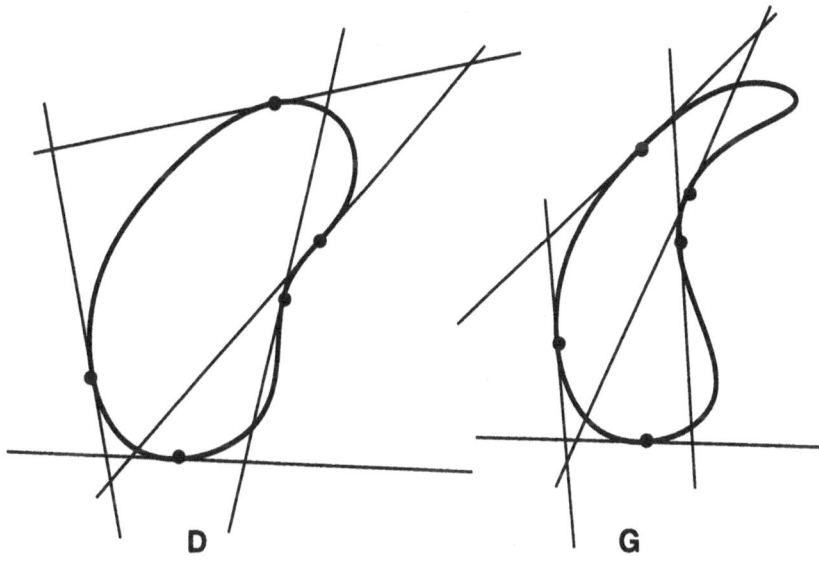

Fig. 3. Equivalent order structure from points and tangent lines shapes D and G

concavity of shapes D-F. The fact that subsets of points and tangent lines can be found with the same order structure is a potential tool for classifying shapes into equivalence classes and for establishing point to point correspondence. Note that there are other subsets of five points and tangents that have the same order structure through all of the shapes A - F. Fig. 4 illustrates that given perceptually corresponding points of two shapes we can get equivalent order structure based on points and tangent lines.

2.2   Point Sets

The order structure of a set of points and lines can be used to define equivalence classes of shapes whose members are qualitatively or topologically similar, i.e. they can be obtained from each other by a deformation that preserves order structure. Order structure is a natural extension of the concepts of affine and projective structure in the sense that all affine and projective transformations that preserve orientation also preserve order structure. Order structure preserving transformations or deformations are much larger than the classes of affine and projective transformation however. For a set of points in that plane, order structure is denoted order type. The order structure defining property for point sets is that of orientation. Three points $1, 2, 3$ have positive orientation if traversing them in order means anti-clockwise rotation. The orientation is negative if the rotation is clockwise. This can be established formally by computing the sign of the determinant:

$$sign[p_1\ p_2\ p_3] \tag{1}$$

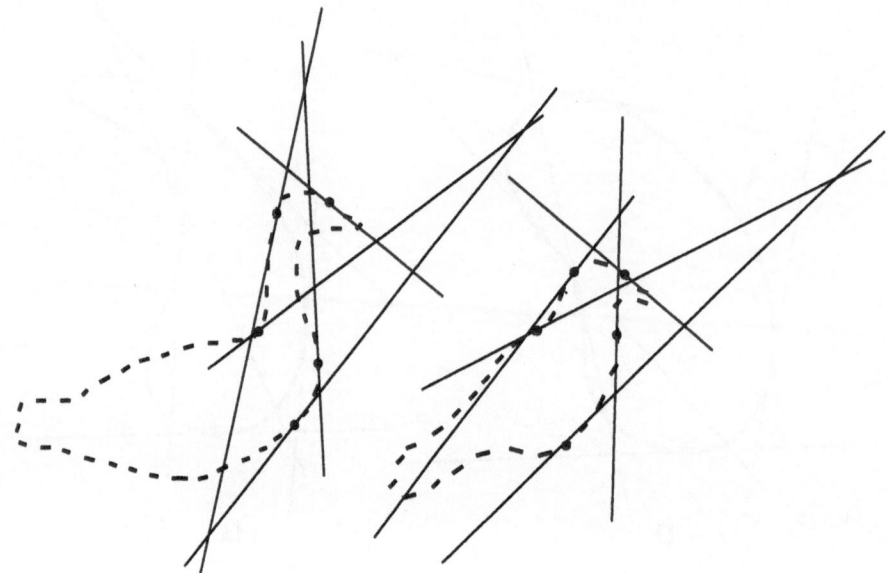

Fig. 4. Equivalent order structure from points and tangent lines

of the oriented homogeneous coordinates:

$$p = \begin{pmatrix} x \\ y \\ 1 \end{pmatrix} \tag{2}$$

For an arbitrary set of points, the order type is uniquely determined by the set of mappings:

$$\chi_p(i,j,k) = sign[p_i \; p_j \; p_k] \;\rightarrow\; \{-1,1\} \tag{3}$$

for all points i, j, k in the set. The various order types that exist for $3, 4$ and 5 points are shown in fig. 5. Note that for five points we get unique canonical orderings of the points for the first two order types. For the third one, ordering is ambiguous up to a cyclic permutation.

2.3 Sets of Lines

Order structure for a set of lines in the plane can be defined in essentially the same way as for points by using the fact that they are projectively dual. Some care must be exercised however since order structure relies on oriented projective geometry where duality does not hold strictly. If p are the homogeneous coordinates for a point, and q the homogeneous line coordinates of a line passing through p, we have

$$q^T p = 0 \tag{4}$$

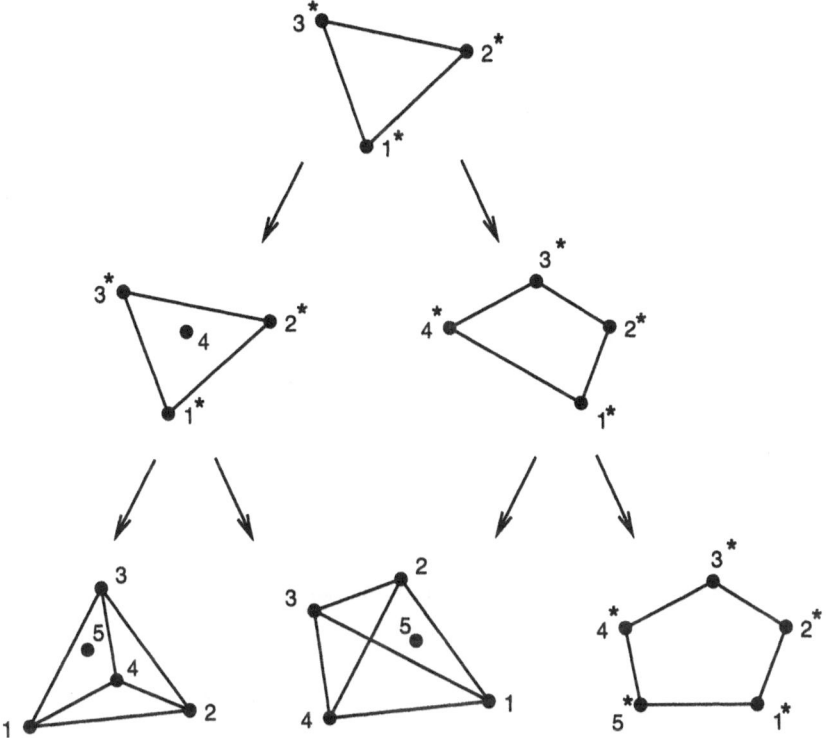

Fig. 5. Order types and canonical orderings for 3, 4, and 5 points. "∗" means that ordering is ambiguous up to cyclic permutations

In order to define order structure for lines in the same way as for points we have to normalise the homogeneous line coordinates q in some way. This will be done by choosing:

$$q = \begin{pmatrix} a \\ 1 \\ b \end{pmatrix} \tag{5}$$

which means that we consider lines of the form:

$$ax + y + b = 0 \tag{6}$$

The vertical line $x + b = 0$ therefore plays the same role as the point at infinity in the point case. All lines therefore become oriented relative to the vertical. The order type for a set of lines can now be represented by the signs:

$$\chi_l(i, j, k) = sign[q_i \; q_j \; q_k] \rightarrow \{-1, 1\} \tag{7}$$

for all triplets of lines i, j, k in the set.

2.4   Combination of Points and Lines

By using oriented homogeneous coordinates for lines we introduce a direction for every line. We can therefore assign a left-right position for every point in the plane relative to every line. For line q_i and point p_j this is given by:

$$\chi_{pl} = sign(q_i^T p_j) \rightarrow \{-1, 1\} \tag{8}$$

For every arrangement of points and lines we can therefore talk about the order structure of combinations of points and lines represented by these signs.

2.5   Order Structure Index from Points and Tangent Lines

An arbitrary set of points and tangent lines can now be assigned a unique order structure based on point, line and point-line order structure given by the sign sets $\chi_p(i,j,k), \chi_l(i,j,k)$ for all triplets of points (i,j,k) in the set, and $\chi_{pl}(i,j)$ for all pairs. If we start by computing the order type for the set of points, we get a unique numbering from the canonical ordering. In the case where ordering is ambiguous up to cyclic permutations we choose the leftmost point as the first point. Given the numbering of the points, we can compute all determinant signs

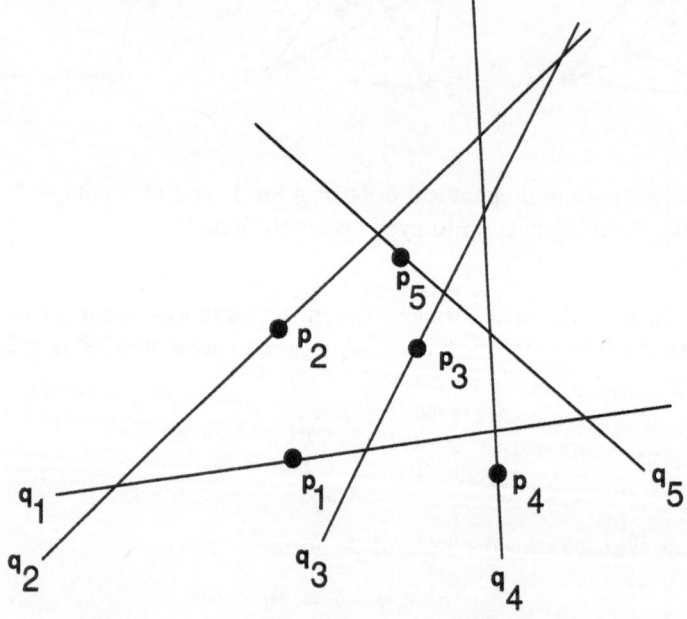

Fig. 6. Arrangement of points and tangent lines

for triplets of oriented line coordinates and inner product signs for lines and points. These signs can be combined into indexes which characterize the order structure of the point-line arrangement. Note that points and lines plays different roles in defining these indexes. The order structure of the points is used for the numbering of the points and lines. By giving an identity to each point and line, we increase the combinatorial richness of the arrangement of lines and thereby its discriminatory power compared to the case when the lines are not numbered.

3   Combinatorial Geometric Hashing - Computing Correspondence

Given subsets of points and lines from two shapes, we can compare their order structure. Order structure equivalence of subsets of points and tangents of an arbitrary shape can be used to establish point correspondence between the shapes. For two grey value images, we only have to sample points and tangents, i.e. there is no specific feature extraction or perceptual grouping stage necessary. The qualitative nature of the order structure concept means that metric accuracy of sampling point positions and tangent line directions is not required, leading to a robust scheme for computing correspondence.

An algorithm for computing point correspondence between arbitrary shapes in grey level images has been implemented using geometric hashing(Lamdan et. al. 1988) based on the combinatorial order structure of subsets of points and tangent lines. The algorithm computes point correspondence of a certain shape and that of a "model-shape" stored in the form of tables that can be indexed. The first part of the algorithm is the construction of the model-shape index table, and the second part is the actual indexing. The steps of the algorithm are illustrated by fig. 7. Both the modeling and indexing stages are based on sampling edge points of a shape and selecting all five point combinations. For a certain five point set, the canonical order type and an order structure index is computed based on the point coordinates and the line coordinates of the tangent lines of the edge points. The order structure index is used to identify the specific point set in the model table. All five point sets with the same order structure index are stored in the same entry given by the index.

Given a model table we can compute correspondence between the points in the table and the points that have been sampled from another shape. From the shape to be matched we sample five point combinations and compute order structure indexes just as in the modeling stage. The order structure index for a certain five point combination is used as a key to the model table and we note all the model five point combinations that are stored in the model table with that index. For each stored five point combination we vote for a correspondence to the five points from the shape to be matched. The end result is therefore a table of correspondence votes between the points of model shape and those of the shape to be matched.

4   Results and Discussion

The algorithm for computing correspondence has been tested on a set of shapes that were generated manually. Fig. 8 shows two shapes (A) and (B) of 12 points

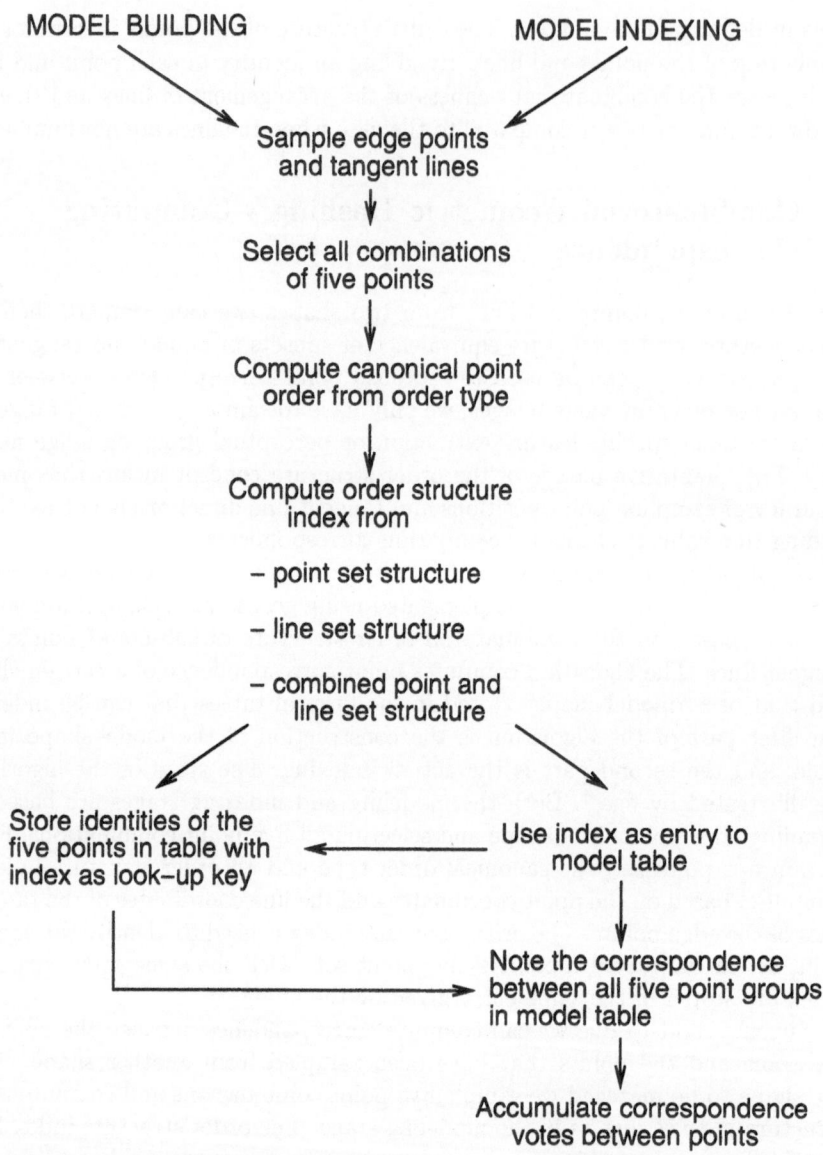

Fig. 7. Combinatorial geometric hashing for computing correspondence

and their tangent lines. (The points are located at the midpoints of the tangent line segments). The first table shows the normalised accumulated correspondence votes for the points when the shape (A) is matched to itself. We see that we get a dominant diagonal in the table as could be expected but we also get votes for incorrect correspondences but these are almost invariably associated with matchings to nearest neighboring points. The second table shows the result of

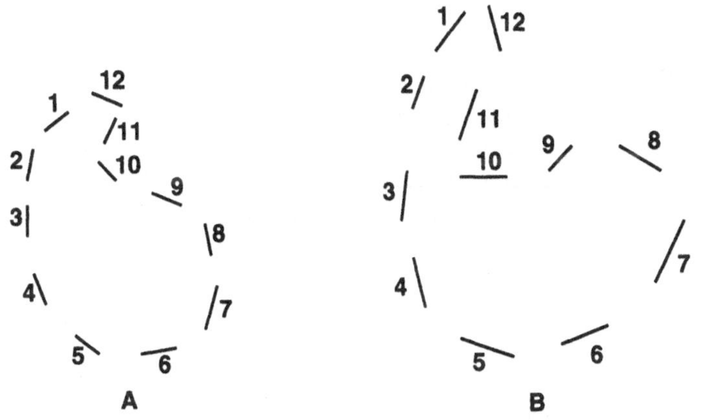

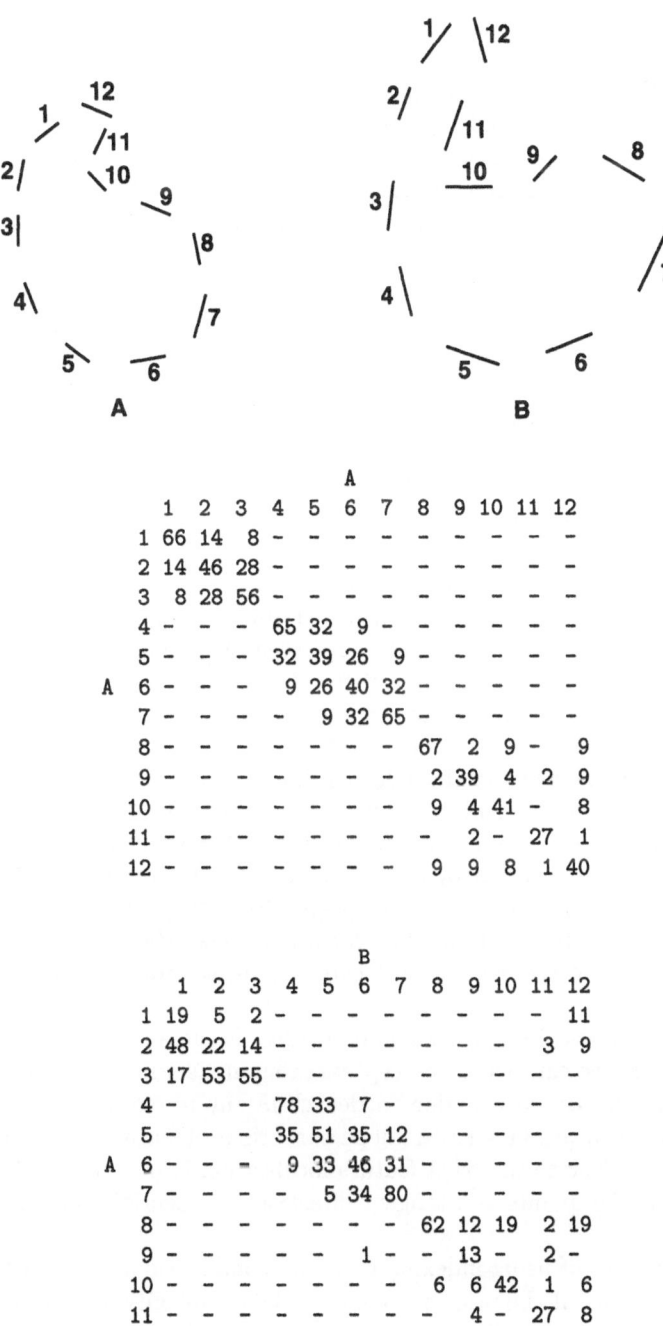

A \ A	1	2	3	4	5	6	7	8	9	10	11	12
1	66	14	8	-	-	-	-	-	-	-	-	-
2	14	46	28	-	-	-	-	-	-	-	-	-
3	8	28	56	-	-	-	-	-	-	-	-	-
4	-	-	-	65	32	9	-	-	-	-	-	-
5	-	-	-	32	39	26	9	-	-	-	-	-
6	-	-	-	9	26	40	32	-	-	-	-	-
7	-	-	-	-	9	32	65	-	-	-	-	-
8	-	-	-	-	-	-	-	67	2	9	-	9
9	-	-	-	-	-	-	-	2	39	4	2	9
10	-	-	-	-	-	-	-	9	4	41	-	8
11	-	-	-	-	-	-	-	-	2	-	27	1
12	-	-	-	-	-	-	-	9	9	8	1	40

A \ B	1	2	3	4	5	6	7	8	9	10	11	12
1	19	5	2	-	-	-	-	-	-	-	-	11
2	48	22	14	-	-	-	-	-	-	-	3	9
3	17	53	55	-	-	-	-	-	-	-	-	-
4	-	-	-	78	33	7	-	-	-	-	-	-
5	-	-	-	35	51	35	12	-	-	-	-	-
6	-	-	-	9	33	46	31	-	-	-	-	-
7	-	-	-	-	5	34	80	-	-	-	-	-
8	-	-	-	-	-	-	-	62	12	19	2	19
9	-	-	-	-	-	1	-	-	13	-	2	-
10	-	-	-	-	-	-	-	6	6	42	1	6
11	-	-	-	-	-	-	-	-	4	-	27	8
12	-	-	-	-	-	-	-	7	-	7	-	6

Fig. 8. Normalised accumulated correspondence votes for a shape (A) matched to itself and a deformed version (B)

correspondence when the shape (A) is matched to a deformed version (B). The peaks in the correspondence table are all at perceptually "correct" correspondences with the exception of point 12. The tables in this figure as well as the following ones are normalised for readability.

Fig. 9 shows a matching between pictures of a mug with a handle and a cup with a handle. From the table we see that most points of the mug are matched to perceptually corresponding points of the cup if peak in the table is used as matching criterion. The table has been partitioned into shape parts and there is a clear "parts" correspondence that can be read out from the table. A major ambiguity is that of the inner and outer parts of the mug's handle that are confused with the corresponding inner and outer parts of the cup's handle and that with the cup itself.

Another example of matching instances of the same object category is shown in fig. 10 where the outlines of the pictures of a goose and a crow are matched to each other. The overall correspondence is perceptually plausible with the exception of the top of gooses back matching to that of the head of the crow.

The results show that order structure of sampled points and tangent lines of a shape can be used to establish point correspondence between between shapes that are projections of instances of the same object category. The basic reason for this is that order structure is well preserved over shape deformations that do not alter the perceptual category of the shape. It is therefore an interesting alternative for use in recognition of shape based categories. Order structure can be considered as relational structure of very low level features. In that respect it is similar to shape category theories based on parts decomposition (Marr and Nishihara 1978, Biederman 1985) where object categories are defined based on relational structure of generic subparts. The fact that we use low level features however, means that we can bypass the stage of perceptual grouping that is necessary to define subparts which has proven to be very difficult to achieve in a robust way in computer vision. The correspondences that can be established between instances of the same object category using order structure indexing could be used to define a similarity measure which could be used as a basis for a system for categorical recognition (Rosch 1988, Edelman 1998) .

The fact that we can bypass perceptual grouping is a major advantage with our approach since this is a major bottleneck in any recognition system. Since order structure is invariant w.r.t. small perturbations of feature locations we also gain in robustness since no exact feature localisation is necessary. The extraction of features, i.e. points and tangent directions is essentially just a sampling process.

The advantages of using indexing based on combinations of features in this way of course comes at the price of combinatorial complexity. By considering all combinations of five point features, the complexity of the algorithm will grow as n^5 where n is the number of features in the image. In practise this means that we cannot consider more than $25 - 30$ features at a time. A major issue is therefore to find means how to reduce this complexity by being selective in the choice of feature combinations and only select a subset of all possibilities.

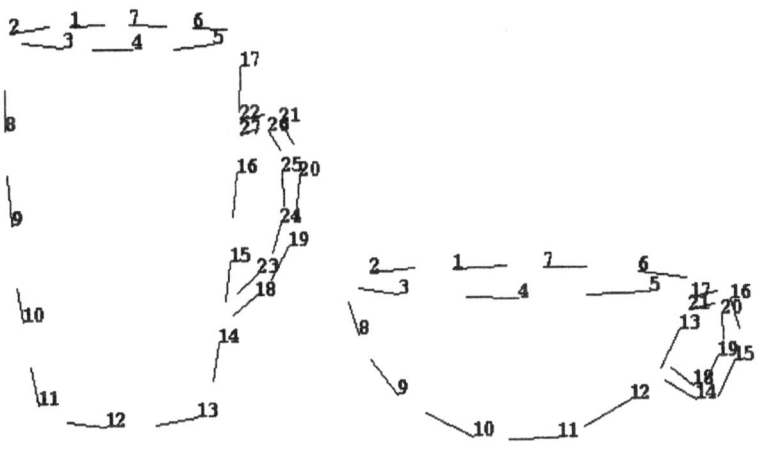

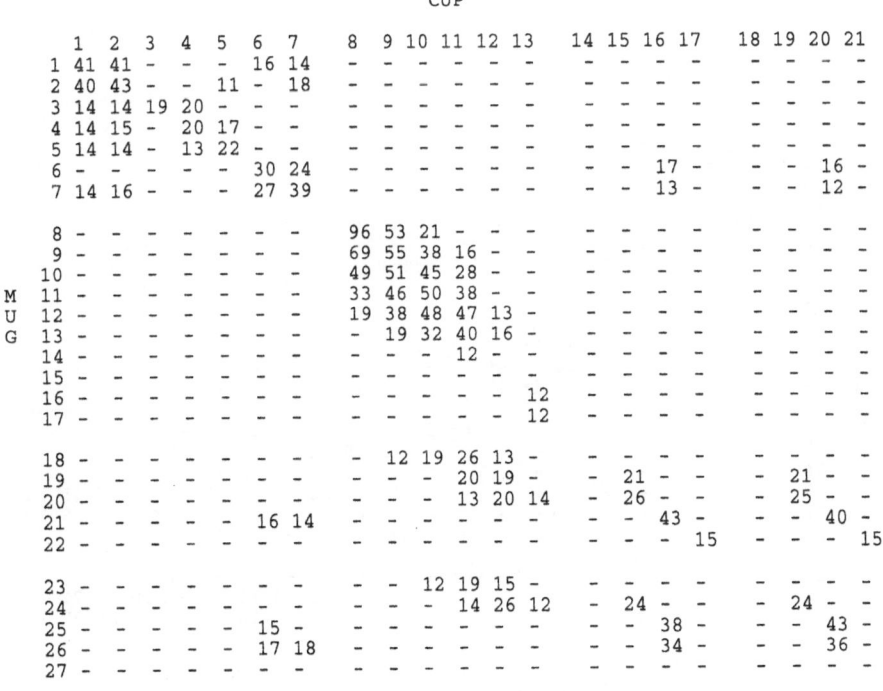

MUG \ CUP	1	2	3	4	5	6	7	8	9	10	11	12	13	14	15	16	17	18	19	20	21
1	41	41	-	-	-	16	14	-	-	-	-	-	-	-	-	-	-	-	-	-	-
2	40	43	-	-	11	-	18	-	-	-	-	-	-	-	-	-	-	-	-	-	-
3	14	14	19	20	-	-	-	-	-	-	-	-	-	-	-	-	-	-	-	-	-
4	14	15	-	20	17	-	-	-	-	-	-	-	-	-	-	-	-	-	-	-	-
5	14	14	-	13	22	-	-	-	-	-	-	-	-	-	-	-	-	-	-	-	-
6	-	-	-	-	-	30	24	-	-	-	-	-	-	-	-	17	-	-	-	16	-
7	14	16	-	-	-	27	39	-	-	-	-	-	-	-	-	13	-	-	-	12	-
8	-	-	-	-	-	-	-	96	53	21	-	-	-	-	-	-	-	-	-	-	-
9	-	-	-	-	-	-	-	69	55	38	16	-	-	-	-	-	-	-	-	-	-
10	-	-	-	-	-	-	-	49	51	45	28	-	-	-	-	-	-	-	-	-	-
11	-	-	-	-	-	-	-	33	46	50	38	-	-	-	-	-	-	-	-	-	-
12	-	-	-	-	-	-	-	19	38	48	47	13	-	-	-	-	-	-	-	-	-
13	-	-	-	-	-	-	-	-	19	32	40	16	-	-	-	-	-	-	-	-	-
14	-	-	-	-	-	-	-	-	-	-	12	-	-	-	-	-	-	-	-	-	-
15	-	-	-	-	-	-	-	-	-	-	-	-	-	-	-	-	-	-	-	-	-
16	-	-	-	-	-	-	-	-	-	-	-	-	12	-	-	-	-	-	-	-	-
17	-	-	-	-	-	-	-	-	-	-	-	-	12	-	-	-	-	-	-	-	-
18	-	-	-	-	-	-	-	-	12	19	26	13	-	-	-	-	-	-	-	-	-
19	-	-	-	-	-	-	-	-	-	-	20	19	-	-	21	-	-	-	21	-	-
20	-	-	-	-	-	-	-	-	-	-	13	20	14	-	26	-	-	-	25	-	-
21	-	-	-	-	-	16	14	-	-	-	-	-	-	-	-	43	-	-	-	40	-
22	-	-	-	-	-	-	-	-	-	-	-	-	-	-	-	-	15	-	-	-	15
23	-	-	-	-	-	-	-	-	-	12	19	15	-	-	-	-	-	-	-	-	-
24	-	-	-	-	-	-	-	-	-	-	14	26	12	-	24	-	-	-	24	-	-
25	-	-	-	-	-	15	-	-	-	-	-	-	-	-	-	38	-	-	-	43	-
26	-	-	-	-	-	17	18	-	-	-	-	-	-	-	-	34	-	-	-	36	-
27	-	-	-	-	-	-	-	-	-	-	-	-	-	-	-	-	-	-	-	-	-

Fig. 9. Normalised accumulated correspondence votes for MUG and CUP

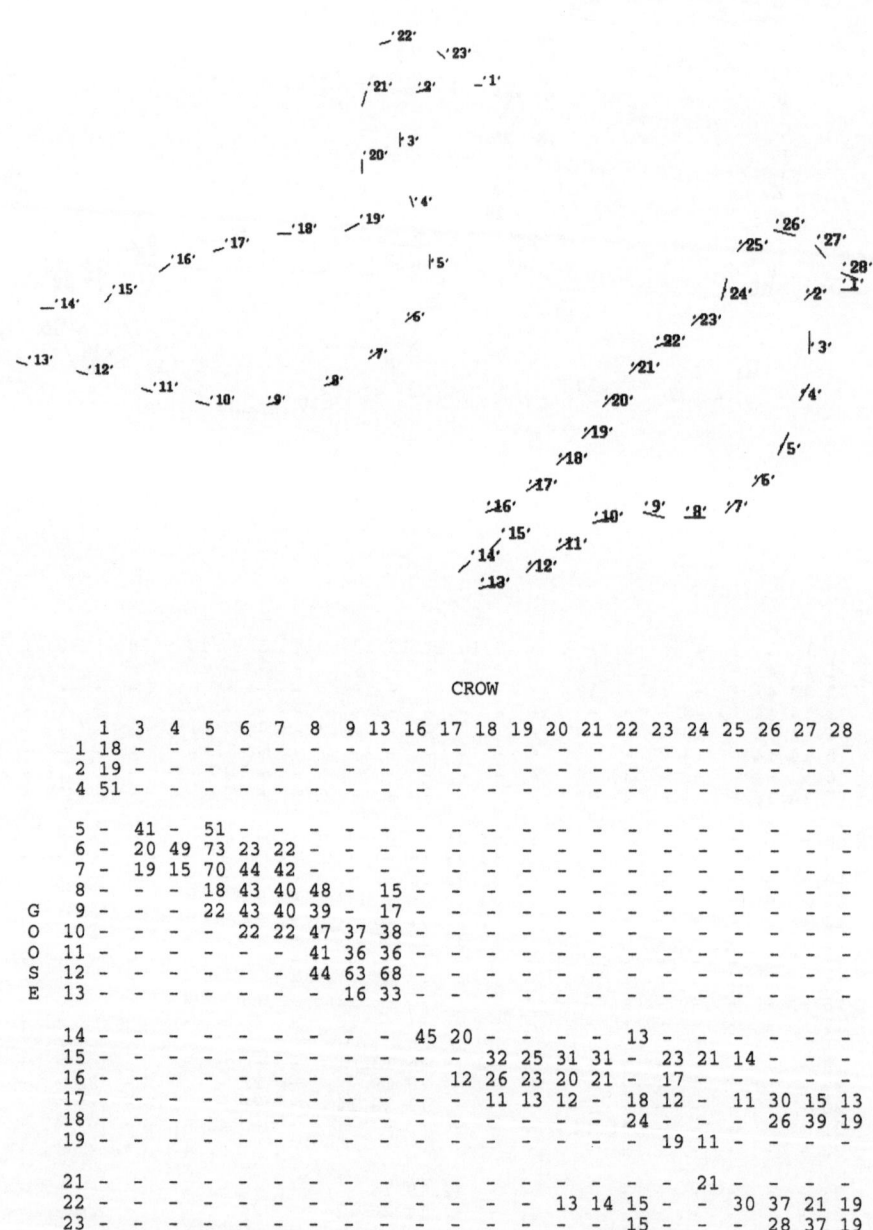

Fig. 10. Normalised accumulated correspondence votes for GOOSE and CROW

CROW

		1	3	4	5	6	7	8	9	13	16	17	18	19	20	21	22	23	24	25	26	27	28
	1	18	-	-	-	-	-	-	-	-	-	-	-	-	-	-	-	-	-	-	-	-	-
	2	19	-	-	-	-	-	-	-	-	-	-	-	-	-	-	-	-	-	-	-	-	-
	4	51	-	-	-	-	-	-	-	-	-	-	-	-	-	-	-	-	-	-	-	-	-
	5	-	41	-	51	-	-	-	-	-	-	-	-	-	-	-	-	-	-	-	-	-	-
	6	-	20	49	73	23	22	-	-	-	-	-	-	-	-	-	-	-	-	-	-	-	-
	7	-	19	15	70	44	42	-	-	-	-	-	-	-	-	-	-	-	-	-	-	-	-
	8	-	-	-	18	43	40	48	-	15	-	-	-	-	-	-	-	-	-	-	-	-	-
G	9	-	-	-	22	43	40	39	-	17	-	-	-	-	-	-	-	-	-	-	-	-	-
O	10	-	-	-	-	22	22	47	37	38	-	-	-	-	-	-	-	-	-	-	-	-	-
O	11	-	-	-	-	-	-	41	36	36	-	-	-	-	-	-	-	-	-	-	-	-	-
S	12	-	-	-	-	-	-	44	63	68	-	-	-	-	-	-	-	-	-	-	-	-	-
E	13	-	-	-	-	-	-	16	33	-	-	-	-	-	-	-	-	-	-	-	-	-	-
	14	-	-	-	-	-	-	-	-	-	45	20	-	-	-	-	13	-	-	-	-	-	-
	15	-	-	-	-	-	-	-	-	-	-	-	32	25	31	31	-	23	21	14	-	-	-
	16	-	-	-	-	-	-	-	-	-	-	12	26	23	20	21	-	17	-	-	-	-	-
	17	-	-	-	-	-	-	-	-	-	-	11	13	12	-	18	12	-	11	30	15	13	-
	18	-	-	-	-	-	-	-	-	-	-	-	-	-	-	-	-	24	-	-	26	39	19
	19	-	-	-	-	-	-	-	-	-	-	-	-	-	-	-	-	19	11	-	-	-	-
	21	-	-	-	-	-	-	-	-	-	-	-	-	-	-	-	-	-	21	-	-	-	-
	22	-	-	-	-	-	-	-	-	-	-	-	-	-	13	14	15	-	-	30	37	21	19
	23	-	-	-	-	-	-	-	-	-	-	-	-	-	-	-	15	-	-	-	28	37	19

In a sense, this is exactly what classical perceptual grouping tries to achieve by using rules of non-accidentalness of image features, (Lowe 1985). Order structure indexing implies a more general approach to this problem since we do not limit ourselves a priori to specific feature relations but can use arbitrary combinations on the basis of their effectiveness in establishing correspondence.

References

[1] R. Basri, L. Costa, D. Geiger and D. Jacobs Determining the similarity of deformed objects, Vision Research, 38, Issue 15-16,pp. 2365-2385 August (1998)

[2] I. Biederman, Human image understanding: recent research and a theory, CVGIP 32, 29-73, (1985)

[3] Bjorner, Las Vergnas, Sturmfels, White and Ziegler, Oriented Matroids, Encyclopedia of Mathematics and its Applications, Vol. 46, C.G.Rota editor, Cambridge University Press, (1993)

[4] D. J. Burr, Elastic Matching of Line Drawings, IEEE Trans. on Pattern Analysis and Machine Intelligence, 3, No. 6, pp. 708-713, November (1981)

[5] H. H Bülthoff, S. Edelman and M. Tarr: How are three-dimensional objects represented in the brain? Cerebral Cortex 5, 247-260 (1995).

[6] S. Carlsson, Combinatorial Geometry for Shape Representation and Indexing, Object Representation in Computer Vision II, Springer Lecture Notes in Computer Science 1144, pp. 53 - 78 Ponce, Zisserman eds. (1996)

[7] S. Carlsson Geometric Structure and View Invariant Recognition Philosophical Transactions of the Royal Society of London Series A, 356, 1233 - 1247 (1998)

[8] S. Edeleman, Representation is representation of similarity, Behavioral and Brain Sciences (to appear) (1998)

[9] J. E. Goodman and R. Pollack Multidimensional sorting SIAM J. Comput. 12 , 484–507, (1983)

[10] J. J. Koenderink and A. von Doorn, The internal representation of solid shape with respect to vision, Biological Cybernetics, 32, 211 - 216, (1979)

[11] Y. Lamdan, J. T. Schwartz, and H. J. Wolfson, Object recognition by affine invariant matching. In: Proc. CVPR-88, pp. 335-344. (1988)

[12] D.G. Lowe, Perceptual Organisation and Visual Recognition, Kluwer, (1984).

[13] D. Marr and K. Nishihara, Representation and recognition of the spatial organisation of three dimensional shapes, Proc. Roy. Soc. B 200: 269 - 294 (1978)

[14] E. Rosch, Principles of categorisation, In: Rosch and Lloyd eds., Cognition and Categorisation, pp. 27 - 48, Erlbaum, Hillsdale, NJ (1988)

[15] M. J. Tarr, W.G. Hayward, I. Gauthier,and P. Williamns, Is object recognition mediated by viewpoint invariant parts or viewpoint dependent features ? Perception, 24, 4, (1995)

[16] K. Yoshida and H. Sakoe , "Online handwritten character recognition for a personal computer system", IEEE Trans. on Consumer Electronics CE-28, (3): 202 - 209, (1982)
1982

Quasi-Invariant Parameterisations and Their Applications in Computer Vision[*]

Jun Sato[1,2] and Roberto Cipolla[2]

[1] Nagoya Institute of Technology, Nagoya 466, Japan
[2] Department of Engineering, University of Cambridge, Cambridge CB2 1PZ, UK

Abstract. In this paper, we show that there exist *quasi-invariant parameterisations* which are not exactly invariant but approximately invariant under group transformations and do not require high order derivatives. The affine quasi-invariant parameterisation is investigated in more detail and exploited for defining general affine semi-local invariants from second order derivatives only. The new invariants are implemented and used for matching curve segments under general affine motions and extracting symmetry axes of objects with 3D bilateral symmetry.

1 Introduction

The relative motion between an observer and the scene causes distortions in images. These distortions can be described by specific *transformation groups* [17], such as Euclidean, affine and projective transformations. Thus, geometric invariants under these transformation groups are very important for object recognition and identification [16, 17, 20, 22, 27].

Although invariants on points have been studied extensively [1, 22, 32], invariants on smooth curves and curved surfaces have not been explored enough [7, 8, 23, 27, 30]. The traditional invariants for smooth curves are differential invariants [7, 30]. Since these invariants require high order derivatives, many methods have been studied to reduce the order of derivatives for defining invariants on curves.

If we have enough number of distinguished points on curves, these points provide coordinate frames to normalise distorted curves without using derivatives [32]. For planar curves, three distinguished points are required for normalising affine distortions, and four points for projective distortions. If we use the differential property of curves, we can reduce the number of distinguished points required for computing invariants on curves [16, 20, 27]. For example, if we have first derivatives, two distinguished points are enough to compute invariants under projective transformations [27]. However, to find correspondences of distinguished points on the original and distorted curves is non-trivial problem.

To cope with these problems, semi-local invariants were also proposed [4, 23]. They showed that it is possible to define invariants semi-locally, by which the order of derivatives in invariants can be reduced from that of group curvatures

---

[*] The authors acknowledge the support of the EPSRC, grant GR/K84202.

D.A. Forsyth et al. (Eds.): Shape, Contour ..., LNCS 1681, pp. 72–92, 1999.
© Springer-Verlag Berlin Heidelberg 1999

to that of group arc-length without using any distinguished points on curves. As we have seen in these works, the invariant parameterisation is important to guarantee unique identification of corresponding intervals on curves.

Although semi-local invariants reduce the order of derivatives required, it is known that the order is still high in the general affine and projective cases (see table 1). In this paper, we introduce a *quasi-invariant parameterisation* and show how it enables us to use second order derivatives instead of fourth and fifth. The idea of quasi-invariant parameterisation is to approximate the group invariant arc-length by lower order derivatives. The new parameterisations are therefore less sensitive to noise, and are approximately invariant under a slightly restricted range of image distortions.

The concept of quasi-invariants was originally proposed by Binford [2], who showed that quasi-invariants enable a reduction in the number of corresponding points required for computing algebraic invariants. For example quasi-invariants require only four points for computing planar projective invariants [2], while exact planar projective invariants require five points [17]. It has also been shown that quasi-invariants exist even under the situation where the exact invariant does not exist [2]. In spite of its potential, the quasi-invariant has not previously been studied in detail. One reason for this is that the concept of *quasiness* is rather ambiguous and is difficult to formalise. Furthermore, the existing method is limited to the quasi-invariants based on point correspondences [2], or the quasi-invariants under specific models [31].

In this paper, we investigate quasi-invariance on smooth manifolds, and show that there exists a *quasi-invariant parameterisation*, that is a parameterisation approximately invariant under group transformations. Although the approximated values are no longer exact invariants, their changes are negligible for a restricted range of transformations. Hence, the aim here is to find in parameterisations the best tradeoff between the error caused by the approximation and the error caused by image noise.

Following the motivation, we investigate a measure of invariance which describes the difference from the exact invariant under group transformations. To formalise a measure of invariance in differential formulae, we introduce the so called *prolongation* [18] of vector fields. We next define a quasi-invariant parameter as a function which minimises the difference from the exact invariant. A quasi invariant parameter under general affine transformations is then proposed. The proposed parameter is applied to semi-local integral invariants and exploited successfully for matching curves under general affine transformations in real image sequences.

2   Semi-local Invariants

If the invariants are too local such as differential invariants [7, 30], they suffer from noise. If the invariants are too global such as moment (integral) invariants [11, 14, 26], they suffer from occlusion and the requirement of correspondences. It has been shown recently [4, 23] that it is possible to define integral

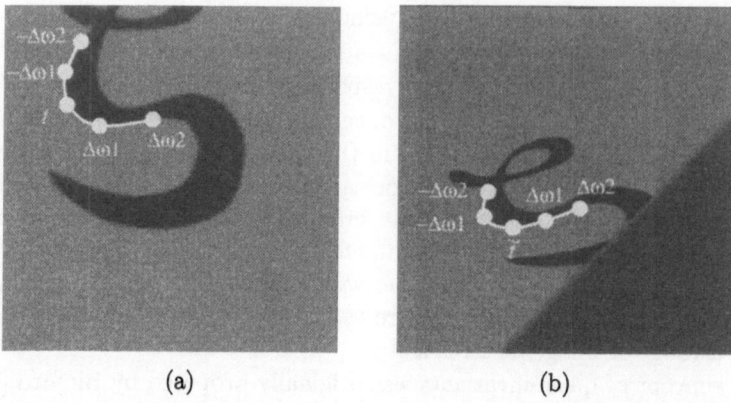

(a)   (b)

Fig. 1. Identifying interval of integration semilocally. (a) and (b) are images of a Japanese character extracted from the first and the second viewpoints. The interval of integration in these two images can be identified uniquely from invariant arc-length, w. For example, an interval, $(t - \Delta w_1, t + \Delta w_1)$, corresponds to an interval $(\tilde{t} - \Delta w_1, \tilde{t} + \Delta w_1)$.

invariants semi-locally, so that they do not suffer from occlusion, image noise and the requirement of correspondences.

Consider a curve, $\mathbf{C} \in \mathbf{R}^2$, to be parameterised by t. It is also possible to parameterise the curve by invariant parameters, w, under specific transformation groups. These are called arc-length of the group. The important property of group arc-length is that it enables us to identify the corresponding interval of curves automatically. Consider a point, $\mathbf{C}(t)$, on a curve $\mathbf{C}$ to be transformed to a point, $\tilde{\mathbf{C}}(\tilde{t})$, on a curve $\tilde{\mathbf{C}}$ by a group transformation as shown in Fig. 1. Since w is an invariant parameterisation, if we take an interval, $(t - \Delta w, t + \Delta w)$, on $\mathbf{C}$ and an interval, $(\tilde{t} - \Delta w, \tilde{t} + \Delta w)$ on $\tilde{\mathbf{C}}$, then these two intervals correspond to each other (see Fig. 1). That is, by integrating with respect to the group arc-length, w, the corresponding interval of integration of the original and the transformed curves can be uniquely identified.

By using the invariant parameterisations, we can define semi-local invariants, I, at point $\mathbf{C}(t)$ with interval $(-\Delta w, \Delta w)$ as follows:

$$I(t) = \int_{t-\Delta w}^{t+\Delta w} F \, dw \tag{1}$$

where, F is any invariant function under the group. The choice of F provides various kinds of semi-local invariants [23]. If we choose the function F carefully, the integral formula (1) can be solved analytically, and the resulting invariants have simpler forms. For example, in the affine case, we have the following semi-local invariants:

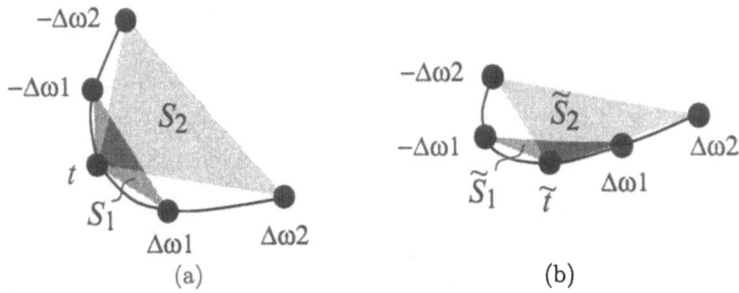

Fig. 2. Semi-local invariants.In affine case, semi-local invariants are defined as the ratio of two areas defined by the invariant parameter.

$$I(t) = \frac{S_1(t)}{S_2(t)} \tag{2}$$

S_1 and S_2 are the areas made of the two sets of two vectors, $\mathbf{C}(t + \Delta w_1) - \mathbf{C}(t)$ and $\mathbf{C}(t - \Delta w_1) - \mathbf{C}(t)$, and $\mathbf{C}(t + \Delta w_2) - \mathbf{C}(t)$ and $\mathbf{C}(t - \Delta w_2) - \mathbf{C}(t)$ as follows:

$$S_1(t) = \frac{1}{2}[\mathbf{C}(t + \Delta w_1) - \mathbf{C}(t), \mathbf{C}(t - \Delta w_1) - \mathbf{C}(t)]$$

$$S_2(t) = \frac{1}{2}[\mathbf{C}(t + \Delta w_2) - \mathbf{C}(t), \mathbf{C}(t - \Delta w_2) - \mathbf{C}(t)]$$

where, $[\mathbf{x}_1, \mathbf{x}_2]$ denotes the determinant of a matrix which consists of two column vectors, $\mathbf{x}_1, \mathbf{x}_2 \in \mathbf{R}^2$.

From table 1 [19], it is clear that the semi-local invariants are useful under Euclidean and special affine cases, but they still require high order derivatives in general affine and projective cases.

The distortion caused by a group transformation is often not so large. For example, the distortion caused by the relative motion between the observer and the scene is restricted because of the finite speed of the camera or object motions. In such cases, parameters approximated by lower order derivatives give us

Table 1. Order of derivatives required for the group arc-length and curvature. In general derivatives more than the second order are sensitive to noise, and are not available from images. Thus, the general affine and projective arc-length as well as curvatures are not practical.

group	arc-length	curvature
Euclidean	1st	2nd
special affine	2nd	4th
general affine	4th	5th
projective	5th	7th

a good approximation of the exact invariant parameterisation. We call such a parameterisation a *quasi-invariant parameterisation*. In the following sections, we define the quasi-invariant parameterisation, and derive an affine quasi-invariant parameterisation.

3   Infinitesimal Quasi-Invariance

Before deriving quasi-invariant parameterisations, we first consider the concept of *infinitesimal quasi-invariance*; that is quasi-invariance under infinitesimal group transformations.

3.1   Vector Fields of the Group

Let G be a *Lie group*, that is a group which carries the structure of a smooth manifold in such a way that both the group operation (multiplication) and the inversion are smooth maps [18]. Transformation groups such as rotation, Euclidean, affine and projective groups are Lie groups.

Consider an image point $\mathbf{x} = [x, y]$ to be transformed to $\tilde{\mathbf{x}} = [\tilde{x}, \tilde{y}]$ by a group transformation, $h \in G$, so that a function, $I(x, y)$, with respect to x and y coordinates is transformed to $\tilde{I}(\tilde{x}, \tilde{y})$ by h.

Infinitesimally this is considered as an action of a 2D vector field, $\mathbf{v}$:

$$\mathbf{v} = \xi \frac{\partial}{\partial x} + \eta \frac{\partial}{\partial y} \tag{3}$$

where, ξ and η are functions of x and y. Locally the orbit of the point, $\mathbf{x}$, caused by the transformation, h, is described by an integral curve, Γ, of the vector field, $\mathbf{v}$, passing through the point (see Fig. 3). The uniqueness of an ordinary differential equation guarantees the existence of such a unique integral curve in the vector field.

Because of its linearity, infinitesimal generator can be described by the summation of a finite number of independent vector fields, $\mathbf{v}_i$ $(i = 1, 2, \cdots, m)$, of the group as follows:

$$\mathbf{v} = \sum_{i=1}^{m} \mathbf{v}_i \tag{4}$$

where $\mathbf{v}_i$ is the ith independent vector field:

$$\mathbf{v}_i = \xi_i \frac{\partial}{\partial x} + \eta_i \frac{\partial}{\partial y} \tag{5}$$

where, ξ_i and η_i are basis coefficients of $\frac{\partial}{\partial x}$ and $\frac{\partial}{\partial y}$ respectively, and are functions of x and y. These independent vector fields form a finite dimensional vector space called a *Lie algebra* [18]. Locally any transformation of the group can be described by an integral of a finite number of independent vector fields, $\mathbf{v}_i$. The vector field described in (3) acts as a differential operator of the Lie derivative.

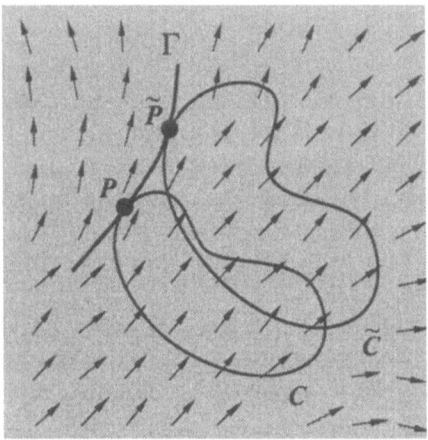

Fig. 3. The vector field, **v**, and an integral curve, Γ. The curve **C** is transformed to $\tilde{\mathbf{C}}$ by a group transformation, so that the point **P** on the curve is transformed to $\tilde{\mathbf{P}}$. Locally the orbit of the point caused by a group transformation coincides with the integral curve, Γ, of the vector field at the point, **P**.

3.2 Exact Invariance

Let **v** be an infinitesimal generator of the group transformation. A real-valued function I is invariant under group transformations, if and only if the Lie derivative of I with respect to any infinitesimal generator, **v**, of the group, G, vanishes as follows [18]:

$$\pounds_{\mathbf{v}}[I] = 0 \qquad (6)$$

where $\pounds_{\mathbf{v}}[\cdot]$ denotes the Lie derivatives with respect to a vector field **v**. Since I is a scalar function, the Lie derivative is the same as the directional derivative with respect to **v**. Thus, the condition of invariance (6) can be rewritten as follows:

$$\mathbf{v}[I] = 0 \qquad (7)$$

where $\mathbf{v}[\cdot]$ is the directional derivative with respect to **v**.

3.3 Infinitesimal Quasi-Invariance

The idea of quasi-invariance is to approximate the exact invariant by a certain function $I(x, y)$, which is not exactly invariant but nearly invariant. If the function, I, is not exactly invariant the equation (7) no longer holds. We can however measure the difference from the exact invariant by using (7). By definition, the change in function I caused by the infinitesimal group transformation induced by a vector field, **v**, is described by the Lie derivative of I as follows:

$$\delta I = \mathbf{v}[I] = \sum_{i=1}^{m} \mathbf{v}_i[I] \tag{8}$$

For measuring the invariance of a function irrespective of the choice of basis vectors, we consider an intrinsic vector field of the group, G. It is known [25] that if the group is semi-simple (e.g. rotation group, special linear group), there exists a non-degenerate symmetric bilinear form called *Killing form*, K, of the Lie algebra as follows:

$$K(\mathbf{v}_i, \mathbf{v}_j) = tr(ad(\mathbf{v}_i)ad(\mathbf{v}_j)) \quad (i, j = 1, 2, \cdots, m) \tag{9}$$

where $ad(\mathbf{v}_i)$ denotes the adjoint representation of $\mathbf{v}_i$, and tr denotes the trace (The adjoint representation, $ad(\mathbf{v}_i)$, provides a $m \times m$ matrix representation of the algebra, whose (j, k) component is described by a structure constant C_{ik}^j [25]). The Killing form provides the metric tensor, g_{ij}, for the algebra:

$$g_{ij} = K(\mathbf{v}_i, \mathbf{v}_j) \tag{10}$$

and the Casimir operator, C_a, defined by the metric tensor is independent of the choice of the basis vectors:

$$C_a = g^{ij}\mathbf{v}_i\mathbf{v}_j$$

where, g^{ij} is the inverse of g_{ij}. That is, the metric, g^{ij}, changes according to the choice of basis vectors, $\mathbf{v}_i$, so that C_a is an invariant. Since g^{ij} is symmetric, there exists a choice of basis vectors, $\mathbf{v}_i (i = 1, 2, \cdots, m)$, by which g^{ij} is diagonalised as follows:

$$g^{ij} = \begin{cases} \pm 1 & \text{if } i = j \\ 0 & \text{if } i \neq j \end{cases}$$

Such vector fields, $\mathbf{v}_i (i = 1, 2, \cdots, m)$, are unique in the group, G, and thus intrinsic. By using the intrinsic vector fields in (8), we can measure the change in value of a function, I, which is intrinsic to the group, G.

For measuring the quasi invariance of a function irrespective of the magnitude of the function, we consider the change in function, δI, normalised by the original function, I. We, thus, define a measure of infinitesimal quasi invariance, Q, of a function I by the squared sum of normalised changes in function caused by the intrinsic vector fields, $\mathbf{v}_i (i = 1, 2, \cdots, m)$, as follows:

$$Q = \sum_{i=1}^{m} \left(\frac{\mathbf{v}_i[I]}{I} \right)^2 \tag{11}$$

This is a measure of how invariant the function, I, is under the group transformation. If Q is small enough, we call I a quasi-invariant under infinitesimal group transformations.

Unfortunately, if the group is not semi-simple (e.g. general affine group, general linear group), the Killing form is degenerate and we do not have such intrinsic vector fields. However, it is known that a non-semi-simple group is decomposed into a semi-simple group and a radical. Thus, in such cases, we choose a set of vector fields which correspond to the semi-simple group and the radical.

4   Quasi-Invariance on Smooth Manifolds

In the last section, we introduced the concept of infinitesimal quasi-invariance, which is the quasi-invariance under infinitesimal group transformations, and derived a measure for the invariance of an approximated function. Unfortunately (11) is valid only for functions which do not include derivatives. In this section, we introduce an important concept known as the *prolongation* [18] of vector fields, and investigate quasi-invariance on smooth manifolds, so that it enables us to define quasi-invariants with a differential formula.

4.1   Prolongation of Vector Fields

The prolongation is a method for investigating the differential world from a geometric point of view. Let a smooth curve $\mathbf{C} \in \mathbf{R}^2$ be described by an independent variable x and a dependent variable y with a smooth function f as follows:

$$y = f(x)$$

The curve, $\mathbf{C}$, is transformed to $\widetilde{\mathbf{C}}$ by a group transformation, h, induced by a vector field, $\mathbf{v}$, as shown in Fig. 4. Consider a kth order prolonged space, whose coordinates are x, y and derivatives of y with respect to x up to kth order, so that the prolonged space is $k + 2$ dimensional. The curves, $\mathbf{C}$ and $\widetilde{\mathbf{C}}$, in 2D space are prolonged and described by space curves, $\mathbf{C}^{(k)}$ and $\widetilde{\mathbf{C}}^{(k)}$, in the $k + 2$ dimensional prolonged space. The prolonged vector field, $\mathbf{v}^{(k)}$, is a vector field in $k + 2$ dimension, which carries the prolonged curve, $\mathbf{C}^{(k)}$, to the prolonged curve, $\widetilde{\mathbf{C}}^{(k)}$ explicitly as shown in Fig. 4. More precisely, the kth order prolongation, $\mathbf{v}^{(k)}$, of a vector field, $\mathbf{v}$, is defined so that it transforms the kth order derivatives, $y^{(k)}$, of a function, $y = f(x)$, into the corresponding kth order derivatives, $\widetilde{y}^{(k)}$, of the transformed function $\widetilde{y} = \widetilde{f}(\widetilde{x})$ geometrically.

Let $\mathbf{v}_i, (i = 1, .., m)$ be m independent vector fields induced by a group transformation, h. Since the prolongation is linear, the kth prolongation, $\mathbf{v}^{(k)}$, of a general vector field, $\mathbf{v}$, can be described by a sum of kth prolongations, $\mathbf{v}_i^{(k)}$, of the independent vector fields, $\mathbf{v}_i$ as follows:

$$\mathbf{v}^{(k)} = \sum_{i=1}^{m} \mathbf{v}_i^{(k)}$$

Consider a vector field (5) in 2D space again. Its first and second prolongations, $\mathbf{v}^{(1)}$, $\mathbf{v}^{(2)}$, are computed as follows [18]:

$$\mathbf{v}_i^{(1)} = \mathbf{v}_i + (D_x(\eta_i - \xi_i y_x) + \xi_i y_{xx})\frac{\partial}{\partial y_x} \tag{12}$$

$$\mathbf{v}_i^{(2)} = \mathbf{v}_i^{(1)} + (D_x^2(\eta_i - \xi_i y_x) + \xi_i y_{xxx})\frac{\partial}{\partial y_{xx}} \tag{13}$$

where D_x and D_x^2 denote the first and the second total derivatives with respect to x, and y_x, y_{xx}, y_{xxx} denote the first, second and the third derivatives of y

original image   **transformed image**

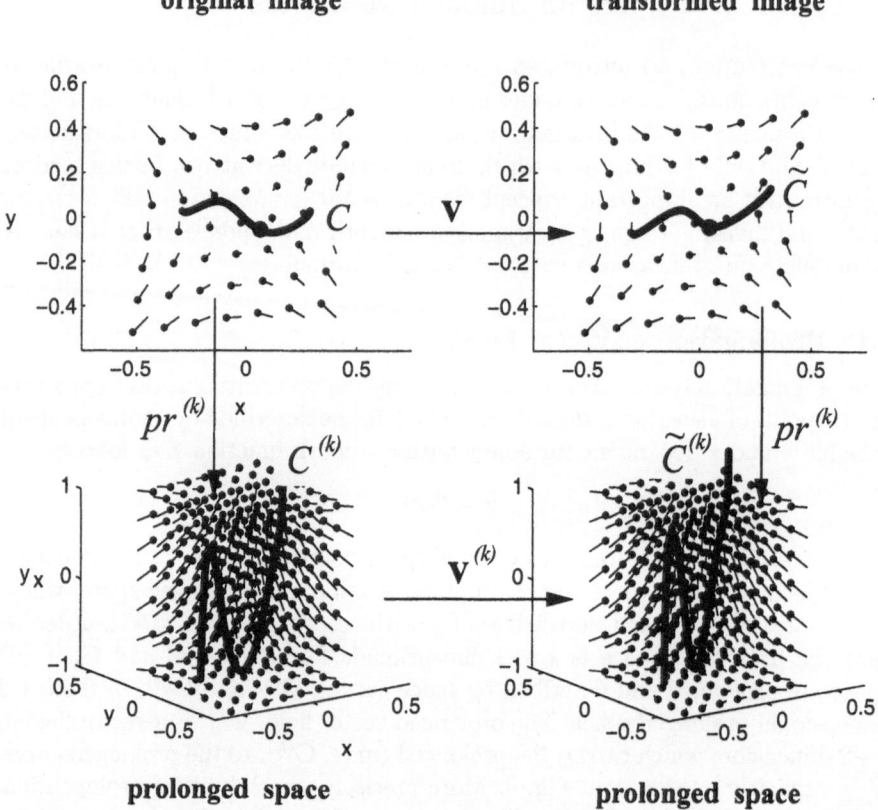

prolonged space   **prolonged space**

Fig. 4. Prolongation of a vector field. The kth order prolonged vector field, $\mathbf{v}^{(k)}$ transforms kth order derivatives of y into kth order derivatives of $\tilde{y}$. That is the prolonged curve, $\mathbf{C}^{(k)}$, is transformed into the prolonged curve, $\widetilde{\mathbf{C}}^{(k)}$, by the prolonged vector field, $\mathbf{v}^{(k)}$. This enables us to investigate derivatives of functions geometrically. $pr^{(k)}$ denotes kth order prolongation. This figure illustrates the first order prolongation ($k = 1$).

with respect to x. Let $F(x, y, y^{(k)})$ be a function of x, y and derivatives of y with respect to x up to kth order, which is denoted by $y^{(k)}$. Since the prolongation describes how the derivatives are going to change under group transformations, we can compute the change in function, δF, caused by the group transformation, h, as follows:

$$\delta F = \mathbf{v}^{(k)}[F]$$

where, $\mathbf{v}^{(k)}$ is the kth order prolongation of the infinitesimal generator, $\mathbf{v}$, of a transformation h. Note that we require only the same order of prolongation as that of the function, F. Since the prolongation describes how derivatives are going to change, it is important for evaluating the quasi-invariance of a differential formula as described in the next section.

4.2 Quasi-Invariance on Smooth Manifolds

Let us consider the curve $\mathbf{C}$ in 2D space again. Suppose $I(y^{(n)})$ is a function on the curve containing the derivatives of y with respect to x up to the nth order, which we denote by $y^{(n)}$. Since the nth order prolongation, $\mathbf{v}^{(n)}$, of the vector field $\mathbf{v}$ transforms nth order derivatives, $y^{(n)}$, of the original curve to nth order derivatives, $\tilde{y}^{(n)}$, of the transformed curve, the change in function, $\delta I_i(y^{(n)})$, caused by the infinitesimal group transformation induced by the ith independent vector field, $\mathbf{v}_i$, is described by:

$$\delta I_i(y^{(n)}) = \mathbf{v}_i^{(n)}[I(y^{(n)})] \tag{14}$$

A quasi-invariant is a function whose variation caused by group transformations is relatively small compared with its original value. We thus define a measure of invariance, Q, on smooth curve, $\mathbf{C}$, by the normalised squared sum of $\delta I_i(y^{(n)})$ integrated along the curve, $\mathbf{C}$, as follows:

$$Q = \int_C \sum_{i=1}^m \left(\frac{\mathbf{v}_i^{(n)}[I(y^{(n)})]}{I(y^{(n)})} \right)^2 dx \tag{15}$$

If $I(y^{(n)})$ is close to the exact invariant, then Q tends to zero. Thus, Q is a measure of how invariant the function, $I(y^{(n)})$, is under the group transformation.

5 Quasi-Invariant Parameterisation

In the last section, we have derived quasi-invariance on smooth manifolds. We now apply the results and investigate the quasi-invariance of parameterisation under group transformations.

A group arc-length, w, of a curve, $\mathbf{C}$, is in general described by a group metric, g, and the independent variable, x, of the curve as follows:

$$dw = gdx$$

where, dw and dx are the differentials of w and x respectively. Suppose the metric, g, is described by the derivatives of y with respect to x up to kth order as follows:

$$g = g(y^{(k)})$$

where $y^{(k)}$ denotes the kth order prolongation of y. The change of the differential, δdw_i, caused by the ith independent vector field, $\mathbf{v}_i$, is thus derived by computing the Lie derivative of dw with respect to the kth order prolongation of $\mathbf{v}_i$:

$$\delta dw_i = \mathbf{v}_i^{(k)}[gdx] = (\mathbf{v}_i^{(k)}[g] + g\frac{d\xi_i}{dx})dx \tag{16}$$

The change in dw normalised by dw itself is described as follows:

$$\delta d\bar{w}_i = \frac{\delta dw_i}{dw} = \frac{1}{g}\mathbf{v}_i^{(k)}[g] + \frac{d\xi_i}{dx} \tag{17}$$

The measure of invariance of the parameter, w, is thus described by integrating the squared sum of $\delta d\bar{w}_i$ along the curve, $\mathbf{C}$, as follows:

$$Q = \int_C \mathcal{L} dx \tag{18}$$

where,

$$\mathcal{L} = \sum_{i=1}^{m} (\frac{1}{g}\mathbf{v}_i^{(k)}[g] + \frac{d\xi_i}{dx})^2 \tag{19}$$

If the parameter is close to the exact invariant parameter, Q tends to zero. Although there is no exact invariant parameter unless it has enough orders of derivatives, there still exists a parameter which minimises Q and requires only lower order derivatives. We call such a parameter a quasi-invariant parameter of the group. The necessary condition of Q to have a minimum is that its first variation, δQ, vanishes:

$$\delta Q_a = 0 \tag{20}$$

This is a variational problem of one independent variable, x, and two dependent variables, y and g. It is known that (20) holds if and only if its Euler-Lagrange vanishes as follows [18]:

$$\mathcal{E}[\mathcal{L}] = 0 \tag{21}$$

where, $\mathcal{E}[\cdot]$ denotes the Euler operator.

In the next section, we consider affine case, and derive a metric g which minimises Q under general affine transformations.

6   Affine Quasi-Invariant Parameterisation

In this section, we apply quasi-invariance to derive a quasi-invariant parameterisation under general affine transformations which requires only second order derivatives and is thus less sensitive to noise than the exact invariant parameter which requires fourth order derivatives.

Suppose the quasi-invariant parameterisation, τ, under general affine transformation is of second order, so that the metric, g, of the parameter, τ, is made of derivatives up to the second:

$$d\tau = g(y_x, y_{xx})dx \tag{22}$$

where, y_x and y_{xx} are the first and the second derivatives of y with respect to x. To find a quasi-invariant parameter is thus the same as finding a second order

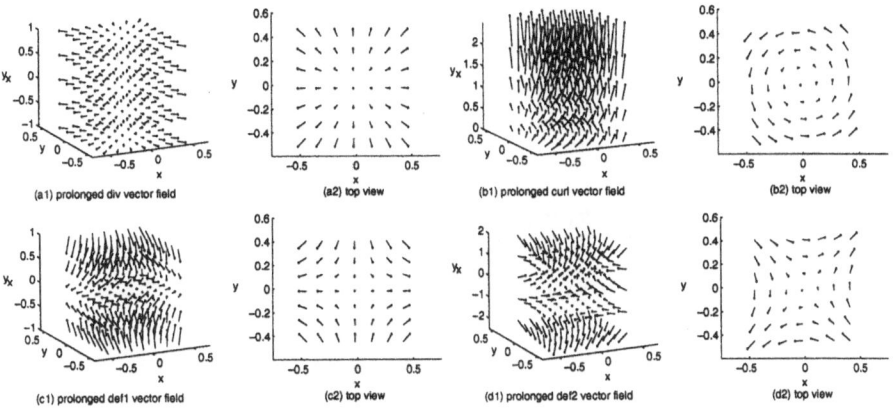

Fig. 5. Prolongation of affine vector fields. (a), (b), (c) and (d) show the original and the prolonged affine vector fields (i.e. divergence, curl and two deformation components).

differential function, $g(y_x, y_{xx})$, which minimises the quasi-invariance, Q, under general affine transformations. Since the metric, g, is of second order, we require the second order prolongation of the vector fields to compute the quasi-invariance of the metric.

6.1   Prolongation of Affine Vector Fields

A two dimensional general affine transformation is described by a 2×2 invertible matrix, $A \in GL(2)$, and a translational component, $t \in \mathbf{R}^2$, and transforms $\mathbf{x} \in \mathbf{R}^2$ into $\tilde{\mathbf{x}} \in \mathbf{R}^2$ as follows:

$$\tilde{\mathbf{x}} = A\mathbf{x} + t$$

Since the differential form, $d\tau$, in (22) does not include x and y components, it is invariant under translations. Thus, we here simply consider the action of $A \in GL(2)$, which can be described by four independent vector fields, $v_i (i = 1, \cdots, 4)$, that is the divergence, curl, and the two components of deformation [6, 13]:

$$\mathbf{v}_1 = x\frac{\partial}{\partial x} + y\frac{\partial}{\partial y} \qquad \mathbf{v}_2 = -y\frac{\partial}{\partial x} + x\frac{\partial}{\partial y}$$

$$\mathbf{v}_3 = x\frac{\partial}{\partial x} - y\frac{\partial}{\partial y} \qquad \mathbf{v}_4 = y\frac{\partial}{\partial x} + x\frac{\partial}{\partial y} \qquad (23)$$

Since the general linear group, $GL(2)$, is not semi-simple, the Killing form (9) is degenerate and there is no unique choice of vector fields for the group (see section 3.3). It is however decomposed into the radical, which corresponds to the divergence, and the special linear group, $SL(2)$, which is semi-simple and whose intrinsic vector fields coincide with $\mathbf{v}_2$, $\mathbf{v}_3$ and $\mathbf{v}_4$ in (23). Thus, we use the vector fields in (23) for computing the quasi-invariance of differential forms under general affine transformations.

From (12), (13), and (23), the second prolongations of these vector fields are computed by:

$$\mathbf{v}_1^{(2)} = \mathbf{v}_1 - y_{xx}\frac{\partial}{\partial y_{xx}}$$

$$\mathbf{v}_2^{(2)} = \mathbf{v}_2 + (1+y_x^2)\frac{\partial}{\partial y_x} + 3y_x y_{xx}\frac{\partial}{\partial y_{xx}}$$

$$\mathbf{v}_3^{(2)} = \mathbf{v}_3 - 2y_x\frac{\partial}{\partial y_x} - 3y_{xx}\frac{\partial}{\partial y_{xx}}$$

$$\mathbf{v}_4^{(2)} = \mathbf{v}_4 + (1-y_x^2)\frac{\partial}{\partial y_x} - 3y_x y_{xx}\frac{\partial}{\partial y_{xx}} \tag{24}$$

These are the vector fields in four dimension, whose coordinates are x, y, y_x and y_{xx}, and the projection of these vector fields onto the $x-y$ plane coincides with the original affine vector fields (23) in two dimension. For readers reference, the first prolongations of affine vector fields are shown in Fig. 5. Unfortunately, the second prolongations cannot be shown in figures, since they are four dimensional vector fields. However, the first prolongations are the projection of second prolongations, and thus Fig. 5 may help readers to infer the structure of second prolongations.

Since gdx is of second order, the prolonged vector fields, $\mathbf{v}_1^{(2)}$, $\mathbf{v}_2^{(2)}$, $\mathbf{v}_3^{(2)}$ and $\mathbf{v}_4^{(2)}$, describe how the parameter, τ, is going to change under general affine transformations.

6.2 Affine Quasi-Invariant Parameterisation

By substituting the affine prolonged vector fields, $\mathbf{v}_1^{(2)}$, $\mathbf{v}_2^{(2)}$, $\mathbf{v}_3^{(2)}$ and $\mathbf{v}_4^{(2)}$ into (19) and solving (21), we find that δQ vanishes for any curve, $y = f(x)$, if the following function, g, is chosen [24]:

$$g = y_{xx}^{\frac{2}{5}}(1+y_x^2)^{-\frac{1}{10}} \tag{25}$$

We conclude that for any curve the following parameter τ is quasi-invariant under general affine transformations:

$$d\tau = y_{xx}^{\frac{2}{5}}(1+y_x^2)^{-\frac{1}{10}}dx \tag{26}$$

By reformalising (26), we find that the parameter, τ, is described by the Euclidean arc-length, dv, and the Euclidean curvature, κ, as follows:

$$d\tau = \kappa^{\frac{2}{5}}dv \tag{27}$$

Thus, $d\tau$, is in fact an exact invariant under rotation, and quasi-invariant under divergence and deformation. Note, it is known that the invariant parameter under similarity transformations is κdv and that of special affine transformations is

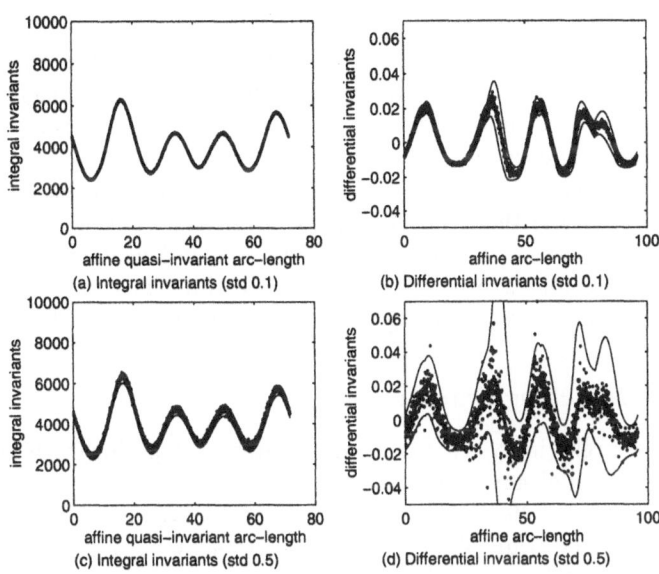

Fig. 6. Results of noise sensitivity analysis. The invariant signatures of an artificial curve are derived from the proposed invariants (semi-local invariants based on affine quasi invariant parameterisation) and the affine differential invariants (affine curvature), and are shown by thick lines in (a) and (b) respectively. The dots in (a) and (b) show signatures after adding random Gaussian noise of std 0.1 pixels, and the dots in (c) and (d) show signatures after adding random Gaussian noise of std 0.5 pixels. The thin lines show the uncertainty bounds of the signatures estimated by the linear perturbation method. The signatures from the proposed method are much more stable than those of differential invariants.

$\kappa^{\frac{1}{3}} dv$; The derived quasi-invariant parameter τ for general affine transformations is between these two as expected. We call τ the *affine quasi-invariant parameter (arc-length)*. Since the new parameter requires only the second order derivatives, it is expected to be less sensitive to noise than the exact invariant parameter under general affine transformations.

By using τ for w in (2), we can define affine quasi semi-local invariants. These invariants require only second order derivatives, and do not require any distinguished points on curves.

7   Experiments

7.1   Noise Sensitivity of Quasi Invariants

We first compare the noise sensitivity of the semi-local invariants based on the proposed affine quasi-invariant parameterisation with that of affine differential invariants, i.e. affine curvature.

The invariant signatures of an artificial curve have been computed from the proposed quasi-invariants and the affine curvature, and are shown by solid lines in Fig. 6 (a) and (b). The dots in (a) and (b) show the invariant signatures after adding random Gaussian noise of standard deviation of 0.1 pixels to the position data of the curve, and the dots in (c) and (d) show those of standard deviation of 0.5 pixels. As we can see in these signatures, the proposed invariants are much less sensitive to noise than the differential invariants. This is simply because the proposed invariants require only second order derivatives while differential invariants require fourth order derivatives. The thin lines show the results of noise sensitivity analysis derived by the linear perturbation method.

7.2   Curve Matching Experiments

Next we show preliminary results of curve matching experiments under relative motion between an observer and objects.

Fig. 7 (a) and (b) show the images of natural leaves taken from two different viewpoints. The white lines in these images show example contour curves extracted from B-spline fitting [5]. As we can see in these curves, because of the viewer motion, the curves are distorted and occluded partially. Since the leaf is nearly flat and the extent of the leaf is much less than the distance from the camera to the leaf, we can assume that the corresponding curves are related by a general affine transformation.

The computed invariant signatures of the original and the distorted curves are shown in Fig. 7 (c). One of these two signatures was shifted horizontally minimising the total difference between these two signatures. The corresponding points on the contour curves were extracted by taking identical points in these two signatures, and are shown in Fig. 7 (d) and (e). Note that the extracted corresponding curves are fairly accurate. In this experiment, we have chosen $\Delta\hat{\tau} = 3.0$ for computing invariant signatures.

7.3   Extracting Symmetry Axes

We next apply the quasi invariants for extracting the symmetry axes of three dimensional objects. Extracting symmetry [9, 10, 28] of objects in images is very important for recognising objects [15, 29], focusing attention [21] and controlling robots [3] reliably. It is well known that the corresponding contour curves of a planar bilateral symmetry can be described by special affine transformations [12, 28]. In this section, we consider a class of symmetry which is described by a general affine transformation.

Consider a planar object to have bilateral symmetry with an axis, L. Suppose the planar object can be separated into two planes at the axis, L, and is connected by a hinge so that two planes can rotate around this axis, L, as shown in Fig. 8 (a). The objects derived by rotating these two planes have a 3D bilateral symmetry. This class of symmetry is also common in artificial and natural objects such as butterflies and other flying insects. Since the distortion in images caused by a three dimensional motion of a planar object can be described by a

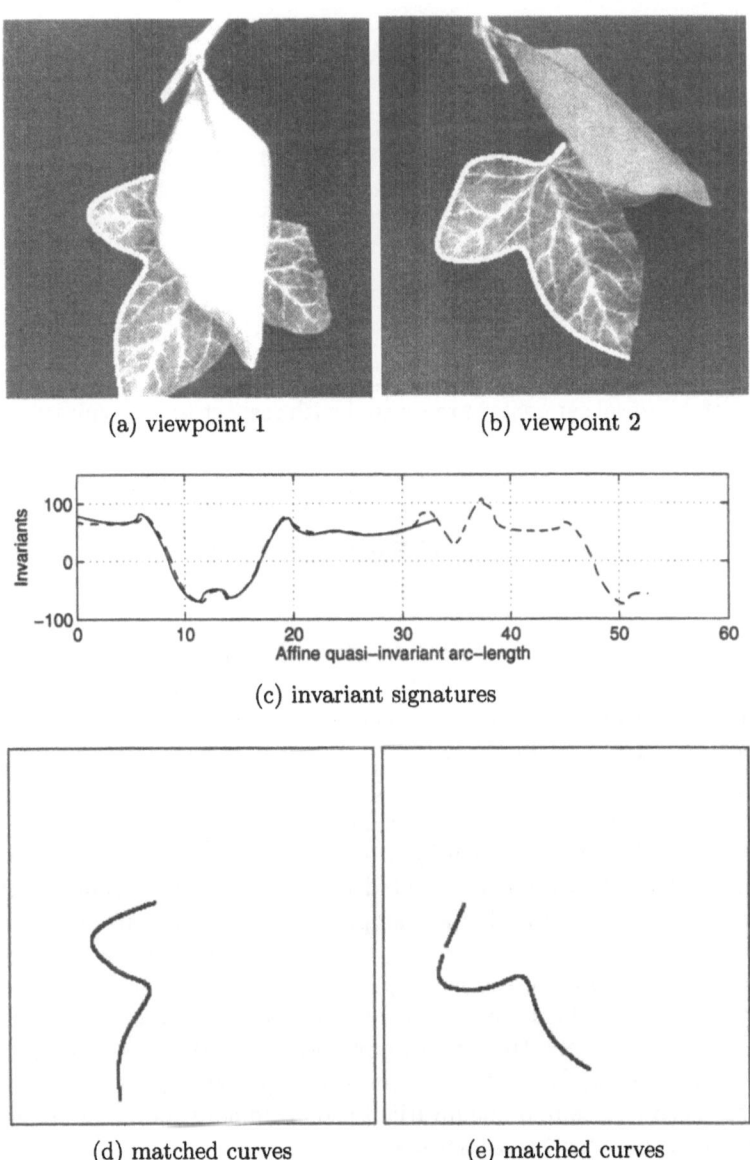

(a) viewpoint 1   (b) viewpoint 2

(c) invariant signatures

(d) matched curves   (e) matched curves

Fig. 7. Curve matching experiment. Images of natural leaves from the first and the second viewpoints are shown in (a) and (b). The white lines in these images show extracted contour curves. The quasi-invariant arc-length and semi-local invariants are computed from the curves in (a) and (b), and are shown in (c) by solid and dashed lines. (d) and (e) show the corresponding curves extracted from the invariant signatures (c).

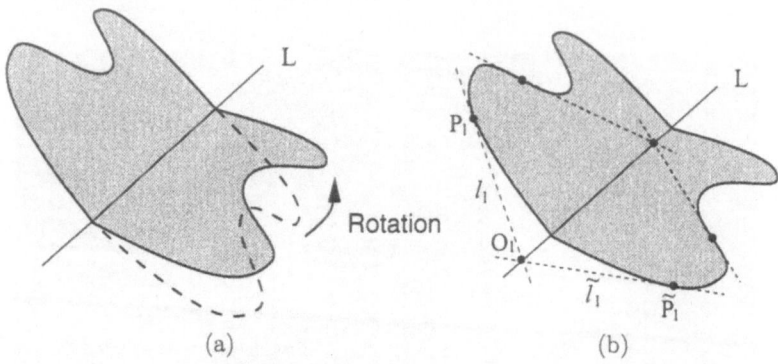

Fig. 8. Bilateral symmetry with rotation. The left and the right parts of an object with bilateral symmetry are rotated with respect to the symmetry axis, L in (a). The intersection point, O_1, of two tangent lines, l_1 and $\tilde{l}_1$, at corresponding points, P_1 and $\tilde{P}_1$, of a bilateral symmetry with rotation lies on the symmetry axes, L in (b). If we have N cross points, O_i $(i = 1, \cdots, N)$, the symmetry axis can be computed by fitting a line to these cross points, $O_1, O_2, \cdots, O_N$.

general affine transformation, this class of symmetry can also be described by general affine transformations under the weak perspective assumption. Thus, the corresponding two curves of this symmetry have the same invariant signatures under general affine transformations.

We next show the results of extracting symmetry axes of 3D bilateral symmetry. Fig. 9 (a) shows an image of a butterfly (*Small White*) with a flower. Since the two wings of the butterfly are not coplanar, the corresponding contour curves of the two wings are related by a general affine transformation as described above. Fig. 9 (b) shows example contour curves extracted from (a). Note that not all the points on the curves have correspondences because of the lack of edge data and the presence of spurious edges. The solid and dashed lines in Fig. 9 (c) show the invariant signatures computed from the left and the right wings in (b) respectively. (In this example, we chose $\Delta \hat{\tau} = 8.0$ for computing semi-local invariants.) Since the signatures are invariant up to a shift, we have simply reflected and shifted one invariant signature horizontally minimising the total difference between two signatures

As shown in these signatures, semi-local invariants based on quasi-invariant parameterisation are quite accurate and stable. Corresponding points are derived by taking the identical points on these two signatures, and shown in Fig. 9 (d) by connecting the corresponding points. Tangent lines at every corresponding pair of points are computed and displayed in Fig. 9 (d) by white lines. The cross points of every pair of tangent lines are extracted and shown in Fig. 9 (d) by square dots. The symmetry axis of the butterfly is extracted by fitting a line to the cross points of tangent lines and shown in Fig. 9 (e). Although the extracted contour curves include asymmetric parts as shown in (b), the computed axis

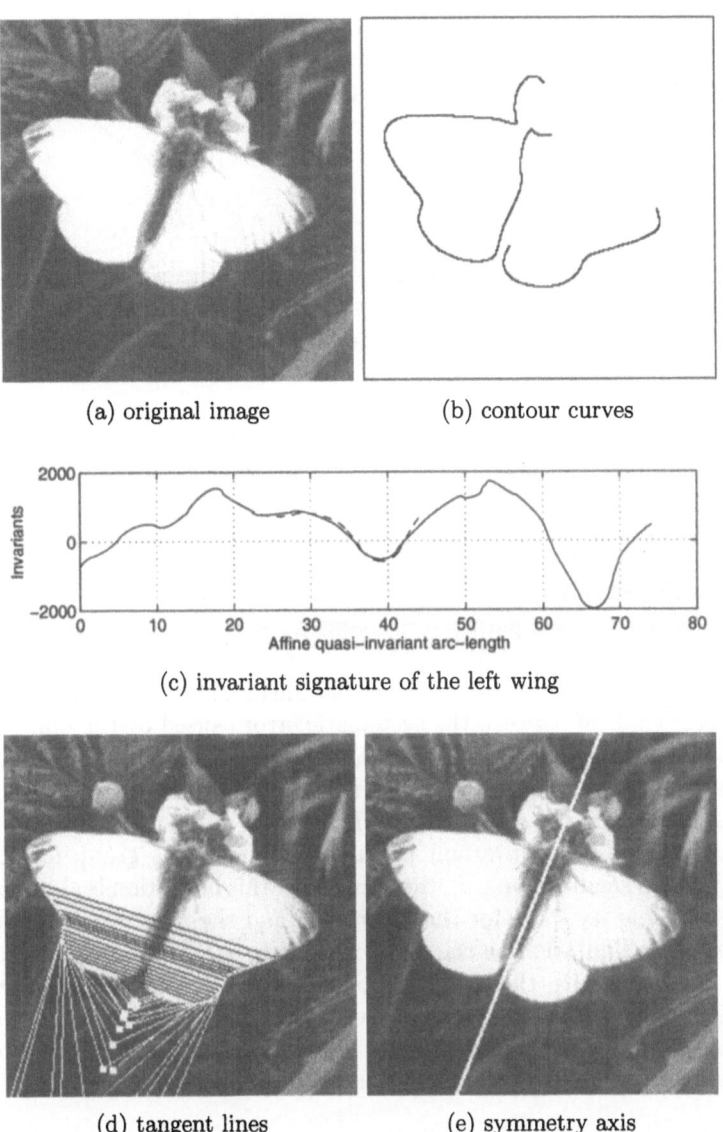

(a) original image   (b) contour curves

(c) invariant signature of the left wing

(d) tangent lines   (e) symmetry axis

Fig. 9. Extraction of axis of bilateral symmetry with rotation. (a) shows the original image of a butterfly (Small White), perched on a flower. (b) shows an example of contour curves. The invariant signatures of these curves are computed from the quasi-invariant arc-length and semi-local invariants. (c) shows the extracted invariant signatures of the left and the right curves in (b). The black lines in (d) connect pairs of corresponding points extracted from the invariant signatures in (c). The white lines and the square dots show the tangent lines for the corresponding points and their cross points. The white line in (e) shows the symmetry axis of the butterfly extracted by fitting a line to the cross points.

of symmetry agrees with the body of the butterfly quite well. Whereas purely global methods, e.g. moment based methods [9, 10], would not work in such cases. These results show the power and usefulness of the proposed semi-local invariants and quasi-invariant parameterisation.

8   Discussion

In this paper, we have shown that there exist quasi-invariant parameterisations which are not exactly invariant but approximately invariant under group transformations and do not require high order derivatives. The affine quasi-invariant parameterisation is derived and applied for matching of curves under the weak perspective assumption.

Although the range of transformations is limited, the proposed method is useful for many cases especially for curve matching under relative motion between a viewer and objects, since the movements of a camera and objects are, in general, limited. We now discuss the properties of the proposed parameterisation.

1. **Noise Sensitivity**
   Since quasi-invariant parameters enable us to reduce the order of derivatives required, they are much less sensitive to noise than exact invariant parameters. Thus using the quasi-invariant parameterisation is the same as finding the best tradeoff between the systematic error caused by the approximation and the error caused by the noise. The derived parameters are more feasible than traditional invariant parameters.

2. **Limitation of the Amount of Motion**
   The proposed quasi-invariant parameter assumes the group motion to be limited to a small amount. In the affine case, this limitation is about $a_1 \leq 0.1$, $a_3 \leq 0.1$ and $a_4 \leq 0.1$ for the divergence and the deformation components (there is no limitation on the curl component, a_2). Since, in many computer vision applications, the distortion of the image is small due to the limited speed of the relative motion between a camera and the scene or the finite distance between two cameras in a stereo system, we believe the proposed parameterisation can be exploited in many applications.

References

[1] E.B. Barrett and P.M. Payton. General methods for determining projective invariants in imagery. *Computer Vision, Graphics and Image Processing*, Vol. 53, No. 1, pp. 46–65, 1991.

[2] T.O. Binford and T.S. Levitt. Quasi-invariant: Theory and exploitation. In *Proc. DARPA Image Understanding Workshop*, pp. 819–829, 1993.

[3] A. Blake. A symmetry theory of planar grasp. *International Journal of Robotics Research*, Vol. 14, No. 5, pp. 425–444, 1995.

[4] A.M. Bruckstein, R.J. Holt, A.N. Netravali, and T.J. Richardson. Invariant signatures for planar shape recognition under partial occlusion. *Computer Vision, Graphics and Image Processing*, Vol. 58, No. 1, pp. 49–65, 1993.

[5] T.J. Cham and R. Cipolla. Automated B-spline curve representation with MDL-based active contours. In *Proc. 7th British Machine Vision Conference*, Vol. 2, pp. 363–372, Edinburgh, September 1996.

[6] R. Cipolla and A. Blake. Surface orientation and time to contact from image divergence and deformation. In G. Sandini, editor, *Proc. 2nd European Conference on Computer Vision*, pp. 187–202, Santa Margherita, Italy, 1992. Springer–Verlag.

[7] D. Cyganski, J.A. Orr, T.A. Cott, and R.J. Dodson. An affine transformation invariant curvature function. In *Proc. 1st International Conference on Computer Vision*, pp. 496–500, London, 1987.

[8] D. Forsyth, J.L. Mundy, A. Zisserman, and C.A. Rothwell. Recognising rotationally symmetric surfaces from their outlines. In G. Sandini, editor, *Proc. 2nd European Conference on Computer Vision*, Santa Margherita, Italy, 1992. Springer–Verlag.

[9] S.A. Friedberg. Finding axes of skewed symmetry. *Computer Vision, Graphics and Image Processing*, Vol. 34, pp. 138–155, 1986.

[10] A.D. Gross and T.E. Boult. Analyzing skewed symmetries. *International Journal of Computer Vision*, Vol. 13, No. 1, pp. 91–111, 1994.

[11] M. Hu. Visual pattern recognition by moment invariants. *IRE Transaction on Information Theory*, Vol. IT-8, pp. 179–187, February 1962.

[12] T. Kanade and J.R. Kender. Mapping image properties into shape constraints: Skewed symmetry, affine-transformable patterns, and the shape-from-texture paradigm. In J. Beck et al, editor, *Human and Machine Vision*, pp. 237–257. Academic Press, NY, 1983.

[13] J.J. Koenderink and A.J. van Doorn. Geometry of binocular vision and a model for stereopsis. *Biological Cybernetics*, Vol. 21, pp. 29–35, 1976.

[14] S. Lie. *Gesammelte Abhandlungen*, Vol. 6. Teubner, Leipzig, 1927.

[15] R. Mohan and R. Nevatia. Perceptual organization for scene segmentation and description. *IEEE Trans. Pattern Analysis and Machine Intelligence*, Vol. 14, No. 6, pp. 616–635, 1992.

[16] T. Moons, E.J. Pauwels, L.J. Van Gool, and A. Oosterlinck. Foundations of semi-differential invariants. *International Journal of Computer Vision*, Vol. 14, pp. 25–47, 1995.

[17] J.L. Mundy and A. Zisserman. *Geometric Invariance in Computer Vision*. MIT Press, Cambridge, USA, 1992.

[18] P.J. Olver. *Applications of Lie Groups to Differential Equations*. Springer–Verlag, 1986.

[19] P.J. Olver, G. Sapiro, and A. Tannenbaum. Differential invariant signatures and flows in computer vision. In B.M. ter Haar Romeny, editor, *Geometry-Driven Diffusion in Computer Vision*, pp. 255–306. Kluwer Academic Publishers, 1994.

[20] E.J. Pauwels, T. Moons, L.J. Van Gool, P. Kempenaers, and A. Oosterlinck. Recognition of planar shapes under affine distortion. *International Journal of Computer Vision*, Vol. 14, pp. 49–65, 1995.

[21] D. Reisfeld, H. Wolfson, and Y. Yeshurun. Contex-free attention operators: The generalized symmetry transform. *International Journal of Computer Vision*, Vol. 14, No. 2, pp. 119–130, 1995.

[22] C.A. Rothwell, A. Zisserman, D.A. Forsyth, and J.L. Mundy. Planar object recognition using projective shape representation. *International Journal of Computer Vision*, Vol. 16, pp. 57–99, 1995.

[23] J. Sato and R. Cipolla. Affine integral invariants for extracting symmetry axes. In *Proc. 7th British Machine Vision Conference*, Vol. 1, pp. 63–72, Edinburgh, September 1996.

[24] J. Sato and R. Cipolla. Quasi-invariant parameterisations and matching of curves in images. *International Journal of Computer Vision*, Vol. 28, No. 2, pp. 117–136, 1998.

[25] D.H. Sattinger and O.L. Weaver. *Lie groups and algebras with applications to physics, geometry and mechanics*. Springer-Verlag, New York, 1986.

[26] G. Taubin and D.B. Cooper. Object recognition based on moment (or algebraic) invariants. In J.L. Mundy and A. Zisserman, editors, *Geometric Invariance in Computer Vision*, pp. 375–397. MIT Press, 1992.

[27] L.J. Van Gool, T. Moons, E. Pauwels, and A. Oosterlinck. Semi-differential invariants. In J.L. Mundy and A. Zisserman, editors, *Geometric Invariance in Computer Vision*, pp. 157–192. MIT Press, 1992.

[28] L.J. Van Gool, T. Moons, D. Ungureanu, and A. Oosterlinck. The characterization and detection of skewed symmetry. *Computer Vision and Image Understanding*, Vol. 61, No. 1, pp. 138–150, 1995.

[29] L.J. Van Gool, T. Moons, D. Ungureanu, and E. Pauwels. Symmetry from shape and shape from symmetry. *International Journal of Robotics Research*, Vol. 14, No. 5, pp. 407–424, 1995.

[30] I. Weiss. Projective invariants of shapes. In *Proc. Image Understanding workshop*, Vol. 2, pp. 1125–1134, 1988.

[31] M. Zerroug and R. Nevatia. Three-dimensional descriptions based on the analysis of the invariant and quasi-invariant properties of come curved-axis generalized cylinders. *IEEE Trans. Pattern Analysis and Machine Intelligence*, Vol. 18, No. 3, pp. 237–253, 1996.

[32] A. Zisserman, D.A. Forsyth, J.L. Mundy, and C.A. Rothwell. Recognizing general curved objects efficiently. In J.L. Mundy and A. Zisserman, editors, *Geometric Invariance in Computer Vision*, pp. 228–251. MIT Press, 1992.

Part III

Shading

Representations for Recognition
Under Variable Illumination*

David J. Kriegman[1], Peter N. Belhumeur[2], and Athinodoros S. Georghiades[2]

[1] Beckman Institute and Department of Computer Science
University of Illinois at Urbana-Champaign
405 N. Mathews Avenue
Urbana, IL 61801, USA
[2] Center for Computational Vision and Control
Department of Electrical Engineering
Yale University
New Haven, CT 06520-8267, USA

Abstract. Due to illumination variability, the same object can appear dramatically different even when viewed in fixed pose. Consequently, an object recognition system must employ a representation that is either invariant to, or models this variability. This chapter presents an appearance-based method for modeling this variability. In particular, we prove that the set of n-pixel monochrome images of a convex object with a Lambertian reflectance function, illuminated by an arbitrary number of point light sources at infinity, forms a convex polyhedral cone in $\mathbb{R}^n$ and that the dimension of this *illumination cone* equals the number of distinct surface normals. For a non-convex object with a more general reflectance function, the set of images is also a convex cone. Geometric properties of these cones for monochrome and color cameras are considered. Here, present a method for constructing a cone representation from a small number of images when the surface is continuous, possibly non-convex, and Lambertian; this accounts for both attached and cast shadows. For a collection of objects, each object is represented by a cone, and recognition is performed through nearest neighbor classification by measuring the minimal distance of an image to each cone. We demonstrate the utility of this approach to the problem of face recognition (a class of non-convex and non-Lambertian objects with similar geometry). The method is tested on a database of 660 images of 10 faces, and the results exceed those of popular existing methods.

1 Introduction

One of the complications that has troubled computer vision recognition algorithms is the variability of an object's appearance from one image to the

* D. J. Kriegman and A.S. Georghiades were supported under NSF NYI IRI-9257990 and ARO DAAG55-98-1-0168. P. N. Belhumeur was supported by a Presidential Early Career Award, an NSF Career Award IRI-9703134, and ARO grant DAAH04-95-1-0494.

D.A. Forsyth et al. (Eds.): Shape, Contour ..., LNCS 1681, pp. 95–131, 1999.
© Springer-Verlag Berlin Heidelberg 1999

next. With slight changes in lighting conditions and viewpoint often come large changes in the object's appearance. To handle this variability methods usually take one of two approaches: either measure some property in the image of the object which is, if not invariant, at least insensitive to the variability in the imaging conditions, or model the object, or part of the object, in order to predict the variability.

Nearly all approaches to object recognition have handled the variability due to illumination by using the first approach; they have, for example, concentrated on edges, i.e. the discontinuities in the image intensity. Because discontinuities in the albedo on the object's surface or discontinuities in albedo across the object's boundary generate edges in images, these edges tend to be insensitive to a range of illumination conditions [5].

Yet, edges do not contain all of the information useful for recognition. Furthermore, objects which are not simple polyhedra or are not composed of piecewise constant albedo patterns often produce inconsistent edge maps. The top of Fig. 1 shows two images of a person with the same facial expression and photographed from the same viewpoint. The variability in these two images due to differences in illumination is dramatic: not only does it lead to a change in contrast, but also to changes in the configuration of the shadows, i.e. certain regions are shadowed in the left image, but illuminated in the right, and vice versa. The edge maps in the bottom half of Fig. 1 are produced from these images. Due to the variation in illumination, only a small fraction of the edges are common between images. Figure 9 shows another example of extreme illumination variation in images; in this case observe the extreme variability in the images of a single individual illuminated by a single light source in different locations.

The reason most approaches have avoided using the rest of the intensity information is because its variability under changing illumination has been difficult to tame. Methods have recently been introduced which use low-dimensional representations of images to perform recognition, see for example [15, 27, 39]. These methods, often termed appearance-based methods, differ from feature-based methods in that their low-dimensional representation is, in a least-squared sense, faithful to the original image. Systems such as SLAM [27] and Eigenfaces [39] have demonstrated the power of appearance-based methods both in ease of implementation and in accuracy. Yet these methods suffer from an important drawback: recognition of an object (or face) under a particular pose and lighting can be performed reliably *provided that object has been previously seen under similar circumstances*. In other words, these methods in their original form have no way of extrapolating to novel viewing conditions. Yet, if one enumerates all possible poses and permutes these with all possible illumination conditions, things get out of hand quite quickly. This raises the question: Is there some underlying "generative" structure to the set of images of an object under varying illumination and pose such that to create the set, the object does not have to be viewed under all possible conditions?

In this chapter we address only part of this question, restricting our investigation to varying illumination. In particular, if an image with n pixels is treated

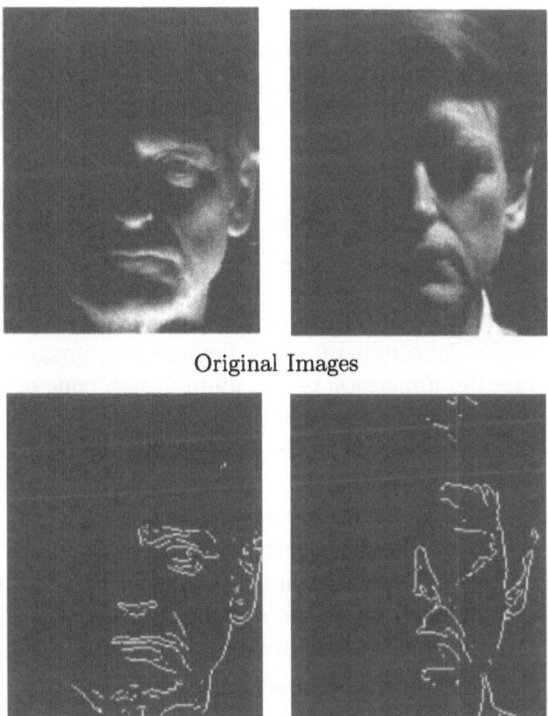

Original Images

Edge Maps

Fig. 1. Effects of Variability in Illumination: The top two images show the same face seen under different illumination conditions. The bottom two images show edge maps of the top two images. Even though the change in light source direction is less than $45°$, the change in the resulting image is dramatic.

as a point in $\mathbb{R}^n$, what is the set of all images of an object under varying illumination? Is this set an incredibly complex, but low-dimensional manifold in the image space? Or does the set have a simple, predictable structure? If the object is convex in shape and has a Lambertian reflectance function, can a finite number of images characterize this set? If so, how many images are needed?

The image formation process for a particular object can be viewed as a function of pose and lighting. Since an object's pose can be represented by a point in $\mathbb{R}^3 \times SO(3)$ (a six dimensional manifold), the set of n-pixel images of an object under constant illumination, but over all possible poses, is at most six dimensional. Murase and Nayar take advantage of this structure when constructing appearance manifolds [27]. However, the variability due to illumination may be much larger as the set of possible lighting conditions is infinite dimensional.

Arbitrary illumination can be modeled as a scalar function on a four dimensional manifold of light rays [25]. However, without limiting assumptions about the possible light sources, the bidirectional reflectance density functions, or object geometry, it is difficult to draw limiting conclusions about the set of images. For example, the image of a perfect mirror can be anything. Alternatively, if the light source is composed of a collection of independent lasers with one per pixel (which is admissible under [25]), then an arbitrary image of any object can be constructed by appropriately selecting the lasers' intensities.

Nonetheless, we will show that the set of images of an object with arbitrary reflectance functions seen under arbitrary illumination conditions is a convex cone in $\mathbb{R}^n$ where n is the number of pixels in each image. Furthermore, if the object has a convex shape and a Lambertian reflectance function and is illuminated by an arbitrary number of point light sources at infinity, this cone is polyhedral and can be determined from as few as three images. In addition, we will show that while the dimension of the illumination cone equals the number of distinct surface normals, the shape of the cone is "flat," i.e. the cone lies near a low dimensional linear subspace of the image space. When the object is non-convex and non-Lambertian, methods for approximating the cone are presented. Throughout the chapter, empirical investigations are presented to complement the theoretical arguments. In particular, experimental results are provided which support the validity of the illumination cone representation and the associated propositions on the illumination cone's dimension and shape. Note that some results in this chapter were originally presented in [4, 14].

The effectiveness of these algorithms and the cone representation is demonstrated within the context of face recognition – it has been observed by Moses, Adini and Ullman that the variability in an image due to illumination is often greater than that due to a change in the person's identity [26]. Figure 9 shows the variability for a single individual. It has also been observed that methods for face recognition based on finding local image features and using their geometric relation are generally ineffective [6]. Hence, faces provide an interesting and useful class of objects for testing the power of the illumination cone representation.

In this chapter we empirically compare this new method to a number of popular techniques and representations such as correlation [6] and Eigenfaces [24, 39] as well as more recently developed techniques such as distance to linear subspace [3, 15, 29, 34]; the latter technique has been shown to be much less sensitive to illumination variation than the former. However, these methods also break down as shadowing becomes very significant. As we will see, the presented algorithm based on the illumination cone outperforms all of these methods on a database of 660 images. It should be noted that our objective in this work is to focus solely on the issue of illumination variation whereas other approaches have been more concerned with issues related to large image databases, face finding, pose, and facial expressions.

We are hopeful that the proposed illumination representation will prove useful for 3-D object recognition under more general conditions. For problems where pose is unknown, we envision marrying the illumination cone representation with a low-dimensional set of image coordinate transformations [40] or with the appearance manifold work of [27], thus allowing both illumination and pose variation. For problems in which occlusion and non-rigid motion cannot be discounted, we envision breaking the image of an object into sub-regions and building "illumination sub-cones." These illumination sub-cones could then be glued together in a manner similar to the recent "body plans" work of [12].

2   The Illumination Cone

In this section, we develop the illumination cone representation. To start, we make two simplifying assumptions: first, we assume that the surfaces of objects have Lambertian reflectance functions; second, we assume that the shape of an object's surface is convex. While the majority of the propositions are based upon these two assumptions, we will relax them in Section 2.2 and show that the set of images is still a convex cone. In addition, the empirical investigations of Section 2.4 will demonstrate the validity of the illumination cone representation by presenting results on images of objects which have neither purely Lambertian reflectance functions nor convex shapes. The cone representation will then be used for face recognition in Section 5.

2.1   Illumination Cones for Convex Lambertian Surfaces

To begin, let us assume a Lambertian model for reflectance with a single point light source at infinity. Let $\mathbf{x}$ denote an image with n pixels. Let $B \in \mathbb{R}^{n \times 3}$ be a matrix where each row of B is the product of the albedo with the inward pointing unit normal for a point on the surface projecting to a particular pixel; here we effectively approximate a smooth surface by a faceted one and assume that the surface normals for the set of points projecting to the same image pixel are identical.

Let $\mathbf{s} \in \mathbb{R}^3$ be a column vector signifying the product of the light source strength with the unit vector for the light source direction. Thus, a convex object with surface normals and albedo given by B, seen under illumination $\mathbf{s}$, produces an image $\mathbf{x}$ given by the following equation

$$\mathbf{x} = \max(B\mathbf{s}, \mathbf{0}), \tag{1}$$

where $\max(\cdot, \mathbf{0})$ zeros all negative components of the vector $B\mathbf{s}$ [18]. Note that the negative components of $B\mathbf{s}$ correspond to the shadowed surface points and are sometimes called *attached shadows* [33]. Also, note that we have assumed that the object's shape is convex at this point to avoid *cast shadows*, i.e. shadows that the object casts on itself.

If the object is illuminated by k point light sources at infinity, the image $\mathbf{x}$ is given by the superposition of images which would have been produced by the individual light source, i.e.

$$\mathbf{x} = \sum_{i=1}^{k} \max(B\mathbf{s}_i, \mathbf{0})$$

where $\mathbf{s}_i$ is a single light source. Note that extended light sources at infinity can be handled by allowing an infinite number of point light sources (i.e., the sum becomes an integral).

The product of B with all possible light source directions and strengths sweeps out a subspace in the n-dimensional image space [17, 29, 33]; we call the subspace created by B the illumination subspace $\mathcal{L}$, where

$$\mathcal{L} = \{\mathbf{x} \mid \mathbf{x} = B\mathbf{s}, \forall \mathbf{s} \in \mathbb{R}^3\}.$$

Note that the dimension of $\mathcal{L}$ equals the rank of B. Since B is an $n \times 3$ matrix, $\mathcal{L}$ will in general be a 3-D subspace, and we will assume it to be so in the remainder of the chapter. When the surface has fewer than three linearly independent surface normals, B does not have full rank. For example, in the case of a cylindrical object, both the rank of B and dimension of $\mathcal{L}$ are two. Likewise, in the case of a planar object, both the rank and dimension are one.

When a single light source is parallel with the camera's optical axis, all visible points on the surface are illuminated, and consequently, all pixels in the image have non-zero values. The set of images created by scaling the light source strength and moving the light source away from the direction of the camera's optical axis such that all pixels remain illuminated can be found as the relative interior of a set $\mathcal{L}_0$ defined by the intersection of $\mathcal{L}$ with the non-negative orthant[1] of $\mathbb{R}^n$.

Lemma 1. *The set of images $\mathcal{L}_0$ is a convex cone in $\mathbb{R}^n$.*

Proof. $\mathcal{L}_0 = \mathcal{L} \cap \{\mathbf{x} \mid \mathbf{x} \in \mathbb{R}^n$, with all components of $\mathbf{x} \geq 0\}$. Both $\mathcal{L}$ and the positive orthant are convex. For the definition of convexity and the definition of a cone, see [7, 31]. Because the intersection of two convex sets is convex, it follows that $\mathcal{L}_0$ is convex.

Because $\mathcal{L}$ is a linear subspace, if $\mathbf{x} \in \mathcal{L}$ then $\alpha\mathbf{x} \in \mathcal{L}$. And, if $\mathbf{x}$ has all components non-negative, then $\alpha\mathbf{x}$ has all components non-negative for every $\alpha \geq 0$. Therefore $\alpha\mathbf{x} \in \mathcal{L}_0$. So it follows that $\mathcal{L}_0$ is a cone.

As we move the light source direction further from the camera's optical axis, points on the object will fall into shadow. Naturally, which pixels are the image of shadowed or illuminated surface points depends on where we move the light source direction. If we move the light source all the way around to the back of the object so that the camera's optical axis and the light source are pointing in opposite directions, then all pixels are in shadow.

Let us now consider all possible light source directions, representing each direction by a point on the surface of the sphere; we call this sphere the *illumination sphere*. For a convex object, the set of light source directions for which a given facet (i.e. pixel in the image) is illuminated corresponds to an open hemisphere of the illumination sphere; the set of light source directions for which the

---

[1] By orthant we mean the high-dimensional analogue to quadrant, i.e., the set $\{\mathbf{x} \mid \mathbf{x} \in \mathbb{R}^n$, with certain components of $\mathbf{x} \geq 0$ and the remaining components of $\mathbf{x} < 0\}$. By non-negative orthant we mean the set $\{\mathbf{x} \mid \mathbf{x} \in \mathbb{R}^n$, with all components of $\mathbf{x} \geq 0\}$.

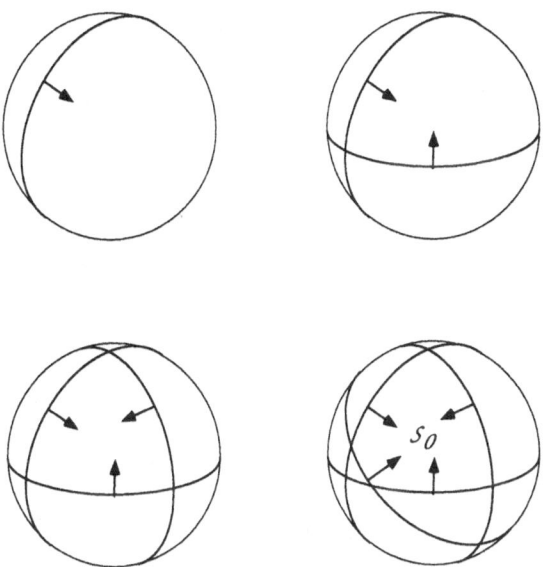

Fig. 2. The Illumination Sphere: The set of all light source directions can be represented by points on the surface of a sphere; we call this sphere the *illumination sphere*. Great circles corresponding to individual pixels divide the illumination sphere into cells of different shadowing configurations. The arrows indicate the hemisphere of light directions for which the particular pixel is illuminated. The cell of light source directions which illuminate all pixels is denoted by S_0. The light source directions within S_0 produce $\mathcal{L}_0$ the set of images in which all pixels are illuminated. Each of the other cells produce the $\mathcal{L}_i$, $0 < i \leq n(n-1)+1$. The extreme rays of the cone are given by the images produced by light sources at the intersection of two circles.

facet is shadowed corresponds to the other hemisphere of points. A great circle on the illumination sphere divides these sets.

For each of the n pixels in the image, there is a corresponding great circle on the illumination sphere. The collection of great circles carves up the surface of the illumination sphere into a collection of cells S_i. See Figure 2. The collection of light source directions contained within a cell S_i on the illumination sphere produces a set of images, each with the same pixels in shadow and the same pixels illuminated; we say that these images have the same "shadowing configurations." Different cells produce different shadowing configurations. Note that this partitioning is reminiscent of the partitioning of the viewpoint space in the construction of orthographic projection aspect graphs of convex polyhedral objects [41].

We denote by S_0 the cell on the illumination sphere containing the collection of light source directions which produce images with all pixels illuminated. Thus, the collection of light source directions from the interior and boundary of S_0 produces the set of images $\mathcal{L}_0$. To determine the set of images produced by another cell on the illumination sphere, we need to return to the illumination subspace $\mathcal{L}$.

The illumination subspace $\mathcal{L}$ not only slices through the non-negative orthant of $\mathbb{R}^n$, but other orthants in $\mathbb{R}^n$ as well. Let $\mathcal{L}_i$ be the intersection of the illumination subspace $\mathcal{L}$ with an orthant i in $\mathbb{R}^n$ through which $\mathcal{L}$ passes. Certain components of $\mathbf{x} \in \mathcal{L}_i$ are always negative and others always greater than or equal to zero. Each $\mathcal{L}_i$ has a corresponding cell of light source directions S_i on the illumination sphere. Note that $\mathcal{L}$ does not slice through all of the 2^n orthants in $\mathbb{R}^n$, but at most $n(n-1)+2$ orthants (see the proof of Proposition 1). Thus, there are at most $n(n-1)+2$ sets $\mathcal{L}_i$, each with a corresponding cell S_i on the illumination sphere.

The set of images produced by the collection of light source directions from a cell S_i other than S_0 can be found as a projection P_i of all points in a particular set $\mathcal{L}_i$. The projection P_i is such that it leaves the non-negative components of $\mathbf{x} \in \mathcal{L}_i$ untouched, while the negative components of $\mathbf{x}$ become zero. We denote the projected set by $P_i(\mathcal{L}_i)$.

Lemma 2. *The set of images $P_i(\mathcal{L}_i)$ is a convex cone in $\mathbb{R}^n$.*

Proof. By the same argument used in the proof of Lemma 1, $\mathcal{L}_i$ is a convex cone. Since the linear projection of a convex cone is itself a convex cone, $P_i(\mathcal{L}_i)$ is a convex cone.

Since $P_i(\mathcal{L}_i)$ is the projection of $\mathcal{L}_i$, it is at most three dimensional. Each $P_i(\mathcal{L}_i)$ is the set of all images such that certain facets are illuminated, and the remaining facets are shadowed. The dual relation between $P_i(\mathcal{L}_i)$ and S_i can be concisely written as $P_i(\mathcal{L}_i) = \{\alpha \max(B\mathbf{s}, \mathbf{0}) : \alpha \geq 0, \mathbf{s} \in S_i\}$ and $S_i = \{\mathbf{s} : |\mathbf{s}| = 1, \max(B\mathbf{s}, \mathbf{0}) \in P_i(\mathcal{L}_i)\}$. Let P_0 be the identity, so that $P_0(\mathcal{L}_0) = \mathcal{L}_0$ is the set of all images such that all facets are illuminated. The number of possible *shadowing configurations* is the number of orthants in $\mathbb{R}^n$ through which the illumination subspace $\mathcal{L}$ passes, which in turn is the same as the number of sets $P_i(\mathcal{L}_i)$.

Proposition 1. *The number of shadowing configurations is at most $m(m-1)+2$, where $m \leq n$ is the number of distinct surface normals.*

Proof. Each of the n pixels in the image has a corresponding great circle on the illumination sphere, but only $m \leq n$ of the great circles are distinct. The collection of m distinct great circles carves the surface of the illumination sphere into cells. Each cell on the illumination sphere corresponds to a particular set of images $P_i(\mathcal{L}_i)$. Thus, the problem of determining the number of shadowing configurations is the same as the problem of determining the number of cells. If every vertex on the illumination sphere is formed by the intersection of only two of the m distinct great circles (i.e., if no more than two surface normals are coplanar), then it can be shown by induction that the illumination sphere is divided into $m(m-1)+2$ cells. If a vertex is formed by the intersection of three or more great circles, there are fewer cells.

Thus, the set $\mathcal{U}$ of images of a convex Lambertian surface created by varying the direction and strength of a *single* point light source at infinity is given by the union of at most $n(n-1)+2$ convex cones, i.e.,

$$\mathcal{U} = \{\mathbf{x} \mid \mathbf{x} = \max(B\mathbf{s}, \mathbf{0}), \forall \mathbf{s} \in \mathbb{R}^3\}$$

$$= \bigcup_{i=0}^{n(n-1)+1} P_i(\mathcal{L}_i). \tag{2}$$

From this set, we can construct the set $\mathcal{C}$ of all possible images of a convex Lambertian surface created by varying the direction and strength of an *arbitrary number* of point light sources at infinity,

$$\mathcal{C} = \{\mathbf{x} : \mathbf{x} = \sum_{i=1}^{k} \max(B\mathbf{s}_i, \mathbf{0}), \forall \mathbf{s}_i \in \mathbb{R}^3, \forall k \in \mathbb{Z}^+\}$$

where $\mathbb{Z}^+$ is the set of positive integers.

Proposition 2. *The set of images $\mathcal{C}$ is a convex cone in $\mathbb{R}^n$.*

Proof. The proof that $\mathcal{C}$ is a cone follows trivially from the definition of $\mathcal{C}$. To prove that $\mathcal{C}$ is convex, we appeal to a proposition for convex cones which states that a cone $\mathcal{C}$ is convex iff $\mathbf{x}_1 + \mathbf{x}_2 \in \mathcal{C}$ for any two points $\mathbf{x}_1, \mathbf{x}_2 \in \mathcal{C}$ [7]. So the proof that $\mathcal{C}$ is convex also follows trivially from the above definition of $\mathcal{C}$.

We call $\mathcal{C}$ the *illumination cone*. Every object has its own illumination cone. Note that each point in the cone is an image of the object under a particular lighting configuration, and the entire cone is the set of images of the object under all possible configurations of point light sources at infinity.

Proposition 3. *The illumination cone $\mathcal{C}$ of a convex Lambertian surface can be determined from as few as three images, each taken under a different, but unknown light source direction.*

Proof. The illumination cone $\mathcal{C}$ is completely determined by the illumination subspace $\mathcal{L}$. If the matrix of surface normals scaled by albedo B were known, then this would determine $\mathcal{L}$ uniquely, as $\mathcal{L} = \{\mathbf{x} \mid \mathbf{x} = B\mathbf{s}, \forall \mathbf{s} \in \mathbb{R}^3\}$. Yet, from images produced by differing, but unknown light source directions, we can not determine B uniquely. To see this, note that for any arbitrary invertible 3×3 linear transformation $A \in GL(3)$,

$$B\mathbf{s} = (BA)(A^{-1}\mathbf{s}) = B^*\mathbf{s}^*.$$

In other words, the same image is produced when the albedo and surface normals are transformed by A, while the light source is transformed by A^{-1}. Therefore, without knowledge of the light source directions, we can only recover B^* where $B^* = BA$, see [10, 17]. Nonetheless B^* is sufficient for determining the subspace $\mathcal{L}$: it is easy to show that $\mathcal{L} = \{\mathbf{x} \mid \mathbf{x} = B^*\mathbf{s}, \forall \mathbf{s} \in \mathbb{R}^3\} = \{\mathbf{x} \mid \mathbf{x} = B\mathbf{s}, \forall \mathbf{s} \in \mathbb{R}^3\}$, see [33].

Thus, for a convex object with Lambertian reflectance, we can determine its appearance under arbitrary illumination from as few as three images of the object – knowledge of the light source strength or direction is *not* needed, see also [33]. To determine the illumination cone $\mathcal{C}$, we simply need to determine the illumination subspace $\mathcal{L}$. In turn, we can choose any three images from the set $\mathcal{L}_0$, each taken under a different lighting direction, as its basis vectors. Naturally, if more images are available, they can be combined to find the best rank three approximation to $\mathcal{L}$ using singular value decomposition (SVD).

We should point out that for many convex surfaces the cone can be constructed from as few as three images; however, this is not always possible. If the object has surface normals covering the Gauss sphere, then there is only one light source direction – the viewing direction – such that the entire visible surface is illuminated. For any other light source direction, some portion of the surface is shadowed. To determine $\mathcal{L}$ each point on the surface of the object must be illuminated in at least three images; for this to be true over the entire visible surface, as many as five images may be required. See [20] and Section 5.1 for algorithms for determining $\mathcal{L}$ from images with shadowed pixels.

What may not be immediately obvious is that any point within the cone $\mathcal{C}$ (including the boundary points) can be found as a convex combination of the rays (images) produced by light source directions lying at the $m(m-1)$ intersections of the great circles on the illumination sphere. Each of these $m(m-1)$ rays (images) is an extreme ray of the convex cone, because it cannot be expressed as a convex combination of two other images in the cone. Furthermore, because the cone is constructed from a finite number of extreme rays (images), the cone is polyhedral.

These propositions and observations suggest the following algorithm for constructing the illumination cone from three or more images:

Illumination Subspace Method: Gather images of the object under varying illumination without shadowing and use these images to estimate the three-dimensional illumination subspace $\mathcal{L}$. After normalizing the images to be of unit length, singular value decomposition (SVD) can be used to estimate the best orthogonal basis in a least squares sense. From the illumination subspace $\mathcal{L}$, the extreme rays defining the illumination cone $\mathcal{C}$ are then computed. Recall that an extreme ray is an image created by a light source direction lying at the intersection of two or more great circles. If there are m independent surface normals, there can be as many as $m(m-1)$ extreme rays (images). Let $\mathbf{b}_i$ and $\mathbf{b}_j$ be rows of B with $i \neq j$, the extreme rays are given by

$$\mathbf{x}_{ij} = \max(B\mathbf{s}_{ij}, \mathbf{0}) \qquad (3)$$

where

$$\mathbf{s}_{ij} = \mathbf{b}_i \times \mathbf{b}_j. \qquad (4)$$

In Section 2.4, we use this method to experiment with images of real objects; we use a small number of images to build the illumination subspace $\mathcal{L}$ and then produce sample images from the illumination cone $\mathcal{C}$. To reduce storage and computational requirements for applications using the cone, the images can be projected down to a low dimensional subspace; any image in the projected cone can be found as convex combinations of the projected extreme rays. Note however, that some of the projected extreme rays are redundant since an extreme ray may project to the interior of the projected cone. As will be seen in the experiments of Section 3.4, the illumination cones of real objects do lie near a low dimensional subspace; thus dimensionality reduction by linear projection may be justified.

A Two-Dimensional Example To illustrate the relationship between an object and its illumination cone, consider the simplified 2-D example in Fig. 3. An object composed of three facets is shown in Fig. 3.a. For facet i, the product of the albedo and surface normal is given by $\mathbf{b}_i \in \mathbb{R}^2$. In this 2-D world, the direction of a light source at infinity can be represented as a point on a circle.

Let us now consider a camera observing the three facets from above such that each facet projects to one pixel yielding an image $\mathbf{x} = (x_1, x_2, x_3)^t \in \mathbb{R}^3$. $\mathcal{L}$ is then a 2-D linear subspace of $\mathbb{R}^3$, and the set of images from a single light source such that all pixels are illuminated $\mathcal{L}_0 \in \mathcal{L}$ is the 2-D convex cone shown in Figure 3.b. The left edge of $\mathcal{L}_0$, where $x_3 = 0$, corresponds to the light source direction where Facet 3 just goes into shadow, and similarly the right edge of $\mathcal{L}_0$, where $x_1 = 0$, corresponds to the light source direction where Facet 1 just goes in shadow. Now, for a single light source, the set of images is formed by projecting $\mathcal{L}$ onto the positive orthant as shown in Figure 3.c. Note for example, that the 2-D cone $P_1(\mathcal{L}_1)$ corresponds to the set of images in which Facets 1 and 2 are illuminated while Facet 3 is in shadow, and the 1-D ray $P_3(\mathcal{L}_3)$ corresponds to the set of image with Facet 1 illuminated and Facets 2 and 3 shadowed. The union $\cup_{i=0}^{i=6} P_i(\mathcal{L}_i)$ defines the walls of the illumination cone $\mathcal{C}$, and the entire cone is formed by taking convex combinations of images on the walls.

As seen in Figure 3.d, the set of light source directions, represented here by a circle, can be partitioned into regions $\mathcal{S}_i$ such that all images produced by light sources within a region have the same shadowing configurations. That is, $\mathcal{S}_i = \{\mathbf{s} : |\mathbf{s}| = 1, \max(B\mathbf{s}, \mathbf{0}) \in P_i(\mathcal{L}_i)\}$. The corresponding partitioning of light source directions is shown in Figure 3.a.

2.2   Illumination Cones for Arbitrary Objects

In the previous sub-section, we assumed that the objects were convex in shape and had Lambertian reflectance functions. The central result was that the set of images of the object under all possible illumination conditions formed a convex cone in the image space and that this illumination cone can be constructed from as few as three images. Yet, most objects are non-convex in shape and have reflectance functions which can be better approximated by more sophisticated

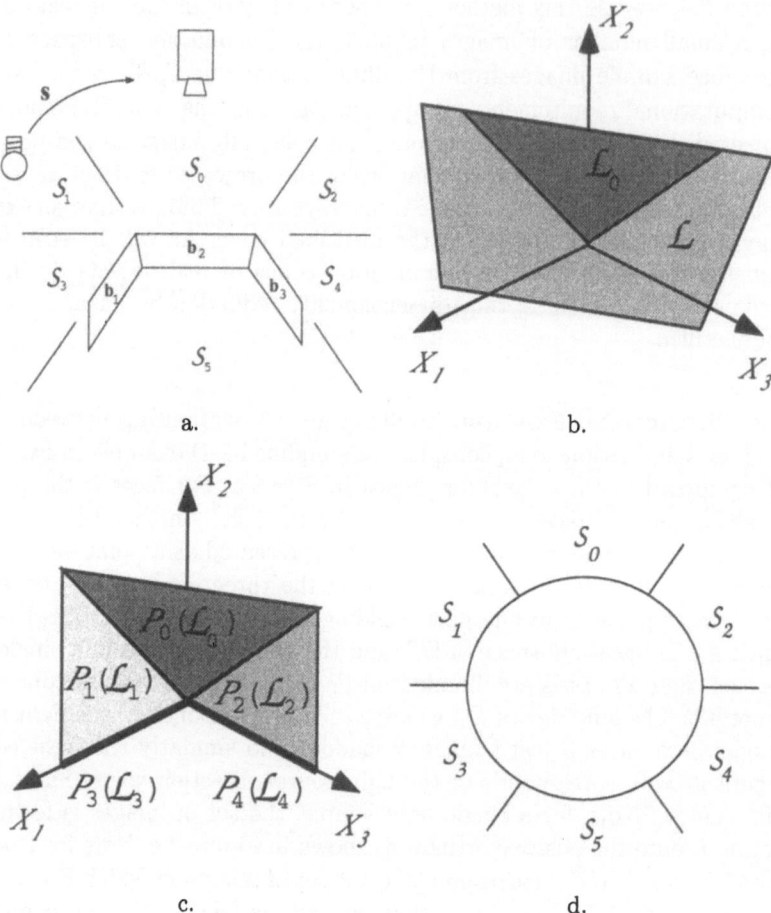

Fig. 3. A 2-D Example: a. A surface with three facets is observed from above and produces an image with pixels x_1, x_2 and x_3.   b. The linear subspace $\mathcal{L}$ and its intersection with the positive quadrant $\mathcal{L}_0$.   c. The "walls" of the cone $P_i(\mathcal{L}_i)$ corresponding to images formed by a single light source. The illumination cone $\mathcal{C}$ is formed by all convex combinations of images lying on the walls. d. The geometry of facets leads to a partitioning of the illumination circle.

physical [30, 36, 38] and phenomenological [22] models. The question again arises: What can we say about the set of images of an object with a non-convex shape and a non-Lambertian reflectance function?

The proof of Proposition 2 required *no* assumptions about the shape of the object, the nature of the light sources, or the reflectance function for the object's surface. Consequently, we can state a more general proposition about the set of images of an object under varying illumination:

Proposition 4. *The set of n-pixel images of any object, seen under all possible lighting conditions, is a convex cone in* $\mathbb{R}^n$.

Therefore, even for a nonconvex object with a non-Lambertian reflectance function, the set of images under all possible lighting conditions still forms convex cone in the image space. This result is in some sense trivial, arising from the superposition property of illumination: the image of an object produced by two light sources is simply the addition of the two images produced by the sources individually.

It is doubtful that the illumination cone for such objects can be constructed from as few as three images. This is not due to the non-convexity of objects and the shadows they cast. The structure of objects with Lambertian reflectance, but non-convex shapes, can be recovered up to a "generalized bas-relief" transformation from as few as three images [2]. From this, it is possible to determine the cast shadows exactly. Rather, the difficulty is due to the fact that the reflectance function is unknown. To determine the reflectance function *exactly* could take an infinite number of images. However, the Illumination Subspace Method developed in Section 2.1 can be used to approximate the cone, as will be seen in the empirical investigation of Section 2.4; such an approximation for a non-convex, non-Lambertian surface is used in the face recognition experiment in Section 5.

An alternative method for approximating the cone is presented below:

Sampling Method: Illuminate the object by a series of light source directions which evenly sample the illumination sphere. The resulting set of images is then used as the set of extreme rays of the approximate cone.

Note that this approximate cone is a subset of the true cone and so any image contained within the approximate cone is a valid image. The Sampling Method has its origins in the linear subspace method proposed by Hallinan [15]; yet, it differs in that the illumination cone restricts the images to be convex – not linear – combinations of the extreme rays. This method is a natural way of extending the appearance manifold method of Murase and Nayar to account for multiple light sources and shadowing [27].

2.3   Illumination Cones for Non-convex Lambertian Surfaces

While the *sampling method* provides the means to approximate the cone for objects with aribtrary geometry and reflectance functions and illuminated by multiple light sources, it is necessary to have observed the object under many lighting conditions to obtain a good approximation. On the other hand, if the object is convex and Lambertian, the *illumination subspace method* can be used to construct the entire cone from only three images. Here we consider an intermediate situation where the surface is Lambertian but non-convex. Most significantly, non-convex objects can cast shadows upon themselves. Whereas attached shadows are defined by a local condition (See Equation 1), cast shadows are global in nature. Nonetheless, from Section 2.2 we know that the set of images must still be a cone; here we show how an approximation of this cone can be constructed from as few as three images.

The illumination subspace method suggests a starting point for constructing the illumination cone: gather three or more images of an object under varying illumination without shadowing and use these images to estimate the three-dimensional illumination subspace $\mathcal{L}$. Note that the estimated basis B^* differs from the true B (rows which are the surface normal scaled by the albedo) by an unknown linear transformation, i.e., $B = B^*A$ where $A \in GL(3)$; for any light source, $B\mathbf{s} = (BA)(A^{-1}\mathbf{s})$. Nonetheless, for a convex object, the extreme rays defining the illumination cone $\mathcal{C}$ can be computed using Equations 3 and 4 using B^*. For a non-convex object, cast shadows can cover significant portions of the visible surface when the angle of the light source with respect to the viewing direction is large (extreme illumination); see the images from Subsets 4 and 5 in Fig. 9. Yet the image formation model (Eq. 1) used to develop the illumination cone in Section 2.1 does not account for cast shadows.

It has been shown in [2, 42] and in this book that from multiple images where the light source directions are *unknown*, one can only recover a Lambertian surface up to a three-parameter family given by the generalized bas-relief (GBR) transformation. This family is a restriction on A, and it has the effect of scaling the relief (flattening or extruding) and introducing an additive plane. Since both shadows and shading are preserved under these transformation [2, 23], images synthesized from a surface whose normal field is given by B^* under light source $\mathbf{s}^*_{ij}$ will have correct shadowing. Thus, to construct the extreme rays of the cone, we first reconstruct a Lambertian surface (a height function plus albedo) from B^*. This surface is not an approximation of the original surface, but rather a representative element of the orbit of the original surface under GBR. For a given light source direction $\mathbf{s}^*$, ray-tracing techniques can be used to determine which surface points lie in a cast shadow. Whereas for convex Lambertian objects, the illumination sphere is partitioned into $m(m-1)+2$ regions by m great circles, the illumination sphere will be partitioned by more complex curves for non-convex Lambertian objects, and so it is expected that there will be many more shadowing configurations. As such, it is unlikely that an exact representation of the cone could be used in practice. This approximate cone is a subset of the true cone when there is no imaging noise.

These observations lead to the following steps for constructing an approximation to the illumination cone of a non-convex Lambertian surface from a set of images taken under unknown lighting.

Cast Shadow Method:

1. Gather images of the object under varying illumination without shadowing.
2. Estimate B^* from training images.
3. Reconstruct a surface up to GBR.
4. For a set of light source directions that uniformly sample the sphere, use ray-tracing to synthesize images from the reconstructed surface that account for both cast and attached shadows.
5. Use synthetic images as extreme rays of cone.

More details of these steps as applied to face recognition will be provided in Section 5.1.

2.4   An Empirical Investigation: Building Illumination Cones

To demonstrate the power of these concepts, we have used the Illumination Subspace Method to construct the illumination cone for two different scenes: a human face and a desktop still life. To construct the cone for the human face, we used images from the Harvard Face Database [15], a collection of images of faces seen under a range of lighting directions. For the purpose of this demonstration, we used the images of one person, taking six images with little shadowing and using singular value decomposition (SVD) to construct a 3-D basis for the illumination subspace $\mathcal{L}$. Note that this 3-D linear subspace differs from the affine subspace constructed using the Karhunen-Loeve transform: the mean image is not subtracted before determining the basis vectors as in the Eigenpicture methods [24, 39].

The illumination subspace was then used to construct the illumination cone $\mathcal{C}$. We generated novel images of the face as if illuminated by one, two, or three point light sources by randomly sampling the illumination cone. Rather than constructing an explicit representation of the half-spaces bounding the illumination cone, we sampled $\mathcal{L}$, determined the corresponding orthant, and appropriately projected the image onto the illumination cone. Images constructed under multiple light sources simply correspond to the superposition of the images generated by each of the light sources.

The top two rows of Fig. 4 show all six low resolution images of a person's face that were used to construct the basis of the linear subspace $\mathcal{L}$. The bottom row of Fig. 4 shows three basis images that span $\mathcal{L}$. Each of the three columns of Fig. 5 respectively comprises of sample images from the illumination cone for the face with one, two, or three light sources.

There is a number of points to note about this experiment. There was almost no shadowing in the training images yet there are strong attached shadows in many of the sample images. These are particularly distinct in the images generated with a single light source. Notice for example the sharp shadow across the ridge of the nose in Column 1, Row 2 or the shadowing in Column 1, Row 4 where the light source is coming from behind the head. Notice also the depression under the cheekbones in Column 2, Row 5, and the cleft in the chin revealed

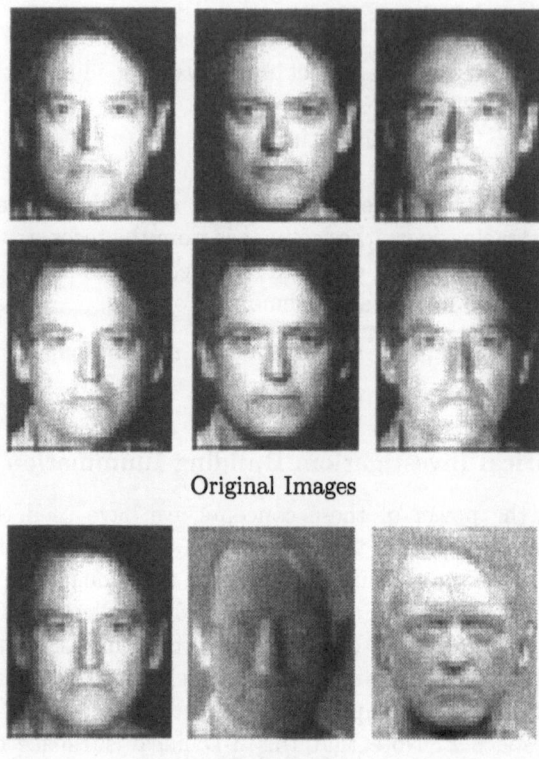

Original Images

Basis Images

Fig. 4. Illumination Subspace Method: The top two rows of the figure show all six of the original images used to construct the illumination subspace $\mathcal{L}$ for the face. The bottom row of the figure shows three basis images, that span the illumination subspace $\mathcal{L}$ for the face.

in Column 1, Row 3. For the image in Column 3, Row 2, two of the light sources are on opposite sides while the third one is coming from below; notice that both ears and the bottom of the chin and nose are brightly illuminated while the rest of the face is darker.

To construct the cone for the desktop still life, we used our own collection of nine images with little shadowing. The top row of Fig. 6 shows three of these images. The second row of Fig. 6 shows the three basis images that span $\mathcal{L}$. Each of the lower three columns of Fig. 6 respectively comprises of sample images from the illumination cone for the desktop still life with one, two, or three light sources.

The variability in illumination in these images is so extreme that the edge maps for these images would differ drastically. Notice in the image in Column 1, Row 4 that the shadow line on the bottle is distinct and that the left sides of the phone, duck, and bottle are brightly illuminated. Throughout the scene, notice that those points having comparable surface normals seem to be similarly

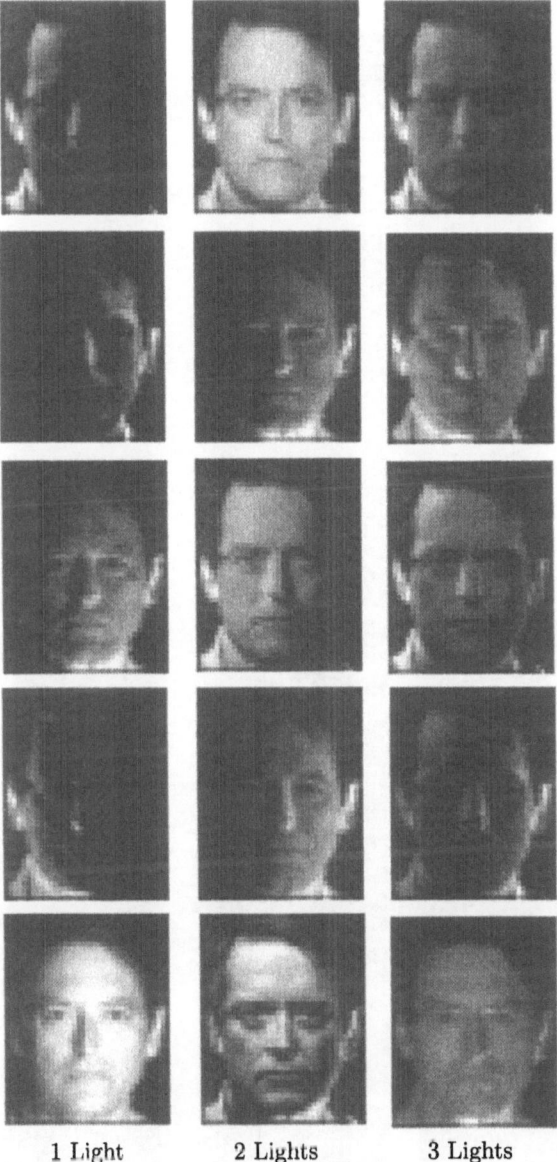

1 Light   2 Lights   3 Lights

Fig. 5. Random Samples from the Illumination Cone of a Face: Each of the three columns respectively comprises of sample images from the illumination cone with one, two, or three light sources.

illuminated. Furthermore, notice that all of the nearly horizontal surfaces in the bottom two images of the first column are in shadow since the light is coming from below. In the image with two light sources shown at the bottom of Column

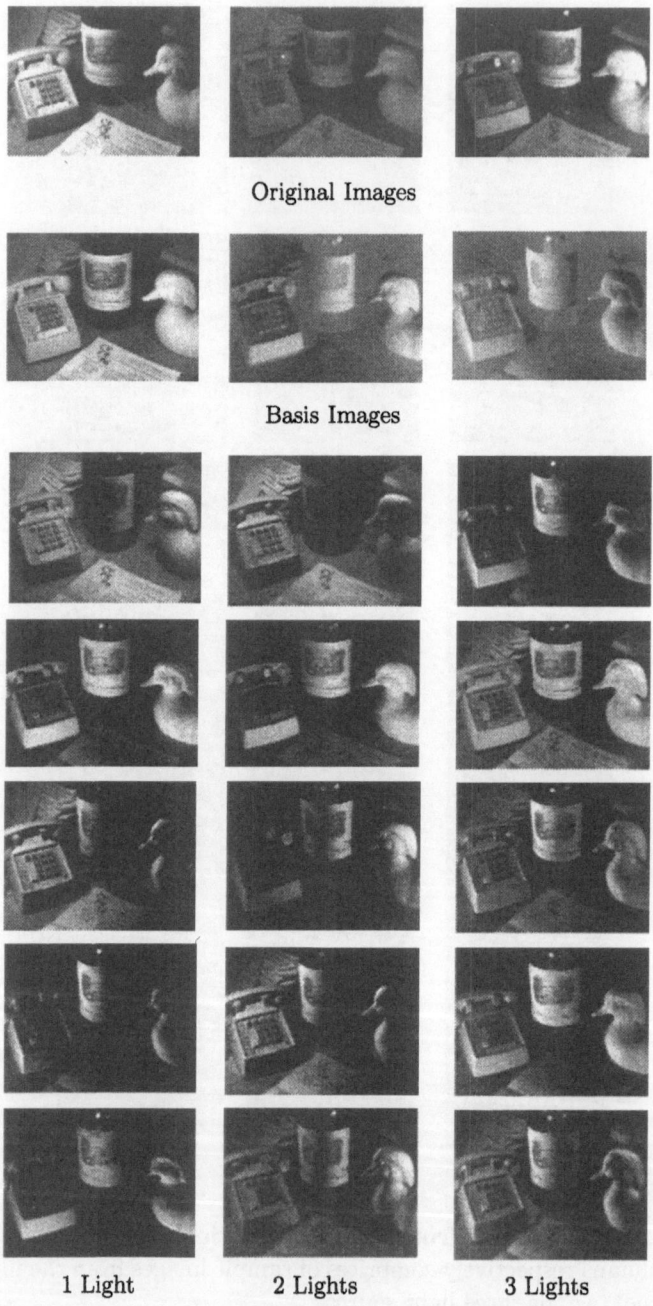

Original Images

Basis Images

1 Light   2 Lights   3 Lights

Fig. 6. Illumination Subspace Method: The top row of the figure shows three of the original nine images used to construct the illumination subspace $\mathcal{L}$ for the still life. The second row shows the three basis images that span the illumination subspace $\mathcal{L}$. Each of the lower three columns respectively comprises of sample images from the illumination cone with one, two, or three light sources.

2, the sources are located on opposite sides and behind the objects. This leads
to a shadow line in the center of the bottle. The head of the wooden duck shows
a similar shadowing where its front and back are illuminated, but not the side.

3 Dimension and Shape of the Illumination Cone

In this section, we investigate the dimension of the illumination cone, and show
that it is equal to the number of distinct surface normals. However, we conjecture
that the shape of the cone is flat, with much of its volume concentrated near a
low-dimensional subspace, and present empirical evidence to support this conjecture. Finally, we show that the cones of two objects with the same geometry,
but with separate albedo patterns, differ by a diagonal linear transformation.

3.1 The Dimension of the Illumination Cone

Given that the set of images of an object under variation in illumination is a
convex cone, it is natural to ask: What is the dimension of the cone in $\mathbb{R}^n$?
By this we mean, what is the span of the vectors in the illumination cone $\mathcal{C}$?
Why do we want to know the answer to this question? Because the complexity
of the cone, may dictate the nature of the recognition algorithm. For example,
if the illumination cones are 1-D, i.e., rays in the positive orthant of $\mathbb{R}^n$, then a
recognition scheme based on normalized correlation could handle all of the variation due to illumination. However, in general the cones are not one dimensional
unless the object is planar. To this end, we offer the following proposition.

Proposition 5. *The dimension of the illumination cone $\mathcal{C}$ is equal to the number of distinct surface normals.*

Proof. As with the proof of Proposition 1, we again represent each light source
direction by a point on the surface of the illumination sphere. Each cell on the
illumination sphere corresponds to the light source directions which produce a
particular set of images $P_i(\mathcal{L}_i)$. For every image in a set $P_i(\mathcal{L}_i)$, certain pixels
are always equal to zero, i.e., always in shadow. There exists a cell S_0 on the
illumination sphere corresponding to the light source directions which produce
$\mathcal{L}_0$, the set of images in which all pixels are always illuminated. There exists a
cell S_d corresponding to the light source directions which produce a set of images
in which all pixels are always in shadow. Choose any point $\mathbf{s}_b \in S_0$. The point
$\mathbf{s}_d = -\mathbf{s}_b$ is antipodal to $\mathbf{s}_b$ and lies within S_d. Draw any half-meridian connecting
$\mathbf{s}_b$ and $\mathbf{s}_d$. Starting at $\mathbf{s}_b$, follow the path of the half-meridian; it crosses m distinct
great circles, and passes through m different cells before entering S_d. Note that
the path of the half-meridian corresponds to a particular path of light source
directions, starting from a light source direction producing an image in which all
pixels are illuminated and ending at a light source direction producing an image
in which all pixels are in shadow. Each time the half-meridian crosses a great
circle, the pixel corresponding to the great circle becomes shadowed.

Take an image produced from any light source direction within the interior of each cell through which the meridian passes, including S_0, but excluding S_d. Arrange each of these m images as column vectors in an $n \times m$ matrix M. By elementary row operations, the matrix M can be converted to its echelon form M^*, and it is trivial to show that M^* has exactly m non-zero rows. Thus, the rank of M is m, and the dimension of $\mathcal{C}$ is at least m. Since there are only m distinct surface normals, the dimension of $\mathcal{C}$ cannot exceed m. Thus, the dimension of $\mathcal{C}$ equals m.

Note that for images with n pixels, this proposition indicates that the dimension of the illumination cone is one for a planar object, is roughly $\sqrt{n}$ for a cylindrical object, and is n for a spherical object. But if the cone spans $\mathbb{R}^n$, what fraction of the positive orthant does it occupy? In Section 3.3, we investigate this question, conjecturing that the illumination cones for most objects occupy little volume in the image space.

3.2   The Connection between Albedo and Cone Shape

If two objects are similar in geometry, but differ in their respective albedo patterns, then there is a simple linear relationship between their corresponding illumination cones. Here, we consider two Lambertian objects that have the same underlying geometry, but have differing albedo patterns (e.g., a Coke can and a Pepsi can). In this case, the product of albedo and surface normals for the two objects can be expressed as $B_1 = R_1 N$ and $B_2 = R_2 N$ where N is an $n \times 3$ matrix of surface normals and R_i is an $n \times n$ diagonal matrix whose diagonal elements are positive and represent the albedo. The following proposition relates the illumination cones of the two objects.

Proposition 6. *If $\mathcal{C}_1$ is the illumination cone for an object defined by $B_1 = R_1 N$ and $\mathcal{C}_2$ is the illumination cone for an object defined by $B_2 = R_2 N$, then*

$$\mathcal{C}_1 = \{R_1 R_2^{-1} \mathbf{x} : \mathbf{x} \in \mathcal{C}_2\} \qquad and$$
$$\mathcal{C}_2 = \{R_2 R_1^{-1} \mathbf{x} : \mathbf{x} \in \mathcal{C}_1\}.$$

Proof. For every light source direction $\mathbf{s}$, the corresponding images are given by $\mathbf{x}_1 = \max(B_1 \mathbf{s}, \mathbf{0}) = R_1 \max(N \mathbf{s}, \mathbf{0})$ and $\mathbf{x}_2 = \max(B_2 \mathbf{s}, \mathbf{0}) = R_2 \max(N \mathbf{s}, \mathbf{0})$. Since R_1 and R_2 are diagonal with positive diagonal elements, they are invertible. Therefore, $\mathbf{x}_1 = R_1 R_2^{-1} \mathbf{x}_2$ and $\mathbf{x}_2 = R_2 R_1^{-1} \mathbf{x}_1$.

Thus, the cones for two objects with identical geometry but differing albedo patterns differ by a diagonal linear transformation. This fact can be applied when computing cones for objects observed by color (multi-band) cameras as noted in Section 4. Note that this proposition also holds when the objects are non-convex; since the partitioning of the illumination sphere is determined by the objects' surface geometry, the set of shadowing configurations is identical for two objects with the same shape. The intensities of the illuminated pixels are related by the transformations given in the proposition.

3.3   Shape of the Illumination Cone

While we have shown that an illumination cone is a convex, polyhedral cone that can span n dimensions if there are n distinct surface normals, we have not said how big it is in practice. Note that having a cone span n dimensions does not mean that it covers $\mathbb{R}^n$, since a convex cone is defined only by convex combinations of its extreme rays. It is conceivable that an illumination cone could completely cover the positive orthant of $\mathbb{R}^n$. However, the existence of an object geometry that would produce this is unlikely. For such an object, it must be possible to choose n light source direction such that each of the n facets are illuminated independently.

On the other hand, if the illumination cones for objects are small and well separated, then recognition should be possible, even under extreme lighting conditions. We believe that the latter is true – that the cone has almost no volume in the image space. We offer the following conjecture:

Conjecture 1. The shape of the cone is "flat," i.e., most of its volume is concentrated near a low-dimensional subspace.

While we have yet to prove this conjecture, the empirical investigations of [9, 15] and the one in the following section seem to support it.

3.4   Empirical Investigation of the Shape of the Illumination Cones

To investigate Proposition 5 and Conjecture 1, we have gathered several images, taken under varying lighting conditions, of two objects: the corner of a cardboard box and a Wilson tennis ball. For both objects, we computed the illumination subspace using SVD their corresponding sets of images. Using the estimated illumination subspaces, we performed two experiments.

In the first experiment, we tried to confirm that the illumination spheres for both objects would appear as we would expect. For both the box and the tennis ball, we drew the great circles associated with each pixel on the illumination sphere, see Fig. 7. From Proposition 5, we would expect the illumination cone produced by the corner of the box to be three dimensional since the corner has only three faces. The illumination sphere should be partitioned into eight regions by three great circles, each meeting the other two orthogonally. This structure is evident in the figure. Yet, due to both image noise and the fact that the surface is not truly Lambertian, there is some small deviation of the great circles. Furthermore, the few pixels from the edge and corner of the box produce a few stray great circles. In contrast, the visible surface normals of the tennis ball should nearly cover half of the Gauss sphere and, therefore, the great circles should nearly cover the illumination sphere. Again, this structure is evident in the figure.

In the second experiment, we plotted the eigenvalues of the matrix of extreme rays for both the box and the tennis ball. The point of this experiment was to compare the size and "flatness" of both cones. As discussed in Section 2.1, an extreme ray $\mathbf{x}_{ij}$ is an image created by a light source direction $\mathbf{s}_{ij}$ lying at the

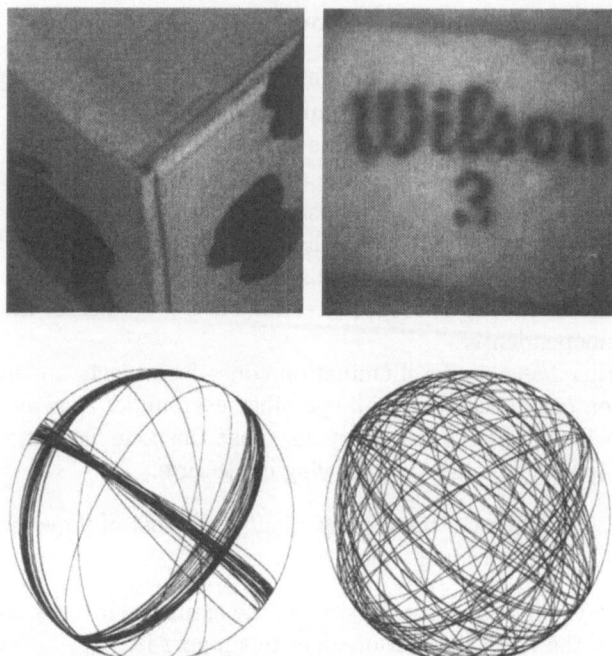

Fig. 7. Examples of Illumination Spheres: On the left, the figure shows an image of the corner of a cardboard box and its corresponding illumination sphere. Note that the illumination sphere is, for the most part, partitioned into eight regions by three great circles, each meeting the other two orthogonally. On the right, the figure shows an image of a Wilson tennis ball and its corresponding illumination sphere. Note that the great circles nearly cover the illumination sphere.

intersection of two or more great circles on the illumination sphere. The matrix of extreme rays is simply the matrix whose columns are the vectorized images $x_{ij}/|x_{ij}|$. We then performed SVD on the matrix of extreme rays for the box corner and the matrix of extreme rays for the tennis ball. The corresponding eigenvalues are plotted in decreasing order in Fig. 8.

From this figure we make the following observations. First, in the plot of the box corner there is a sharp drop-off after the third eigenvalue, indicating that most of the illumination cone is concentrated near a 3-D subspace of the image space. Second, the eigenvalues for the tennis ball do not drop-off as quickly as those for the box, indicating that the illumination cone for the tennis ball is larger than that for the box. And, third, the eigenvalues for both the box corner and the tennis ball diminish by at least two orders of magnitude within the first fifteen eigenvalues. Thus, in agreement with the above conjecture, the illumination cones appear to be concentrated near a low dimensional subspace.

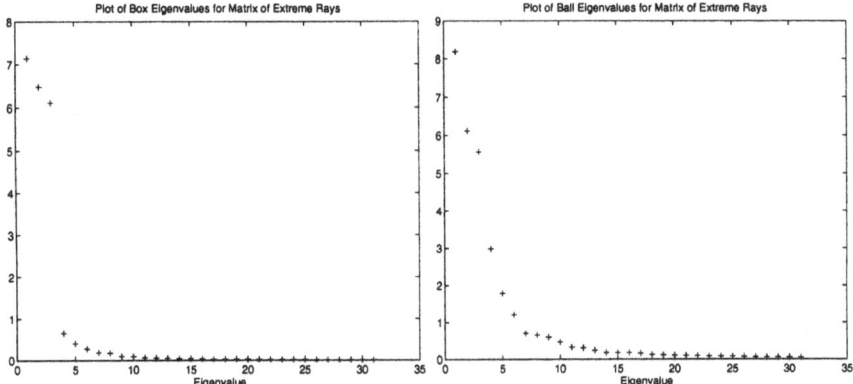

Fig. 8. Eigenvalues for the Matrix of Extreme Rays: The figure shows a plot in decreasing order of the eigenvalues of the matrix of extreme rays for the illumination cone of the corner of a box and for the illumination cone of a tennis ball.

We should point out that Epstein *et al.* [9] and Hallinan [15] performed a related experiment on images created by *physically* moving the light source to evenly sample the illumination sphere. They, too, found that the set of images of an object under variable illumination lies near a low dimensional subspace. Our results using synthesized images from the cone seem to complement their findings.

4   Color

Until now, we have neglected the spectral distribution of the light sources, the color of the surface, and the spectral response of the camera; here we extend the results of Section 2 to multi-spectral images.

Let λ denote the wavelength of light. Let $\rho_i(\lambda)$ denote the response for all elements of the ith color channel. Let $R(\lambda)$ be a diagonal matrix whose elements are the spectral reflectance functions of the facets, and let the rows of $N \in \mathbb{R}^{n \times 3}$ be the surface normals of the facets. Finally, let $\tilde{s}(\lambda)$ and $\hat{s}$ be the power spectrum and direction of the light source, respectively. Then, ignoring attached shadows and the associated max operation, the n-pixel image $\mathbf{x}_i$ produced by color channel i of a convex Lambertian surface from a single colored light is [18, 21]

$$\mathbf{x}_i = \int \rho_i(\lambda)(R(\lambda)N)(\tilde{s}(\lambda)\hat{s})d\lambda. \tag{5}$$

It is difficult to make limiting statements about the set of possible images of a colored object when $\rho(\lambda)$, $R(\lambda)$ and $\tilde{s}(\lambda)$ are arbitrary. For example, if we consider a particular object with a spectral reflectance function $R(\lambda)$ and surface normals N, then without constraining assumptions on $\rho_i(\lambda)$ and $\tilde{s}(\lambda)$, any image x_i is obtainable. Consequently, we will consider two specific cases: cameras with narrow-band spectral response and light sources with identical spectral distributions.

4.1   Narrow-Band Cameras

Following [29], if the sensing elements in each color channel have narrow-band spectral response or can be made to appear narrow band [11], then $\rho_i(\lambda)$ can be approximated by a Dirac delta function about some wavelength λ_i, and Eq. 5 can be rewritten as

$$\begin{aligned} \mathbf{x}_i &= \rho(\lambda_i)(R(\lambda_i)N)(\tilde{s}(\lambda_i)\hat{\mathbf{s}}) \\ &= \rho_i(R_iN)(\tilde{s}_i\hat{\mathbf{s}}). \end{aligned} \tag{6}$$

Note that ρ_i, R_i and N are constants for a given surface and camera whereas $\tilde{s}_i$ and $\hat{\mathbf{s}}$ depend on properties of the light source. Eq. 6 can be expressed using the notation of Eq. 1 where $B = \rho_i R_i N$ and $\mathbf{s} = \tilde{s}_i \hat{\mathbf{s}}$. The diagonal elements of $\rho_i R_i$ are the effective albedo of the facets for color channel i. For c narrow-band color channels, the color image $\mathbf{x} = [\mathbf{x}_1^t \,|\, \mathbf{x}_2^t \,|\, \cdots \,|\, \mathbf{x}_c^t]^t$ formed by stacking up the c images for each channel can be considered as a point in $\mathbb{R}^{cn}$. Under a single light source, $\mathbf{x}$ is a function of $\hat{\mathbf{s}}$ and $\tilde{s}_1 \cdots \tilde{s}_c$. Taken over all light source directions and spectral distributions, the set of images from a single light source without shadowing is a $c + 2$ dimensional manifold in $\mathbb{R}^{cn}$. It is easy to show that this manifold is embedded in a $3c$-dimensional linear subspace of $\mathbb{R}^{cn}$, and that any point (image) in the intersection of this linear subspace with the positive orthant of $\mathbb{R}^{cn}$ can be achieved by three colored light sources.

A basis for this $3c$-dimensional subspace can be constructed from three color images without shadowing. This is equivalent to independently constructing c three-dimensional linear subspaces in $\mathbb{R}^n$, one for each color channel. Note that $\rho_i R_i N$ spans subspace i. When attached shadows are considered, an illumination cone can be constructed in $\mathbb{R}^n$ for each color channel independently. The cones for each color channel are closely related since they arise from the same surface; effectively the albedo matrix R_i may be different for each color channel, but the surface normals N are the same. As demonstrated in Section 3.2, the cones for two surfaces with the same geometry, but different albedo patterns differ by a diagonal linear transformation. Now, the set of all multi-spectral images of a convex Lambertian surface is a convex polyhedral cone in $\mathbb{R}^{cn}$ given by the Cartesian product of the c individual cones. Following Proposition 5, this color cone spans at most cm dimensions where m is the number of distinct surface normals.

4.2   Light Sources with Identical Spectra

Consider another imaging situation in which a color camera (c channels, not necessarily narrow-band) observes a scene where the number and location of the light sources are unknown, but the power spectral distributions of all light sources are identical (e.g., incandescent bulbs). Equation 5 can then be rewritten as

$$\mathbf{x}_i = \left(\int \rho_i(\lambda)\tilde{s}(\lambda)R(\lambda)d\lambda \right) N\hat{\mathbf{s}}. \qquad (7)$$

In this case, the integral is independent of the light source direction and scales with its intensity. If we define the intensity of the light source to be $\tilde{s} = \int \tilde{s}(\lambda)d\lambda$, then $\mathbf{s} = \tilde{s}\hat{\mathbf{s}}$ and $R_i = \frac{1}{\tilde{s}} \int \rho_i(\lambda)\tilde{s}(\lambda)R(\lambda)d\lambda$. Equation 7 can then be expressed as

$$\mathbf{x}_i = R_i N\mathbf{s}.$$

For c color channels, the color image $\mathbf{x} \in \mathbb{R}^{cn}$ is given by

$$\mathbf{x} = [R_1 \,|\, R_2 \,|\, \cdots \,|\, R_c]^t \, N\mathbf{s}.$$

Consequently, the set of images of the surface without shadowing is a three-dimensional linear subspace of $\mathbb{R}^{cn}$ since R_i and N are constants. Following Section 2, the set of all images with shadowing is a convex polyhedral cone that spans m dimensions of $\mathbb{R}^{cn}$. Thus, when the light sources have identical power spectra (even if the camera is not narrow-band), the set of all images is significantly smaller than considered above since the color measured at each pixel is independent of the light source direction.

5   Face Recognition Using the Illumination Cone

Until this point, we have focused on properties of the set of images of an object under varying illumination. Here, we utilize these properties to develop representations and algorithms for recognizing objects, namely faces, under different lighting conditions. Face recognition is a challenging yet well-studied problem [8, 32]; the difficulty in face recognition arises from the fact that many faces are geometrically and photometrically very similar, yet there is a great deal of variability in the images of an individual due to changes of pose, lighting, facial expression, facial hair, hair style, makeup, age, etc. Here we focus solely on illumination, and in this section, we empirically compare these new methods to a number of popular techniques such as correlation [6] and Eigenfaces [24, 39] as well as more recently developed techniques such as distance to linear subspace [3, 15, 20, 34].

5.1   Constructing the Illumination Cone Representation of Faces

In the experiments reported below, illumination cones are constructed using variations of the *illumination subspace method* and the *cast shadow method*. When implementing these methods, there are two problems which must be addressed.

The first problem that arises with these two methods is with the estimation of B^*. For even a convex object whose Gaussian image covers the Gauss sphere, there is only one light source direction – the viewing direction – for which no point on the surface is in shadow. For any other light source direction, shadows

Subset 1   Subset 2   Subset 3   Subset 4   Subset 5

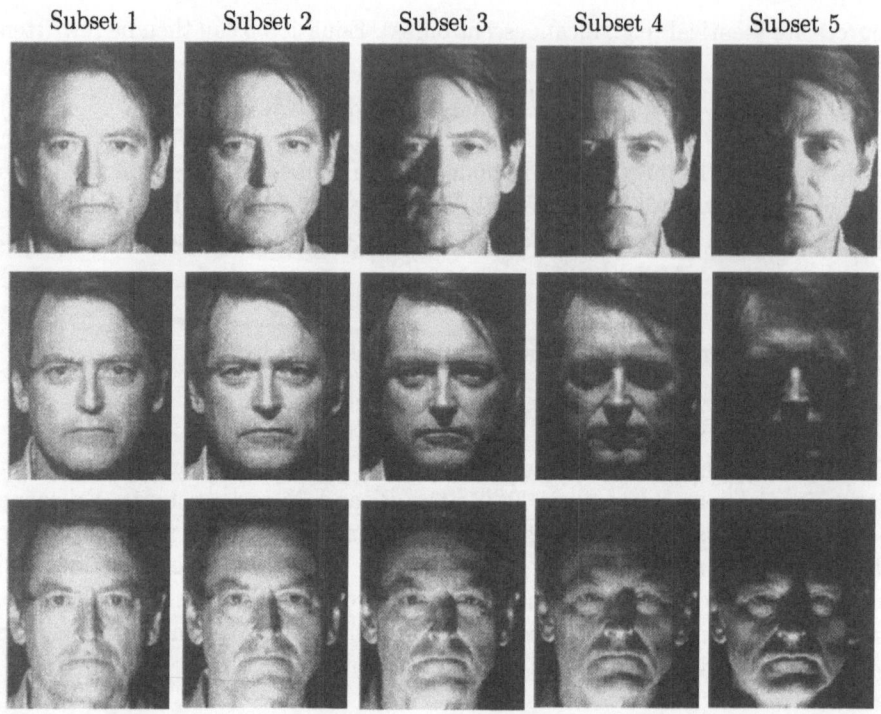

Fig. 9. Example images from each subset of the Harvard Database used to test the algorithms.

will be present. For faces, which are not convex, shadowing in the modeling images is likely to be more pronounced. When SVD is used to estimate B^* from images with shadows, these systematic errors can bias the estimation significantly. Therefore, alternative ways are needed to estimate B^* that take into account the fact that some data values should not be used in the estimation.

The next problem is that usually m, the number of independent normals in B, can be large (more than a thousand) hence the number of extreme rays needed to completely define the illumination cone can run in the millions. Therefore, we must approximate the cone in some fashion; in this work, we choose to use a small number of extreme rays (images). In Section 3.4 it was shown empirically that the cone is flat (i.e., elements lie near a low dimensional linear subspace), and so the hope is that a sub-sampled cone will provide an approximation that leads to good recognition performance. In our experience, around 60-80 images are sufficient, provided that the corresponding light source directions s_{ij} more or less uniformly sample the illumination sphere. The resulting cone C^* is a subset of the object's true cone C. In the *Sampling Method* described in Section 2.2, an alternative approximation to C is obtained by directly sampling the space of light source directions rather than generating the extreme rays through Eq. 4. While the resulting images form the extreme rays of the representation C^* and lie on the boundary of the true cone $\mathcal{C}$, they are not necessarily extreme rays of $\mathcal{C}$.

Estimating B^* Using singular value decomposition directly on the images leads to a biased estimate of B^* due to shadows. In addition, portions of some of the images from the Harvard database used in our experiments were saturated. Both shadows formed under a single light source and saturations can be detected by thresholding and labeled as "missing" – these pixels do not satisfy the linear equation $\mathbf{x} = B\mathbf{s}$. Thus, we need to estimate the 3-D linear subspace B^* from images with missing values.

Define the data matrix for c images of an individual to be $X = [\mathbf{x}_1 \ldots \mathbf{x}_c]$. If there were no shadowing, X would be rank 3, and we could use SVD to decompose X into $X = B^*S^*$ where S^* is the $3 \times c$ matrix of the light source direction for all c images. To estimate a basis B^* for the 3-D linear subspace $\mathcal{L}$ from image data with missing elements, we have implemented a variation of [35]; see also [37, 20].

The overview of this method is as follows: without doing any row or column permutations sift out all the full rows (with no invalid data) of matrix X to form a full sub-matrix $\tilde{X}$. Perform SVD on $\tilde{X}$ and get an initial estimate of S^*. Fix S^* and estimate each of the rows of B^* independently using least squares. Then, fix B^* and estimate each of the light source direction $\mathbf{s}_i$ independently. Repeat last two steps until estimates converge. The inner workings of the algorithm are given as follows: Let $\mathbf{b}_i$ be the ith row of B^*, let $\mathbf{x}_i$ be the ith row of X. Let p be the indices of non-missing elements in $\mathbf{x}_i$, and let $\mathbf{x}_i^p$ be the row obtained by taking only the non-missing elements of $\mathbf{x}_i$, and let S^p similarly be the submatrix of S^* consisting of rows with indices in p. Then, the ith row of B^* is given by,

$$\mathbf{b}_i = (\mathbf{x}_i^p)(S^p)^\dagger$$

where $(S^p)^\dagger$ is the pseudo-inverse of S^p. With the new estimate of B^* at hand, let $\mathbf{x}_j$ be the jth column of X, let p be the indices of non-missing elements in $\mathbf{x}_j$, and let $\mathbf{x}_j^p$ be the column obtained by taking only the non-missing elements of $\mathbf{x}_j$. Let B^p similarly be the submatrix of B^* consisting of rows with indices in p. Then, the jth light source direction is given by,

$$\mathbf{s}_j = (B^p)^\dagger(\mathbf{x}_j^p)$$

After the new set of light sources S^* has been calculated, the last two steps can be repeated until the estimate of B^* converges. The algorithm is very well behaved, converging to the global minimum within 10-15 iterations. Though it is possible to converge to a local minimum, we never observed this in simulation or in practice.

Enforcing Integrability To predict cast shadows, we must reconstruct a surface and to do this, the vector field B^* must correspond to an integrable normal field. Since no method has been developed to enforce integrability during the

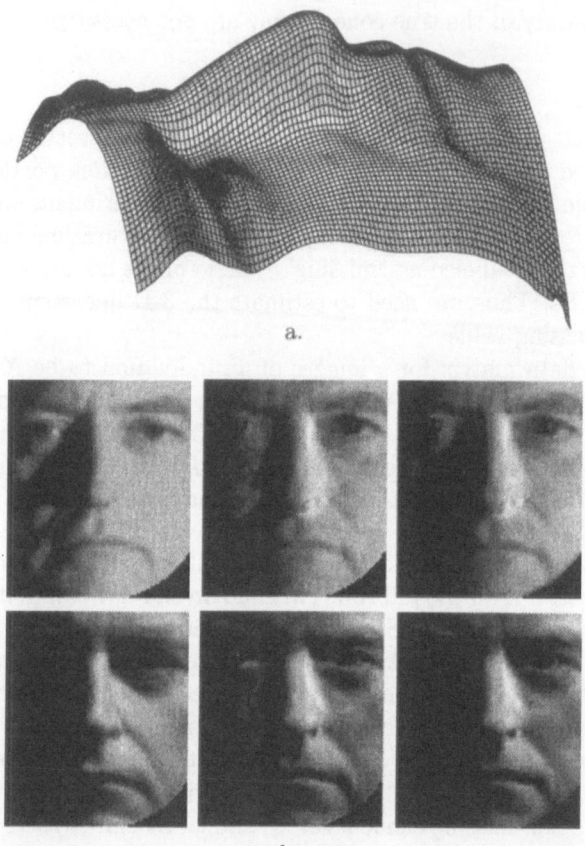

a.

b.

Fig. 10. Figure 4 showed six original images of a face and three images spanning the linear subspace B^*. a) From B^*, the surface is reconstructed up to a GBR transformation. b) Sample images from database (left column); closest image in illumination cone without cast shadows (middle column); and closest image in illumination cone with cast shadows (right column)

estimation of B^*, we enforce it afterwards. That is, given B^* computed as described above, we estimate a matrix $A \in GL(3)$ such that B^*A corresponds to an integrable normal field; the development follows [42].

Consider a continuous surface defined as the graph of $z(x, y)$, and let $\mathbf{b}$ be the corresponding normal field scaled by an albedo (scalar) field. The integrability constraint for a surface is $z_{xy} = z_{yx}$ where subscripts denote partial derivatives. In turn, $\mathbf{b}$ must satisfy:

$$\left(\frac{b_1}{b_3}\right)_y = \left(\frac{b_2}{b_3}\right)_x$$

To estimate A such that $\mathbf{b}^T(x, y) = \mathbf{b}^{*^T}(x, y)A$, we expand this out. Letting the columns of A be denoted by A_1, A_2, A_3 yields

$$(\mathbf{b}^{*^T}A_3)(\mathbf{b}_x^{*^T}A_2) - (\mathbf{b}^{*^T}A_2)(\mathbf{b}_x^{*^T}A_3) =$$
$$(\mathbf{b}^{*^T}A_3)(\mathbf{b}_y^{*^T}A_1) - (\mathbf{b}^{*^T}A_1)(\mathbf{b}_y^{*^T}A_3)$$

which can be expressed as

$$\mathbf{b}^{*^T}S_1\mathbf{b}_x^* = \mathbf{b}^{*^T}S_2\mathbf{b}_y^* \tag{8}$$

where $S_1 = A_3A_2^T - A_2A_3^T$ and $S_2 = A_3A_1^T - A_1A_3^T$.

S_1 and S_2 are skew-symmetric matrices and have three degrees of freedom. Equation 8 is linear in the six elements of S_1 and S_2. From the estimate of B^* obtained using the method in Section 5.1, discrete approximations of the partial derivatives ($\mathbf{b}_x^*$ and $\mathbf{b}_y^*$) are computed, and then SVD is used to solve for the six elements of S_1 and S_2. In [42], it was shown that the elements of S_1 and S_2 are cofactors of A, and a simple method for computing A from the cofactors was presented. This procedure only determines six degrees of freedom of A. The other three correspond to the generalized bas relief (GBR) transformation [2] and can be chosen arbitrarily since GBR preserves integrability. The surface corresponding to B^*A differs from the true surface by GBR, i.e., $z^*(x,y) = \lambda z(x,y) + \mu x + \nu y$ for arbitrary λ, μ, ν with $\lambda \neq 0$.

Generating a GBR Surface The preceding sections give a method for estimating the matrix B^* and then enforcing integrability; we now reconstruct the corresponding surface $\hat{z}(x,y)$. Note that $\hat{z}(x,y)$ is not a Euclidean reconstruction of the face, but a representative element of the orbit under a GBR transformation. Recall that both shading and shadowing will be correct for images synthesized from a transformed surface.

To find $\hat{z}(x,y)$, we use the variational approach presented in [19]. A surface $\hat{z}(x,y)$ is fit to the given components of the gradient $p = \frac{\partial z}{\partial x} = -\frac{b_{i1}}{b_{i3}}$ and $q = \frac{\partial z}{\partial y} = -\frac{b_{i2}}{b_{i3}}$ by minimizing the functional

$$\int\int_\Omega (\hat{z}_x - p)^2 + (\hat{z}_y - q)^2 \, dx \, dy.$$

whose Euler equation reduces to $\nabla^2 z = p_x + q_y$. By enforcing the right natural boundary conditions and employing an iterative scheme that uses a discrete approximation of the Laplacian, we can generate the surface $\hat{z}(x,y)$ [19]. Then, it is a simple matter to construct an illumination cone representation that incorporates cast shadows. Using ray-tracing techniques for a given light source direction, we can determine the cast shadow regions and correct the extreme rays of C^*.

Figures 4 and 10 demonstrate the process of constructing the cone C^*. Figure 4 shows the training images for one individual in the databaseas as well as the columns of the matrix B^*. Figure 10.a shows the reconstruction of the surface up to a GBR transformation. The left column of Fig. 10.b shows sample images in the database; the middle column shows the closest image in the illumination cone without cast shadows; and the right column shows the closest image in the illumination cone with cast shadows. Note that the background and hair have been masked.

5.2   Recognition

The cone C^* can be used in a natural way for face recognition, and in experiments described below, we compare three recognition algorithms to the proposed method. From a set of face images labeled with the person's identity (*the learning set*) and an unlabeled set of face images from the same group of people (*the test set*), each algorithm is used to identify the person in the test images. For more details of the comparison algorithms, see [3]. We assume that the face has been located and aligned within the image.

The simplest recognition scheme is a nearest neighbor classifier in the image space [6]. An image in the test set is recognized (classified) by assigning to it the label of the closest point in the learning set, where distances are measured in the image space. If all of the images are normalized to have zero mean and unit variance, this procedure is equivalent to choosing the image in the learning set that best *correlates* with the test image. Because of the normalization process, the result is independent of light source intensity.

As correlation methods are computationally expensive and require great amounts of storage, it is natural to pursue dimensionality reduction schemes. A technique now commonly used in computer vision – particularly in face recognition – is principal components analysis (PCA) which is popularly known as *Eigenfaces* [15, 27, 24, 39]. Given a collection of training images $\mathbf{x}_i \in \mathbb{R}^n$, a linear projection of each image $\mathbf{y}_i = W\mathbf{x}_i$ to an f-dimensional feature space is performed. A face in a test image $\mathbf{x}$ is recognized by projecting $\mathbf{x}$ into the feature space, and nearest neighbor classification is performed in $\mathbb{R}^f$. The projection matrix W is chosen to maximize the scatter of all projected samples. It has been shown that when f equals the number of training images, the Eigenface and Correlation methods are equivalent (See [3, 27]). One proposed method for handling illumination variation in PCA is to discard from W the three most significant principal components; in practice, this yields better recognition performance [3].

A third approach is to model the illumination variation of each face as a three-dimensional linear subspace $\mathcal{L}$ as described in Section 2.1. To perform recognition, we simply compute the distance of the test image to each linear subspace and choose the face corresponding to the shortest distance. We call this recognition scheme the *Linear Subspace* method [2]; it is a variant of the photometric alignment method proposed in [34] and is related to [16, 29]. While this models the variation in intensity when the surface is completely illuminated, it does not model shadowing.

Finally, given a test image $\mathbf{x}$, recognition using *illumination cones* is performed by first computing the distance of the test image to each cone, and then choosing the face that corresponds to the shortest distance. Since each cone is convex, the distance can be found by solving a convex optimization problem. In particular, the non-negative linear least squares technique contained in Matlab was used in our implementation, and this algorithm has computational complexity $O(n e^2)$ where n is the number of pixels and e is the number of extreme rays. Two different vatiations for constructing the cone and a method for increasing the speed are considered.

Subset 1

Subset 2

Subset 3

Subset 4

Subset 5

Fig. 11. The highlighted lines of longitude and latitude indicate the light source directions for Subsets 1 through 5. Each intersection of a longitudinal and latitudinal line on the right side of the illustration sphere has a corresponding image in the database.

5.3   Experiments and Results

To test the effectiveness of these recognition algorithms, we performed a series of experiments on a database from the Harvard Robotics Laboratory in which lighting had been systematically varied [15, 16]. In each image in this database, a subject held his/her head steady while being illuminated by a dominant light source. The space of light source directions, which can be parameterized by spherical angles, was then sampled in 15° increments. See Figure 11. From this database, we used 660 images of 10 people (66 of each). We extracted five subsets to quantify the effects of varying lighting. Sample images from each subset are shown in Fig. 9. Subset 1 (respectively 2, 3, 4, 5) contains 60 (respectively 90, 130, 170, 210) images for which both the longitudinal and latitudinal angles of light source direction are within 15° (respectively 30°, 45°, 60°, 75°) of the camera axis.

All of the images were cropped (96 by 84 pixels) within the face so that the contour of the head was excluded. For the Eigenface and correlation tests, the images were normalized to have zero mean and unit variance, as this improved the performance of these methods. For the Eigenface method, we used twenty principal components – recall that performance approaches correlation as the dimension of the feature space is increased [3, 27]. Since the first three principal components are primarily due to lighting variation and since recognition rates can be improved by eliminating them, error rates are also presented when principal components four through twenty-three are used. For the cone experiments, we tested two variations: in the first variation (Cones-attached), the representation was constructed ignoring cast shadows by essentially using the illumination subspace method except that B^* is estimated using the technique described in Section 5.1. In the second variation (Cones-cast), the representation was constructed using the cast shadow method as described in Section 5.1. In both variations, recognition was performed by choosing the face corresponding to the smallest computed distance to cone.

In our quest to speed up the recognition process using cones, we also employed principal components analysis (PCA). The collection of *all* images in the cones (with cast shadows) is projected down to a 100-dimensional feature space. This is achieved by performing a linear projection of the form $\mathbf{y}_i = W\mathbf{x}_i$, where the projection matrix W is chosen to maximize the scatter of all projected samples. A face in an image, normalized to have zero mean and unit variance, is recognized by first projecting the image down to this 100-dimensional feature space and then performing nearest neighbor classification.

Mirroring the extrapolation experiment described in [3], each method was trained on samples from Subset 1 (near frontal illumination) and then tested using samples from Subsets 2, 3, 4 and 5. (Note that when tested on Subset 1, all methods performed without error). Figure 12 shows the result from this experiment.

5.4   Discussion of Face Recognition Results

From the results of this experiment, we draw the following conclusions:

- The illumination cone representation outperforms all of the other techniques.
- When cast shadows are included in the illumination cone, error rates are improved.
- PCA of cones with cast shadows outperforms all of the other methods except distance to cones with cast shadows. The small degradation in error rates is offset by the considerable speed up of more than one order of magnitude.
- For very extreme illumination (Subset 5), the Correlation and Eigenface methods completely break down, and exhibit results that are slightly better than chance (90% error rate). The cone method performs significantly better, but certainly not well enough to be usable in practice. At this point, more experimentation is required to determine if recognition rates can be improved by either using more sampled extreme rays or by improving the image formation model.

6   Conclusions and Discussion

In this chapter we have shown that the set of images of a convex object with a Lambertian reflectance function, under all possible lighting conditions at infinity, is a convex, polyhedral cone. Furthermore, we have shown that this cone can be learned from three properly chosen images and that the dimension of the cone equals the number of distinct surface normals. We have shown that for objects with an arbitrary reflectance function and a non-convex shape, the set of images is still a convex cone and that these results can be easily extended to color images. For non-convex Lambertian surfaces, three images is still sufficient for

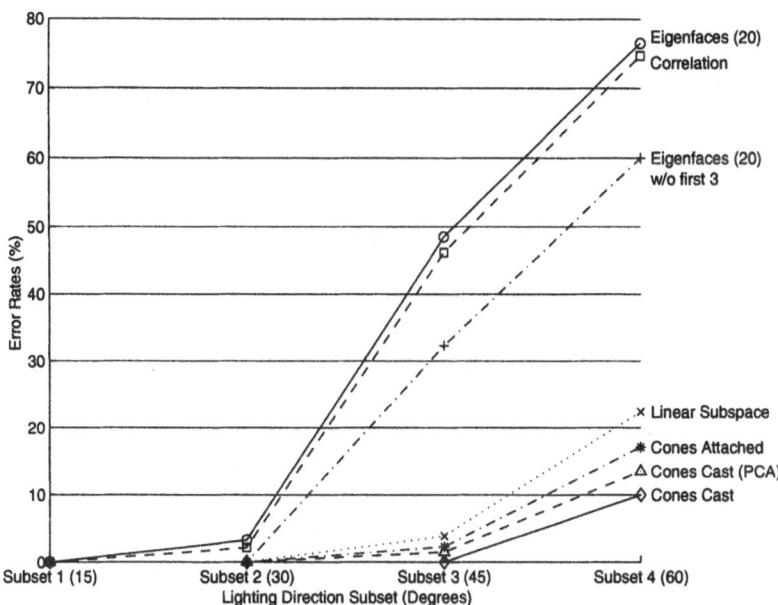

Fig. 12. Extrapolation: When each of the methods is trained on images with near frontal illumination (Subset 1), the graph and corresponding table show the relative performance under more extreme light source conditions.

EXTRAPOLATING FROM SUBSET 1				
Method	Error Rate (%)			
	Subset 2 30°	Subset 3 45°	Subset 4 60°	Subset 5 75°
Correlation	2.2	46.2	74.7	86.6
Eigenface	3.3	48.5	76.5	86.6
Eigenface w/o 1st 3	0.0	32.3	60.0	80.6
Linear subspace	0.0	3.9	22.4	50.8
Cones-attached	0.0	2.3	17.1	43.8
Cones-cast (PCA)	0.0	1.5	13.5	39.8
Cones-cast	0.0	0.0	10.0	37.3

constructing the cone, and this is accomplished by first reconstructing the surface up to a shadow-preserving generalized bas relief transformation. We have applied these results to develop a face recognition technique based on computing distance to cone, and have demonstrated that the method is superior to methods which do not model illumination effects, particularly the role of shadowing. Nevertheless, there remain a number of extensions and open issues which we discuss below.

6.1   Interreflection

A surface is not just illuminated by the light sources but also through inter-reflections from points on the surface itself [1, 13]. For a Lambertian surface, the image with interreflection $\mathbf{x}'$ is related to the image that would be formed without interreflection $\mathbf{x}$ by

$$\mathbf{x}' = (I - RK)^{-1}\mathbf{x}$$

where I is the identity matrix, R is a diagonal matrix whose diagonal elements denote the albedo of facet i, and K is known as the interreflection kernel [28]. When there is no shadowing, all images lie in a 3-D linear space that would be generated from Eq. 1 by a pseudo-surface whose normals and albedo B' are given by $B' = (I - RK)^{-1}B$ [28, 29]. From Proposition 4, the set of all possible images is still a cone. While B' can be learned from only three images, the set of shadowing configurations and the partitioning of the illumination sphere is generated from B, not B'. So, it remains an open question how the cone can be constructed from only three images.

6.2   Effects of Change in Pose

All of the previous analysis in the chapter has dealt solely with variation in illumination. Yet, a change in the object's pose creates a change in the perceived image. If an object undergoes a rotation or translation, how does the illumination cone deform? The illumination cone of the object in the new pose is also convex, but almost certainly different from the illumination cone of the object in the old pose. Which raises the question: Is there a simple transformation, obtainable from a small number of images of the object seen from different views, which when applied to the illumination cone characterizes these changes? Alternatively, is it practical to simply sample the pose space constructing an illumination cone for each pose? Nayar and Murase have extended their appearance manifold representation to model illumination variation for each pose as a 3-D linear subspace [29]. However, their representation does not account for the complications produced by attached shadows.

6.3   Object Recognition

It is important to stress that the illumination cones are convex. If they are non-intersecting, then the cones are linearly separable. That is, they can be separated by $n-1$ dimensional hyperplanes in $\mathbb{R}^n$ passing through the origin. Furthermore since convex sets remain convex under linear projection, then for any projection direction lying in a separating hyperplane, the projected convex sets will also be linearly separable. For d different objects represented by d linearly separable convex cones, there always exists a linear projection of the image space to a $d-1$ dimensional space such that all of the projected sets are again linearly separable. So, an alternative to classification based on measuring distance to the cones in

$\mathbb{R}^n$ is to find a much lower dimensional space in which to do classification. In our Fisherface method for recognizing faces under variable illumination and facial expression, projection directions were chosen to maximize separability of the object classes [3]; a similar approach can be taken here.

The face recognition experiment was limited to the available dataset from the Harvard Robotics Laboratory. To perform more extensive experimentation, we are constructing a geodesic lighting rig that supports 64 computer controlled xenon strobes. Using this rig, we will be able to modify the illumination at frame rates and gather an extensive image database covering a broader range of lighting conditions including multiple sources. Note that the images in the Harvard face database were obtained with a single source, and so all of the images in the test set were on or near the boundary of the cone. Images formed with multiple light sources may lie in the interior, and we have not tested these methods with multiple light sources. Our new database will permit such experimentation.

Acknowledgments

The authors would like to thank David Mumford and Alan Yuille for their many comments, David Forsyth for his insights on interreflections, and David Jacobs, Michael Langer, João Hespanha and Elena Dotsenko for many relevant discussions. The authors would also like to thank Peter Hallinan for providing images from the Harvard Face Database.

References

[1] R. Bajcsy, S. Lee, and A. Leonardis. Detection of diffuse and specular interface reflections and inter-reflections by color image segmentation. *Int. J. Computer Vision*, 17(3):241–272, March 1996.

[2] P. Belhumeur, D. Kriegman, and A. Yuille. The bas-relief ambiguity. In *Proc. IEEE Conf. on Comp. Vision and Patt. Recog.*, pages 1040–1046, 1997.

[3] P. N. Belhumeur, J. P. Hespanha, and D. J. Kriegman. Eigenfaces vs. Fisherfaces: Recognition using class specific linear projection. *IEEE Trans. Pattern Anal. Mach. Intelligence*, 19(7):711–720, 1997. Special Issue on Face Recognition.

[4] P. N. Belhumeur and D. J. Kriegman. What is the set of images of an object under all possible lighting conditions. In *Proc. IEEE Conf. on Comp. Vision and Patt. Recog.*, pages 270–277, 1996.

[5] T. Binford. Generic surface interpretation: Observability model. In *Proc. of the 4th International Symposium on Robotics Research*, Santa Cruz, CA, August 1987.

[6] R. Brunelli and T. Poggio. Face recognition: Features vs templates. *IEEE Trans. Pattern Anal. Mach. Intelligence*, 15(10):1042–1053, 1993.

[7] M. Canon, C. Cullum Jr., and E. Polak. *Theory of Optimal Control and Mathematical Programming*. McGraw-Hill, New York, 1970.

[8] R. Chellappa, C. Wilson, and S. Sirohey. Human and machine recognition of faces: A survey. *Proceedings of the IEEE*, 83(5):705–740, 1995.

[9] R. Epstein, P. Hallinan, and A. Yuille. 5 ± 2 Eigenimages suffice: An empirical investigation of low-dimensional lighting models. Technical Report 94-11, Harvard University, 1994.

130   David J. Kriegman, Peter N. Belhumeur, and Athinodoros S. Georghiades

[10] R. Epstein, A. Yuille, and P. N. Belhumeur. Learning object representations from lighting variations. In *Proc. of the Int. Workshop on Object Representation for Computer Vision*, page 179, 1996.

[11] G. Finlayson, M. Drew, and B. Funt. Spectral sharpening: Sensor transformations for improved color constancy. *J. Opt. Soc. Am. A*, 11:1553–1563, 1994.

[12] D. Forsyth and M. Fleck. Body plans. In *Proc. IEEE Conf. Computer Vision and Pattern Recognition*, 1997.

[13] D. Forsyth and A. Zisserman. Reflections on shading. *IEEE Trans. Pattern Anal. Mach. Intelligence*, 13(7):671–679, 1991.

[14] A. Georghiades, D. Kriegman, and P. Belhumeur. Illumination cones for recognition under variable lighting: Faces. In *Proc. IEEE Conf. on Comp. Vision and Patt. Recog.*, pages 52–59, 1998.

[15] P. Hallinan. A low-dimensional representation of human faces for arbitrary lighting conditions. In *Proc. IEEE Conf. on Comp. Vision and Patt. Recog.*, pages 995–999, 1994.

[16] P. Hallinan. *A Deformable Model for Face Recognition Under Arbitrary Lighting Conditions*. PhD thesis, Harvard University, 1995.

[17] H. Hayakawa. Photometric stereo under a light-source with arbitrary motion. *JOSA-A*, 11(11):3079–3089, Nov. 1994.

[18] B. Horn. *Computer Vision*. MIT Press, Cambridge, Mass., 1986.

[19] B. Horn and M. Brooks. The variational approach to shape from shading. *Computer Vision, Graphics and Image Processing*, 35:174–208, 1992.

[20] D. Jacobs. Linear fitting with missing data: Applications to structure from motion and characterizing intensity images. In *Proc. IEEE Conf. on Comp. Vision and Patt. Recog.*, pages 206–212, 1997.

[21] G. Klinker, S. Shafer, and T. Kanade. Image segmentation and reflection analysis through color. *Int. J. Computer Vision*, 2(1):7–32, June 1988.

[22] J. Koenderink and A. van Doorn. Bidirectional reflection distribution function expressed in terms of surface scattering modes. In *Proc. European Conf. on Computer Vision*, pages II:28–39, 1996.

[23] D. Kriegman and P. Belhumeur. What shadows reveal about object structure. In *Proc. European Conf. on Computer Vision*, pages 399–414, 1998.

[24] L. Sirovitch and M. Kirby. Low-dimensional procedure for the characterization of human faces. *J. Optical Soc. of America A*, 2:519–524, 1987.

[25] M. Langer and S. Zucker. A ray-based computational model of light sources and illumination. In *Physics Based Modeling Workshop in Computer Vision*, 1995.

[26] Y. Moses, Y. Adini, and S. Ullman. Face recognition: The problem of compensating for changes in illumination direction. In *Proc. European Conf. on Computer Vision*, pages 286–296, 1994.

[27] H. Murase and S. Nayar. Visual learning and recognition of 3-D objects from appearence. *Int. J. Computer Vision*, 14(1):5–24, 1995.

[28] S. Nayar, K. Ikeuchi, and T. Kanade. Shape from interreflections. *IJCV*, 6(3):173–195, August 1991.

[29] S. Nayar and H. Murase. Dimensionality of illumination in appearance matching. *IEEE Conf. on Robotics and Automation*, 1996.

[30] M. Oren and S. Nayar. Generalization of the Lambertian model and implications for machine vision. *Int. J. Computer Vision*, 14:227–251, 1996.

[31] R. Rockafellar. *Convex Analysis*. Princeton University Press, Princeton, 1970.

[32] A. Samal and P. Iyengar. Automatic recognition and analysis of human faces and facial expressions: A survey. *Pattern Recognition*, 25:65–77, 1992.

[33] A. Shashua. *Geometry and Photometry in 3D Visual Recognition.* PhD thesis, MIT, 1992.

[34] A. Shashua. On photometric issues to feature-based object recognition. *Int. J. Computer Vision*, 21:99–122, 1997.

[35] H. Shum, K. Ikeuchi, and R. Reddy. Principal component analysis with missing data and its application to polyhedral object modeling. *PAMI*, 17(9):854–867, September 1995.

[36] H. Tagare and R. deFigueiredo. A framework for the construction of reflectance maps for machine vision. *Comp. Vision, Graphics, and Image Proces.*, 57(3):265–282, May 1993.

[37] C. Tomasi and T. Kanade. Shape and motion from image streams under orthography: a factorization method. *International Journal of Computer Vision*, 9(2):134–154, 1992.

[38] K. Torrance and E. Sparrow. Theory for off-specular reflection from roughened surfaces. *JOSA*, 57:1105–1114, 1967.

[39] M. Turk and A. Pentland. Eigenfaces for recognition. *J. of Cognitive Neuroscience*, 3(1), 1991.

[40] S. Ullman and R. Basri. Recognition by a linear combination of models. A.I. Memo 1152, MIT, Aug. 1989.

[41] N. Watts. Calculating the principal views of a polyhedron. Technical Report CS Tech. Report 234, Rochester University, 1987.

[42] A. Yuille and D. Snow. Shape and albedo from multiple images using integrability. In *Proc. IEEE Conf. on Comp. Vision and Patt. Recog.*, pages 158–164, 1997.

Shadows, Shading, and Projective Ambiguity

Peter N. Belhumeur[1], David J. Kriegman[2], and Alan L. Yuille[3]

[1] Center for Computional Vision and Control, Yale University, New Haven CT 06520
[2] Beckman Institute, University of Illinois, Urbana-Champaign, Urbana, IL 61801
[3] Smith-Kettlewell Eye Research Institute, San Francisco, CA 94115

Abstract. In a scene observed from a fixed viewpoint, the set of shadow curves in an image changes as a point light source (nearby or at infinity) assumes different locations. We show that for any finite set of point light sources illuminating an object viewed under either orthographic or perspective projection, there is an equivalence class of object shapes having the same set of shadows. Members of this equivalence class differ by a four parameter family of projective transformations, and the shadows of a transformed object are identical when the same transformation is applied to the light source locations. Under orthographic projection, this family is the generalized bas-relief (GBR) transformation, and we show that the GBR transformation is the only family of transformations of an object's shape for which the complete set of imaged shadows is identical. Furthermore, for objects with Lambertian surfaces illuminated by distant light sources, the equivalence class of object shapes which preserves shadows also preserves surface shading. Finally, we show that given multiple images under differing and unknown light source directions, it is possible to reconstruct an object's shape up to these transformations from the shadows alone.

1 Introduction

In his fifteenth century *Treatise on Painting* [15], Leonardo da Vinci errs in his analysis of shadows while comparing painting and relief sculpture:

> As far as light and shade are concerned low relief fails both as sculpture and as painting, because the shadows correspond to the low nature of the relief, as for example in the shadows of foreshortened objects, which will not exhibit the depth of those in painting or in sculpture in the round.

It is true that – when illuminated by the same light source – a relief surface and a surface "in the round" will cast different shadows. However, Leonardo's statement appears to overlook the fact that for any flattening of the surface relief, there is a corresponding change in the light source direction such that the shadows appear the same. This is not restricted to classical reliefs but, as we will later show, applies equally to a greater set of projective transformations.

D.A. Forsyth et al. (Eds.): Shape, Contour ..., LNCS 1681, pp. 132–151, 1999.
© Springer-Verlag Berlin Heidelberg 1999

Original   Transformed   Original (2)   Transformed (2)

Fig. 1. An illustration of the effect of applying a generalized perspective bas-relief (GPBR) transformation to a scene composed of a teapot resting on a supporting plane. The first image shows the original teapot. The second image shows the teapot after having undergone a GPBR transformation with $(a_1, a_2, a_3, a_4) = (.05, .05, .05, 1))$ with respect to the viewpoint used to generate the first image. (The GPBR transformation is defined in Eq. 2.) Note that the attached and cast shadows as well as the occluding contour are identical in first two images. The third image shows the original teapot from a second viewpoint. The fourth image reveals the nature of the GPBR transformation, showing the transformed teapot from the same viewpoint as used for the third image.

More specifically, when an object is viewed from a fixed viewpoint, there is a four parameter family of projective transformations of the object's structure and the light source locations such that the images of the shadows remain the same. This family of projective transformations is such that it restricts surface points to move along the lines of sight, i.e. it fixes the lines passing through the focal point. Furthermore, if the surface has a Lambertian reflectance [19, 12] and is viewed orthographically, then for any of the above mentioned transformations of the surface, there is a corresponding transformation of the surface albedo such that the surface shading remains constant.

It follows that when light source positions are unknown neither shadows nor shading (for orthographically viewed objects with Lambertian reflecantance) reveal the object's Euclidean structure. Yet in all past work on reconstruction from shadows [11, 17, 31, 6, 13, 14, 21], shape from shading [12, 23], and photometric stereo [12, 27, 30], it is explicitly assumed that the direction or location of the light source *is known*.

In Section 2, we explain the details of the shadowing ambiguity. We show that seen from a fixed viewpoint under perspective projection, two surfaces produce the same shadows if they differ by a particular projective transformation – which we call the Generalized Perspective Bas-Relief (GPBR) transformation. See Figure 1 for an example of this transformation. This result holds for any number of proximal or distant point light sources. Furthermore, under conditions where perspective projection can be approximated by orthographic projection, this transformation is the Generalized Bas-Relief (GBR) transformation [3].

In Section 3, we explain the details of the shading ambiguity. We show that seen from a fixed viewpoint under orthographic projection and illuminated by light sources at infinity, two surfaces produce the same shading if they differ by a GBR transformation. As with the result on shadows, this result holds for any number of point light sources.

In Section 4, we show that the GBR transformation is unique in that any two smooth surfaces which produce the same shadows must differ by a GBR. (The result is developed only for surfaces which are convex in shape.)

Finally, in Section 5, we propose an algorithm for reconstructing, from the attached shadow boundaries, the structure of an object up to a GBR transformation. The algorithm assumes that the object is viewed orthographically and that it is illuminated by a set of point light sources at infinity. We do not propose this algorithm with the belief that its present form has great applicability, but rather we give it to demonstrate that, under ideal conditions, information from shadows alone is enough to determine the structure of the object up to a GBR transformation.

2   Shadowing Ambiguity

Let us define two objects as being *shadow equivalent* if there exist two sets of point light sources S and S' such that for every light source in S illuminating one object, there exists a light source in S' illuminating the second object, such that the shadowing in both images is identical. Let us further define two objects as being *strongly shadow equivalent* if for *any* light source illuminating one object, there exists a source illuminating the second object such that shadowing is identical – i.e., S is the set of all point light sources. In this section we will show that two objects are shadow equivalent if they differ by a particular set of projective transformations.

Consider a camera-centered coordinate system whose origin is at the focal point, whose x- and y-axes span the image plane, and whose z-axis points in the direction of the optical axis. Let a smooth surface f be defined with respect to this coordinate system and lie in the halfspace $z > 0$. Since the surface is smooth, the surface normal $\mathbf{n(p)}$ is defined at all points $\mathbf{p} \in f$.

We model illumination as a collection of point light sources, located nearby or at infinity. Note that this is a restriction of the lighting model presented by Langer and Zucker [20] which permits anisotropic light sources whose intensity is a function of direction. In this paper, we will represent surfaces, light sources, and the camera center as lying in either a two or three dimensional real projective space ($\mathbb{RP}^2$ or $\mathbb{RP}^3$). (For a concise treatment of real projective spaces, see [22].) This allows a unified treatment of both point light sources that are nearby (proximal) or distant (at infinity) and camera models that use perspective or orthographic projection.

When a point light source is proximal, its coordinates can be expressed as $\mathbf{s} = (s_x, s_y, s_z)^T$. In projective (homogeneous) coordinates, the light source $\mathbf{s} \in \mathbb{RP}^3$ can be written as $\mathbf{s} = (s_x, s_y, s_z, 1)^T$. (Note that different fonts are used to distinguish between Euclidean and projective coordinates.) When a point light source is at infinity, all light rays are parallel, and so one is concerned with the direction of the light source. The direction can be represented as a unit vector in $\mathbb{R}^3$ or as point on an illumination sphere $s \in S^2$. In projective coordinates, the fourth homogeneous coordinate of a point at infinity is zero, and so the light source can be expressed as $s = (s_x, s_y, s_z, 0)^T$. (Note that when the light source at infinity is represented in projective coordinates, the antipodal points from S^2 must be equated.)

For a single point source $s \in \mathbb{RP}^3$, let us define the set of *light rays* as the lines in $\mathbb{RP}^3$ passing through s. For any $p \in \mathbb{RP}^3$ with $p \neq s$, there is a single light ray passing through p. Naturally it is the intersection of the light rays with the surface f which determine the shadows. We differentiate between two types of shadows: *attached shadows* and *cast shadows* [2, 26]. See Figures 2 and 3.

A surface point p lies on the border of an *attached shadow* for light source s if and only if it satisfies both a local and global condition:

Local Attached Shadow Condition: The light ray through p lies in the tangent plane to the surface at p. Algebraically, this condition can be expressed as $n(p) \cdot (p - s) = 0$ for a nearby light source (here p and s denote Euclidean coordinates) and as $n(p) \cdot s = 0$ for a distant light source (here s denotes the direction of the light source). A point p which satisfies at least the local condition is called a *local attached shadow boundary point*.

Global Attached Shadow Condition: The light ray does not intersect the surface between p and s, i.e., the light source is not occluded at p.

Now consider applying an arbitrary projective transformation $a : \mathbb{RP}^3 \rightarrow \mathbb{RP}^3$ to both the surface and the light source. Under this transformation, let $p' = a(p)$ and $s' = a(s)$.

Lemma 1. *A point p on a smooth surface is a local attached shadow boundary point for point light source s iff p' on a transformed surface is a local attached shadow boundary point for point light source s'.*

Proof. At a local attached shadow boundary point p, the line defined by $p \in \mathbb{RP}^3$ and light source $s \in \mathbb{RP}^3$ lies in the tangent plane at p. Since the order of contact (e.g., tangency) of a curve and surface is preserved under projective transformations, the line defined by p' and s' lies in the tangent plane at p'.

Cast shadows occur at points on the surface that face the light source, but where some other portion of the surface lies between the shadowed points and the light source. A point p lies on the boundary of a cast shadow for light source s if and only if it similarly satisfies both a local and global condition:

Local Cast Shadow Condition: The light ray through **p** grazes the surface at some other point **q** (i.e., **q** lies on an attached shadow boundary). A point **p** which satisfies at least the local condition is called a *local cast shadow boundary point*.

Global Cast Shadow Condition: The only intersection of the surface and the light ray between **p** and **s** is at **q**.

Lemma 2. *A point* **p** *on a smooth surface is a local cast shadow boundary point for point light source* **s** *iff* **p**′ *on a transformed surface is a local cast shadow boundary point for point light source* **s**′.

Proof. For a local cast shadow boundary point $\mathbf{p} \in \mathbb{RP}^3$ and light source $\mathbf{s} \in \mathbb{RP}^3$, there exists another point $\mathbf{q} \in \mathbb{RP}^3$ on the line defined by **p** and **s** such that **q** lies on an attached shadow. Since collinearity is preserved under projective transformations, **p**′, **q**′ and **s**′ are collinear. Hence from Lemma 1, **q**′ is also an attached shadow point.

Taken together, Lemmas 1 and 2 indicate that under an arbitrary projective transformation of a surface and light source, the set of local shadow curves is a projective transformation of the local shadow curves of the original surface and light source. However, these two lemmas do not imply that the two surfaces are shadow equivalent since the transformed points may project to different image points, or the global conditions may not hold.

2.1   Perspective Projection: GPBR

We will further restrict the set of projective transformations. Modeling the camera as a function $\pi : \mathbb{RP}^3 \to \mathbb{RP}^2$, we require that for any point **p** on the surface $\pi(\mathbf{p}) = \pi(a(\mathbf{p}))$ where a is a projective transformation – that is **p** and $a(\mathbf{p})$ must project to the *same* image point. We will consider two specific camera models in turn: perspective projection π_p and orthographic projection π_o.

Without loss of generality, consider a pinhole perspective camera with unit focal length located at the origin of the coordinate system and with the optical axis pointed in the direction of the z-axis. Letting the homogeneous coordinates of an image point be given by $\mathbf{u} \in \mathbb{RP}^2$, then pinhole perspective projection of $\mathbf{p} \in \mathbb{RP}^3$ is given by $\mathbf{u} = \Pi_p \mathbf{p}$ where

$$\Pi_p = \begin{bmatrix} 1 & 0 & 0 & 0 \\ 0 & 1 & 0 & 0 \\ 0 & 0 & 1 & 0 \end{bmatrix}. \tag{1}$$

For $\pi_p(\mathbf{p}) = \pi_p(a(\mathbf{p}))$ to be true for any point **p**, the transformation must move **p** along the optical ray between the camera center and **p**. This can be accomplished by the projective transformation $a : \mathbf{p} \mapsto A\mathbf{p}$ where

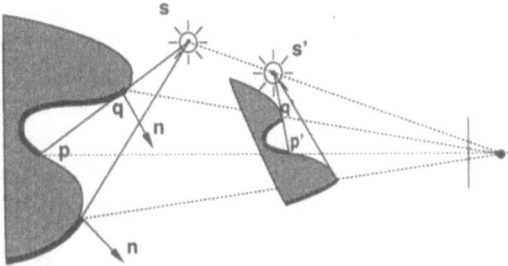

Fig. 2. In this 2-d illustration of the generalized perspective bas-relief transformation (GPBR), the lower shadow is an attached shadow while the upper one is composed of both attached and cast components. A GPBR transformation has been applied to the left surface, yielding the right one. Note that under GPBR, all surface points and the light source are transformed along the optical rays through the center of projection. By transforming the light source from **s** to **s′**, the shadows are preserved.

$$A = \begin{bmatrix} 1 & 0 & 0 & 0 \\ 0 & 1 & 0 & 0 \\ 0 & 0 & 1 & 0 \\ a_1 & a_2 & a_3 & a_4 \end{bmatrix}. \tag{2}$$

We call this transformation the Generalized Perspective Bas-Relief (GPBR) transformation. In Euclidean coordinates, the transformed surface and light source are given by

$$\mathbf{p}' = \frac{1}{\mathbf{a} \cdot \mathbf{p} + a_4} \mathbf{p} \qquad \mathbf{s}' = \frac{1}{\mathbf{a} \cdot \mathbf{s} + a_4} \mathbf{s} \tag{3}$$

where $\mathbf{a} = (a_1, a_2, a_3)^T$. Figure 2 shows a 2-d example of GPBR being applied to a planar curve and a single light source. The effect is to move points on the surface and the light sources along lines through the camera center in a manner that preserves shadows. The sign of $\mathbf{a} \cdot \mathbf{p} + a_4$ plays a critical role: if it is positive, all points on f move inward or outward from the camera center, remaining in the halfspace $z > 0$. On the other hand, if the sign is negative for some points on f, these points will move through the camera center to points with $z < 0$, i.e., they will not be visible to the camera. The equation $\mathbf{a} \cdot \mathbf{p} + a_4 = 0$ defines a plane which divides $\mathbb{R}^3$ into these two cases; all points on this plane map to the plane at infinity. A similar effect on the transformed light source location is determined by the sign of $\mathbf{a} \cdot \mathbf{s} + a_4$.

Proposition 1. *The image of the shadow curves for a surface f and light source* **s** *is identical to the image of the shadow curves for a surface f' and light source* **s′** *transformed by a GPBR if* $\mathbf{a} \cdot \mathbf{s} + a_4 > 0$ *and* $\mathbf{a} \cdot \mathbf{p} + a_4 > 0$ *for all* $\mathbf{p} \in f$.

Proof. Since GPBR is a projective transformation, Lemmas 1 and 2 show that the local attached and cast shadow curves on the transformed surface f' from light source $\mathbf{s}'$ are a GPBR transformation of the local shadow curves on f from light source $\mathbf{s}$. For any point $\mathbf{p}$ on the surface and any GPBR transformation A, we have $\Pi_p \mathbf{p} = \Pi_p A \mathbf{p}$, and so the images of the local shadow curves are identical.

To show that the global condition for an attached shadow is also satisfied, we note that projective transformations preserve collinearity; therefore, the only intersections of the line defined by $\mathbf{s}'$ and $\mathbf{p}'$ with f' are transformations of the intersections of the line defined by $\mathbf{s}$ and $\mathbf{p}$ with f. Within each light ray (a projective line), the points are subjected to a projective transformation; in general, the order of the transformed intersection points on the line may be a combination of a cyclic permutation and a reversal of the order of the original points. However, the restriction that $\mathbf{a} \cdot \mathbf{p} + a_4 > 0$ for all $\mathbf{p} \in f$ and that $\mathbf{a} \cdot \mathbf{s} + a_4 > 0$ has the effect of preserving the order of points between $\mathbf{p}$ and $\mathbf{s}$ on the original line and between $\mathbf{p}'$ and $\mathbf{s}'$ on the transformed line.

It should be noted for that for any $\mathbf{a}$ and a_4, there exists a light source $\mathbf{s}$ such that $\mathbf{a} \cdot \mathbf{s} + a_4 < 0$. When f is illuminated by such a source, the transformed source passes through the camera center, and the global shadowing conditions may not be satisfied. Hence two objects differing by GPBR are not strongly shadow equivalent. On the other hand, for any bounded set of light sources and bounded object f, there exists a set of $a_1, \ldots, a_4$ such that $\mathbf{a} \cdot \mathbf{s} + a_4 > 0$ and $\mathbf{a} \cdot \mathbf{p} + a_4 > 0$. Hence, there exist a set of objects which are *shadow equivalent*.

Since the shadow curves of multiple light sources are the union of the shadow curves from the individual light sources, this also holds for multiple light sources. It should also be noted that the occluding contours (silhouette) of f and f' are identical, since the camera center is a fixed point under GPBR and the occluding contour is the same as the attached shadow curve produced by a light source located at the camera center.

Figure 1 shows an example of the GPBR transformation being applied to a scene containing a teapot resting on a support plane. The images were generated using the VORT ray tracing package – the scene contained a single proximal point light source, the surfaces were modeled as Lambertian, and a perspective camera model was used. When the light source is transformed with the surface, the shadows are the same for both the original and transformed scenes. Even the shading is similar in both images, so much so that it is nearly impossible to distinguish the two surfaces. However, from another viewpoint, the effect of the GPBR transformation on the object's shape is apparent.

This result compliments past work on structure from motion in which the aim of structure recovery is a weaker, non-Euclidean representation, such as affine [18, 24, 25, 28], projective [9], or ordinal [10].

2.2   Orthographic Projection: GBR

When a camera is distant and can be modeled as orthographic projection, the visual rays are all parallel to the direction of the optical axis. In $\mathbb{RP}^3$, these

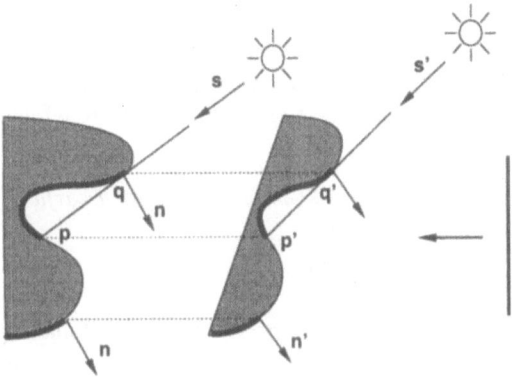

Fig. 3. The image points that lie in shadow for a surface under light source s are identical to those in shadow for a transformed surface under light source s'. In this 2-d illustration, the lower shadow is an attached shadow while the upper one is composed of both attached and cast components. A generalized bas-relief transformation with both flattening and an additive plane has been applied to the left surface, yielding the right one.

rays intersect at the camera center which is a point at infinity. Without loss of generality consider the viewing direction to be in the direction of the z-axis and the x- and y-axes to span the image plane. Again, letting the homogeneous coordinates of an image point be given by $u \in \mathbb{RP}^2$, orthographic projection of $p \in \mathbb{RP}^3$ can be expressed as $u = \Pi_o p$ where

$$\Pi_o = \begin{bmatrix} 1 & 0 & 0 & 0 \\ 0 & 1 & 0 & 0 \\ 0 & 0 & 0 & 1 \end{bmatrix}. \tag{4}$$

Now, let us consider another set of projective transformations $g : \mathbb{RP}^3 \to \mathbb{RP}^3$. For $\pi_o(p) = \pi_o(g(p))$ to be true for any point p, the transformation g must move p along the viewing direction. This can be accomplished by the projective transformation $g : p \mapsto Gp$ where

$$G = \begin{bmatrix} 1 & 0 & 0 & 0 \\ 0 & 1 & 0 & 0 \\ g_1 & g_2 & g_3 & g_4 \\ 0 & 0 & 0 & 1 \end{bmatrix} \tag{5}$$

with $g_3 > 0$. The mapping g is an affine transformation which was introduced in [3] and was called the generalized bas-relief (GBR) transformation. Consider the effect of applying GBR to a surface parameterized as the graph of a depth function, $(x, y, f(x, y))$. This yields a transformed surface

$$\begin{bmatrix} x' \\ y' \\ z' \end{bmatrix} = \begin{bmatrix} x \\ y \\ g_1 x + g_2 y + g_3 f(x, y) + g_4 \end{bmatrix}. \tag{6}$$

See Figure 3 for an example. The parameter g_3 has the effect of scaling the relief of the surface, g_1 and g_2 characterize an additive plane, and g_4 provides a depth offset. As described in [3], when $g_1 = g_2 = 0$ and $0 < g_3 < 1$, the resulting transformation is simply a compression of the surface relief, as in relief sculpture.

Proposition 2. *The image of the shadow curves for a surface f and light source s are identical to the image of the shadow curves for a surface f' and light source s' transformed by any GBR.*

Proof. The proof follows that of Proposition 1.

It should be noted that Proposition 2 applies to both nearby light sources and those at infinity. However, in contrast to the GPBR transformation, nearby light source do not move to infinity nor do light sources at infinity become nearby light sources since GBR is an affine transformation which fixes the plane at infinity. Since Proposition 2 holds for *any* light source, all objects differing by a GBR transformation are *strongly shadow equivalent*.

An implication of Propositions 1 and 2 is that when an object is observed from a fixed viewpoint (whether perspective or orthographic projection), one can at best reconstruct its surface up to a four parameter family of transformations (GPBR or GBR) from shadow or occluding contour information, irrespective of the number of images and number of light sources. Under the same conditions, it is impossible to distinguish (recognize) two objects that differ by these transformations from shadows or silhouettes.

3   Shading Ambiguity

Let us define two objects as being *strongly shading equivalent* if for *any* light source illuminating one object, there exists a source illuminating the second object such that shading is identical. In this section we will show that two objects with surfaces having Lambertian reflectance [19, 12] are strongly shading equivalent if they differ by any of the set of GBR transformations described in the previous section. Here we consider distant illumination (parallel illuminating rays) of objects viewed under orthographic projection (parallel lines of sight).

Consider again a camera-centered coordinate system whose origin is at the focal point, whose x- and y-axes span the image plane, and whose z-axis points in the direction of the optical axis. In this coordinate system, the depth of every visible point in the scene can be expressed as

$$z = f(x, y)$$

where f is a piecewise differentiable function. The graph $(x, y, f(x, y))$ defines a surface which will also be denoted by f. The direction of the inward pointing surface normal $\mathbf{n}(x, y)$ can be expressed as

$$\mathbf{n}(x, y) = \begin{bmatrix} -f_x \\ -f_y \\ 1 \end{bmatrix} \tag{7}$$

where f_x and f_y denote the partial derivatives of f with respect to x and y respectively.

Once we restrict ourselves to orthographic projection, we no longer need the full machinery of projective coordinates. A visible point $\mathbf{p}$ on the surface has Euclidean coordinates $\mathbf{p} = (x, y, f(x, y))^T$. As done in Eq. 6, we write the GBR transformation on a surface point $\mathbf{p}$ as $\mathbf{p}' = G\mathbf{p} + (0, 0, g_4)^T$ where G has been rewritten as

$$G = \begin{bmatrix} 1 & 0 & 0 \\ 0 & 1 & 0 \\ g_1 & g_2 & g_3 \end{bmatrix}. \tag{8}$$

Under the matrix product operation, the set $GBR = \{G\}$ forms a subgroup of $GL(3)$ with

$$G^{-1} = \frac{1}{g_3} \begin{bmatrix} g_3 & 0 & 0 \\ 0 & g_3 & 0 \\ -g_1 & -g_2 & 1 \end{bmatrix}.$$

Also note that for image point (x, y), the relation between the direction of the surface normal of f' and f is given by $\mathbf{n}' = G^{-T}\mathbf{n}$ where $G^{-T} \equiv (G^T)^{-1} = (G^{-1})^T$. (As shown in [3], this is the only linear transformation of the surface's normal field which preserves integrability.)

Letting the albedo of a Lambertian surface f be denoted by $a(x, y)$, the intensity image produced by a light source $\mathbf{s}$ can be expressed as

$$\mathbf{I}_{f,a,\mathbf{s}}(x, y) = \Psi_{f,\mathbf{s}}(x, y)\mathbf{b}^T(x, y)\mathbf{s}$$

where $\mathbf{b}(x, y)$ is the product of the albedo $a(x, y)$ of the surface and the inward pointing unit surface normal $\hat{\mathbf{n}}(x, y)$; the vector $\mathbf{s}$ denotes a point light source at infinity, with the magnitude of $\mathbf{s}$ proportional to the intensity of the light source; and $\Psi_{f,\mathbf{s}}(x, y)$ is a binary function such that

$$\Psi_{f,\mathbf{s}}(x, y) = \begin{cases} 0 & \text{if } (x, y) \text{ is shadowed} \\ 1 & \text{otherwise.} \end{cases}$$

We now show that shading on a surface f for some light source $\mathbf{s}$ is identical to that on a GBR transformed surface f' for a light source $\mathbf{s}'$ when f' has albedo $a(x, y)'$ given by

$$a' = \frac{a}{g_3}\sqrt{(g_3 n'_x - g_1 n'_z)^2 + (g_3 n'_y - g_2 n'_z)^2 + n'^2_z} \tag{9}$$

where $\mathbf{n}' = (n'_x, n'_y, n'_z)^T$. The effect of applying Eq. 9 to a classical bas-relief transformation $0 < g_3 < 1$ is to darken points on the surface where $\mathbf{n}$ points away from the optical axis.

This transformation on the albedo is subtle and warrants discussion. For g_3 close to unity, the transformation on the albedo is nearly impossible to detect. That is, if you transform the shape of a surface by a GBR transformation, but leave the albedo unchanged, then the differences in the images produced under varying illumination are too small to reveal the difference in the structure. In Fig. 4, we left the albedo unchanged, $a'(x, y) = a(x, y)$, and even though g_3 ranges from 0.5 to 1.5, the differences in shape cannot not be discerned from the frontal images. However, when the albedo is unchanged and the flattening is more severe, e.g., tenfold ($g_3 = 0.1$), the shading patterns can reveal the flatness of the surface. This effect is often seen on very low relief sculptures (e.g., Donatello's *rilievo schiacciato*) which reproduce shadowing accurately, but shading poorly.

Note that for the shadowing to be identical it is necessary that $g_3 > 0$. When $g_3 < 0$, the surface f' is inverted (as in *intaglio*). For a corresponding transformation of the light source $\mathbf{s}'$, the illuminated regions of the original surface f and the transformed surface f' will be the same if the albedo is transformed as described above. (This is the well known "up/down" (convex/concave) ambiguity.) However, the shadows cast by f' and f may differ quite dramatically.

Proposition 3. *For each light source* $\mathbf{s}$ *illuminating a Lambertian surface* $f(x, y)$ *with albedo* $a(x, y)$, *there exists a light source* $\mathbf{s}'$ *illuminating a surface* $f'(x, y)$ *(a GBR transformation of* f*) with albedo* $a'(x, y)$ *(as given in Eq. 9), such that* $I_{f,a,\mathbf{s}}(x, y) = I_{f',a',\mathbf{s}'}(x, y)$.

Proof. The image of f is given by

$$I_{f,a,\mathbf{s}}(x, y) = \Psi_{f,\mathbf{s}}(x, y)\mathbf{b}^T(x, y)\mathbf{s}$$

For any 3×3 invertible matrix A, we have that

$$I_{f,a,\mathbf{s}}(x, y) = \Psi_{f,\mathbf{s}}(x, y)\mathbf{b}^T(x, y)A^{-1}A\mathbf{s}.$$

Since GBR is a subgroup of $GL(3)$ and $\Psi_{f,\mathbf{s}}(x, y) = \Psi_{f',\mathbf{s}'}(x, y)$,

$$\begin{aligned}
I_{f,a,\mathbf{s}}(x, y) &= \Psi_{f,\mathbf{s}}(x, y)\mathbf{b}^T(x, y)G^{-1}G\mathbf{s} \\
&= \Psi_{f',\mathbf{s}'}(x, y)\mathbf{b}'^T(x, y)\mathbf{s}' \\
&= I_{f',a',\mathbf{s}'}(x, y)
\end{aligned}$$

where $\mathbf{b}'(x, y) = G^{-T}\mathbf{b}(x, y)$ and $\mathbf{s}' = G\mathbf{s}$.

Hence, two objects with Lambertian surfaces differing in shape by a GBR transformation and differing in albedo by Eq. 9 are indeed strongly shading equivalent.

The three preceding propositions have shown that when a Lambertian surface f with albedo $a(x, y)$ is illuminated by a single light source, the set of images it can produce by varying the light source strength and direction are equivalent to those produced by a GBR transformed surface f' with albedo $a'(x, y)$ given by Eq. 9. Yet, due to the superposition of images, this result holds not simply for images produced by a single point light source, but also for images produced by any, possibly infinite, combination of point light sources.

These results demonstrate that when both the surface and light source directions are transformed by G, both the shadowing and shading are identical in the images of the original and transformed surface. An implication of this result is that given any number of images taken from a fixed viewpoint, neither

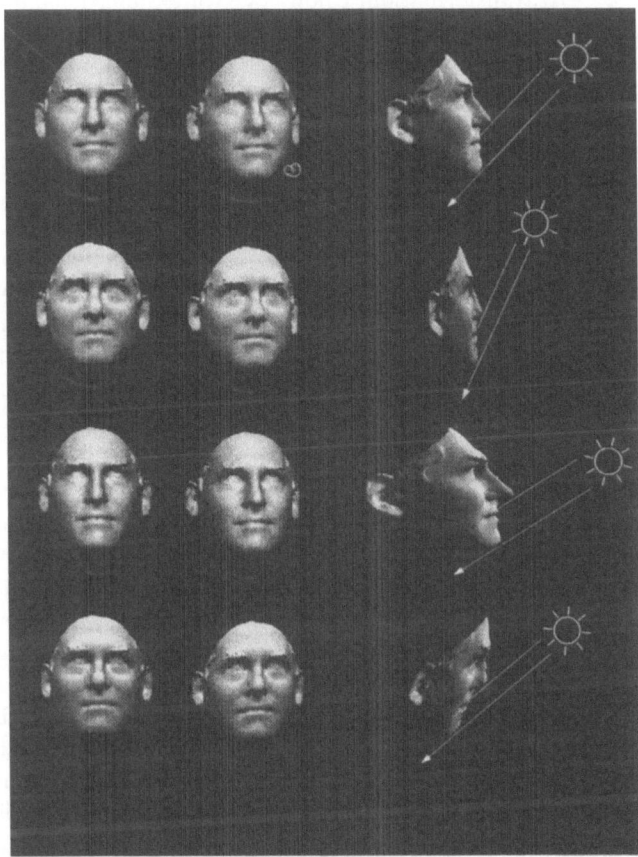

Fig. 4. Three-dimensional data for a human head was obtained using a laser scan (Cyberwave) and rendered (top row) as a Lambertian surface with constant albedo (equal grey values for all surface points). The subsequent three rows show images of the head whose shape has been transformed by different generalized bas-relief transformations, but whose albedo has not been transformed. The profile views of the face in the third column reveal the nature of the individual transformations and the direction of the light source. The top row is the true shape; the second from top is a flattened shape ($g_3 = 0.5$) (as are classical bas-reliefs); the third is an elongated shape ($g_3 = 1.5$); and the bottom is a flattened shape plus an additive plane ($g_3 = 0.7$, $g_2 = 0.5$, and $g_1 = 0.0$). The first column shows frontal views of the faces in the third column. From this view the true 3-d structure of the objects cannot be determined; in each image the shadowing patterns are identical, and even though the albedo has not been transformed according to Eq. 9, the shading patterns are so close as to provide few cues to the true structure. The second column shows near frontal views of the faces in the first column, after having been separately rotated to compensate for the degree of flattening or elongation. Note that even small rotations appear not to reveal the 3-d structure.

a computer vision algorithm nor biological process can distinguish two objects that differ by a GBR transformation. Knowledge (or assumptions) about surface shape, surface albedo, light source direction, or light source intensity must be employed to resolve this ambiguity. See again Fig. 4.

4   Uniqueness of the Generalized Bas-Relief Transformation

Here we prove that under orthographic projection the generalized bas-relief (GBR) transformation is unique in that there is no other transformation of an object's surface which preserves the set of shadows produced by illuminating the object with all possible point sources at infinity. We consider only the simplest case – an object with convex shape casting no shadows on its own surface – and show that the set of attached shadow boundaries are preserved *only* under a GBR transformation of the object's surface.

Recall that an attached shadow boundary is defined as the contour of points $(x, y, f(x, y))^T$ satisfying $\mathbf{n} \cdot \mathbf{s} = 0$, for some $\mathbf{s}$. For a convex object, the global attached shadow condition holds everywhere. Here the magnitude and the sign of the light source are unimportant as neither effects the location of the attached shadow boundary. Thus, let the vector $\mathbf{s} = (s_x, s_y, s_z)^T$ denote in homogeneous coordinates a point light source at infinity, where all light sources producing the same attached shadow boundary are equated, i.e., $(s_x, s_y, s_z)^T \equiv (ks_x, ks_y, ks_z)^T \; \forall k \in \mathbb{R}, k \neq 0$. With this, the space of light source directions $\mathcal{S}$ is equivalent to the real projective plane ($\mathbb{RP}^2$), with the line at infinity given by coordinates of the form $(s_x, s_y, 0)^T$. Note that in Section 2, we represented light sources as points in $\mathbb{RP}^3$; here, we restrict ourselves only to distant light sources lying in the plane at infinity of $\mathbb{RP}^3$, (a real projective plane).

Let $\mathbf{n} = (n_x, n_y, n_z)^T$ denote the direction of a surface normal. Again, the magnitude and sign are unimportant, so we have $(n_x, n_y, n_z)^T \equiv (kn_x, kn_y, kn_z)^T \; \forall k \in \mathbb{R}, k \neq 0$. Thus, the space of surface normals $\mathcal{N}$ is, likewise, equivalent to $\mathbb{RP}^2$. Note that under the equation $\mathbf{n} \cdot \mathbf{s} = 0$, the surface normals are the dual of the light sources. Each point in the $\mathbb{RP}^2$ of light sources has a corresponding line in the $\mathbb{RP}^2$ of surface normals, and vice versa.

Let us now consider the image contours defined by the points (x, y) satisfying $\mathbf{n} \cdot \mathbf{s} = 0$, for some $\mathbf{s}$. These image contours are the attached shadow boundaries orthographically projected onto the image plane. For lack of a better name, we will refer to them as the imaged attached shadow boundaries.

The set of imaged attached shadow boundaries for a convex object forms an abstract projective plane $\mathbb{P}^2$, where a "point" in the abstract projective plane is a single attached shadow boundary, and a "line" in the abstract projective plane is the collection of imaged attached shadow boundaries passing through a common point in the image plane. To see this, note the obvious projective isomorphism between the real projective plane of light source directions $\mathcal{S}$ and the abstract projective plane of imaged attached shadow boundaries $\mathbb{P}^2$. Under this isomorphism, we have bijections mapping points to points and lines to lines.

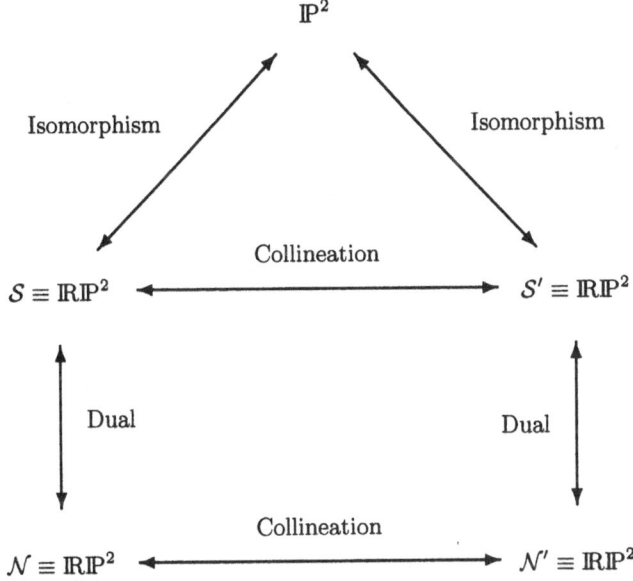

Fig. 5. The relation of different spaces in proof of Proposition 4.

Now let us say that we are given two objects whose visible surfaces are described by respective functions $f(x,y)$ and $f'(x,y)$. If the objects have the same set of imaged attached shadow boundaries as seen in the image plane (i.e., if the objects are strongly shadow equivalent), then the question arises: How are the two surfaces $f(x,y)$ and $f'(x,y)$ related?

Proposition 4. *If the visible surfaces of two convex objects f and f' are strongly shadow equivalent, then the surfaces are related by a generalized bas-relief transformation.*

Proof. As illustrated in Figure 5, we can construct a projective isomorphism between the set of imaged attached shadow boundaries $\mathbb{P}^2$ and the real projective plane of light source directions $\mathcal{S}$ illuminating surface $f(x,y)$. The isomorphism is chosen to map the collection of imaged attached shadow boundaries passing through a common point (x,y) in the image plane (i.e., a line in $\mathbb{P}^2$) to the surface normal $\mathbf{n}(x,y)$. In the same manner, we can construct a projective isomorphism between $\mathbb{P}^2$ and the real projective plane of light source directions $\mathcal{S}'$ illuminating the surface $f'(x,y)$. The isomorphism is, likewise, chosen to map the same collection of imaged attached shadow boundaries passing through (x,y) in the image plane to the surface normal $\mathbf{n}'(x,y)$. Under these two mappings, we have a projective isomorphism between $\mathcal{S}$ and $\mathcal{S}'$ which in turn is a projective transformation (collineation) [1]. Because $\mathcal{N}$ and $\mathcal{N}'$ are the duals of $\mathcal{S}$ and $\mathcal{S}'$ respectively, the surface normals of $f(x,y)$ are also related to the surface normals of $f'(x,y)$ by a projective transformation, i.e., $\mathbf{n}'(x,y) = P\mathbf{n}(x,y)$ where P is a 3×3 invertible matrix.

The transformation P is further restricted in that the surface normals along the occluding contour of f and f' are equivalent, i.e., the transformation P pointwise fixes the line at infinity of surface normals. Thus, P must be of the form

$$P = \begin{bmatrix} 1 & 0 & p_1 \\ 0 & 1 & p_2 \\ 0 & 0 & p_3 \end{bmatrix}$$

where $p_3 \neq 0$. The effect of applying P to the surface normals is the same as applying G in Eq. 5 to the surface if $p_1 = -g_1/g_3$, $p_2 = -g_2/g_3$ and $p_3 = 1/g_3$. That is, P has the form of the generalized bas-relief transformation. Note that the shadows are independent of the translation g_4 along the line of sight under orthographic projection.

5   Reconstruction from Attached Shadows

In the previous section, we showed that under orthographic projection with distant light sources, the only transformation of a surface which preserves the set of imaged shadow contours is the generalized bas-relief transformation. However, Proposition 4 does not provide a prescription for actually reconstructing a surface up to GBR. In this section, we consider the problem of reconstruction from the attached shadow boundaries measured in n images of a surface, each illuminated by a single distant light source. We will show that it is possible to estimate the n light source directions and the surface normals at a finite number of points, all up to GBR. In general, we expect to reconstruct the surface normals at $O(n^2)$ points. From the reconstructed normals, an approximation to the underlying surface can be computed for a fixed GBR. Alternatively, existing shape-from-shadow methods can be used to reconstruct the surface from the estimated light source directions (for a fixed GBR) and from the measured attached and cast shadow curves [11, 17, 31].

First, consider the occluding contour (silhouette) of a surface which will be denoted C_0. This contour is equivalent to the attached shadow produced by a light source whose direction is the viewing direction. Define a coordinate system with $\hat{\mathbf{x}}$ and $\hat{\mathbf{y}}$ spanning the image plane, and with $\hat{\mathbf{z}}$ pointing in the viewing direction. For all points $\mathbf{p}$ on the occluding contour, the viewing direction lies in the tangent plane (i.e., $\mathbf{n}(\mathbf{p}) \cdot \hat{\mathbf{z}} = 0$), and the surface normal $\mathbf{n}(\mathbf{p})$ is parallel to the image normal. Hence if the normal to the image contour is $(n_x, n_y)^T$, the surface normal is $\mathbf{n} = (n_x, n_y, 0)^T$. In $\mathbb{RP}^2$, the surface normals to all points on the occluding contour correspond to the line at infinity.

Now consider the attached shadow boundary C_1 produced by a light source whose direction is $\mathbf{s}_1$. See Figure 6.a. For all points $\mathbf{p} \in C_1$, $\mathbf{s}_1$ lies in the tangent plane, i.e., $\mathbf{s}_1 \cdot \mathbf{n}(\mathbf{p}) = 0$. Where C_1 intersects the occluding contour, the normal $\mathbf{n}_1$ can be directly determined from the measured contour as described above. It should be noted that while C_1 and the occluding contour intersect transversally on the surface, their images generically share a common tangent and form the

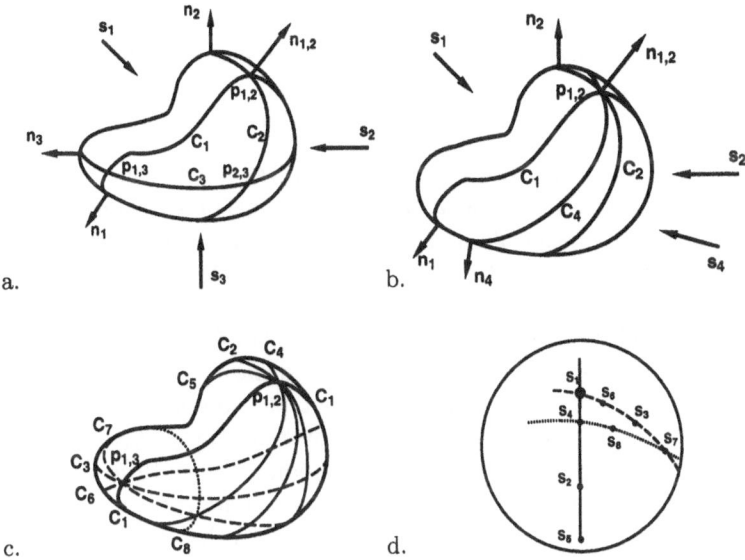

Fig. 6. Reconstruction up to GBR from attached shadows: For a single object in fixed pose, these figures show superimposed attached shadow contours C_i for light source directions s_i. The surface normal where C_i intersects the occluding contour is denoted by n_i. The normal at the intersection of C_i and C_j is denoted by $n_{i,j}$. a) The three contours intersect at three points in the image. b) The three contours meet at a common point implying that s_1, s_2 and s_3 lie on a great circle of the illumination sphere. c) Eight attached shadow boundaries of which four intersect at $p_{1,2}$ and four intersect at $p_{1,3}$; the direction of the light sources $s_1 \ldots s_8$ and the surface normals at the intersection points can be determined up to GBR. d) The structure of the illumination sphere S^2 for the light source directions generating the attached shadow boundaries in Fig. 6.c.

crescent moon image singularity [8]. Note that by measuring n_1 along the occluding contour, we obtain a constraint on the light source direction, $s_1 \cdot n_1 = 0$. This restricts the light source to a line in $\mathbb{RP}^2$ or to a great circle on the illumination sphere S^2. The source s_1 can be expressed parametrically in the camera coordinate system as

$$s_1(\theta_1) = \cos\theta_1(n_1 \times \hat{z}) + \sin\theta_1\hat{z}.$$

From the shadows in a single image, it is not possible to further constrain s_1 nor does it seem possible to obtain any further information about points on C_1.

Now, consider a second attached shadow boundary C_2 formed by a second light source direction s_2. Again, the measurement of n_2 (where C_2 intersects C_0) determines a projective line in $\mathbb{RP}^2$ (or a great circle on S^2) that the light source s_2 must lie on. In general, C_1 and C_2 will intersect at one or more visible surface points. If the object is convex and the Gauss map is bijective, then they only intersect at one point $\mathbf{p}_{1,2}$. For a non-convex surface, C_1 and C_2 may intersect more than once. However in all cases, the direction of the surface normal $\mathbf{n}_{1,2}$ at the intersections is

$$\mathbf{n}_{1,2} = \mathbf{s}_1(\theta_1) \times \mathbf{s}_2(\theta_2). \tag{10}$$

Thus from the attached shadows in two images, we directly measure $\mathbf{n}_1$ and $\mathbf{n}_2$ and obtain estimates for $\mathbf{n}_{1,2}$, $\mathbf{s}_1$, and $\mathbf{s}_2$ as functions of θ_1 and θ_2.

Consider a third image illuminated by $\mathbf{s}_3$, in which the attached shadow boundary C_3 *does not* pass through $\mathbf{p}_{1,2}$ (Fig. 6.a). Again, we can estimate a projective line (great circle on S^2) containing $\mathbf{s}_3$. We also obtain the surface normal at two additional points, the intersections of C_3 with C_1 and C_2. From the attached shadow boundaries for a convex surface measured in n images – if no three contours intersect at a common point – the surface normal can be determined at $n(n-1)$ points as a function of n unknowns $\theta_i, i = 1 \ldots n$.

However, the number of unknowns can be reduced when three contours intersect at a common point. Consider Fig. 6.b where contour C_4 intersects C_1 and C_2 at $\mathbf{p}_{1,2}$. In this case, we can infer from the images that $\mathbf{s}_1, \mathbf{s}_2$ and $\mathbf{s}_4$ all lie in the tangent plane to $\mathbf{p}_{1,2}$. In $\mathbb{RP}^2$, this means that $\mathbf{s}_1, \mathbf{s}_2, \mathbf{s}_4$ all lie on the same projective line. Since $\mathbf{n}_4$ can be measured, $\mathbf{s}_4$ can be expressed as a function of θ_1 and θ_2, i.e.,

$$\mathbf{s}_4(\theta_1, \theta_2) = \mathbf{n}_4 \times (\mathbf{s}_1(\theta_1) \times \mathbf{s}_2(\theta_2)).$$

Thus, a set of attached shadow curves (C_1, C_2, C_4 in Fig. 6.b) passing through a common point ($\mathbf{p}_{1,2}$) is generated by light sources ($\mathbf{s}_1, \mathbf{s}_2, \mathbf{s}_4$ in Fig. 6.d) located on a great circle of S^2. The light source directions can be determined up to two degrees of freedom θ_1 and θ_2. Now, if in addition a second set of light sources lies along another projective line (the great circle in Fig 6.d containing $\mathbf{s}_1, \mathbf{s}_3, \mathbf{s}_6, \mathbf{s}_7$), the corresponding shadow contours (C_1, C_3, C_6, C_7 in Fig 6.c) intersect at another point on the surface ($\mathbf{p}_{1,3}$). Again, we can express the location of light sources ($\mathbf{s}_6, \mathbf{s}_7$) on this great circle as functions of the locations of two other sources ($\mathbf{s}_1$ and $\mathbf{s}_3$):

$$\mathbf{s}_i(\theta_1, \theta_3) = \mathbf{n}_i \times (\mathbf{s}_1(\theta_1) \times \mathbf{s}_3(\theta_3)).$$

Since $\mathbf{s}_1$ lies at the intersection of both projective lines, we can estimate the direction of any light source located on either line up to just three degrees of freedom θ_1, θ_2, and θ_3. Furthermore, the direction of any other light source ($\mathbf{s}_8$ on Fig. 6.d) can be determined if it lies on a projective line defined by two light sources whose directions are known up to θ_1, θ_2 and θ_3. From the estimated light source directions, the surface normal can be determined using Eq. 10 at all points where the shadow curves intersect. As mentioned earlier, there are $O(n^2)$ such points – observe the number of intersections in Fig. 6.c. It is easy to verify algebraically that the three degrees of freedom θ_1, θ_2 and θ_3 correspond to the degrees of freedom in GBR g_1, g_2, and g_3. The translation g_4 of the surface along the line of sight cannot be determined under orthographic projection.

6   Discussion

We have defined notions of shadow equivalence for object, showing that two objects differing by a four parameter family of projective transformations (GPBR) are shadow equivalent under perspective projection. Furthermore, under orthographic projection, two objects differing by a generalized bas-relief (GBR) transformation are strongly shadow equivalent – i.e., for any light source illuminating an object, there exists a light source illuminating a transformed object such that the shadows are identical. We have proven that GBR is the only transformation having this property. While we have shown that the occluding contour is also preserved under GPBR and GBR, it should be noted that image intensity discontinuities (step edges) arising from surface normal discontinuities or albedo discontinuities are also preserved under these transformations since these points move along the line of sight and are viewpoint and (generically) illumination independent. Consequently, edge-based recognition algorithms should not be able to distinguish objects differing by these transformations, nor should edge-based reconstruction algorithms be able to perform Euclidean reconstruction without additional information.

In earlier work where we concentrated on light sources at infinity [4, 3], we showed that for any set of point light sources, the shading as well as the shadowing of an object with Lambertian reflectance are identical to the shading and shadowing of any generalized bas-relief transformation of the object, i.e., the illumination cones [4] are identical. This is consistent with the effectiveness of well-crafted relief sculptures in conveying a greater sense of the depth than is present. It is clear that shading is not preserved for GPBR or for GBR when the light sources are proximal; the image intensity falls off by the reciprocal of the squared distance between the surface and light source, and distance is not preserved under these transformations. Nonetheless, for a range of transformations and for some sets of light sources, it is expected that the intensity may only vary slightly.

Furthermore, we have shown that it is possible to reconstruct a surface up to GBR from the shadow boundaries in a set of images. To implement a reconstruction algorithm based on the ideas in Section 5 requires detection of cast and attached shadow boundaries. While detection methods have been presented [5, 29], it is unclear how effective these techniques would be in practice. In particular, attached shadows are particularly difficult to detect and localize since, for a Lambertian surface with constant albedo, there is a discontinuity in the intensity gradient or shading flow field, but not in the intensity itself. On the other hand, there is a step edge at a cast shadow boundary, and so extensions of the method described in Section 5 which use information about cast shadows to constrain the light source direction may lead to practical implementations.

Leonardo da Vinci's statement that shadows of relief sculpture are "foreshortened" is, strictly speaking, incorrect. However, reliefs are often constructed in a manner such that the cast shadows will differ from those produced by sculpture in the round. Reliefs have been used to depict narratives involving numerous figures located at different depths within the scene. Since the sculpting medium is usually not thick enough for the artist to sculpt the figures to the proper relative depths, sculptors like Donatello and Ghiberti employed rules of perspective to determine the size and location of figures, sculpting each figure to the proper relief [16]. While the shadowing for each figure is self consistent, the shadows cast from one figure onto another are incorrect. Furthermore, the shadows cast onto the background, whose orientation usually does not correspond to that of a wall or floor in the scene, are also inconsistent. Note, however, that ancient Greek sculpture was often painted; by painting the background of the Parthenon Frieze a dark blue [7], cast shadows would be less visible and the distortions less apparent. Thus, Leonardo's statement is an accurate characterization of complex reliefs such as Ghiberti's East Doors on the Baptistery in Florence, but does not apply to figures sculpted singly.

Acknowledgments

Many thanks to David Mumford for leading us to the proof of Proposition 4. P. N. Belhumeur was supported by a Presidential Early Career Award, an NSF Career Award IRI-9703134, and ARO grant DAAH04-95-1-0494. D. J. Kriegman was supported by NSF under NYI IRI-9257990. A. L. Yuille was supported by ARO grant DAAH04-95-1-0494 and NSF grant IRI-93-17670.

References

[1] E. Artin. *Geometric Algebra*. Interscience Publishers, Inc., New York, 1957.

[2] M. Baxandall. *Shadows and Enlightenment*. Yale University Press, New Haven, 1995.

[3] P. Belhumeur, D. Kriegman, and A. Yuille. The bas-relief ambiguity. In *Proc. IEEE Conf. on Comp. Vision and Patt. Recog.*, 1997. in press.

[4] P. N. Belhumeur and D. J. Kriegman. What is the set of images of an object under all possible lighting conditions. In *Proc. IEEE Conf. on Comp. Vision and Patt. Recog.*, pages 270–277, 1996.

[5] P. Breton and S. Zucker. Shadows and shading flow fields. In *CVPR96*, pages 782–789, 1996.

[6] F. Cheng and K. Thiel. Delimiting the building heights in a city from the shadow in a panchromatic spot-image. 1 test of 42 buildings. *JRS*, 16(3):409–415, Feb. 1995.

[7] B. F. Cook. *The Elgin Marbles*. Harvard University Press, Cambridge, 1984.

[8] L. Donati and N. Stolfi. Singularities of illuminated surfaces. *Int. J. Computer Vision*, 23(3):207–216, 1997.

[9] O. Faugeras. Stratification of 3-D vision: Projective, affine, and metric representations. *J. Opt. Soc. Am. A*, 12(7):465–484, 1995.

[10] C. Fermuller and Y. Aloimonos. Ordinal representations of visual space. In *Proc. Image Understanding Workshop*, pages 897–904, 1996.

[11] M. Hatzitheodorou. The derivation of 3-d surface shape from shadows. In *Proc. Image Understanding Workshop*, pages 1012–1020, 1989.

[12] B. Horn. *Computer Vision*. MIT Press, Cambridge, Mass., 1986.

[13] A. Huertas and R. Nevatia. Detection of buildings in aerial images using shape and shadows. In *Proc. Int. Joint Conf. on Art. Intell.*, pages 1099–1103, 1983.

[14] R. Irvin and D. McKeown. Methods for exploiting the relationship between buildings and their shadows in aerial imagery. *IEEE Systems, Man, and Cybernetics*, 19(6):1564–1575, 1989.

[15] M. Kemp, editor. *Leonardo On Painting*. Yale University Press, New Haven, 1989.

[16] M. Kemp. *The Science of Art: Optical Themes in Western Art from Brunelleschi to Seurat*. Yale University Press, New Haven, 1990.

[17] J. Kender and E. Smith. Shape from darkness. In *Int. Conf. on Computer Vision*, pages 539–546, 1987.

[18] J. Koenderink and A. Van Doorn. Affine structure from motion. *JOSA-A*, 8(2):377–385, 1991.

[19] J. Lambert. *Photometria Sive de Mensura et Gradibus Luminus, Colorum et Umbrae*. Eberhard Klett, 1760.

[20] M. Langer and S. Zucker. What is a light source? In *Proc. IEEE Conf. on Comp. Vision and Patt. Recog.*, pages 172–178, 1997.

[21] G. Medioni. Obtaining 3-d from shadows in aerial images. In *CVPR83*, pages 73–76, 1983.

[22] J. Mundy and A. Zisserman. *Geometric invariance in computer vision*. MIT Press, 1992.

[23] J. Oliensis. Uniqueness in shape from shading. *Int. J. Computer Vision*, 6(2):75–104, June 1991.

[24] R. Rosenholtz and J. Koenderink. Affine structure and photometry. In *Proc. IEEE Conf. on Comp. Vision and Patt. Recog.*, pages 790–795, 1996.

[25] L. Shapiro, A. Zisserman, and M. Brady. 3D motion recovery via affine epipolar geometry. *Int. J. Computer Vision*, 16(2):147–182, October 1995.

[26] A. Shashua. *Geometry and Photometry in 3D Visual Recognition*. PhD thesis, MIT, 1992.

[27] W. Silver. *Determining Shape and Reflectance Using Multiple Images*. PhD thesis, MIT, Cambridge, MA, 1980.

[28] S. Ullman and R. Basri. Recognition by a linear combination of models. *IEEE Trans. Pattern Anal. Mach. Intelligence*, 13:992–1006, 1991.

[29] A. Witkin. Intensity-based edge classification. In *Proc. Am. Assoc. Art. Intell.*, pages 36–41, 1982.

[30] R. Woodham. Analysing images of curved surfaces. *Artificial Intelligence*, 17:117–140, 1981.

[31] D. Yang and J. Kender. Shape from shadows under error. In *Proc. Image Understanding Workshop*, pages 1083–1090, 1993.

Part IV

Grouping

Grouping in the Normalized Cut Framework

Jitendra Malik, Jianbo Shi, Serge Belongie, and Thomas Leung

Computer Science Division, University of California at Berkeley
Berkeley, CA 94720
{malik,jshi,sjb,leungt}@cs.berkeley.edu

Abstract. In this paper, we study low-level image segmentation in the normalized cut framework proposed by Shi and Malik (1997). The goal is to partition the image from a big picture point of view. Perceptually significant groups are detected first while small variations and details are treated later. Different image features — intensity, color, texture, contour continuity, motion and stereo disparity are treated in one uniform framework. We suggest directions for intermediate-level grouping on the output of this low-level segmentation.

1 Introduction

Suppose we are interested in the recognition of objects in complex backgrounds. As a canonical example, consider finding a leopard in the dappled light of a jungle.

In addition to attaching semantic labels–leopard, tree–at some stage of visual perception, we also have an awareness of which pixels in the image belong together–the spots as one region, the leaves of the tree as another and so on. Whether such a grouping of pixels into regions that belong to a single object is done as a precursor to recognition or is a consequence of recognition has been the subject of much debate in both human vision and machine vision.

We view this to be a false dichotomy–grouping is aided by recognition and vice versa–and the most fruitful approach to adopt is one in which grouping and recognition are intertwined processes. The successful application of Hidden Markov Models in speech to simultaneously guide grouping and recognition suggests the power of such an approach.

Such a framework is not yet available for vision. However we can sketch what must be essential components—an integrated treatment of

1. low-level cues: coherence of brightness, color and texture;
2. intermediate level cues: symmetry, parallelism, repeated structures and convexity; as well as
3. higher level cues: specific object knowlege or context information.

This view of hierarchical grouping was first emphasized by researchers in the Gestalt school of psychology in the early part of the twentieth century. They stated the various factors of grouping — proximity, similarity, good continuation, symmetry, parallelism, convexity, common fate and familiar configuration.

D.A. Forsyth et al. (Eds.): Shape, Contour ..., LNCS 1681, pp. 155–164, 1999.

Though they did not have mathematically precise formulations, it is fair to say that they had a strong intuitive sense of what is important about the problem.

It is important to note that the Gestalt factors are *not* rules, instead they have probabilistic interpretations. The factor of proximity only means that pixels nearby are *more likely* to belong to the same group. Obviously, it is absurd to say that nearby pixels *always* belong together. Moreover, a probabilistic framework can naturally resolve conflicting cues and allow for multiple hypotheses.

In computer vision, there has not yet been a successful demonstration of a unified architecture for grouping and recognition which combines the various low-level, intermediate-level and high-level cues in an effective manner. In this paper we review normalized cuts, which provides a unified framework for the low-level cues. We also outline how intermediate level grouping could operate on the results of normalized cuts. How to incorporate high-level knowledge remains very much an open question.

In the past, low-level cues have typically been treated in isolation, one or two of the cues at a time. We will review some representative examples here. The most widely used segmentation algorithm is edge detection [3]. An edge detector marks all the pixels where there are big discontinuities in intensity, color or texture. The cue of contour continuity is exploited to link the edgels together to form long contours [9]. Texture information is encoded as the responses to a set of linear filters [6]. Another formulation for segmentation is the *variational formulation*. Pixel similarities are defined locally, but the final segmentation is obtained by optimizing a global functional [8]. For motion segmentation, one popular algorithm is the motion layer approach — the goal is to simultaneously estimate multiple global motion models and their spatial supports. The Expectation-Maximization (EM) algorithm allows one to achieve this goal[4].

Our approach is based on the normalized cut framework proposed by Shi and Malik [11]. The goal is to partition the image from a "big picture" point of view. Perceptually significant groups are detected first while small variations and details are treated later. Different image features — intensity, color, texture, contour continuity, motion and stereo disparity are treated in one uniform framework.

2   Segmentation Using Normalized Cuts

In this section, we review the normalized cut framework for grouping proposed by Shi and Malik in [11]. Shi and Malik formulate visual grouping as a graph partitioning problem. The nodes of the graph are the entities that we want to partition, for example, in image segmentation, they will be the pixels; in video segmentation, they will be a space-time triplet. The edges between two nodes correspond to the *strength* with which these two nodes belong to one group, again in image segmentation, the edges of the graph will correspond to how much two pixels agree in intensity, color, etc; while in motion segmentation, the edges describe the similarity of the motion. Intuitively, the criterion for partitioning the graph will be to minimize the sum of weights of connections *across* the groups and maximize the sum of weights of connections *within* the groups.

Let $G = \{V, E\}$ be a weighted undirected graph, where V are the nodes and E are the edges. Let A, B be a partition of the graph: $A \cup B = V, A \cap B = \emptyset$. In graph theoretic language, the similarity between these two groups is called the *cut*:

$$cut(A, B) = \sum_{u \in A, v \in B} w(u, v)$$

where $w(u, v)$ is the weight on the edge between nodes u and v. Shi and Malik proposed to use a *normalized* similarity criterion to evaluate a partition. They call it the *normalized cut*:

$$Ncut(A, B) = \frac{cut(A, B)}{asso(A, V)} + \frac{cut(B, A)}{asso(B, V)}$$

where $asso(A, V) = \sum_{u \in A, t \in V} w(u, t)$ is the total connection from nodes in A to all the nodes in the graph. For more discussion on this criterion, please refer to [11].

One key advantage of using the normalized cut is that a good approximation to the optimal partition can be computed very efficiently. [1] Let W be the association matrix, i.e. W_{ij} is the weight between nodes i and j in the graph. Let D be the diagonal matrix such that $D_{ii} = \sum_j W_{ij}$, i.e. D_{ii} is the sum of the weights of all the connections to node i. Shi and Malik showed that the optimal partition can be found by computing:

$$
\begin{aligned}
y &= \arg\min Ncut \\
&= \arg\min_y \frac{y^T(D - W)y}{y^T Dy}
\end{aligned}
\tag{1}
$$

where $y = \{a, b\}^N$ is a binary indicator vector specifying the group identity for each pixel, i.e. $y_i = a$ if pixel i belongs to group A and $y_j = b$ if pixel j belongs to B. N is the number of pixels. Notice that the above expression is the Rayleigh quotient. If we relax y to take on real values (instead of two discrete values), we can optimize Equation 1 by solving a generalized eigenvalue system. Efficient algorithms with polynomial running time are well-known for solving such problems. Therefore, we can compute an approximation to the optimal partition very efficiently. For details of the derivation of Equation 1, please refer to [11].

3   The Mass-Spring Analogy

As we have just seen, the Normalized Cut algorithm requires the solution of a generalized eigensystem involving the weighted adjacency matrix. In this section, we develop the intuition behind this process by considering a physical interpretation of the eigensystem as a mass-spring system.

---

[1] Finding the true optimal partition is an NP-complete problem.

One can readily verify that the symmetric positive semi-definite matrix ($\mathbf{D}-\mathbf{W}$), known in graph theory as the *Laplacian* of the graph $\mathbf{G}$, corresponds to a *stiffness matrix* while the diagonal positive semidefinite matrix $\mathbf{D}$ represents a *mass matrix*. These matrices are typically denoted by $\mathbf{K}$ and $\mathbf{M}$, respectively, and appear in the equations of motion as

$$\mathbf{M}\ddot{\mathbf{x}}(t) = -\mathbf{K}\mathbf{x}(t)$$

If we assume a solution of the form $\mathbf{x}(t) = \mathbf{v}_k \cos(\omega_k t + \phi)$, we obtain the following generalized eigenvalue problem for the time-independent part,

$$\mathbf{K}\mathbf{v}_k = \omega_k^2 \mathbf{M}\mathbf{v}_k$$

in analogy to Equation (1).

The intuition is that each pixel represents a mass and each connection weight represents a Hooke spring constant. If the system is shaken, tightly connected groups of pixels will tend to shake together.

In light of this connection, the generalized eigenvectors in Equation (1) represent normal modes of vibration of an equivalent mass-spring system based on the pairwise pixel similarities.[2] For illustrative purposes, a few normal modes for the landscape test image in Figure 2 are shown in Figure 1, together with a snapshot of a superposition of the modes.

Using the mass-spring analogy, one can proceed to define a measure of similarity within the space of modes by considering the maximum extension of each spring over all time. We refer to this as the *inter-group distance*. As described in [2], the inter-group distance between two pixels i and j may be defined as the following weighted L_1 norm:

$$d_{IG}(i,j) = \sum_{k=2}^{K} \frac{1}{\omega_k} |\mathbf{v}_k^i - \mathbf{v}_k^j| \tag{2}$$

Since the springs have large extensions between groups and small extensions within groups, an obvious application of the inter-group distance is to define a measure of local "edginess" at each pixel. Please refer to [2] for a more detailed discussion of this idea.

4   Local Image Features

In region-based segmentation algorithms, similarity between pixels are encoded locally and there is a global routine that makes the decision of partitioning. In the normalized cut framework, local pixel similarities are encoded in the *weight* matrix W discussed in section 2. In this section, we will describe how local pixel similarities are encoded to take into account the factors of similarity in intensity, color, texture; contour continuity and common motion (or common disparity in stereopsis).

---

[2] Note that since we assume free boundary conditions around the edges of the image, we ignore the first mode since it corresponds to uniform translation.

(a)   (b)

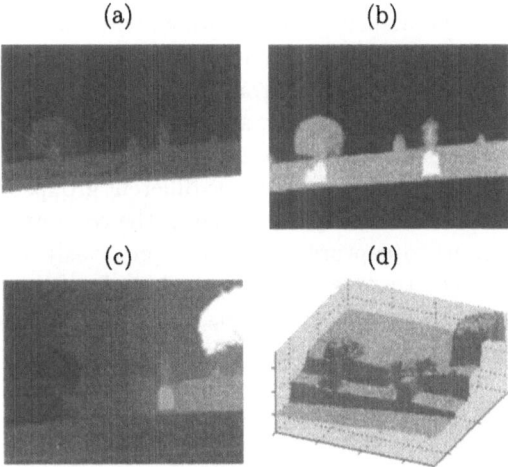

(c)   (d)

Fig. 1. Three generalized eigenvectors (v_2, v_3 and v_4) for the landscape test image are shown in (a)-(c). As an illustration of the connection between Normalized Cuts and the analysis of mass-spring systems, a superposition of the modes at an arbitrary time instant is shown in (d) as a surface plot.

4.1 Brightness, Color, and Texture

We first look at how we measure pixel similarities due to brightness, color and texture. Texture information is measured as the responses to a set of zero-mean difference of Gaussian (DOG) and difference of offset Gaussian (DOOG) kernels, similar to those used for texture analysis in [6]. We call the vector of filter responses the texture feature vector: $u_{tex} = (f_1 * I, f_2 * I, \ldots, f_N * I)^T$. Intensity and color are measured using histograms with soft binning. We write the intensity/color feature vector as u_{col}. The combined texture and intensity/color feature vector at pixel i is thus given by: $u_i = (u_{tex}^T, u_{col}^T)^T$. This feature vector is normalized to have L_2 norm equal to 1: $\hat{u}_i = u_i/\|u_i\|$. Notice that $\|u_{col}\|$ is approximatly equal to a constant. The normalization step can then be seen as a form of gain control, which diminishes the contribution of the intensity/color components when there is a lot of activity in the texture components. The dissimilarity between two pixels is then defined as:

$$d_{tex,col} = (\hat{u}_i - \hat{u}_j)^T \Sigma^{-1}(\hat{u}_i - \hat{u}_j)$$

4.2 Contour Continuity

Information about curvilinear continuity can also be incorporated into the similarity measure between two pixels. Contour information can be computed "softly" through *orientation energy* [7] ($OE(x)$). Orientation energy is strong at an extended contour of sharp contrast, while it will be weak at low contrast gaps along the contour. We enhance the orientation energy at low contrast gaps by propagating the energy from neighboring pixels along an extended contour. The probability of propagation is derived from the energy of the *elastica* curve completion model [13]. Orientation energy, after propagation, provides us with soft information about the presence of contours. Intuitively, the factor of curvilinear continuity says that two pixels belong to two different groups if there is a contour separating them. The dissimilarity is stronger if the contour is extended. Orientation energy allows us to capture this notion very easily. Given pixels p_1 and p_2, dissimilarity between them is defined to be high[5], if the orientation energy along the line joining them is strong. Thus, if l is the straight line between p_1 and p_2 and x is a pixel on l, we define the dissimilarity due to contour continuity as:

$$d_{edg}(p_1, p_2) = \max_{x \in l}\{OE(x) - 0.5(OE(p_1) + OE(p_2))\}$$

As an alternative to this definition, one can restrict the evaluation of the orientation energy to points lying on edge contours. The edge contours can be detected and localized using, for example, maxima of oriented energy [10]. Such a definition leads to sharper segmentation at the expense of a small amount of added computation.

4.3 Motion and Stereo Disparity

For motion segmentation (or binocular segmentation for a stereo pair), the nodes of the graph are the triplet (x, y, t), where (x, y) denote image location and t is time. The weights between two nodes describe the similarity of the motion at the two pixel locations at that time. We propose to compute these weights softly through *motion profile*. Instead of trying to determine exactly where each pixel moves to in the next frame (as in optical flow), we compute a *probability distribution* over the locations where the pixel might move to. Similarity between two nodes is then measured as the similarity of the motion profiles.

This technique can be made computationally efficient for long image sequences by considering only a fixed number of image frames centered around each incoming image frame in the time domain to compute the segmentation. Because there is a significant overlap of the image frames used to compute the segmentation from one time step to another, we can use it to our advantage to speed up our computation. Specifically, when solving the generalized eigensystem using the Lanczos method, the eigenvectors from a previous time step can provide us with a good guess for the initial vectors at the next time step, and we can arrive at the solution very quickly. An example of the motion segmentation results for the flower garden sequence is shown in 4. For details, please refer to [12].

4.4 Results

Results are shown in Figure 2 using texture and intensity and in Figure 3 using contour continuity. For more results, the reader is encouraged to look at our Web site: *http://www.cs.berkeley.edu/~jshi/Grouping/*.

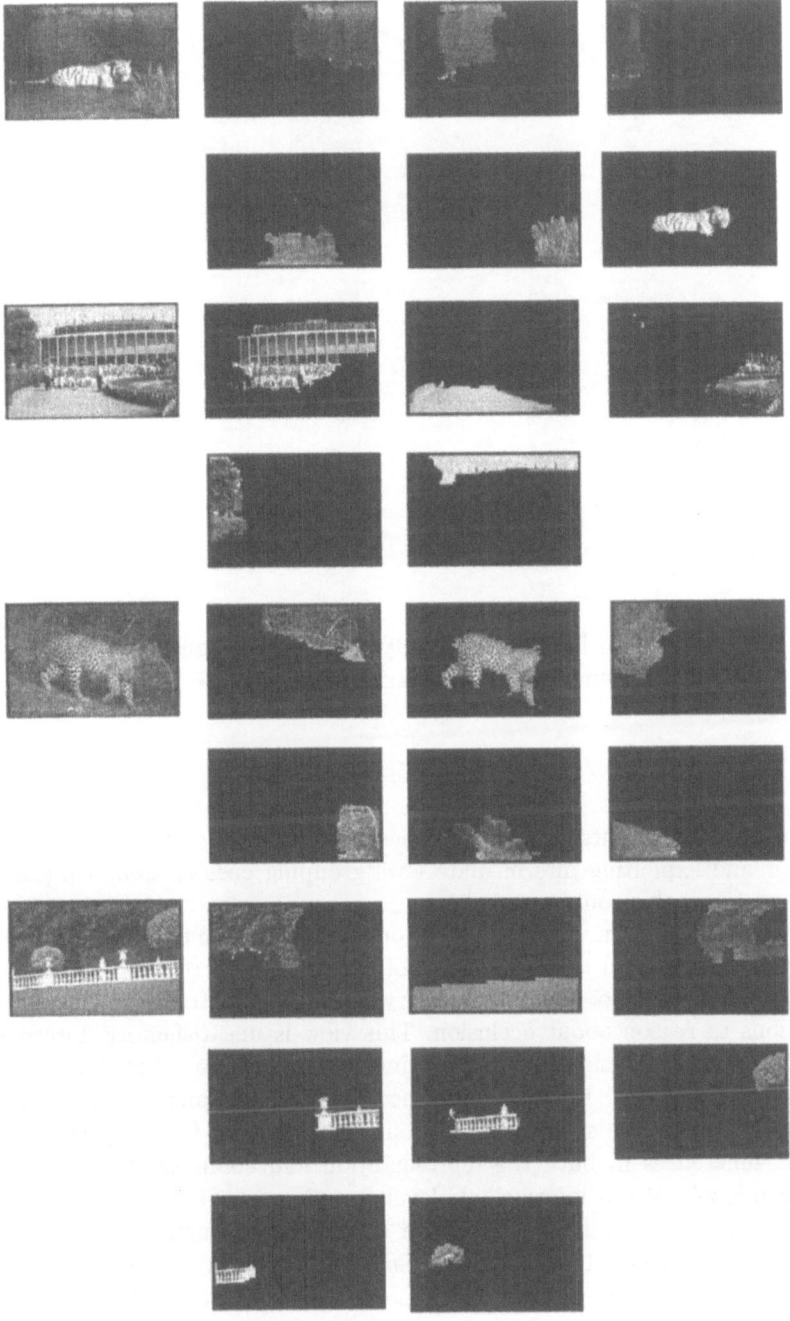

Fig. 2. Segmentation using intensity and texture. Original image shown on the left and the segments on the right.

Fig. 3. Segmentation based on intensity and contour continuity. Left: original image; middle: segments; right: boundaries of segments.

5   Discussion

Whiel normalized cuts provides the basic regions, we are interested in going further and exploiting intermediate level grouping cues as well. We sketch an outline of how this could proceed.

The traditional way to extend the grouping mechanism to intermediate grouping cues would be to take the curves of the segmented regions (or edges from a simple edge detector) as given and try to find symmetric pairs or to look for junctions to reason about occlusion. This view is unsatisfactory. Intermediate level grouping can and should affect image segmentation. Low-level grouping is to provide "hints" to invoke intermediate level grouping. A pathway to go back and change the segmentation should be provided. However, there are intrinsic differences in both the representation and computational mechanisms between low-level and intermediate level grouping. Low-level grouping operates in a continuous domain (pixels) and at least in our framework is deterministic (given a graph, compute the best segmentation), while intermediate-level grouping operates in a discrete, symbolic domain (regions and curves) and needs to be probablistic to allow for multiple interpretations (resolving the different interpretations involves higher-level knowledge in the form of object specific knowledge or domain and context information.)

(a)   (b)

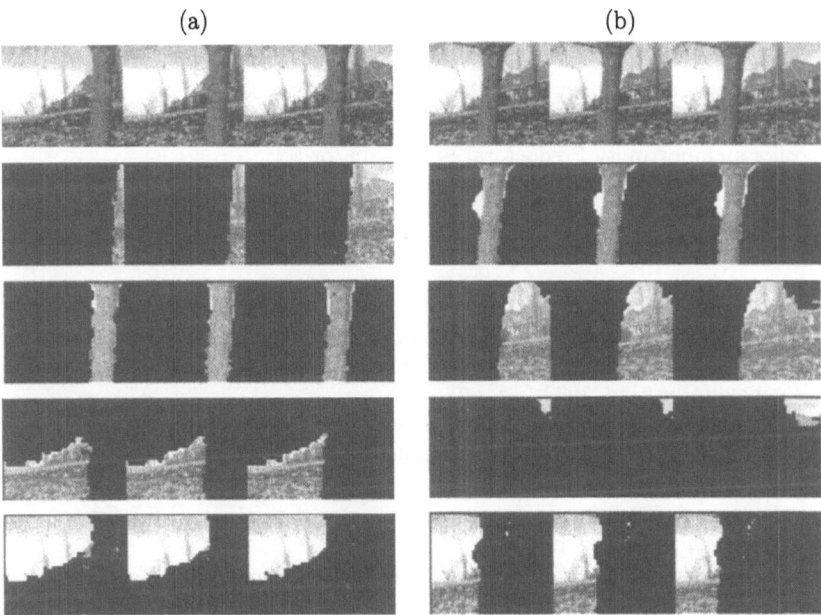

Fig. 4. Subplot (a) shows three of the first six frames of the "flower garden" sequence along with the segmentation. The original image size is 120×175, and image patches of size 3×3 are used to construct the partition graph. Each of the image patches are connected to others that are less than 5 superpixels and 3 image frames away. Subplot (b) shows the 15th to the 18th frame of the sequence and the motion segmentation using tracking algorithm with the sliding time window method.

Our approach is to represent the probabilistic symbolic world as a Markov Random Field (MRF), while maintaining a link to the graph representation for the segmentation. Grouping based purely on low-level cues is used to construct the nodes of the MRF, which correspond to regions in the image produced by normalized cuts, as well as their bounding curves. Each configuration of values of the random variables in the MRF is a different interpretation of the scene and can be mapped to a particular grouping. We can encode intermediate level grouping factors in the clique potentials associated with the MRF, and thus model different configurations as being more or less likely. Markov Chain Monte Carlo (MCMC) methods allow us to compute the probability distribution of these configurations efficiently by sampling.

Working out the details of such an architecture, and how to incorporate object category specific knowledge in this framework, promises research challenges for many years to come.

6   Acknowledgements

This work was supported by an NSF Digital Library Grant (IRI 94-11334), (ARO) DAAH04-96-1-0341, an NSF Graduate Fellowship for J.S. and S.B., and a U.C. Berkeley Chancellor's Opportunity Predoctoral Fellowship for S.B.

References

[1] S. Belongie, C. Carson, H. Greenspan, and J. Malik. Color- and texture-based image segmentation using the expectation-maximization algorithm and its application to content-based image retrieval. In *Proc. Int. Conf. Computer Vision*, Bombay, India, Jan. 1998.

[2] S. Belongie and J. Malik. Finding boundaries in natural images: a new method using point descriptors and area completion. In *Proc. of Fifth ECCV*, Freiberg, 1998.

[3] J. Canny. A computational approach to edge detection. *IEEE Trans. Pattern Anal. Mach. Intell.*, 8, 1986.

[4] A.P. Dempster, N.M. Laird, and D.B. Rubin. Maximum likelihood from incomplete data via the em algorithm. *J. Royal Statistical Society*, 39(B), 1977.

[5] T. Leung and J. Malik. Contour Continuity in region based image segmentation. In *Proc. of Fifth ECCV*, Freiberg, pp. 544-559, 1998.

[6] J. Malik and P. Perona. Preattentive texture discrimination with early vision mechanisms. *J. Optical Society of America*, 7(2):923–32, May 1990.

[7] M.C. Morrone and R.A. Owens. Feature detection from local energy. *Pattern Recognition Letters*, 6:303–13, 1987.

[8] D. Mumford and J. Shah. Optimal approximations by piecewise smooth functions, and associated variational problems. *Comm. Pure Math.*, pages 577–684, 1989.

[9] P. Parent and S.W. Zucker. Trace inference, curvature consistency, and curve detection. *IEEE Trans. Pattern Anal. Mach. Intell.*, 11(8):823–39, Aug. 1989.

[10] P. Perona and J. Malik. Detecting and localizing edges composed of steps, peaks and roofs. In *Proc. Int. Conf. Computer Vision*, pages 52–7, Osaka, Japan, Dec 1990.

[11] J. Shi and J. Malik. Normalized cuts and image segmentation. In *Proc. IEEE Conf. Computer Vision and Pattern Recognition*, pages 731–7, San Juan, Puerto Rico, June 1997.

[12] J. Shi and J. Malik. Motion segmentation and tracking using normalized cuts. In *Proc. Int. Conf. Computer Vision*, Bombay, India, Jan. 1998.

[13] S. Ullman. Filling-in the gaps: the shape of subjective contours and a model for their generation. *Biological Cybernetics*, 25:1–6, 1976.

Geometric Grouping of Repeated Elements within Images

Frederik Schaffalitzky and Andrew Zisserman

Department of Engineering Science
University of Oxford, UK
{fsm,az}@robots.ox.ac.uk

Abstract. The objective of this work is the automatic detection and grouping of imaged elements which repeat on a plane in a scene (for example tiled floorings). It is shown that structures that repeat on a scene plane are related by particular parametrized transformations in perspective images. These image transformations provide powerful grouping constraints, and can be used at the heart of hypothesize and verify grouping algorithms. The parametrized transformations are global across the image plane and may be computed without knowledge of the pose of the plane or camera calibration.

Parametrized transformations are given for several classes of repeating operation in the world as well as groupers based on these. These groupers are demonstrated on a number of real images, where both the elements and the grouping are determined automatically.

It is shown that the repeating element can be learnt from the image, and hence provides an image descriptor. Also, information on the plane pose, such as its vanishing line, can be recovered from the grouping.

1 Introduction

Grouping is one of the most fundamental objectives of Computer Vision and pervades most of the disparate sub-disciplines; for example object recognition always involves perceptual organization (or figure/ground separation) to some extent; shape-from-texture involves grouping texels; boundary detection involves grouping edgels (e.g. saliency of curves); motion segmentation involves grouping independently moving objects over multiple frames etc.

In this paper we investigate the grouping of repeated structures. The motivation for this are three-fold: first, repetitions are common in the world — examples include parquet floor tilings, windows, bricks, patterns on fabrics, wallpaper; second, the groupings provide a compact image descriptor, essentially a 'high level' feature, which may be used for image matching — for example in image database retrieval, model based recognition, and stereo correspondence; third, the retrieved repeating operation can provide shape and pose information — for example the vanishing line of a plane — in a similar manner to that of shape-from-texture.

D.A. Forsyth et al. (Eds.): Shape, Contour ..., LNCS 1681, pp. 165–181, 1999.
© Springer-Verlag Berlin Heidelberg 1999

To be specific the objective is quite simply stated: suppose a structure is repeated in the world a number of times by some operation (for example a translation); then identify this structure and all its repetitions from a perspective image. The outcome is the imaged *element*, and a *grouping* over the imaged repetitions. This simple statement does belie the actual difficulty of a computational procedure since *a priori* the element is unknown — in fact the element only 'exists' because it is repeated by the (unknown) image operation.

For the body of the paper we specialize the operation to repetitions on a plane, and return to a more general setting in section 4. In particular it is shown in section 2 that the operation of repeating by a translation on a scene plane induces relations between the imaged elements. These relations are represented by a parametrized transformation. There are only four parameters that need be specified, and these may be determined from the image.

The significance of this transformation is that it provides a *necessary condition* that must be satisfied by imaged elements related by a translation operation on a scene plane. The transformation is powerful as a basis for a grouping algorithm (a *grouper*) because of the following properties: it is global across the image plane; the class of transformation is independent of camera calibration; and, the class is independent of the pose of the scene plane. Furthermore, the transformation is exact under perspective projection, i.e. it does not require a weak perspective approximation. A grouper for this parametrized transformation is described in section 3

Image relations of this type have appeared before in the literature. For example, "1D relations" such as that a line is imaged as a line; that collinear points are imaged as collinear points; and, that parallel lines are imaged as concurrent lines; all have the above useful properties. These 1D relations have been used by Lowe [6], amongst others, as a basis for perceptual grouping. The relations described in this paper may be thought of as "2D relations", and have been investigated previously by [4, 13]. Repeated 3D (i.e. non-planar) structures also induce image relations [7]. For example, points on objects with bilateral symmetry (they are repeated by a reflection operation), or more generally points repeated by any 3D projective transformation, satisfy an epipolar geometry constraint in the image [5, 7, 9]. There are also relations on the image outlines of particular classes of curved surfaces, such as straight homogeneous generalized cylinders, and these have been employed in grouping algorithms [8, 15, 16].

2   The Image Relation Induced by Repetitions on a Plane

In this section we describe the image transformation that arises from the operation of repeating by a translation on a scene plane. The derivation is very short.

In general the scene plane and image plane are related by a planar homography (a plane projective transformation). This map is written $\mathbf{x} = P\mathbf{X}$ where P is a 3×3 homogeneous matrix, and $\mathbf{x}$ and $\mathbf{X}$ are homogeneous 3-vectors representing corresponding points on the image and scene plane respectively. The transformation P has 8 degrees of freedom (dof).

On the scene plane the repeating translation is represented as $\mathbf{X'} = T\mathbf{X}$, where

$$T = \begin{bmatrix} 1 & 0 & t_x \\ 0 & 1 & t_y \\ 0 & 0 & 1 \end{bmatrix} = \begin{bmatrix} 1 & 0 & 0 \\ 0 & 1 & 0 \\ 0 & 0 & 1 \end{bmatrix} + \begin{pmatrix} t_x \\ t_y \\ 0 \end{pmatrix} (0\;0\;1)$$

The image transformation H between the points $\mathbf{x}$ and $\mathbf{x'}$, which are the images of $\mathbf{X}$ and $\mathbf{X'}$, will be called a *conjugate translation*. The reason for this is evident from $\mathbf{x'} = P\mathbf{X'} = PT\mathbf{X} = PTP^{-1}\mathbf{x}$, so that $\mathbf{x'} = H\mathbf{x}$, where $H = PTP^{-1}$. See figure 1.

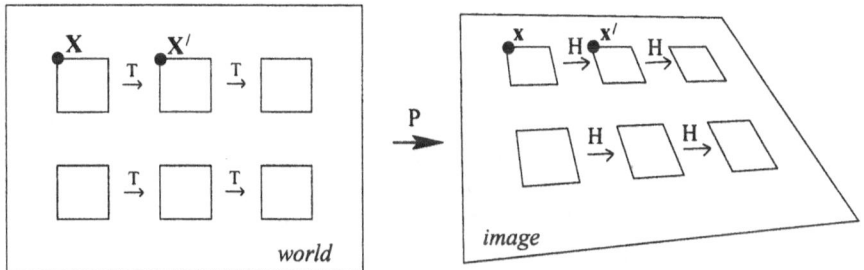

Fig. 1. A translation T on a world plane induces a conjugate translation H in the image.

The conjugate translation H may be written as

$$H = PTP^{-1} = P\begin{bmatrix} 1 & 0 & 0 \\ 0 & 1 & 0 \\ 0 & 0 & 1 \end{bmatrix}P^{-1} + P\begin{pmatrix} t_x \\ t_y \\ 0 \end{pmatrix}\left[P^{-\mathsf{T}}\begin{pmatrix} 0 \\ 0 \\ 1 \end{pmatrix}\right]^{\mathsf{T}}$$

$$= I + \lambda\mathbf{v}\mathbf{l}_\infty^{\mathsf{T}} \quad \text{with } \mathbf{v}.\mathbf{l}_\infty = 0 \tag{1}$$

where I is the 3×3 identity, and

- The 3-vector $\mathbf{v}$ is the vanishing point of the translation direction. It is a fixed point of H.
- The 3-vector $\mathbf{l}_\infty$ is the vanishing line of the scene plane. It is a line of fixed points under H.
- The scalar λ represents the translation magnitude.

The geometric interpretation is illustrated in figure 2

The transformation has only 4 dof, and these may be specified by the line $\mathbf{l}_\infty$ (2 dof), a point $\mathbf{v}$ on $\mathbf{l}_\infty$ (1 dof), and λ (1 dof). This is four less dof than a general homography, and two less dof than the canonical and 'simple' affine transformation used by many authors in the past for this type of grouping [4],

168   Frederik Schaffalitzky and Andrew Zisserman

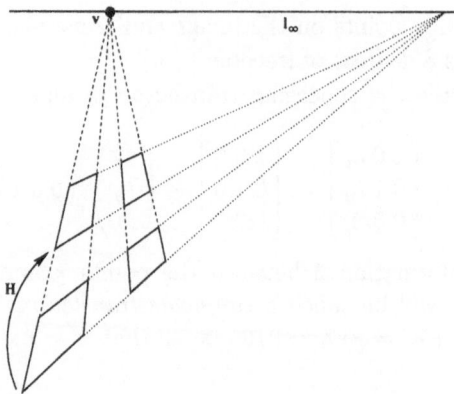

Fig. 2. Geometric interpretation of the parameters of a conjugate translation (elation).

— yet the transformation H exactly models perspective effects which are not accounted for by an affine transformation.

A few remarks on this transformation: The transformation applies to two elements repeated by the translation anywhere on the image plane. If there is a line of repetitions (as in figure 1) then the zeroth element is mapped to the n-th as $H = I + n\lambda \mathbf{v}\mathbf{l}_\infty^T$. The transformation (1) can be determined from two point or two line correspondences. Once the transformation is determined, then so is $\mathbf{l}_\infty$. A planar projective transformation with a line of fixed points, and fixed points only on this line is known in the literature as an *elation* [10, 11].

2.1 Grids

An extension to repeating by a single translation is where there is a repetition in two directions so that the world pattern is a grid of repeated elements. The image is then a conjugate grid. This mapping can be thought of as being composed of two elements

$$H_\mathbf{v} = I + \lambda \mathbf{v}\mathbf{l}_\infty^T \quad H_\mathbf{u} = I + \mu \mathbf{u}\mathbf{l}_\infty^T$$

one for each direction $\mathbf{u}, \mathbf{v}$, i.e. a total of six degrees of freedom. However, note that $\mathbf{l}_\infty$ is common to both, so that once the transformation is determined in one direction only two degrees of freedom remain for the transformation in the other direction. These two degrees of freedom can be determined by one point correspondence.

3   Grouping Imaged Repeated Patterns

In the previous section it has been shown that elements that repeat by a translation on the plane are related in the image by an elation. Thus the problem of grouping repeated patterns can be reduced to that of finding image elements related by an elation, and the rest of this section describes a grouping algorithm for elations.

Initially we do not know the elements or the transformation. This is the chicken and egg problem that often arises in computer vision: if we know the elements we can easily determine the four parameters of the transformation; conversely, if we know the transformation we can (relatively) easily identify elements. In essence then the grouping algorithm must determine simultaneously a transformation (model) and elements consistent with that transformation. A similar situation arises in estimating multiple view relations from several images of a scene, for example the epipolar geometry [12], and ideas can be borrowed from there.

In outline the idea is to first hypothesize a set of elements and associations between these elements. This set is then explored to evaluate if it contains groupings consistent with an elation. This is a search, but it can be made very efficient by a hypothesize and verify approach: the four parameters of the elation are determined from a small number (one or two) of associations, and this hypothesized elation is then verified by testing how many members of the set are mapped under it. This search is equivalent to the problem of robustly fitting a model to data containing outliers. In this case the model is the transformation, and the outliers are the members of the set which are not mapped under the transformation. Depending on how the elements and associations are obtained, a very large proportion of the set may consist of outliers.

The algorithm is summarized in the following section, and illustrated by working through an example.

3.1   Elation Grouping Algorithm

There are five stages to the algorithm. The first two stages are aimed at obtaining *seed* correspondences. The seeds are elements and their associations, and should be sufficiently plentiful that some of the actual elements and associations of the sought elation are included. It is not the aim at this stage that all seed correspondences are correct.

1. Compute interesting features. These may include interest points (e.g. corners), edges, closed regions, oriented texture determined by a set of filter banks etc. The aim is simply to identify regions of the image that are sufficiently interesting. See figures 3 – 5

2. Associate features. An affinity score is then employed to associate features that may be related. Generally the affinity is based on 'similarity' and proximity. An example would be cross-correlation of nearby interest point intensity neighbourhoods. Primarily the choice of affinity score is driven by the invariance sought on the scene plane. For example, that the albedo (reflectance) of an element should be exactly repeated in the scene. However, illumination and imaging effects require that the affinity score has a greater degree of photometric and geometric invariance. At the most basic level the aim is to use photometric cues to filter out obvious mismatches (e.g. matching a predominantly black region with a predominantly white region), but to retain plausible matches. It is important that the affinity score is at least partially geometrically invariant to the transformation sought : if the affinity score is too sensitive to the effects of the transformation, it could reject correct matches. For example, intensity cross-correlation is invariant to translation, but is variant to the rotation and skewing which occur under an elation.

One approach is to use combined affine/photometric invariants [14]. These can be applied to regions bounded by automatically detected closed curves. The advantage of such invariants are two fold: first, invariants can be matched efficiently using indexing; second they can be associated globally across the image. An example is shown in figure 3. Another approach is to determine geometric features, since these are largely invariant to photometric conditions, and then associate the features based on the intensity cross correlation of their neighbourhoods. An example of this is shown in figure 6.

| original | closed curves | clustered invariants |
| one cluster | verified grouping | enlarged grouping |

Fig. 3. Seed matches using closed curves. The idea here is to identify interesting regions by detecting closed Canny [1] edge contours, and then determine if these regions are related by affine transformations by computing their affine texture moment invariants [14]. Regions which are related by an affine transformation have the same value for affine invariants. Thus clustering on the invariants yields a putative grouping of regions. Eight affine invariants are computed, so each curve gives a point in an 8-dimensional space. The points are clustered in this 8D space by the k-means clustering algorithm. The plot shows the distribution and clustering of the zeroth order moments of shape (horizontal axis) and intensity (vertical axis). The cluster used as a hypothesised grouping is the bottom leftmost one.

The next stage is a robust estimation of the elation based on the seed corre-spondences.

3. RANSAC [2] robust estimation. An elation can be instantiated from a minimal number of correspondences that provide either (a) two line correspondences, no two of which are collinear or (b) two line correspondences, two lines of which are collinear, and one point correspondence on the other two lines. The robust estimation then proceeds as follows:

1. Select a random minimal sample of seed correspondences and compute the elation H.
2. Compute the number of inliers consistent with H, i.e. the number of other seed correspondences that map under H.
3. Choose the H with the largest number of inliers.

For example, in figure 7, the white lines denote the initial seed correspondence chosen and the darker[1] lines denotes the correspondences found to be consistent with the elation estimated from the seed.

The RANSAC fit provides an initial estimate of the elation. This estimate is then refined by the following stage.

4. Maximum Likelihood Estimation (MLE). Re-estimate the four parameters of H from all correspondences classified as inliers by minimizing a ML cost func-tion. A ML estimation requires the estimation of the elation together with a set of auxiliary points which map exactly under the estimated elation. The cost function is the image distance between the measured and auxiliary points. As-suming the measurement error is Gaussian, then minimizing this cost function provides the ML estimate of the elation. See [12] for a description of MLE for homographies.

For the example at hand, the vanishing line and vanishing point of the MLE are shown in figure 8.

5. Guided matching. Using the estimated parameters search for new elements consistent with the model by defining a search region about the transferred element position. As figure 8 shows, the location of new elements predicted by the MLE can be very accurate.

Further examples of elation grouping, using exactly the same algorithm, are shown for other images in figures 9 and 10.

3.2   Grid Grouping Algorithm

A similar hypothesize and verify algorithm to the elation grouper may be applied to the case of a conjugate grid, described in section 2.1. Examples of the grid grouper are shown in figures 11 – 14.

---

[1] Blue in the luxury edition of this paper.

Original image.   Fitted lines.

Fig. 4. The sought (but unknown) element/grouping is the repeated floor tiling. The features which successfully provide this element/grouping are line pair intersections. The first stage in determining the features is fitting straight lines to Canny edge detector output.

Line intersections   Lines and points together

Fig. 5. Left: points of intersection of the lines found above. The line segments are extended slightly to allow intersections just beyond their endpoints. Right: lines and intersection points together. Note that line intersections do identify the corners of the floor tilings, but these points are only a small proportion of all the intersections detected.

Closeup of features   Seed matches

Fig. 6. Left: a closeup of the computed intersections. Right: the black lines join pairs of intersections which are deemed to look similar on the basis of intensity neighbourhood correlation. Line pairs which reverse orientation are excluded, since these cannot map under an elation.

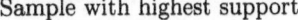

Sample with highest support   Sample with next highest support

Fig. 7. These two images demonstrate the core of the method : each seed match (shown in white) is sufficient to determine an elation in the image. These putative elations can be verified or rejected by scoring them according to the number of feature correspondences consistent with them. The two seed matches whose corresponding elations received the highest support are shown.

Fig. 8. Given the inliers to the elation grouping, the parameters of the elation can be estimated (MLE) more accurately. Left: the ground plane vanishing line and vanishing point of the translation direction. Note that the horizontal line is a very plausible horizon line and that the feature tracks all pass through the vanishing point. Right: the accuracy of the estimated parameters is also demonstrated by transferring elements under the elation: the extended tiling is obtained by mapping the original image lines under the estimated elation.

Fig. 9. More examples of the elation grouper in action. The corners of the windows of the building on the left have been grouped together by the elation constraint. The wall on the right has two sizes of brick, but they are grouped together here by virtue of satisfying the same elation constraint.

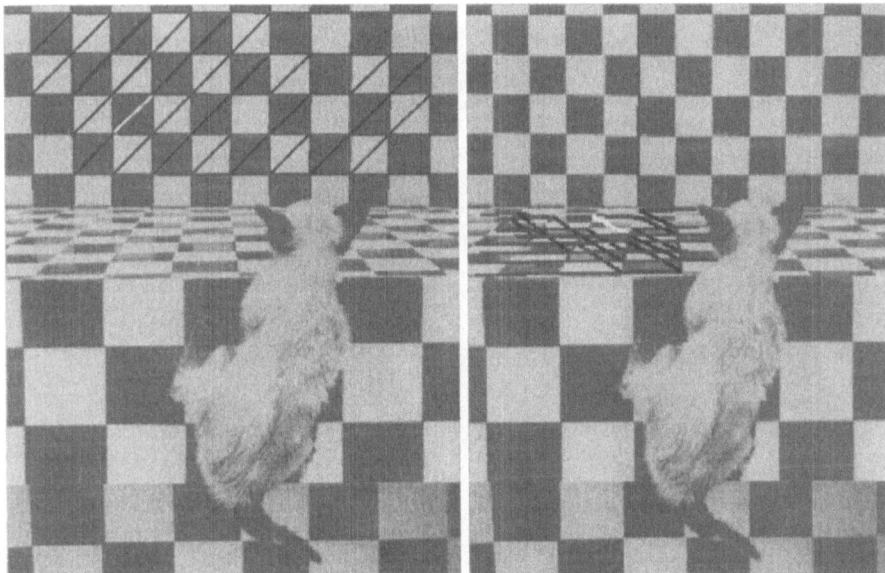

Fig. 10. These figures show two groupings found in the same image by the elation grouper. Despite the difference in pose of the planes in the world, the same grouping algorithm is successful for both cases.

The importance of guided matching, which is the final stage of the algorithm, is very well illustrated in these examples. The previous stages of the algorithm have delivered a ML estimate of the transformation, and a number of elements which are mapped under the estimated transformation. In the case of a grid it is a simple matter to determine which of the integer grid positions is unoccupied, and then search the image for evidence of an element at the corresponding image point.

In detail an element is verified by comparing its similarity to the nearest (in the image) existing element of the grid. In figure 12 the similarity is measured by cross-correlation. This procedure identifies elements which have been missed in the initial feature detection. There may well not be any features present, but because the transformation and intensity are tightly estimated false positives are not generated. Another possibility is to reapply the segmentation in the indicated region, but with the segmentation parameters suitably modified to allow for a perspective scaling. For example, suppose a square is 50% of the size of its neighbour then the Gaussian width of a Canny edge detector could be reduced to detect sharper edges, and the line length thresholds also reduced.

The output of the grid grouper provides many examples of the imaged element. From these we can now estimate the frontoparallel intensity on the tile : each projectively distorted element is warped into the unit square and the resulting textures are averaged in the unit square. The image can then be synthetically

Fig. 11. The first stage of the grid grouping algorithm. From the original image (left), an initial grouping (right) is computed by associating features using only correlation of intensity neighbourhoods.

Grid structure found in the grouping   New elements found by guided search

Fig. 12. The second stage of the grid grouping algorithm. The initial grouping found is processed to elucidate the spatial organisation, namely the grid-like structure of the locations of the elements. This structure is then used to guide a *global* search for new elements. Note that although only half of the potential elements are determined by the initial fit of figure 11, the tight constraints on geometry and intensity provided by the transformation enable virtually every visible element to be identified.

Fig. 13. The floor is generated from the learnt element and spatial organization of the grid.

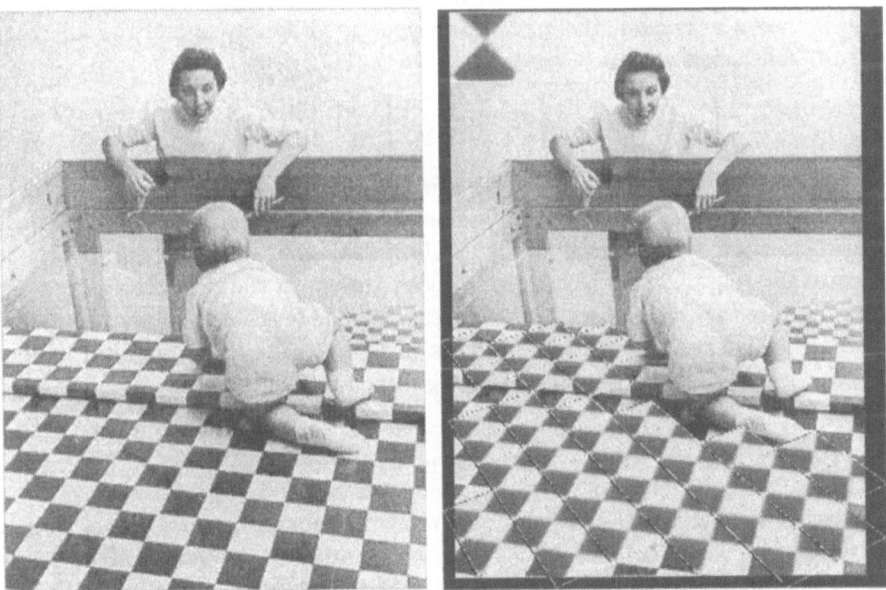

Fig. 14. Another example of the grid grouper. Left: original image. Right: the pattern is generated from the element (which is included as an inset) and grouping determined by the algorithm. Note the algorithm only selects elements belonging to the grid. The two planes in the scene are geometrically indistinguishable.

generated by applying the learnt transformation to the estimated intensity of the element. This is demonstrated in both figure 13 and figure 14. It demonstrates that the element plus grouping does provide a succinct description for substantial parts of the image.

3.3   Grouping Performance

It is evident from these examples that the elation and grid groupers perform extremely well — e.g. the grid grouper identifies all the non-occluded elements with no false positives. This success can be attributed largely to the fact that the transformation has been modelled exactly, and that it is very over determined by the available image data, i.e. there are many more correspondences, which provide constraints, than the four parameters which must be determined.

Ideally the algorithm should return a description of the element and a spatial organisation of the grouping. It is easier to determine the element for the grid than for the elation, because in the case of the grid the element is delineated in both directions, whereas for the elation the element is only demarked in the translation direction.

The organization of the grouping is quite primitive at present, consisting of little more than the grid positions occupied. A more compact description would be the element and a set of operations which generate the grid. Such a description is not uniquely defined of course, as the same grid can be generated by repeating an element by one unit or by repeating a pair of elements at two units of spacing. In fact, for the group of integer displacements on the plane along the two coordinate axes, the grid can be generated by any one of the following sets of translation vectors

$$\left\{ \begin{pmatrix} 1 \\ 0 \end{pmatrix}, \begin{pmatrix} 0 \\ 1 \end{pmatrix} \right\}, \left\{ \begin{pmatrix} 1 \\ 0 \end{pmatrix}, \begin{pmatrix} 1 \\ 1 \end{pmatrix} \right\}, \left\{ \begin{pmatrix} 100 \\ 101 \end{pmatrix}, \begin{pmatrix} 99 \\ 100 \end{pmatrix} \right\}$$

Although clearly the first two are a more suitable choice as a basic generator.

One idiosyncrasy of using the number of inliers as a scoring mechanism in RANSAC is that generators at the smallest repeating distance will always be selected because there will be more of these present in the seed set.

There are also various meta-groupings that could be used to spatially organize the data. For example the top windows in figure 3 may be organized as four meta-groupings, each consisting of nine grouped elements.

4   Conclusions and Extensions

Here we have investigated in detail one repeating operation on a plane, namely a translation, for which the induced transformation is an elation. This serves as an exemplar for the other wall paper groups (discrete subgroups of the 2D affine group) of repeating operations on a plane, such as glide, rotation and reflection groups [3]. Indeed the operation need not be restricted to a single plane. Examples of similar repeating operations and the induced image relation are shown in the table below.

Transformation	Example image	Schematic
Elation $\mathrm{I} + \mathbf{v}\mathbf{l}_\infty^{\mathsf{T}}$, where $\mathbf{l}_\infty . \mathbf{v} = 0$. 4 dof		
Family of Planar Homologies $\mathrm{I} + k\mathbf{v}\mathbf{l}_\infty^{\mathsf{T}}(\mathbf{l}_\infty^{\mathsf{T}}\mathbf{v})$ for integers k 5 dof		
Conjugate Rotation $\mathrm{H}^n = \mathrm{I}$ for an n-fold symmetry 6 dof		
Parallel Lines The imaged lines are concurrent. Equal spacing in world determines world plane vanishing line		

Similar grouping strategies can be developed for each of these examples. Since in man made scenes there are a plentiful supply of elements that do exactly repeat on planes, it is certainly worth building groupers for those repeating operations that commonly occur. It is clear there are always two aspects that must be considered when designing such groupers:

1. **Grouping geometry**: Given a repeating operation in the world, determine the geometric relationships that are induced in the image between the imaged repeated elements.
2. **Grouping strategy**: Develop a grouping strategy based on these relations. This will usually involve a choice on the degree of geometric and photometric invariance required for related elements.

It is certainly plausible that efficient and reliable groupers can be built for virtually any class of exact repeating operation. However, several degrees of greater generality will be required for the non-exact repetitions that also commonly occur: even if the repeating operation is on a plane, it is often the case that either the repetition is not exact, or the element is not exactly repeated by the repetition. A brick wall has both these problems. This type of non-exactness can be modelled by drawing the repeating parameter from a suitable statistical distribution. A far more demanding extension is to the type of repetition that occurs for leaves on a tree, where the colour, shape and size will vary from leaf to leaf (trees are like that), there is a wide (but not uniform) distribution of element poses and there are complex lighting effects produced by both leaves and branches.

Acknowledgements

We are grateful to T. Leung for providing the building image of figure 9, and for comments by Henrik Christensen. The algorithms in this paper were implemented using the IUE/targetjr software packages. This work was supported by the EPSRC IUE Implementation Project GR/L05969, an EPSRC studentship and EU ACTS Project Vanguard.

References

[1] J. Canny. A computational approach to edge detection. *IEEE T-PAMI*, 8(6):679–698, 1986.

[2] M. A. Fischler and R. C. Bolles. Random sample consensus: A paradigm for model fitting with applications to image analysis and automated cartography. *Comm. ACM*, 24(6):381–395, 1981.

[3] D. Hilbert and S. Cohn-Vossen. *Geometry and the Imagination*. Chelsea, NY, 1956.

[4] T. Leung and J. Malik. Detecting, localizing and grouping repeated scene elements from an image. In *Proc. ECCV*, LNCS 1064, pages 546–555. Springer-Verlag, 1996.

[5] J. Liu, J. Mundy, and A. Zisserman. Grouping and structure recovery for images of objects with finite rotational symmetry. In *Proc. Asian Conf. on Computer Vision*, volume I, pages 379–382, 1995.

[6] D. G. Lowe. *Perceptual Organization and Visual Recognition*. Kluwer Academic Publishers, 1985.

[7] J. Mundy and A. Zisserman. Repeated structures: Image correspondence constraints and ambiguity of 3D reconstruction. In J. Mundy, A. Zisserman, and D. Forsyth, editors, *Applications of invariance in computer vision*, pages 89–106. Springer-Verlag, 1994.

[8] J. Ponce, D. Chelberg, and W. B. Mann. Invariant properties of straight homogeneous generalized cylinders and their contours. *IEEE T-PAMI*, 11(9):951–966, 1989.

[9] C. Rothwell, D. Forsyth, A. Zisserman, and J. Mundy. Extracting projective structure from single perspective views of 3D point sets. In *Proc. ICCV*, pages 573–582, 1993.

[10] J. Semple and G. Kneebone. *Algebraic Projective Geometry*. Oxford University Press, 1979.

[11] C. E. Springer. *Geometry and Analysis of Projective Spaces.* Freeman, 1964.

[12] P. H. S. Torr and A. Zisserman. Robust computation and parameterization of multiple view relations. In *Proc. ICCV*, pages 727–732, January 1998.

[13] L. Van Gool, T. Moons, and M. Proesmans. Groups, fixed sets, symmetries and invariants, part i. Technical Report KUL/ESAT/MI2/9426, Katholieke Universiteit Leuven, ESAT/MI2, 1994.

[14] L. Van Gool, T. Moons, and D. Ungureanu. Affine / photometric invariants for planar intensity patterns. In *Proc. ECCV*, pages 642–651. Springer-Verlag, 1995.

[15] M. Zerroug and R. Nevatia. From an intensity image to 3-d segmented descriptions. In J. Ponce, A. Zisserman, and M. Hebert, editors, *Object Representation in Computer Vision*, LNCS 1144, pages 11–24. Springer-Verlag, 1996.

[16] A. Zisserman, J. Mundy, D. Forsyth, J. Liu, N. Pillow, C. Rothwell, and S. Utcke. Class-based grouping in perspective images. In *Proc. ICCV*, 1995.

Constrained Symmetry for Change Detection

Rupert W. Curwen and Joe L. Mundy*

G.E. Corporate Research and Development
1 Research Circle
Niskayuna, NY   12309

Abstract. The automation of imagery analysis processes leads to the
need to detect change between pairs of aerial reconnaissance images. Approximate camera models are available for these images, accurate up to
a translation, and these are augmented with further constraints relat-
ing to the task of monitoring vehicles. Horizontal, bilateral, Euclidean
symmetry is used as a generic object model by which segmented curves
are grouped, first in a 2-d approximation, and then in 3-d, resulting in a
sparse 3-d Euclidean reconstruction of a symmetric object from a single
view. The method is applied to sample images of parked aircraft.

1   Introduction

1.1   Change Detection and Aerial Surveillance

Much of our work in image understanding at General Electric is driven by the
need to automate the process of aerial imagery analysis. This need is an in-
evitable result of the growth in imagery sources for the intelligence community,
combined with post cold-war economics. The bandwidth of data available for
analysis continues to grow, but at the same time the need for increased productivity has constrained the growth of the intelligence work-force. These two
conflicting pressures have generated a vital need for productivity tools for imagery analysis.

The current level of understanding of computer vision is still far from being
able to replace the analyst. Instead we have attempted to identify certain areas of
the analyst's work which are more mechanistic and are amenable to automation.
Our aim is to generate a set of productivity tools which will allow the analyst to
concentrate on the task at hand, somewhat in the style of an office productivity
suite. Those tasks which can be automated should be automated. A trivial example is the location of a site within an image. If the image is of a wide area,
say of a whole city, and the analyst wishes to examine one specific building, then
there is considerable effort involved in simply finding the target building, before

---

* This work was supported by DARPA contract F33615-94-C-1021, monitored by
Wright Patterson Airforce Base, Dayton, OH. The views and conclusions contained
in this document are those of the authors and should not be interpreted as representing the official policies, either expressed or implied, of the Defense Advanced
Research Projects Agency, the United States Government, or General Electric.

D.A. Forsyth et al. (Eds.): Shape, Contour ..., LNCS 1681, pp. 182–195, 1999.

the analyst can even begin to work on producing a report. A productivity tool, using simple spatial models of the regions of the city, combined with a sensor model, can quickly locate and orient the building and present only that region to the user.

This functionality is firmly in the domain of a Geographic Information System (GIS), and at first glance does not appear to involve any image understanding. However, on further study, it becomes apparent that whilst the imagery sources do provide physically derived camera models, these models are seldom exact. For example, when the source is a satellite or high altitude aircraft, the camera has a very long focal length (know colloquially as "the Soda-Straw Model") and a slight error in angular calibration will result in a large translation on the ground. Thus the camera given with the imagery is usually off by a translation and it is sufficient to detect and correct this translation in order to bring the 3-d world into exact alignment with the image.

This problem is one of geographical registration. In the terminology of the computer vision community, this is known as camera calibration, ie. finding the camera models for the images, in terms of the geographical coordinate system. Thus we must be able to map global latitude, longitude and elevation into image coordinates. A geometric description of the region to be monitored in the global coordinate system can then be projected into each image. However, we are provided with a good estimate of the camera *a priori*, so the problem can certainly be solved in most cases with a minimum of additional contextual information.

The are many possibilities for automatic image exploitation once an image stream is registered with a 3-d world model. We have concentrated on a common analysis task, which is to detect, identify and report the changes which occur at a facility. The RADIUS system[6] introduced a number of such context based change detectors. However, these change detectors are either not object specific, or require accurate 3-d models of the objects to be monitored. Recently we have been exploring the use of generic descriptions of objects, and in this paper we show how one such model, symmetry, can be used to produce accurate, object specific change detection.

1.2   Symmetry as a Generic Object Model

Symmetry has long been recognized as a well-defined, intuitively accessible generic model[1]. It is pervasive in imagery because a symmetrical object is both statically and dynamically more stable. For this reason, even natural objects such as flowers and trees exhibit a high degree of symmetry. We have explored the detection of unconstrained symmetries in both man-made and natural scenes[5, 4].

In imagery analysis there are many relevant objects which exhibit strong bilateral symmetry. Most vehicles, including aircraft, and many man-made structures are symmetric in a 3-d plane perpendicular to the ground plane. But in this domain we also have the camera model, and these combined constraints enable the grouping of the symmetric object and even some sparse 3-d Euclidean reconstruction from a single view.

Prior work, such as that of Rothwell[16], demonstrates that is is possible to reconstruct a bilaterally symmetric object up to a projectivity. However, this work does not deal with the complexities of a real world image, with clutter and occlusion. With the additional camera constraints, we are able to automatically detect such bilaterally symmetric objects, without the need to provide detailed geometric descriptions.

As an example, we will use symmetry to detect the presence or absence of an aircraft in a given view. One such view is shown in Figure 1. Note that the quality of the image is not good, and the pixel resolution is low compared to the size of the object. In this example, the aircraft is around a hundred pixels in length.

Fig. 1. An example image event: the analysis should report whether the aircraft is present or absent

In our operational task, a typical use-case might be:

1. The operator (image analyst) specifies a 3-d region of a site which they wish to monitor for the presence of aircraft.
2. Each incoming image of the site contains camera information which allows the system to locate that 3-d region in the image. This is typical of images from the IDEX system, delivered in NITFv2.0 format.
3. The region is segmented in each image, and curves matched to find the strongest axes of symmetry.
4. The strong symmetry axes are used to group the curves in the image, and to attempt to generate some 3-d measurements of the object. These are compared to the generic aircraft model to determine whether an aircraft is present. If so then the image is placed in a queue for the operator to view.

2   Recovering the Symmetry

2.1   Related Work

Previous approaches to grouping using symmetry were based on the "skewed symmetry" model[8]. A skewed symmetry may be generated by taking a planar object with bilateral symmetry, and applying an orthographic projection. Certain non-generic perspective projections also produce a skewed symmetry. A common approach is to use moment properties of the shape to constrain the symmetry parameters, and then apply some evaluation of symmetry quality over all allowed parameters of the symmetry to recover the best description.

Another approach[12] treats the shape as a set of vectors, and derives new images by taking the nth powers of each vector. The nth such derived image is shown to have a mean which is either centered on the origin, or offset, according to how many symmetries the object exhibits. This analysis allows the number of axes, and eventually their orientation, to be recovered.

More recently, many authors[11, 7, 3] have tackled the problems of detecting such transforms and of grouping using a transform as the object class. For example, Cham and Cipolla[3] detect local affine symmetries and evaluate their stability along the curve as a salience criterion. Symmetries which are stable along extended sections of curve are less salient than those which are very localized, since the latter more exactly constrain the transform. For example, a pair of curves which are segments of a single circular arc do not give a unique axis of symmetry.

2.2   Unconstrained Problem

We investigated the unconstrained recovery of planar symmetric curve segments under a projectivity in earlier work[5, 4]. Our approach was based on finding a representation of the curve which was invariant to the symmetry transform.

For a projectivity, a natural representation is the set of inflection points on the curve. However, the recovery of such points on a curve is highly sensitive to noise. The tangent directions are far more stable, and this leads to a method in which the curve segments are parameterized by using the tangents at two inflection points. The curve, thus parameterized, may be matched trivially with any affine transform of the same curve, given just the correspondence for the pair of inflection points. The affine transform may then be iteratively refined to solve for a limited set of projectivities: those which are topologically equivalent to the closest affine transform.

One problem with this approach is the curve representation. Inflection points may not exist for extended sections of curve, and are difficult to recover robustly. We have performed some experiments using a non-local affine invariant curve representation based on the Ramer approximation[15]. In the original form, a curve is approximated by a polygon, where the polygon vertices are chosen to lie along the curve. The approximation is generated recursively by selecting, at each stage, the point on the curve which is furthest from the polygonal approximation.

The initial approximation is just the line through the curve end points. This approximation may be computed very rapidly, and gives a good visual match with the curve. Regions of curve which are high curvature tend to be sampled more densely in arc length than those with low curvature.

2.3 Invariance of the Ramer Approximation

In generating the approximation, we note that for any segment of curve, the point picked as the next polygon vertex is that for which the perpendicular distance from the line joining the curve endpoints is maximal. This point will be such that the tangent to the curve is parallel to the line joining the end points. But parallel lines remain parallel under an affine transform, so the points picked on an affine transformed curve will correspond to the same points on the original curve.

We also must specify the terminating condition for the approximation. Let A_0 be the area between the curve and the line joining its endpoints. Let A_n be the area between the curve and its approximation when there are n spans in the approximation. Then terminate the approximation when A_n/A_0 falls below a constant value. Since the ratios of areas are also affine invariant, this termination condition is guaranteed to give an affine invariant approximation.

In the presence of occlusion, this representation will not be invariant, since the end points define the line segment used as the first approximation. However, we have had some success with this method in recovering symmetries such as tilings and butterfly wings, as shown in Figure 2. The major limitation of these approaches is the combinatorial search for pairs of matching inflection points. This can be eased somewhat by the use of local curve properties, such as colour and texture. In Figure 2 statistics of the local colour properties are computed along each section of curve in the approximation, and these are used to constrain the match.

Further, these methods can only recover a limited set of symmetries, including an affine or projective transformation of a planar curve. Here we explore the use of additional constraint to solve for a 3-d bilateral symmetry.

2.4 Constrained Problem

In our problem domain, the recovery of symmetry is made much simpler by the two constraints available. The camera is known and the symmetry is assumed to be about a plane perpendicular to the ground plane. Further, this ground plane is exactly the 3-d region of interest provided by the analyst.

These constraints allow us to project the image back onto the ground plane. Symmetric curves which are approximately in the ground plane will then form a 2-d Euclidean bilateral symmetry on the ground plane. This is illustrated in Figure 3.

This does not assume a perspective camera. The projection is performed by solving numerically for the intersection of the camera ray with the 3-d ground plane.

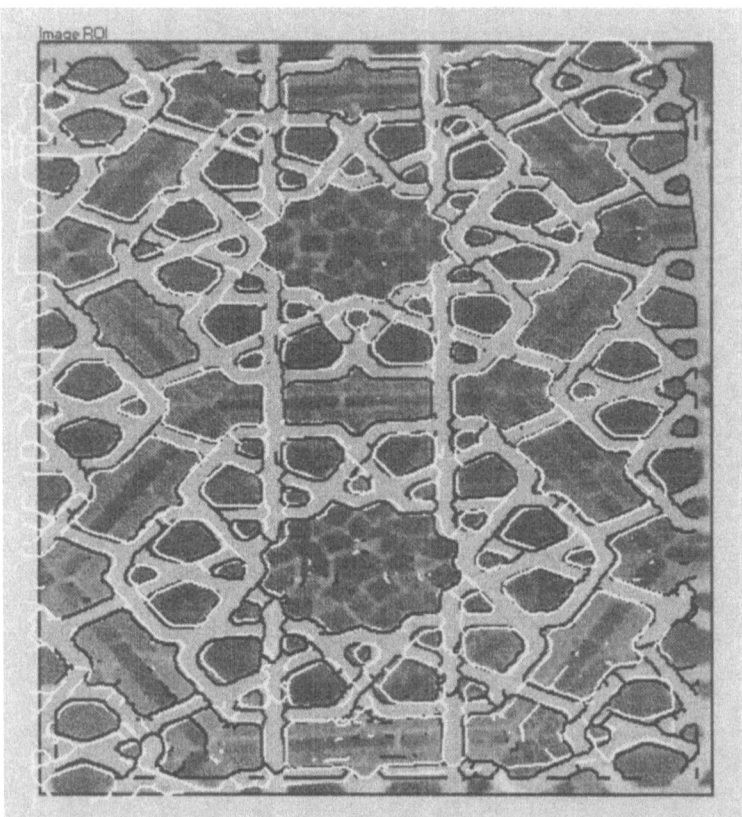

Fig. 2. A planar symmetry recovered using the modified Ramer approximation. The church floor tiles are from Palermo, Sicily. In black are the original edges segmented from the image. In white are the same edges after the strongest affine symmetry transform recovered has been applied.

Furthermore, having recovered the bilateral symmetry axis on the ground plane, we can use the constraint that the 3-d plane of bilateral symmetry is perpendicular to the ground to search for a 3-d reconstruction of the curves in the image.

2.5   Recovering the 2-d Symmetry Axis

Edge detection was performed in the image using the segmentation algorithm of Rothwell[17], and straight lines were fitted to the data. The lines were then projected onto the ground plane to remove perspective skew, and the top 100 longest lines L selected for further processing. This gave an approximate bilateral Euclidean symmetry in 2-d, as shown in Figure 3. This symmetry has only two degrees of freedom, being the parameters of the 2-d axis of symmetry on the plane. A Hough space technique was used to find the strongest axes of symmetry.

a)

b)

Fig. 3. Strong lines in the image (a) are projected along the camera rays onto the ground plane using the known camera (b), where they form an approximate Euclidean bilateral symmetry

Consider a pair of line segments, l_1 and l_2, as shown in Figure 4. The two lines, if images of each other under the symmetry, would have an axis of symmetry given by their bisecting line b. A check was first made to ensure that the projections of l_1 and l_2 onto b overlap. Voting was performed in a 2-d line Hough space where the coordinates in the space corresponded to the angle and length of the perpendicular from the origin to the line. Thus horizontal lines were represented by points along one axis, and lines through the origin were represented by points along the other axis.

Once votes were accumulated for all pairs of lines, the Hough space was smoothed and then normalized so that a uniform distribution of lines in space gave a uniform Hough space. Then non-maximal suppression was performed, and the top 20 possible axes were extracted.

The putative axes were then ranked according to the total length of line explained by each symmetry. Thus for each line $l \in L$, the reflection l' was

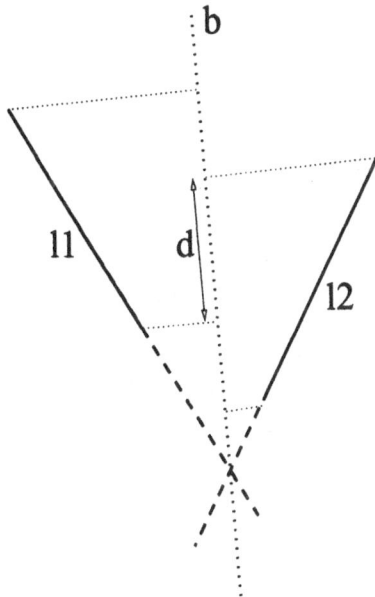

Fig. 4. Each pair of image lines votes for the bisecting line b, provided that the projections of each line onto that bisecting line overlap, ie. span d exists.

found, and all lines which were collinear with l' were recovered from L. The collinear lines were then projected onto l', and the sum of the projected lengths was calculated. This sum, taken over all lines in the group L, was the score for putative axis of symmetry.

2.6   Grouping by 2-d Symmetry

It is interesting to note that the 2-d symmetry is a powerful grouping mechanism. Figure 5 demonstrates the recovery of a symmetry axis from a camouflaged C130 aircraft. The edgels in the original image are dense and most are not symmetric. But the strongest axis of symmetry is still correct, and the features which match under that symmetry are those which are symmetric out of functional necessity. The engine casings, and portions of the airfoils were recovered.

3   Recovering 3-d Shape from Symmetry

Once a 2-d axis of symmetry has been extracted, it is only a small step to recover the 3-d shape of the structure. The axis of symmetry recovered in 2-d x is a projection of a line X which lies on the true plane of bilateral symmetry P in 3-d, the line being at some unknown height above the ground plane. Also P is assumed to be perpendicular to the ground plane. These two facts constrain the plane P to a one-dimensional pencil of planes, where the parameter of the pencil

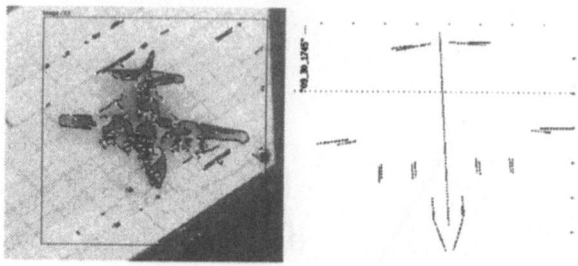

Fig. 5. The edges for a c130 are dense and for the most part do not match under the symmetry. However, the strongest symmetry axis recovers straight lines which must be symmetric in order to be functional, such as the engines and airfoils

corresponds to the position X along the the camera rays. The family of planes is perpendicular to the ground, and sweeps towards the camera as X sweeps from the ground plane towards the camera. Since the symmetric object is expected to lie within the region of interest given by the analyst, the pencil of planes of symmetry to be considered is also bounded.

For a given plane of symmetry from this pencil, and the known camera model, the epipolar geometry of the object is fully determined. Figure 6 illustrates the formation of the epipolar curves. A point u on a segmented curve corresponds with a ray from the camera R. The 3-d generating point U may be any point on R. Each such point can be reflected in the plane of symmetry P and then projected using the virtual camera R', which is the reflection of the camera R in P. Thus the point u maps to the image under $R'P$ of the original ray R. This curve is the epipolar line. For a perspective camera it is a straight line, which passes through the vanishing point for the symmetry.

The epipolar geometry constrains the possible correspondences under a given symmetry. For a point drawn from the set of segmented curves in the image, only those points which lie on the epipolar line may correspond. Whilst this is sufficient to establish correspondence if only one other point is found along the epipolar line for each point in a curve, it is insufficient if there are multiple points along the epipolar line. Any two curve segments which obey the epipolar constraint may be used to reconstruct a 3-d curve, even if they are not the true correspondence. Further constraints are then required.

It is interesting to note that whilst Porrill and Pollard [14, 13] found that if a curve is tangential to the epipolar line, then the corresponding curve must also be tangential, this does not invalidate the previous statement. Provided the 3-d curve is allowed to lie in the direction of the camera ray, a family of corresponding 3-d curves can be generated from any pair of 2-d curve segments which obey the epipolar constraint. However, since a family of curves is generated, we exclude such correspondences from consideration here, concentrating only on those matches which give a unique 3-d curve.

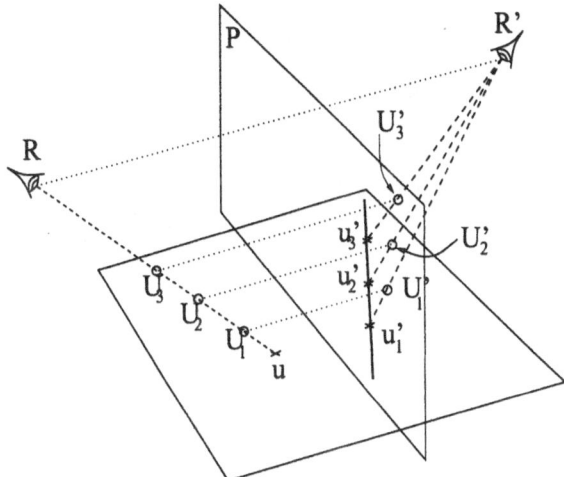

Fig. 6. The epipolar geometry for a given bilateral Euclidean symmetry in 3-d. A single 2-d point u on the left, may in general map to any 2-d point u' on the right, as the position of the 3-d generating point U moves along the camera ray R. Three such mappings are illustrated here.

Once a pair of points has been identified as corresponding, the 3-d curve may be reconstructed. For a perspective camera, Hartley and Sturm[10, 9] show that a closed-form solution exists for finding the 3-d point which minimizes the error in each image. Since we do not restrict our solution to a perspective camera, we simply minimize this 2-d error using standard numerical minimization methods, checking to make sure that convergence was satisfactory and that the resulting error was small enough. A more robust method would be to linearize our camera to find the local perspective model, and then solve using Hartley-Sturm, iterating, if necessary, to convergence.

We used the epipolar geometry to reconstruct all possible 3-d curves, assuming for this experiment that the axis of symmetry X lies on the ground plane. This assumption will result in some distortion of the 3-d reconstruction, the nature of which depends on the camera model used and the height of the original 2-d symmetry above the ground plane. These effects were ignored in our experiments, and will be addressed in future work.

We sampled each curve, and for each point found all corresponding curve points in the segmentation, excluding those correspondences which gave locally indeterminate 3-d curves. Once all such possible correspondences had been calculated, we then discarded all curve points which had many widely separated possible correspondences. The remaining curve segment correspondences were then used to generate seed 3-d curves. These curves are shown in Figure 7 for the aircraft shown in Figure 1. Note that the regions of the airfoils tangential to the epipolar lines of the symmetry were not recovered: these were regions of curve which resulted in a family of 3-d solutions. However, the end points of the wings and tailplane were recovered, as was the section of fuselage leading up to the tailplane. The main portion of the fuselage was inaccurately recovered because of the open hatch and, of course, because the 2-d curves were actually occluding contours and did not correspond to the same 3-d curve. Furthermore, in the region around the engines of the aircraft there were many possible correspondences for each edge. This resulted in a cluster of 3-d curves jutting towards the camera above the front of the aircraft.

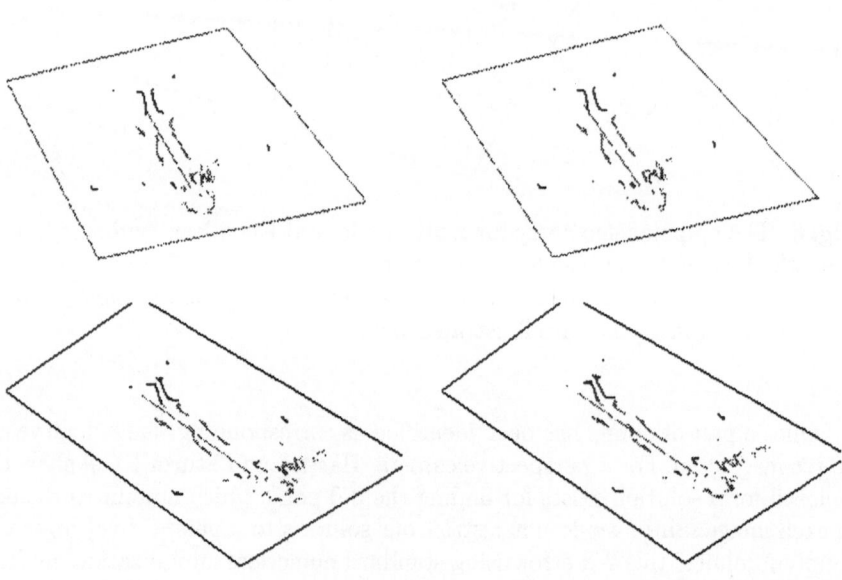

Fig. 7. Cross-eyed stereograms of the reconstructed 3-d seed curves. Note the end points of the wings and tailplane. There are several curves generated by incorrect correspondences in the region around the engines of the aircraft, which form a "jet" of curves above the nose, sweeping towards the cameras on either side of the plane of symmetry.

A second aircraft reconstruction, for the jet in Figure 8, is shown in Figure 9. Here the camera is quite close to the plane of the symmetry, and errors in the 3-d location of curve points are worse, but the reconstruction is still quite stable. The dihedral downward sweep of the tailplane is well captured, as are the sharp edges of the fuselage near the cockpit and the the nose. There are false correspondences in the area around the cockpit, generating multiple curves above the aircraft in 3-d.

Despite these deficiencies, we are currently investigating further constraints which may be applied, given each seed curve in 3-d, to discard incorrect correspondences. One possible approach is to attempt to trace around corresponding

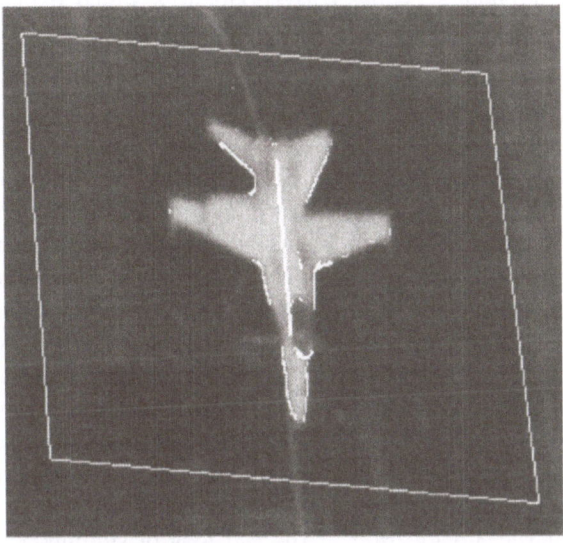

Fig. 8. The jet image with 2-d axis of symmetry and 3-d structure projected.

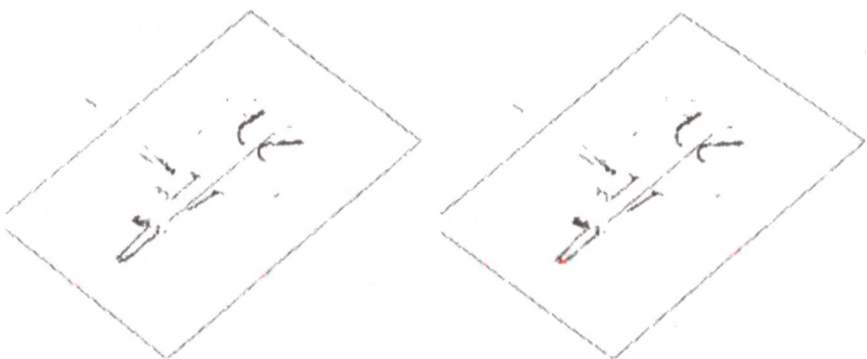

Fig. 9. A second example, showing the 3-d reconstruction projection back into the original image, and a cross-eyed stereogram of the reconstructed 3-d curves. The area around the cockpit has several false correspondences, but the dihedral sweep of the tailplane is well recovered, as are the tips of the wings.

curves and allow only a unique correspondence for each curve point. We can recover segments which gave indeterminant 3-d curves by assuming straight lines between their end points. Those correspondences which explain the greatest length curve will then be chosen as the correct interpretation.

4 Further Work

From a change detection perspective, the 3-d curves can be reconstructed from a single view (the historical or reference image) and then projected into a new view (the current image). If there is support for the projected curves, then the object is still there. If not, then the object has moved. We currently use a 2-d version of this algorithm within the FOCUS system, in which the segmentation is assumed to lie on the ground plane, and is forward projected into the new image and matched. The reconstruction from symmetry will allow us to apply the same approach to 3-d symmetrical objects. Additional views can also be used, once registered, to refine the 3-d model of the object. Edges which are occluding contours are not true 3-d curves, and can be eliminated, or used to generate a surface representation of the object.

The effect of the 3-d location of the 2-d axis of symmetry X was ignored in these experiments. Moving this axis along the camera rays will result in a different plane of symmetry in 3-d and thus in some distortion of the 3-d reconstruction. Selection of the correct plane from this pencil of planes is yet to be investigated.

5 Acknowledgements

Conversations with Peter Tu and Richard Hartley were influential during the formative stages of this paper.

References

[1] H. Blum and R. Nagel. Shape description using weighted symmetric axis features. *Pattern Recognition*, 10:167–180, 1978.
[2] Bernard Buxton and Roberto Cipolla, editors. *Lecture Notes in Computer Science*, volume 1064, Cambridge, UK, April 1996. Springer-Verlag.
[3] T-J. Cham and R. Cipolla. Symmetry detection though local skewed symmetries. *Image and Vision Computing*, 13(5):439–450, 1995.
[4] R.W. Curwen and J.L. Mundy. Grouping planar projective symmetries. In *Image Understanding Workshop*, pages 595–606, 1997.
[5] R.W. Curwen, C.V. Stewart, and J.L. Mundy. Recognition of plane projective symmetry. In *International Conference on Computer Vision*, pages 1115–1122, 1998.
[6] O. Firschein and T.M. Strat. Radius: Image understanding for imagery intelligence. In *Morgan Kaufmann*, 1997.
[7] M. Fleck, D. Forsyth, and C. Bregler. Finding naked people. In Buxton and Cipolla [2], pages 593–602.

[8] S.A. Friedberg. Finding axis of skewed symmetry. *Computer Vision Graphics and Image Processing*, 34(2):138–155, May 1986.

[9] R.I. Hartley and P. Sturm. Triangulation. In *Image Understanding Workshop*, pages II:957–966, 1994.

[10] R.I. Hartley and P. Sturm. Triangulation. *Computer Vision and Image Understanding*, 68(2):146–157, November 1997.

[11] T. Leung and J. Malik. Detecting, localizing and grouping repeated scene elements from an image. In Buxton and Cipolla [2], pages 546–555.

[12] G. Marola. On the detection of the axes of symmetry of symmetric and almost symmetric planar images. *IEEE Trans. Pattern Analysis and Machine Intelligence*, 11(1):104–108, January 1989.

[13] J. Porrill and S. Pollard. Curve matching and stereo calibration. In *British Machine Vision Conference*, pages 37–42, 1990.

[14] J. Porrill and S. Pollard. Curve matching and stereo calibration. *Image and Vision Computing*, 9:45–50, 1991.

[15] U. Ramer. An iterative procedure for the polygonal approximation of plane curves. *Computer Graphics and Image Processing*, 1:244–256, 1972.

[16] C.A. Rothwell. Object recognition through invariant indexing. In *Oxford University Press*, 1995.

[17] C.A. Rothwell, J.L. Mundy, W. Hoffman, and V.D. Nguyen. Driving vision by topology. In *Symposium on Computer Vision*, pages 395–400, 1995.

Grouping Based on Coupled Diffusion Maps

Marc Proesmans[1] and Luc Van Gool[1,2]

[1] ESAT/PSI-VISICS, Univ. of Leuven, Belgium;
[2] D-ELEK, ETH, Switzerland

Abstract. Systems of coupled, non-linear diffusion equations are proposed as a computational tool for grouping. Grouping tasks are divided into two classes – local and bilocal – and for each a prototypical set of equations is presented. It is shown how different cues can be used for grouping given these two blueprints plus cue-specific specialisations. Results are shown for intensity, texture orientation, stereo disparity, optical flow, mirror symmetry, and regular textures. The proposed equations are particularly well suited for parallel implementations. They also show some interesting analogies with basic architectural characteristics of the cortex.

1 Introduction

Vision, more than any other sensory input, enables us to cope with the variablity of our surroundings. The performance of biological vision systems is unrivalled by any computer vision system. One task they are particularly better at is so-called 'grouping'. This is the crucial step of identifying segments that have a high chance of belonging together. Grouping acts as a kind of shortcut between low-level features and high-level scene interpretations, quickly assembling relvant parts. Unfortunately, little is known about the underlying 'computational' principles.

In this paper, an attempt is made to formulate a set of working principles that seem to underly biological vision. These are discussed in section 3. Then, in sections 4 and 5 a computational framework is proposed that seems apt to turn these principles into computer vision algorithms that work on real images. This is an important restriction, that rules out detailed modeling of the actual neural processes. The human visual system owes at least part of its power to the huge amount of processing units and connections. The result is not a faithful copy of biological visual processing but a model that exhibits useful functional analogies. But first, section 2 looks at the implications of defining grouping as redundancy reduction.

2 Grouping as Redundancy Reduction

Perception and grouping in particular have often been regarded as processes of redundancy reduction. Statistical information theory has been invoked to supply

D.A. Forsyth et al. (Eds.): Shape, Contour ..., LNCS 1681, pp. 196–213, 1999.

objective functions to be optimised by these processes, such as Shannon's entropy and mutual information (for a recent example see Phillips and Singer [14]).

Yet, statistical information theory does not tackle the core problem, which is to define redundancy in the first place. Consider the following strings of bits: '1011010010010111011001' and '1010101010101010101010'. In terms of Shannon entropy, both yield the same 'redundancy'. There are 50% 0's and 50% 1's in both cases. The second string definitely seems more ordered, i.e. seems to contain more redundancy, however. Dealing with such differences is the realm of algorithmic information theory. Of course, one could assign new codes to pairs of subsequent bits, like '00'-'01'-'10'-'11', in which case the second bit string would suddenly seem very ordered from the viewpoint of statistical information theory as well. But this requires to appropriately recode the string.

Algorithmic information theory is precisely dealing with this problem. Simply put, it tries to find the shortest computer program (which amounts to a bit string) that produces the given bit string. It would not be easy to find a program that produces the first bit string and that would be shorter. For the second string a simple *repeat '10' eleven times* would suffice. The longer such regular string, the greater the gain in bits would be. The real complexity of the data is defined as the length of the shortest program that generates them. Hence, the second string is of less complexity than the first.

The ideal grouping device would solve this problem from algorithmic information theory. Such device would come up with an ordering principle (the program) that maximally compresses and thereby 'explains' the data. Algorithmic information theory states that only a very small fraction of strings will allow an appreciable degree of compression [3]. This underpins the 'non-accidentalness' idea in that random data have a very low chance of showing appreciable order [8, 9].

Unfortunately, algorithmic information theory also shows that in general maximal redundancy reduction cannot be achieved. Quoting from Chaitin [3]: 'The recognition problem for minimal descriptions is, in general, unsolvable, and a practical induction machine will have to use heuristic methods'.

One might argue that image data are far from random and that appreciable degrees of redundancy reduction are possible right away, e.g. based on correlated feature values at nearby pixels. Segments can quickly emerge that way and higher order groupings could be formed based on these initial results. One could abandon further attempts once the search for further order gets difficult and hence the problem of having to deal with random data is not an issue. Nevertheless, almost all grouping phenomena in human vision have been demonstrated to work with stimuli like random dot patterns. Hence, the human visual system doesn't seem to constrain the input data it can handle, but rather the regularities it can find. Indeed, introducing heuristics in the search for order is the only approach that can prevent the system from performing exhaustive search and thus becoming inacceptably slow. Thus, we have to accept the idea of applying a restricted class of regularity detecting schemes and letting other types of redundancy go by unnoticed.

An example of how also human vision exhibits such behaviour is given by symmetry detection. See fig. 1. Mirror symmetry in random dot patterns is known to be very salient. However, if a small region around the symmetry axis is replaced by a non-symmetrical random dot pattern, the overall impression of symmetry is seriously weakened. Although the level of redundancy has been decreased only slightly by this simple change, the redundancy is much harder to detect [6].

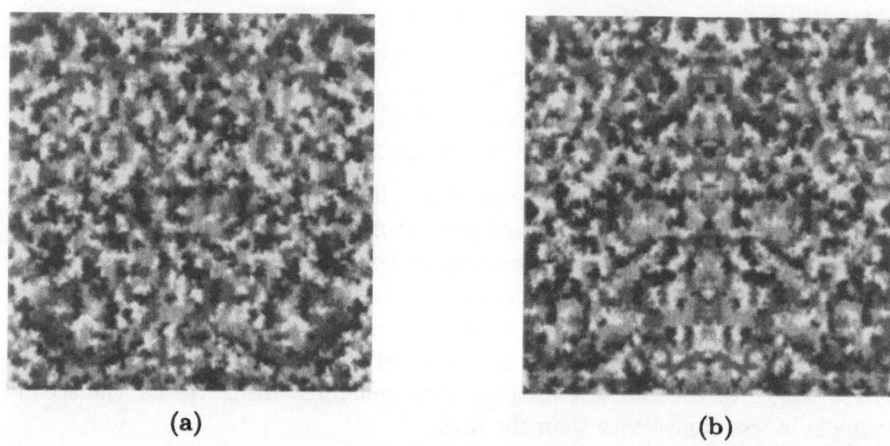

(a)   (b)

Fig. 1. *(a) asymmetric random dot pattern; (b) symmetric random dot pattern; actually (a) is symmetrical except for a vertical strip around the symmetry axis.*

Algorithmic information theory gives justification to a tradition of listing separate grouping principles known from introspection and perception research. Examples are the 'Prägnanz' rules of the Gestaltists [23] and Lowe's non-accidental properties [9]. Grouping methods should focus on mechanisms with maximal effect, avoiding a proliferation of grouping rules. Then computation time and resources are well spent. Emulating the grouping principles that nature applies seems a sound strategy to that end. The next section deals with the guidelines one might extract from the brain's architecture and behaviour.

3   Computational Grouping Principles

This section tries to draw conclusions from the best grouping systems known to date: biological vision systems. It focuses on macro-properties of visual processing, as we are interested in computational principles rather than their actual implementation in the brain.

Massive, but structured parallelism   Neurophysiological observations of mammalian vision systems show that neural structures perform a massively parallel kind of processing. Moreover, the neuronal substrate is not like a soup of millions of these small processors. From the retina, over the lateral geniculate nucleus

(LGN), up to the striate, prestriate, and further cortical areas, one finds a high degree of organisation. Neurons work in parallel within layers, which are simultaneously active and together form modules and areas, which in turn jointly create the visual percept. This fine-grain spatial parallelism in combination with functional parallelism also seem prerequisite for the fast responses of human vision.

Local Interconnections Parallelism does not imply highly connected networks. In the case of the brain, there are an estimated 10^{15} synaptic connections, for an estimated total of 10^{11} neurons. This leaves us with an average of about 10,000 connections for each neuron. Then also take into account that there typically are multiple connections between the same two neurons and the picture is one of sparse rather than dense connectivity. In summary, a neuron's connections are laid very parsimoniously, with an emphasis on local connections in a retinotopic sense (and within a layer and area also in a physical sense for that reason).

Data Driven Processing The responses of human vision to random dot data suggest there is a strong data-driven aspect to early vision. Such data can yield strong impressions of symmetry, coherent motion, and depth. Treisman [19, 20] carried out experiments with artificial stimuli, where simple cues like colour, orientation, etc. were sufficient to let deviating components pop out immediately. It is hard to see how such performance could be due to the extensive use of expectations about the world. Far from suggesting that bottom-up and top-down processes ought not collaborate, there nevertheless is good reason to believe that the initial visual stages depend primarily on the retinal input.

Specialized modules Both neurophysiology and phsychophysics indicate the existence of more or less independent channels for processing of different aspects of vision (colour, orientation, motion, depth, ...) [21]. The existence of specialized visual modules and areas in the cortex is well-established by now [25]. This specialisation of areas is backed up by the selective connections between them. From this one can conclude that the visual information is processed in parallel in different areas or modules therein, and that special attention is paid to each of a number of basic cues.

Bi-directional coupling Neurophysiological terms like 'visual pathways' suggest a model with 'lower' areas feeding into 'higher' areas. But as Zeki [24] puts it: "most connections in the cortex are reciprocal, and in the visual cortex there is no known exception to this rule". Such reciprocal connections form the anatomical basis for feedback and can also help to arrive at an effective integration of information (cue integration/data fusion).

Non-Linearity Many of the convolution masks used in computer vision have their counterpart in the brain, so it seems. However, already quite early in the visual cortex neurons are found with a markedly non-linear response to the intensity and spectral pattern in their receptive fields. Complex and hypercomplex cells are well-known examples. Also increasingly one became aware of influences that stimuli in a wider surround can have. Effects like illusory contours also suggest non-linear processing and all the more so as they may appear or disappear upon small changes to the stimulus.

Explicit representation of boundaries Basic features such as luminance, colour, motion, depth, etc. can all generate the impression of discontinuities that separate regions homogeneous in that cue [21]. The presence of orientation sensitive cells in areas that are specialised in the detection of different cues [24] can also be interpreted as indications that contour mechanisms operate in each of these basic feature maps separately. It seems there is a distinction to be made between at least two types of processes: those that detect homogeneity of some sort within image segments and those that detect their boundaries. Zucker [26] referred to these processes as Type II and Type I processes, resp., and Grossberg [4] called them feature and boundary systems. In the case of the luminance cue, the brain adds the capacity to form illusory contours [22].

Local and Bilocal grouping One can distinguish two types of detectable order. One corresponds to regions with homogeneous local characteristics, such as luminance, colour, or texture orientation. The second type combines cues at two different locations. Mirror symmetry detection is a good case in point. It requires the detection of similar cues at position *pairs*. Similar processes seem called for in the case of Glass patterns [12]. The visual system seems to extract displacement fields (vector fields). Motion and stereo are cues where a similar process would be useful, with the addition of having the two locations defined at different moments in time or in the input from two eyes. The particular relevance of both local and bilocal processes could also be reflected in the particular importance of 1st and 2nd-order statistics in Julesz's texture segmentation experiments. It is also interesting to speculate about the local/bilocal divide as an alternative for the 'what' and 'where' pathways, resp..

Maximal usage of a limited number of grouping mechanisms Separate, specialised modules do not imply that the underlying implementational mechanisms are completely different. From an evolutionary point of view one could expect that a successful computational scheme is duplicated to solve other tasks. There are good anatomical indications for this [7], emphasised by the term 'isocortex'. This suggests that the different types of grouping exhibited by the brain can be implemented as variations of a few basic blueprints. Of course, variations between areas are to be expected as a result of specialisation.

Compliant regularity detection Maximal usage of grouping principles also implies some degree of flexibility. Grouping methods should tolerate deviations from the ideal regularities, in order to be useful in natural environments. Hardly any of the observed, real-world regularities are of an all-or-nothing nature. Human observers are e.g. capable of detecting mildly skewed symmetry in random dot patterns.

In conclusion, the aim of this work was to create a grouping framework according to the following guidelines:

- Allow fine-grain parallelism,
- with mainly local interconnections between retinotopically organised nodes.
- The processes are primarily data driven, based on a restricted number of basic image cues.
- Processing should be carried out by different, specialized feature maps,
- including non-linear processing,
- bidirectional coupling between maps, and
- explicit representations of both feature homegeneity within segments and variations that signal boundaries.
- Grouping processes will be of two main types – local or bilocal – and
- will be based as much as possible on but a few computational blueprints.
- They will also allow for deviations from ideal regularities.

In the next two sections, two blueprints for local and bilocal grouping are described. For each, specialisations towards specific grouping applications are discussed and results on real images are shown.

4 Local Grouping

Probably the most straightforward example of a local grouping process is the detection of regions of approximately constant intensity. This first example is also selected because it best shows the relation of the proposed grouping framework with regularisation based techniques and anisotropic diffusion, of which it could be considered a combination.

The original intensity $g(x, y)$ of the different image points with coordinates (x, y) will be changed into new values $f(x, y)$ such that small variations are suppressed. The function $f(x, y)$ will be referred to as the *intensity map*. Simultaneously, a *discontinuity map* $d(x, y)$ is constructed. Both processes are governed by a nonlinear diffusion equation and they evolve while influencing eachother through bidirectional connections.

These equations have been derived as follows. Regularisation functionals are the point of departure. They typically impose a solution that should strike a balance between smoothness and faithfulness to the input-signal (g in our case). The more sophisticated regularisation schemes also include discontinuities but penalise for their creation in order to avoid over-fragmentation. Such functionals typically are non-convex, which makes them difficult to extremize. The most studied of these functionals is [2, 11]

$$E(f, B) = \int_{R-B} \left(\alpha \|\nabla f\|^2 + \beta(f - g)^2 \right) \, dx \, dy + \nu \, |B| \ .$$

In the image region R boundaries B can be introduced at discrete locations. The first term pushes for an f that is smooth, while the second will keep it from drifting far from the original intensity. Where boundaries are introduced, these terms are put to zero. The third term penalises the introduction of a boundary pixel. This functional regularises f and B simultaneously.

There are at least two problems with such functionals. The first has already been pointed out and is the difficulty of finding the optimum. A second, major problem are the unexpected characteristics that the optimum may have. In the case of this particular functional edges will always intersect as triples in vertices with 120° between them [11]. This is neither desirable nor intuitively clear.

There is not much one can do about the second problem if one works via functionals that prescribe global behaviour. Here we work through local prescriptions of grouping behaviour. The first problem can be reduced by going via related, convex problems. The graduated non-convexity technique (GNC) captures the solution as a limit case of a series of convex approximations [2]. Ambrosio and Tortorelli [1] introduced a discontinuity indicator d which is a kind of smoothed version of B. They replaced the term $\nu|B|$ by

$$\frac{1}{2} \int \left(\rho \|\nabla d\|^2 + \frac{d^2}{\rho} \right) \, dx \, dy$$

The first term is a smoothing term and the second a term that tries to keep boundaries localised. Shah [18] proposed to replace this single functional by a pair of functionals, that are minimised together. The original, difficult optimisation problem is replaced by the solution of a system of diffusion equations:

$$\frac{\partial f}{\partial t} = d^2 \nabla^2 f - \frac{1}{\sigma^2}(f - g) \ , \qquad \frac{\partial d}{\partial t} = \rho \nabla^2 d - \frac{d}{\rho} + 2\alpha(1 - d) \parallel \nabla f \parallel \ .$$

These evolution equations are calculated for all image pixels. At each iteration, only information from neighbouring pixels is needed. The first equation strikes a balance between smoothing f (first term) and keeping it close to the initial intensities g (second term). The second equation governs the boundary strength d. Again, d is smoothed (first term), kept small (second term) unless the local intensity gradient is large (third term). Near edges d will be pulled towards 1, elsewhere towards 0. Spatially, it varies smoothly between these extreme values. Note that f influences d but not vice versa.

A drawback is that both the intensity map and the discontinuity map are blurred. This problem can be alleviated by replacing the linear diffusion operators by the anisotropic diffusion operator of Perona and Malik [13]. In the first equation, this is $\text{div}(c_f \nabla f)$, with c_f a decreasing function of $\|\nabla f\|$ or d. In the second equation a similar change is made, with c_d a function that decreases with $\|\nabla d\|$:

$$\frac{\partial f}{\partial t} = \psi \text{div}(c_f \nabla f) - \frac{\phi}{\sigma^2}(f - g), \qquad \frac{\partial d}{\partial t} = \rho \text{div}(c_d \nabla d) - \frac{d}{\gamma} + 2\alpha(1 - d) \parallel \nabla f \parallel$$

The modulation factors ψ and ϕ can be different functions of d. They can be chosen $\psi = d^2$ and $\phi = 1$, thereby staying close to Shah's equations. If one prefers stronger edge detection and less variations within regions $\psi = 1$ and $\phi = 1 - d$ is a better choice [16]. The effect of the modified equations is shown in

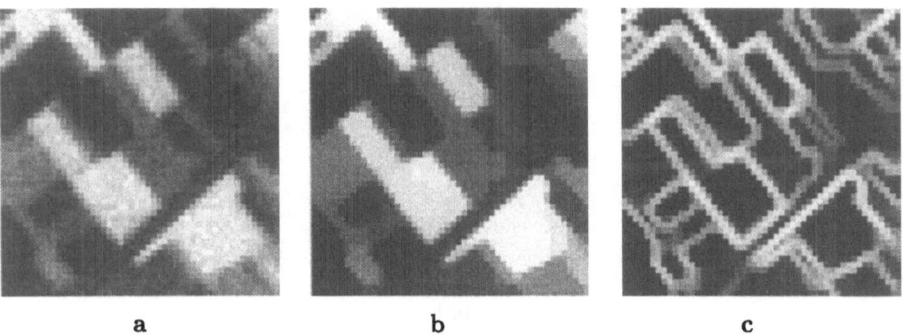

        a   b   c

Fig. 2. *a: Part of a SPOT satellite image (of an agricultural area). b: Intensity map (ψ = constant, $\phi(d) = 1 - d$). c: Discontinuity map.*

fig. 2. The original image is shown in (a), the f-map after 30 iterations in (b), and the d-map in (c), The noise in the intensity values has been reduced, while edges have been sharpened. The d-map has values close to 1 (bright regions in (c)) near the boundaries of regions with homogeneous intensity.

The basic cue used in the previous example was intensity. The orientation of local texture is another basic cue. As orientation is defined modulo π (contrast polarity is discarded) differences can better be measured as $\sin 2(\theta_i - \theta_j)$ [17]. A second difference with intensity is that orientation has to be estimated from the outputs of a whole bank of oriented filters with a discrete series of preferred orientations. The modified equations are

$$\frac{\partial \theta}{\partial t} = div(c_f(d)\sin(2\nabla\theta)) - \frac{1}{\sigma^2} \sum_{j=0}^{N-1} \sum_{k=0}^{N-1} G_j \sin(2\theta - (\theta_j + \theta_k)) ,$$
$$\frac{\partial d}{\partial t} = \rho\nabla^2 d - \frac{d}{\gamma} + 2\alpha(1 - d) \parallel \sin(2\nabla\theta) \parallel .$$

In these equations G_j stands for the output of the filter with preferred orientation θ_j. There are N filters, with orientations π/N apart. Both equations have the same structure as before. For instance, in the first one term imposes continuity on the feature at hand, the second tries to keep the estimated orientation close to that suggested by the raw filter data [16].

An example of orientation based grouping is shown in fig. 3. Figure 3(a) shows a microscope image of a metallic structure. The texture consists of several subparts with homogeneous orientation. Six filters were used, with preferred orientations $30°$ apart. The end state of the orientation map (first equation) is shown in fig. 3(b). The orientation is coded as intensity. The different segments are clearly visible. Fig. 3(c) shows the end state of the discontinuity map (second equation). Bright parts are where boundary strength is high (close to 1). As in the human visual system, the effect of combining the outputs of the filters by these equations is that orientation can be determined with better precision than their orientation differences might suggest (so-called "hyperacuity").

Human perception of intensity shows a number of pecularities, such as Mach band effects (a percept of over- and undershoots of intensity near boundaries)

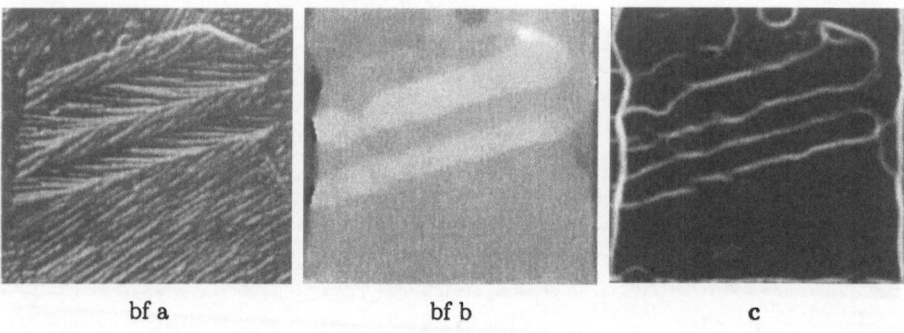

bf a   bf b   c

Fig. 3. *(a) texture of a slice of metallic material, as seen through a microscope; (b) result for the orientation map, with orientation coded as intensities; (c) result for the discontinuity map.*

and illusory contours (a percept of edges where they are completely absent). We have not tried to model the latter in this grouping framework yet. The Mach band effect can be produced if also higher derivatives of intensity are used in the equations [16].

5   Bilocal Grouping

5.1   The Bilocal Blueprint

Bilocal grouping processes such as the extraction of motion vectors, stereo disparities and symmetric point pairs involve combining points at two different positions, albeit maybe at different instances or in different images. These point pairs are constrained to have similar values for a basic feature, such as intensity or orientation. Here only intensity will be used for the illustration of the different bilocal processes.

In order to fix ideas, we present a bilocal process for optical flow. The equations of Horn & Schunck [5] serve as our point of departure. The optical flow vectors (u, v) are found as the solution of

$$\frac{\partial u}{\partial t} = \nabla^2 u - \lambda I_x(I_x.u + I_y.v + I_t) \ , \qquad \frac{\partial v}{\partial t} = \nabla^2 v - \lambda I_y(I_x.u + I_y.v + I_t) \ , \quad (1)$$

with I intensity and subscripts indicating partial derivatives. A problem with this system is that the linear diffusion operators force the displacement field to blur motion boundaries. Furthermore, it is only effective in guiding the search for optical flow in as far as the local intensity profile varies linearly within a neighbourhood of dimensions comparable to the motion distance. Both these problems are tackled by adapting the equations.

The first problem can be alleviated if the diffusion operators are replaced by anisotropic diffusion. The second problem can be handled precisely by switching to a bilocal rather than H&S's local formulation. The underlying idea can easiest be explained for the 1D case. Suppose we are interested in the motion for a point with surrounding intensity profile as shown in fig. 4(a). According to the optical

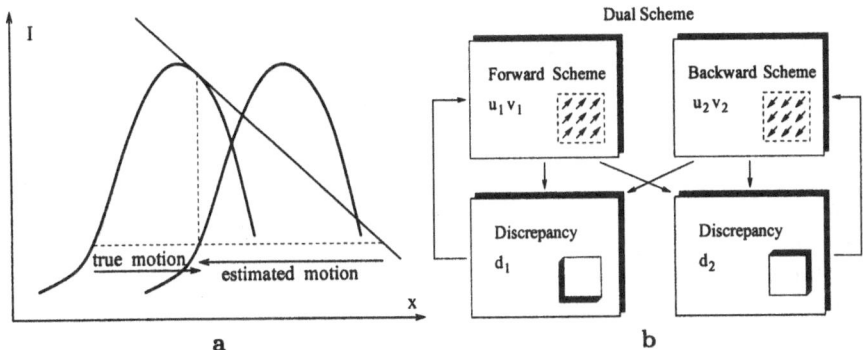

Fig. 4. a) *The assumption that the intensity profile varies linearly may cause big errors for larger motions.* b) *Schematic overview of the proposed bilocal scheme.*

flow constraint that H&S use $u = -(\frac{\partial I}{\partial t})/(\frac{\partial I}{\partial x})$. This is correct over infinitely short time lapses, but deviations can be severe with images are taken at video rate or slower. The problem lies in the fact that the intensity profile is not linear over the distances traveled by the points between the two images. The problem could be reduced if we had a good approximation of the motion. A similar optical flow constraint can then be formulated for the residual motion, which is much smaller and for which the intensity profile therefore has a higher chance of obeying the linearity condition. In [15] the following, mathematical reformulation of the optical flow constraint is derived:

$$I_x u + I_y v + J(u_0, v_0) = 0$$

where

$$J(u_0, v_0) = -I_x \cdot u_0 - I_y \cdot v_0 + \frac{I(x, y, t) - I(x - u_0 \Delta t, y - v_0 \Delta t, t - \Delta t)}{\Delta t}$$

and with (u_0, v_0) the approximation for the motion vector. The result is a bilocal expression that needs information at (x, y) in the second image and at $(x - u_0 \Delta t, y - v_0 \Delta t)$ in the first. The procedure consists of successively updating the displacement estimates and using them to compute the spatial (or temporal) gradients at a shifted location which changes with the latest displacement estimates.

There are different ways to obtain the initial guess for the displacements. One is to first apply the traditional H&S equations. Even if the motion vectors are imprecise at places, here and there the estimated motions will be close to the real ones. These spots allow the process to lock on to the correct motion field and the correct solution will spread through the diffusion process. Secondly, multi-scale techniques can help to quickly bridge larger distances. Thirdly, there always is the possibility to kickstart the system from an initial, random field. Again, places where the motion happens to be close to the real solution can suffice to bootstrap the whole process.

Apart from the anisotropic diffusion and the bilocal optical flow constraint, a third difference with the H&S system is an additional boundary process [15]. Creating such a map is more intricate for the bilocal processes. Near boundaries, parts of the background get occluded or become visible. These areas have no corresponding points in the other image. Hence, in one of the images the displacement field is undefined. This creates an interesting asymmetry between the images for such points, that does not exist for points that are visible in both images. Indeed, one can consider two displacement fields: where points in the first image go to in the second and v.v. Consider a displacement vector from the first image to its corresponding point in the second and then adding the displacement vector from this latter point to its corresponding point in the first image. The two displacement vectors will annihilate eachother, except in boundary regions. The displacement vector for a point only visible in one image will make no sense. The vector in whatever point is assigned to it will not obey the annihilation rule. The magnitude of the sum C of the two vectors can therefore be used to detect boundaries. Indeed, we can let this magnitude drive a discontinuity map of the type that we used for the local processes. In this case, it might be more appropriate to call it a discrepancy map, as complete regions might obtain high values as they are only visible in one of the images. In fact, there are two such sum vectors: one can start either from the first or the second image and take the corresponding point's vector to form the sum. In order to detect occluded ánd disoccluded regions such a dual scheme is necessary. Displacements from the first to the second image ánd displacements from the second to the first image are extracted. The overall system is schematically shown in fig. 4(b). It consists of six coupled diffusion equations, four of which describe the feature maps, i.e. the motion vectors of the dual scheme (both forward and backward, indicated with a and b). the other two measure the discrepancy from the point of view of each of the images.

$$
\begin{aligned}
\frac{\partial u_a}{\partial t} &= div(c(d_a)\nabla u_a) - \lambda I_x(I_x u_a + I_y v_a + J(\boldsymbol{w}_{a0})) \\
\frac{\partial u_b}{\partial t} &= div(c(d_b)\nabla u_b) - \lambda I_x(I_x u_b + I_y v_b + J(\boldsymbol{w}_{b0})) \\
\frac{\partial v_a}{\partial t} &= div(c(d_a)\nabla v_a) - \lambda I_y(I_x u_a + I_y v_a + J(\boldsymbol{w}_{a0})) \\
\frac{\partial v_b}{\partial t} &= div(c(d_b)\nabla v_b) - \lambda I_y(I_x u_b + I_y v_b + J(\boldsymbol{w}_{b0})) \\
\frac{\partial d_a}{\partial t} &= \rho\nabla^2 d_a - \frac{d_a}{\rho} + 2\alpha(1 - d_a) \parallel \boldsymbol{C}_a(\boldsymbol{w}_a, \boldsymbol{w}_b) \parallel \\
\frac{\partial d_b}{\partial t} &= \rho\nabla^2 d_b - \frac{d_b}{\rho} + 2\alpha(1 - d_b) \parallel \boldsymbol{C}_b(\boldsymbol{w}_a, \boldsymbol{w}_b) \parallel
\end{aligned} \tag{2}
$$

The discrepancies d_a and d_b (again one for each of the dual schemes) guide the anisotropic diffusion in the maps that extract the motion components u and v. For a detailed account the reader is referred to [15].

5.2 Bilocal Specialisations

As mentioned earlier, the bilocal processes are introduced to handle grouping based on cues such as motion, stereo, and symmetry. The detection of regular texture is another example. Each of these benefit from certain adaptations.

Motion sequences typically consist of more than two images. Better precision is obtained by considering frames that are separated by a larger time lapse. Displacements between such frames should be the sum of frame-to-frame displacements and hence a good initialisation is available. Computation speed from frame to frame can be increased as well, as motion fields will normally not change drastically from one frame to the next. The latest displacement field can serve as an excellent initialisation for the next frame. For the examples in this paper, a multiview approach was used.

For stereo the two images have to suffice. If disparities are rather large, there might be a problem of initialisation. A multi-scale approach can alleviate this problem [10]. At all scales a bilocal strategy is used, however. Just applying blurring linearises the intensity profile but also increases problems of intensities getting 'contaminated' by parts not visible in the other image. Also precise localisation still benefits from the possibility to work locally around two different positions in the two images. A further specialisation is possible for camera configurations yielding horizontal epipolar lines. In that case the vertical disparity components v can be put to zero and the system reduces to a set of 4 coupled equations. Even if epipolar lines do not run perfectly horizontal, it is often useful to start the system up with only these 4 equations active, to get a good initialisation more rapidly, and then plug in the additional equations for v.

For symmetry a more fundamental adaptation is required, as ideally nearby displacement vectors are not the same but vary in a specific way. Corresponding points lie diametrically along a symmetry axis. This means that the displacement field shows a rather steep gradient which can not be handled by a simple smoothness operator. Furthermore, the actual position of the axis is not known beforehand, which complicates the search process. The bilocal process can be adapted to look for symmetry of a predefined orientation (or an orientation close to that predefined orientation for that matter). This might seem a rather clumsy solution, but orientation effects in human symmetry detection suggest that also the brain has to perform a kind of scan over possible orientations. The order of this scan has been the subject of intensive debate in perception research. To give an idea of how the bilocal scheme can be adapted, a vertical symmetry module is discussed. In that case we only have to deal with a horizontal displacement. The following changes are made:

- First of all, the smoothing operator is replaced by $\operatorname{div}\left(c(d)\nabla(u(x,y) - 2x)\right)$ which takes the desired change in the horizontal displacement u with x into account.

- The horizontal gradient I_x in the equations (2) has to be inversed, since along the horizontal direction corresponding points have mirrored intensity profiles.
- Two opposite displacement fields with relatively short displacements are taken as initialisation of the dual displacement scheme.

This modified bilocal process successfully locks on to the symmetry near its axis. From there it spreads to areas further from the axis. Psychophysical findings with human symmetry perception suggest a similar process. It would explain why a disruption of symmetry near the axis has such a profound impact on symmetry detection. The model is also consistent with human vision in the sense that symmetry need not be perfect. The axis can be somewhat curved, intensity at symmetric positions doesn't need to be identical, etc.

For the detection of regular texture the main difference from the basic scheme lies in the fact that several displacement fields – each corresponding to one type of periodicity – can coexist. We want to find all the different, smallest periods in the pattern. This is achieved by initialising several constant displacement fields with different orientations and vector lengths. They will lock on to the periodic structure if there is local agreement. These matches propagate to other areas as the initial displacement fields get distorted in order to follow the variations in texture orientation and spacing. Several of the initialisation fields may lock on to the same periodicity, but if they sample different orientations and displacements densely enough, every type of periodicity will be 'detected' by at least one initialisation field. Finding out whether a periodicity has been detected is easy, as the discrepancy maps will show low values.

5.3 Examples of Bilocal Grouping

Fig. 5 shows an example of motion extraction. Cars drive with different speeds on a crossroad. Part (a) shows one of the frames of the video input. Part (b) shows the magnitudes of the extracted motion vectors. Brighter means faster. The outlines are sharp, but due to the moving shadows on the ground they do

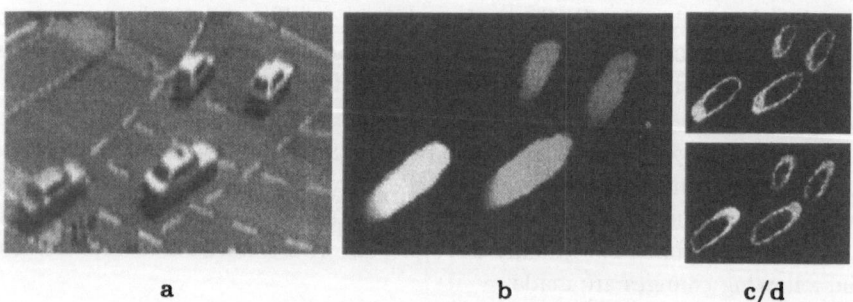

a   b   c/d

Fig. 5. *a: Frame from a video of a traffic scene. b: Magnitudes of the extracted motion vectors. c,d: Discrepancies for each of the dual schemes.*

not precisely coincide with the outlines of the cars. Parts (c) and (d) shows the discrepancies for each of the dual schemes. One (c) detects the parts of the road that become visible again, while the other (d) shows parts that are getting occluded. In fact, one can AND both maps and get the contours of the cars. An EXOR operation of the maps yields the regions that are not visible in one of the views.

Fig. 6 gives a second example of motion extraction. Five frames of a swimming fish were taken as input. Part (a) shows one of the frames. The velocities calcu-

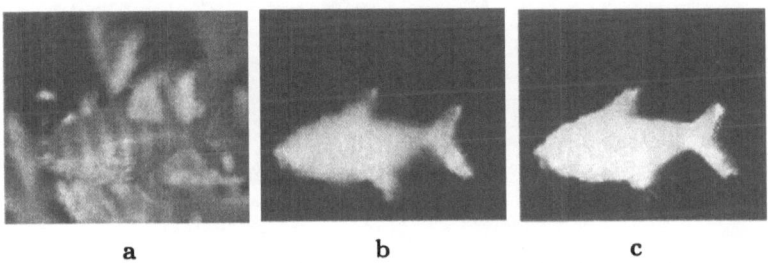

a   b   c

Fig. 6. *a: One of 5 frames with a swimming fish. b: Velocity magnitude when motion is only calculated between two frames. c: Velocity magnitude when motion between the first and the fifth frame.*

lated for two subsequent frames are shown in (b). Part (c) shows the result for the velocity from the first to the fifth frame, based on the sum of frame-to-frame motions as initial displacement field. As can be seen, the object is delineated very sharply from the background and the velocity is very homogeneous over the fish's body.

Fig. 7(a) shows a stereo pair of two manikins. As part (b) shows, the depth discontinuities are precisely localised in the discrepancy maps. Note that the background is also highlighted as yielding irrelevant disparity data. This is achieved by an additional 'texture map', another diffusion process that divides the scene into textured and untextured parts [17]. Disparities are suppressed for untextured parts. Part (c) shows two views of the 3D reconstruction made on the basis of the extracted disparities. The disparities were found with the help of a multi-resolution approach. A three-level image pyramid was used.

Fig. 8 shows an example for a face, which is only weakly textured compared to the manikins. Nevertheless, the reconstruction is reasonable. Again, disparities on the background were suppressed through the texture map.

Figure 9 shows two scenes with symmetry. Part (a) shows an X-ray of a human thorax. The symmetry is not perfect. The places with zero displacement indicate the position of the symmetry axis. They are highlighted in the figure. The same was done for the head-shoulder scene ('Claire') in part (b). The process is seen to be quite tolerant to deviations from ideal symmetry.

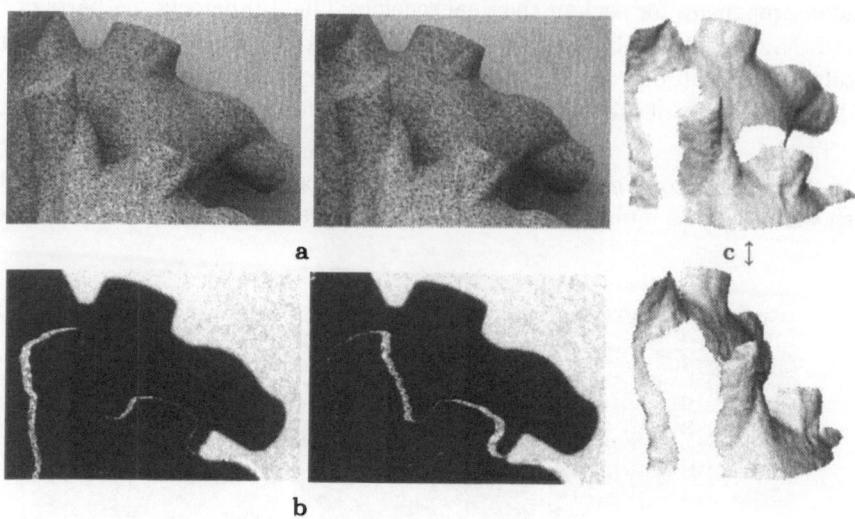

Fig. 7. *a: Original stereo image pair. b: Resulting discrepancies. c: Two views of the 3D reconstruction.*

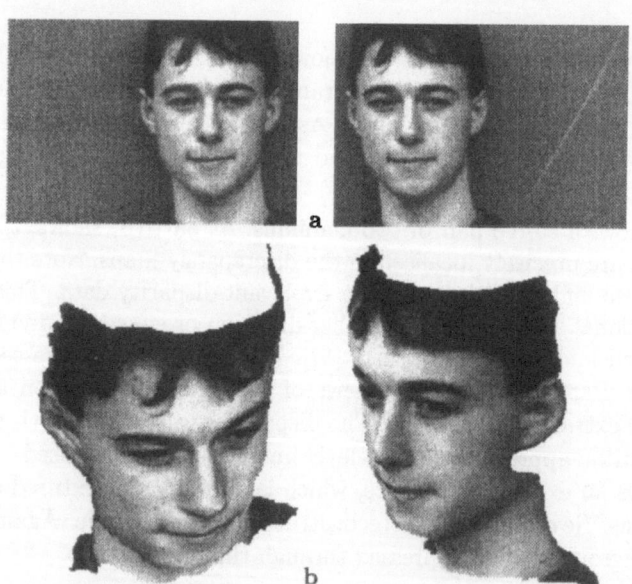

Fig. 8. *a: Original stereo image pair of a face. b: Two views of the reconstructed surface.*

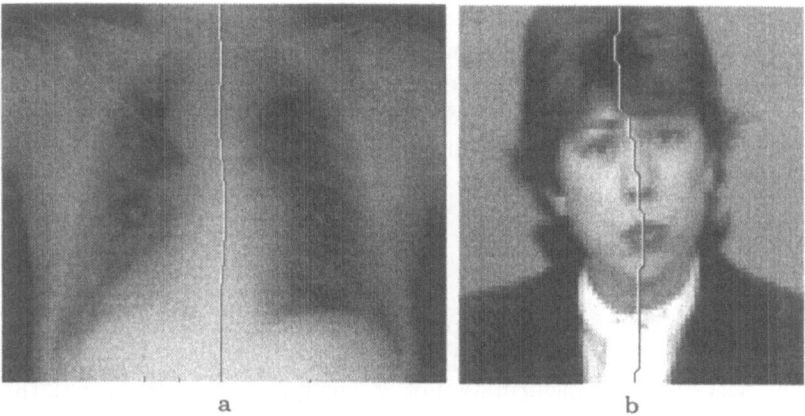

Fig. 9. *Examples of symmetry detection; b: X-ray image of a thorax, c: head-shoulder scene.*

The detection of regular texture is illustrated in fig. 10. Part (a) shows the input image. The goal is to find the repeated textures of the shirt. Part (b) highlights regions where regular texture was found. Darker zones separate the different pieces of textile where they are knitted together. Part (c) gives an idea of the precision of the extracted periodicities. Using a shape-from-texture approach local surface orientations are given for points clicked on by the user. The orientations fit our visual expectations.

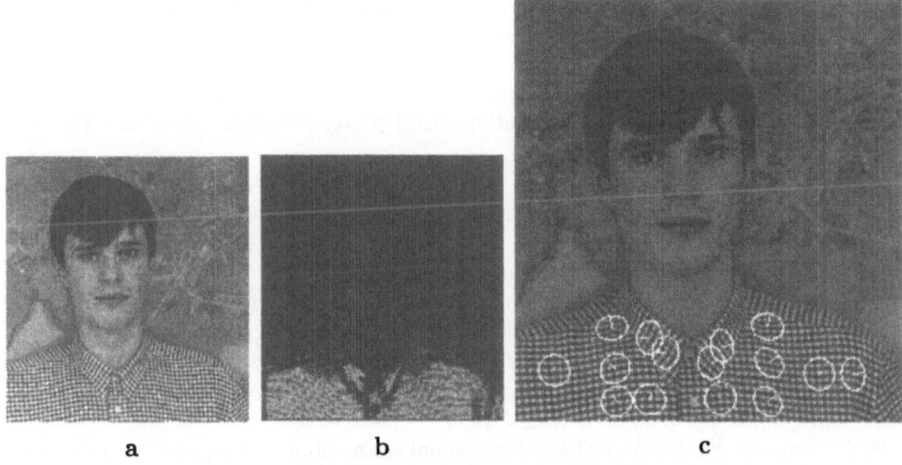

Fig. 10. *a: Original image, b: Segmentation of relevant periodical texture areas, c: Estimated surface orientation using shape-from-texture.*

In the bilocal processes described so far, point pairs are preferred with identical values for the basic feature (here only intensity). When presented with different options the visual system need not even prefer the solution with identical values, however [12]. We have built extended bilocal schemes that allow intensities to change between views (with spatially varying scale + offset). A discussion is out of the scope of this paper.

6   Conclusions

In this paper we have argued that grouping is necessarily based on task-oriented sets of rules, not a universal principle. We have then tried to set out guidelines for the selection and implementation of grouping rules. The framework that we propose is based on the evolution of coupled, non-linear diffusion equations. In these systems, each of the equations determines the evolution of a relevant image cue, such as intensity, local texture orientation, motion components, etc. Feature maps come with discontinuity maps of their own, which make explicit the boundaries of segments that are homogeneous in those features. The maps are organised retinotopically and the number of connections each pixel would need for such equations to be implemented on hardware with fine-grain parallelism can be kept low.

Future research will be aimed at combining different maps into a single system. Work will be needed on the connections between cues. As an example, 3D reconstruction of the face in fig. 8 can be improved by exploiting its symmetry.
Acknowledgment: Support by Esprit-LTR 'Improofs' is gratefully acknowledged.

References

[1] L. Ambrosio, V. Tortorelli, *Approximation of functionals depending on jumpls by elliptic fnctionals via Γ-convergence.* Comm.. Pure and Appl. Math., vol.43, pp. 999-1036, 1990
[2] A. Blake and A. Zisserman, *Visual Reconstruction,* MIT Press, 1987
[3] G. Chaitin, Randomness and mathematical proof, *Scientific American,* Vol. 232, No. 5, pp. 47-52, 1975
[4] S. Grossberg and D. Todorovic, Neural dynamics of 1-D and 2-D brightness perception: A unified model of classical and recent phenomena, Perception & Psychophysics, 43, 241-277, 1988
[5] Horn B.K.P. and Schunck G.: Determining optical flow. AI. **17**, 185–203, 1981.
[6] B. Jenkins, Redundancy in the perception of bilateral symmetry in dot patterns, Perception & Psychophysics, Vol. 32, No. 2, pp. 171-177, 1982
[7] E. Jones, Determinants of the cytoarchitecture of the cerebral cortex, ch. 1 in *Signal and sense, local and global order in perceptual maps,* eds. Edelman, Gall, and Cowan, pp. 3-50, Wiley-Liss, 1990
[8] T. Kanade, Recovery of the 3-dimensional shape of an object from a single view, Artificial Intelligence, Vol.17, pp.75-116, 1981
[9] D. Lowe, Perceptual Organization and Visual Recognition Stanford University technical report STAN-CS-84-1020, 1984

[10] D. Marr and T. Poggio, A therory of human stereopsis, Proc. Royal Soc. B, 204, pp.301-328, 1979.

[11] D. Mumford and J. Shah, Ootimal approximation by piecewise smooth functions and associated variational problems, Comm. on Pure and Applied Math., Vol.42, pp. 577-685, 1989

[12] T. Papathomas, I. Kovacs, A. Gorea, and B. Julesz, A unified approach to the perception of motion, stereo, and static-flow patterns, *Behavior Research Methods, Instruments, & Computers*, Vol. 27, No. 4, pp. 419-432, 1995

[13] P. Perona and J. Malik, Scale-Space and Edge Detection Using Anisotropic Diffusion, PAMI Vol.12, No.7, July 1990.

[14] W. Phillips and W. Singer, In search of common foundations for cortical computation, *Behavioral and Brain Sciences*, Vol. 20, pp. 657-722, 1997

[15] M. Proesmans, L. Van Gool, and A. Oosterlinck, Determination of optical flow and its discontinuities using non-linear diffusion, ECCV, 295-304, may 1994

[16] M. Proesmans, E. Pauwels, and L. Van Gool, Coupled geometry-driven diffusion equations for low-level vision, in Geometry-Driven Diffusion in Computer Vision, Kluwer Academic Publishers, pp.191–228, 1994.

[17] M. Proesmans, L. Van Gool, and A. Oosterlinck, Grouping through local, parallel interactions, SPIE Int. Symp. on Optical Science, Appl. of Digital Image Processing XVIII, Vol.2564, pp.458-469, 1995

[18] J. Shah, Segmentation by non-linear diffusion. CVPR, 1991.

[19] A. Treisman and G. Gelade, A feature integration theory of attention, Cognitive Psychology, Vol. 12, pp. 97-136, 1980

[20] A. Treisman, Preattentive processing in vision, CVIP, 31, 156-177, 1985

[21] A. Treisman, P. Cavanagh, B. Fischer, V. Ramachandran, and R. von der Heydt, Form perception and attention, striate cortex and beyond, in *Visual Perception: The Neurophysiological Foundations*, Academic Press, 1990

[22] R. von der Heydt, E. Peterhans, and G. Baumgartner, Illusory contours and cortical neuron responses, Science, Vol.224, pp.1260-1262, 1984

[23] M. Wertheimer, Laws of organization in perceptual forms, in *A source-book of Gestalt Psychology*, ed. D. Ellis, Harcourt, Brace and Co., pp.71-88, 1938

[24] S. Zeki, Functional specialisation in the visual cortex: the generation of separate constructs and their multistage integration, ch. 4 in *Signal and sense, local and global order in perceptual maps*, eds. Edelman, Gall, and Cowan, pp. 85-130, Wiley-Liss, 1990

[25] S. Zeki, *A Vision of the Brain*, Blackwell Scientific Publications, 1994.

[26] S. Zucker, Early processes for orientation selection and grouping, in *From Pixels to Predicates*, ed. A. Pentland, pp.170-200, Ablex, New Jersey, 1986

Part V

Representation and Recognition

Integrating Geometric and Photometric Information for Image Retrieval

Cordelia Schmid[1], Andrew Zisserman[2], and Roger Mohr[1]

[1] INRIA Rhône-Alpes,655 av. de l'Europe, 38330 Montbonnot,France
[2] Dept of Engineering Science, 19 Parks Rd, Oxford OX1 3PJ, UK

Abstract. We describe two image matching techniques that owe their success to a combination of geometric and photometric constraints. In the first, images are matched under similarity transformations by using local intensity invariants and semi-local geometric constraints. In the second, 3D curves and lines are matched between images using epipolar geometry and local photometric constraints. Both techniques are illustrated on real images.

We show that these two techniques may be combined and are complementary for the application of image retrieval from an image database. Given a query image, local intensity invariants are used to obtain a set of potential candidate matches from the database. This is very efficient as it is implemented as an indexing algorithm. Curve matching is then used to obtain a more significant ranking score. It is shown that for correctly retrieved images many curves are matched, whilst incorrect candidates obtain very low ranking.

1 Introduction

The objective of this work is efficient image based matching. Suppose we have a large database of images and wish to retrieve images based on a supplied 'query' image. The supplied image may be identical to one in the database. However, more generally the supplied image may differ both geometrically and photometrically from any in the database. For example, the supplied image may only be a sub- or super-part of a database image, or be related by a planar projective transformation, or the images may be two views of the same scene acquired from different viewpoints.

An example application to keep in mind is the retrieval and matching of aerial views of cities. If the supplied image is acquired from a large distance, by a satellite for example, then the geometric distortions with respect to the database images are planar projective and partial overlap. However, if the supplied image is acquired at a distance where motion parallax is significant, by a low flying plane for example, then the geometric distortion can not be covered by a planar transformation and 3D effects must be taken into account. The illumination conditions (sun, clouds etc) may well also differ between the supplied and image database images.

D.A. Forsyth et al. (Eds.): Shape, Contour ..., LNCS 1681, pp. 217–233, 1999.
© Springer-Verlag Berlin Heidelberg 1999

There are two key ideas explored here. The first is that matching can be made more robust by using both geometric and photometric information. This is illustrated in two ways: first, in section 2, we describe a method of image retrieval based on local interest point descriptors which is invariant to image similarity transformations; second, in section 3, we describe a method of curve matching between images of 3D scenes acquired from different viewpoints.

The second idea is that the efficiency of indexing using interest points can be supplemented by the verification power of curve matching. This is illustrated in section 4 where it is shown that the interest point matcher provides fast access to an image database, and that the retrieved images may be ranked by the number of matched curves.

2   Image Retrieval Based on Intensity Invariants

The key contribution of several recognition systems has been a method of cutting down the complexity of matching. For example tree search is used in [2]. In indexing, the feature correspondence and search of the model database are replaced by a look-up table mechanism [10]. The major difficulty of these approaches is that they are geometry based which implies that they require CAD-like representations such as line groupings or polyhedra. These representations are not available for objects such as trees or paintings, and can often be difficult to extract even from images of suitable CAD-like objects.

An alternative approach is to not impose what has to be seen in the image (points, lines ...) but rather to use the photometric information in the image to characterise an object. Previous approaches have used histograms [18] and related measures which are less sensitive to illumination changes [5, 11].

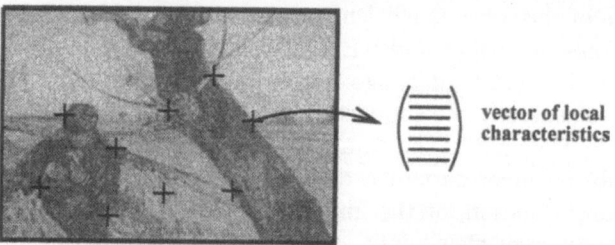

vector of local characteristics

Fig. 1. Representation of an image.

The idea reviewed here, which originally appeared in [13, 14], is to use local intensity invariants as image descriptors. These descriptors are computed at automatically detected interest points (cf. figure 1). Interest points are local features with high informational content [15] and enable differentiation between many objects. Image retrieval based on the intensity invariants can be structured efficiently as an indexing task.

Experimental results show correct retrieval in the case of partial visibility, similarity transformations, extraneous features, and small perspective deformations.

2.1   Interest Points

Computing image descriptors for each pixel in the image creates too much information. Interest points are local features at which the signal changes two-dimensionally. In the context of matching, detectors should be repeatable, that is a 3D point should be detected independently of changes in the imaging conditions. A comparison of different detectors under varying conditions [13] has shown that most repeatable results are obtained for the detector of Harris [6]. The basic idea of this detector is to use the auto-correlation function in order to determine locations where the signal changes in two directions.

Figure 2 shows interest points detected on the same scene under rotation. The repeatability rate is 92% which means that 92% of the points detected in the first image are detected in the second one. Experiments with images taken under different conditions show that the average repeatability rate is about 90%. Moreover, 50% repeatability is sufficient for the remaining process if we use robust methods.

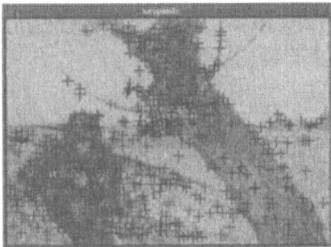 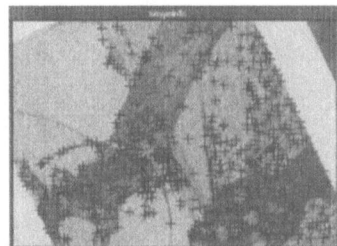

Fig. 2. Interest points detected on the same scene under rotation of the world plane. The image rotation between the left image and right image is 155 degrees. The repeatability rate is 92%.

2.2   Intensity Invariants

The neighbourhood of each interest point is described by a vector of local intensity derivatives. These derivatives are computed stably by convolution with Gaussian derivatives. In order to obtain invariance under rigid displacements in the image, differential invariants are computed [4, 9]. The invariants used here are limited to third order. The vector which contains these invariants is denoted $\mathcal{V}$. Among the components of $\mathcal{V}$ are the average luminance, the square of the gradient magnitude and the Laplacian.

To deal with scale changes, invariants are inserted into a multi-scale framework, that is the vector of invariants is computed at several scales [21]. Scale quantisation is of course necessary for a multi-scale approach. Experiments have shown that matching based on invariants is tolerant to a scale change of 20% [13]. We have thus chosen a scale quantisation which ensures that the difference between consecutive sizes is less than 20%.

Our characterisation is now invariant to similarity transformations which are additionally quasi-invariant to 3D projection [1].

2.3   Retrieval Algorithm

Vector comparison Similarity of two invariant vectors is quantified using the Mahalanobis distance d_M. This distance takes into account the different magnitude as well as the covariance matrix Λ of the components. For two vectors $\mathbf{a}$ and $\mathbf{b}$, $d_M(\mathbf{b}, \mathbf{a}) = \sqrt{(\mathbf{b} - \mathbf{a})^T \Lambda^{-1}(\mathbf{b} - \mathbf{a})}$.

In order to obtain accurate results for the distance, it is important to have a representative covariance matrix which takes into account signal noise, luminance variations, as well as imprecision of the interest point location. As a theoretical computation seems impossible to derive given realistic hypotheses, it is estimated statistically here by tracking interest points in image sequences.

The Mahalanobis distance is impractical for implementing a fast indexing technique. However, a base change makes conversion into the standard Euclidean distance d_E possible.

Image database A database contains a set $\{M_k\}$ of models. Each model M_k is defined by the vectors of invariants $\{\mathcal{V}_j\}$ calculated at the interest points of the model images. During the storage process, each vector $\mathcal{V}_j$ is added to the database with a link to the model k for which it has been computed. Formally, the simplest database is a table of couples $(\mathcal{V}_j, k)$.

Voting algorithm Recognition consists of finding the model $M_{\hat{k}}$ which corresponds to a given query image I, that is the model which is most similar to this image. For this image a set of vectors $\{\mathcal{V}_l\}$ is computed which corresponds to the extracted interest points. These vectors are then compared to the $\mathcal{V}_j$ of the base by computing: $d_M(\mathcal{V}_l, \mathcal{V}_j) = d_{l,j} \; \forall (l, j)$. If this distance is below a threshold t, the corresponding model gets a vote.

The idea of the voting algorithm is to sum the number of times each model is selected. This sum is stored in the vector $T(k)$. The model that is selected most often is considered to be the best match: the image represents the model $M_{\hat{k}}$ for which $\hat{k} = \arg\max_k T(k)$.

Figure 3 shows an example of a vector $T(k)$ in the form of a histogram. Image 0 is correctly recognised. However, other images have obtained almost equivalent scores.

Multi-dimensional indexing Without indexing the complexity of the voting algorithm is of the order of $l \times N$ where l is the number of features in the query image and N the total number of features in the data base. As N is large (about 150,000 in our tests) an indexing technique needs to be used.

Our search structure is a variant of k-d trees. Each dimension of the space is considered sequentially. Access to a value in one dimension is made through fixed size 1-dimensional buckets. Corresponding buckets and their neighbours can be directly accessed. Accessing neighbours is necessary to take into account

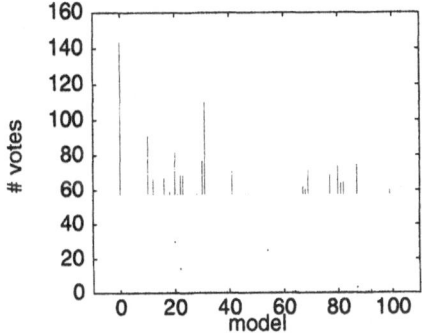

Fig. 3. Result of the voting algorithm: the number of votes are displayed for each of the 100 model images. Image 0 is recognised correctly.

uncertainty. The complexity of such an indexing is of the order of 1 (number of features of the query image).

This indexing technique leads to a very efficient recognition. The mean retrieval time for our database containing 1020 objects (see figure 6) is less than 5 seconds on a UltraSparc 30.

2.4   Semi-local Constraints

Having a large number of models or many very similar ones raises the probability that a feature will vote for several models. We therefore add the use of local shape configurations (see figure 4).

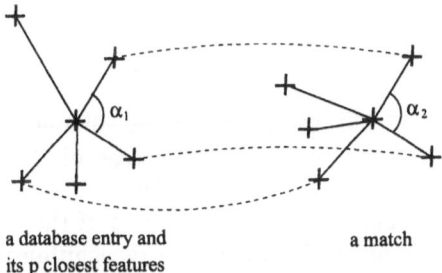

a database entry and
its p closest features   a match

Fig. 4. Semi-local constraints: neighbours of the point have to match and angles have to correspond. Note that not all neighbours have to be matched correctly.

For each feature (interest point) in the database, the p closest features in the image are selected. If we require that all p closest neighbours are matched correctly, we suppose that there is no miss-detection of points. Therefore, we require that at least 50% of the neighbours match. In order to increase the recognition rate further, geometric constraints are added. As we suppose that the transformation can be locally approximated by a similarity transformation, angles and length ratios of the semi-local shape configurations have to be consistent.

An example using the geometrical coherence and the semi-local constraints is displayed in figure 5. It gives the votes if semi-local constraints are applied to the example in figure 3. The score of the object to be recognised is now much more distinctive.

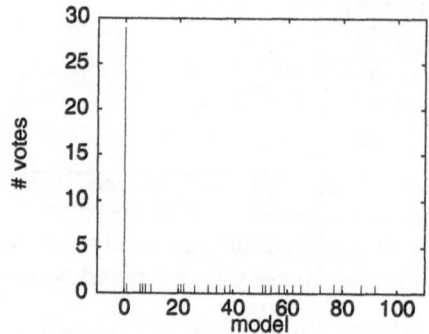

Fig. 5. Result of applying semi-local constraints: the number of votes are displayed for each model image. Semi-local constraints decrease the probability of false votes. Image 0 is recognised much more distinctively than in figure 3.

2.5   Experimental Results

Experiments have been conducted for an image database containing 1020 images. They have shown the robustness of the method to image rotation, scale change, small viewpoint variations, partial visibility and extraneous features. The obtained recognition rate is above 99% for a variety of test images taken under different conditions.

Content of the database The database includes different kinds of images such as 200 paintings, 100 aerial images and 720 images of 3D objects (see figure 6). 3D objects include the Columbia database. These images are of a wide variety. However, some of the painting images and some of the aerial images are very similar. This leads to ambiguities which the recognition method is capable of dealing with.

Fig. 6. Some images of the database. The database contains more 1020 images.

In the case of a planar 2D object, an object is represented by one image in the database. This is also the case for nearly planar objects as for aerial images. A 3D object has to be represented by images taken from different viewpoints. Images are stored in the database with 20 degrees viewpoint changes.

Recognition results Three examples are now given, one for each type of image. For all of them, the image on the right is stored in the database. It is correctly retrieved using any of the images on the left. Figure 7 shows recognition of a painting image in the case of image rotation and scale change. It also shows that correct recognition is possible if only part of an image is given.

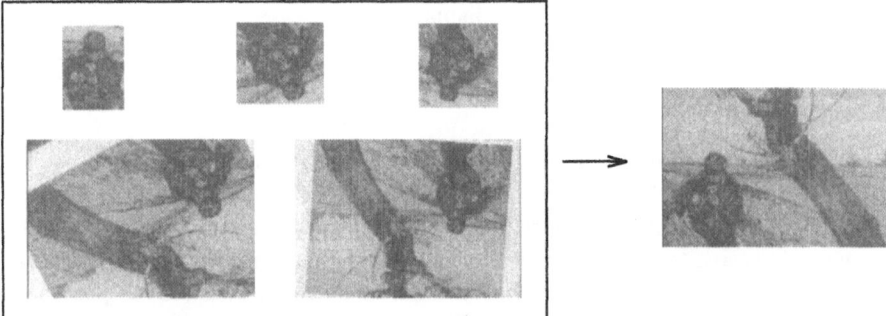

Fig. 7. The image on the right is correctly retrieved using any of the images on the left. Images are rotated, scaled and only part of the image is given.

In figure 8 an example of an aerial image is displayed. It shows correct retrieval in the case of image rotation and if part of an image is used. In the case of aerial images we also have to deal with a change in viewpoint and extraneous features. Notice that buildings appear differently because viewing angles have changed and cars have moved. Figure 9 shows recognition of a 3D object.

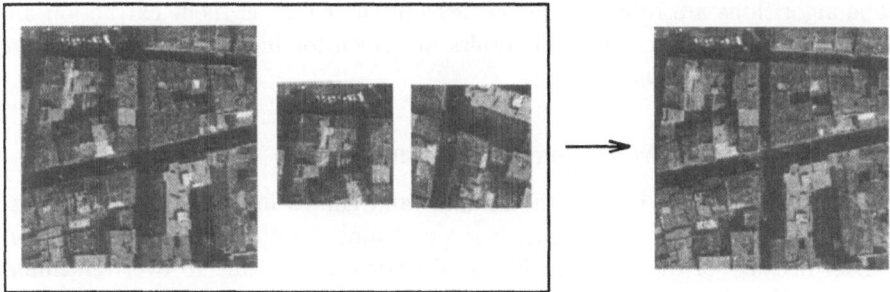

Fig. 8. The image on the right is correctly retrieved using any of the images on the left. Images are seen from a different viewpoint (courtesy of Istar).

Fig. 9. On the left the image used for retrieval and on the right the retrieved image. Matched interest points are displayed.

3 Curve Matching

In this section we review a method for line and curve matching between two perspective images of a 3D scene acquired from different viewpoints. It is assumed that 3D effects can not be ignored, and that the fundamental matrix, F, for the image pair is available. We return to how the fundamental matrix is obtained in section 4, where it is shown that the number of matched curves provides a ranking score in image retrieval.

Previous criteria for stereo curve matching have included epipolar and ordering constraints, figural continuity [12], variation in disparity [23], and consistency of curve groups [3, 7]. The method reviewed here, which originally appeared in [16, 17], is to supplement such geometric constraints by photometric constraints on the intensity neighbourhood of the curve. In particular the similarity of the curves is assessed by cross-correlation of the curve intensity neighbourhoods at corresponding points. This is described in more detail in the following section.

We will describe two algorithms: the first is applicable to nearby views; the second to wide baselines where account must be taken of the viewpoint change. The algorithms are robust to deficiencies in the curve segment extraction and partial occlusion. Experimental results are given for image pairs with varying motions between views.

3.1 Basic Curve Matching Algorithm

We suppose that we have obtained lines and curves in each image. The task is then to determine which lines/curves, if any, match. The problem is nontrivial because of the usual problems of fragmentation due to over and under segmentation. The algorithm proceeds by computing a pair-wise similarity score between each curve (or line) in the first image, and each curve (or line) in the second. The matches are decided by a winner takes all scheme based on the similarity scores.

The photometric information is employed in computing the similarity score. Consider two possibly corresponding curves c and c' in the first and second images respectively. The curves are corresponding if they are images of the same 3D curve. If they are corresponding, then a point to point correspondence on the curves may be determined using the epipolar geometry : for an image point x on the curve c, the epipolar line in the second image is $l'_e = Fx$, and this line intersects the curve c' in the point x' corresponding to x, i.e. x and x' are images of the same 3D point. Consequently, the image intensity neighbourhoods of x and x' should be similar. Then the similarity score for c and c' is determined by averaging the similarity of neighbourhoods for all corresponding points on the curves. The similarity of neighbourhoods is determined by cross-correlation.

If the curves are indeed corresponding, then the similarity score will be high — certainly in general it will be higher than the score for images of two different 3D curves. This is the basis of the winner takes all allocation of curve matches.

Matching performance The algorithm is demonstrated here on the two image pairs shown in figures 10 and 12. The ground-truth matches are assessed by hand.

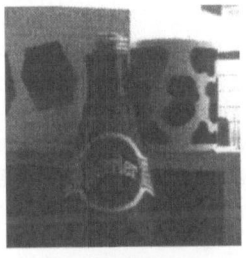  

| frame 11 | frame 15 | frame 19 |

Fig. 10. The "bottle" sequence. Frames are selected from this sequence to form image pairs. The camera motion between the frames is fairly uniform, so that the frame number is a good indicator of the distance between views.

Figure 11 shows a typical matching result for two bottle images (frame 11 and 15). Only the parts of the matched contours for which there are corresponding edgels in both views are shown. This excludes the parts of the chains along epipolar lines (where one-to-one point correspondences are not available), and also those parts of the chain which are detected as edgels in one view but not in the other. Only corresponding parts are shown for the rest of the examples in this paper.

The performance of the algorithm depends on the number and quality of the curves detected in each image. However, as shown in table 1, over a 100% variation in the curve segmentation parameters the algorithm performs extremely well. The two parameters are the minimum intensity gradient at which edgels are included in the linked contour — a high value excludes weak edges; and the minimum number of edgels in the linked chain — a high value excludes short

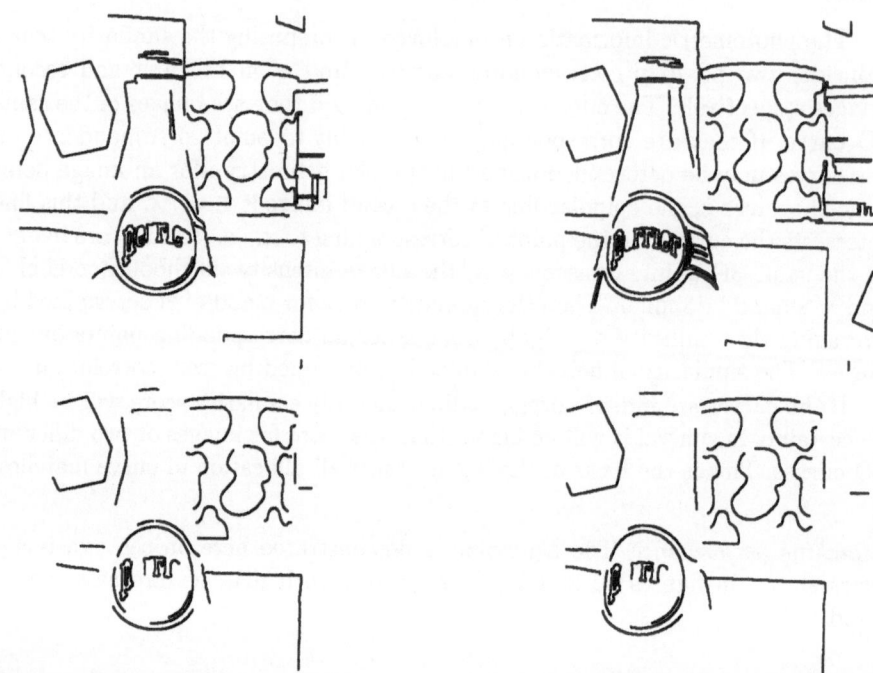

Fig. 11. Short baseline matching for frames 11 and 15 of the bottle sequence. Upper pair : The curves which are input to the matching algorithm. The contours extracted are with a gradient threshold of 60 and a length threshold of 60 pixels. There are 37 and 47 contours in the left and right images respectively. Lower pair : The 29 contours matched by the algorithm, showing only the parts which have corresponding edgels in both views. 97% of the 29 matches are correct.

chains. Most of the mismatches may be attributed to specularities on the bottle. Curves arising from specularities can be removed by a pre-process.

Figure 12 shows matched line segments for aerial images of an urban scene. 248 and 236 line segments are obtained for the left and right images, respectively, 122 of the lines are matched, and 97.5% of the 122 matches obtained are correct.

It is evident from these examples that for all choices of the parameters shown a large proportion ($> 80\%$) of the potential line/curve matches are successfully obtained.

3.2   Wide Base Line Matching Algorithm

If there is a significant rotation of the camera or a wide baseline between views, then the simple correlation of image intensities employed above will fail as a measure of the similarity of the neighbourhoods of corresponding image points on the curve. Think of a camera motion consisting of a translation parallel to the image x-axis, followed by a 90° rotation about the camera principal axis (i.e.

min intensity grad	min curve length	number curves left	number curves right	number curves matched	correct matches
60	60	37	47	29	97%
60	30	59	72	41	90%
30	30	85	85	41	85%

Table 1. Edge detection parameters and curve matching results for the short baseline algorithm applied to frames 11 and 15 of the "bottle" sequence. For the 60/60 case there is one false match, for the 60/30 case there is one false match, the other three are due to specularities; and for the 30/30 case there are two false matches, the other four are due to specularities.

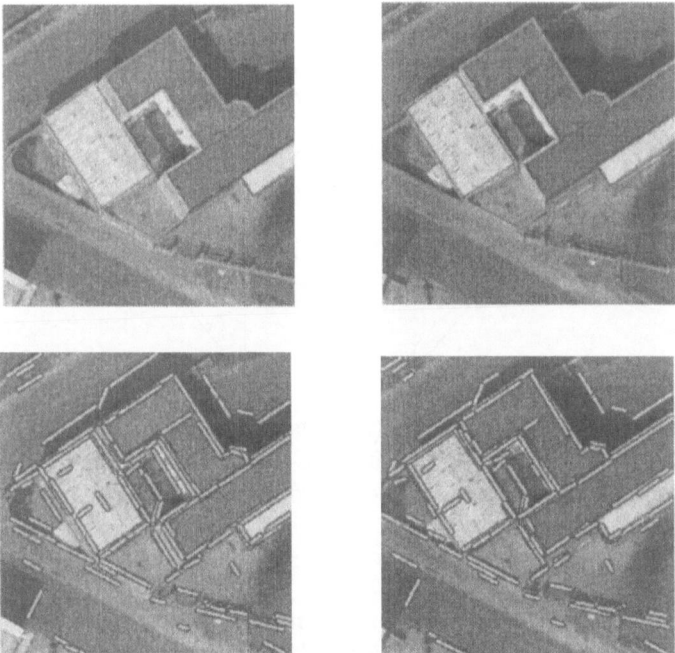

Fig. 12. Upper pair: Two aerial views of a building acquired from different viewpoints. Lower pair: Matched segments using the short range motion algorithm. 97.5% of the 122 matches shown are correct.

a rotation axis perpendicular to the image plane). The cross-correlation of the neighbourhoods will be very low if the rotation is not corrected for.

Suppose the 3D curve lies on a surface, then the rotation, and in general all perspective distortion, can be corrected for, if the cross-correlation is computed as follows: for each point in the intensity neighbourhood of $\mathbf{x}$ in the first image, compute the intersection of the back projected ray with the surface, then determine the image of this intersection in the second view. The surface defines a mapping between the neighbourhoods of $\mathbf{x}$ and $\mathbf{x}'$, and the cross-correlation is computed over points related by this map. We don't know the surface, and so don't know this map, but a very good approximation to the map is provided by the homography induced by the tangent plane of the surface at the 3D point of interest.

In the case of line matching [16] this homography can only be determined up to a one parameter family because a line in 3D only determines the plane inducing the homography up to a one parameter family. This means that for lines a one dimensional search over homographies is required. However, in the case of curve matching, the curve osculating plane provides a homography that may be used, and no search over homographies is required.

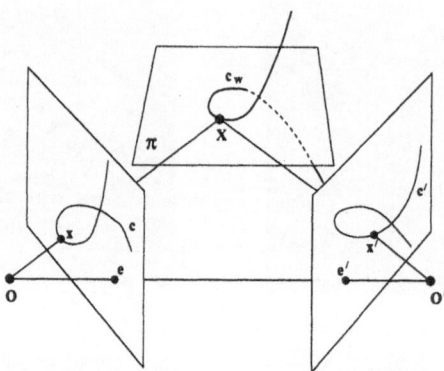

Fig. 13. The osculating plane of a (non-planar) curve varies, but is always defined in 3-space provided the curvature is not zero. This plane is determined uniquely from the image of the curve in two views. The plane induces a homography between the images.

In more detail suppose a plane curve is imaged in two views, as illustrated in figure 13, then given the tangent lines and curvatures at corresponding points, $\mathbf{x} \leftrightarrow \mathbf{x}'$, of the curves in each image, and the fundamental matrix between views; the the homography H induced by the osculating plane may be computed uniquely [17].

An example of wide baseline matching for frames 11 and 19 of the "bottle" sequence (cf. figure 10) is shown in figure 14. Of 37 and 48 curves in the left and right images, respectively, 16 are matched, and 14 of these matches are correct.

Fig. 14. Wide base line matching for frames 11 and 19 of the bottle sequence. 88% of the 16 matched contour chains are correct.

4   Image Matching Using Curve Verification

It has been shown in section 2 that given a query image, a set of possible matching images can be retrieved from an image data base. This retrieval is efficient because it is based on indexing of interest points invariants. It then remains to determine which images in the set of possible matches do indeed match the query image, and to rank the matching images. We show in this section that curve matching may be used to verify image matches and also provide a ranking. These verification tests require a multi-view relation (such as a planar projective transformation or fundamental matrix) and the point correspondences provide this.

Suppose the query and database images are views of a 3D scene acquired from different points. A first verification test is to determine if the interest point correspondences satisfy epipolar geometry constraints. This is equivalent to seeing if a large proportion of the matches are consistent with a fundamental matrix. Robust methods are now well established for simultaneously computing the fundamental matrix and a set of consistent point matches, from a set of putative point matches, many of which may be incorrect [19, 20, 24]. It can be a weak test as correspondences can accidentally line up with epipolar lines, and if there are a limited number of interest points it is always possible to obtain a consistent solution for the fundamental matrix.

If the images pass the first verification test then a fundamental matrix is available between the query and database image. A second verification test is then to use the line/curve matcher described in section 3, to see if a large proportion of the lines and curves match. The retrieved images may then be ranked by this proportion. A higher number indicating a greater overlap in viewpoints of the 3D scene.

These two verification steps are demonstrated in the following example. For the query image on the left of figure 15 there are 11 images in the database with more than 7 interest point correspondences (the minimum number required to compute the fundamental matrix). These images are determined by indexing on local intensity invariants and semi-local geometric constraints. The database images with the highest and next highest voting scores are shown on the right of figure 15 and in figure 16. The match with highest vote is actually correct, whilst the other is incorrect. Both images pass the first verification test, so a fundamental matrix is available between the query image and each of the database images. The curve matcher of section 3 is then applied to each image pair. In the case of the match with highest vote, 802 curve edgels are matched (see figure17). In the case of the match with the second highest vote no edgels are matched. The correct match is therefore very clearly identified.

Computing the fundamental matrix as a means of object recognition has been proposed before by Xu and Zhang [22] amongst others. However, combining the fundamental matrix with the additional geometric and photometric constraints provided by curves delivers a powerful image matcher: it has the indexing advantage of interest points combined with the verification strength of curves.

Fig. 15. Left: the query image. Right: the best match using intensity invariants. Interest points used during the matching process are displayed.

5   Discussion and Extensions

The interplay between geometric and photometric constraints has been illustrated at a number of points throughout this paper.

First, it has been shown that under image similarity transformations point correspondences can be established between two images simply by employing the

Fig. 16. The second best match using intensity invariants – which is in fact incorrect. Matched interest points are displayed. This match is rejected by the curve verification test.

Fig. 17. Verification test : Matched edges for the image pair in figure 15. 802 edgels have been matched.

discriminance of local intensity patterns. However, blindly voting on individual invariants is not sufficient to guarantee the correctness of the image match in database indexing. It is crucial to introduce further geometric constraints in the form of semi-local coherence on the point patterns.

Second, it has been shown that although the matching of 3D curves between two images would appear to be very ambiguous – since a point on a curve in one image could potentially match with any of the points at which its epipolar line intersects curves in the other image – the introduction of photometric constraints on the curve neighbourhoods virtually eliminates the ambiguity.

These two techniques have been combined for the application of matching images of a 3D scene from a large set of images acquired from different viewpoints. Curves, more than points, capture the structure of the scene, and the number of curve matches may be used to rank the image matches. Indeed an extension of this technique would be to detect change between the images (such as the addition or removal of a building [8]) by the spatial arrangement of the unmatched curves and lines.

In the context of image retrieval 3D effects can often be ignored, as a scene may be planar or 3D effects are not significant. The map between images is then a simple planar homography (projective transformation). This homography may be computed from the interest point correspondences. Curve matching using both geometry and photometric information can then proceed in much the same manner as that of section 3, with the homography providing the curve point correspondences.

Acknowledgements

We are grateful for discussions with Joe Mundy. The algorithms in this paper were implemented using the IUE/targetjr software packages. Financial support for this work was provided by the UK EPSRC IUE Implementation Project GR/L05969, and EU Esprit Project IMPACT. Cordelia Schmid has been partially supported by the HCM program of the European Community.

References

[1] T.O. Binford and T.S. Levitt. Quasi-invariants: Theory and exploitation. In DARPA *Image Understanding Workshop*, pages 819–829, 1993.
[2] R.C. Bolles and R. Horaud. 3DPO : A three-dimensional Part Orientation system. *The International Journal of Robotics Research*, 5(3):3–26, 1986.
[3] R.C.K. Chung and R. Nevatia. Use of monocular groupings and occlusion analysis in a hierarchical stereo system. In *Computer Vision and Pattern Recognition*, pages 50–56, 1991.
[4] L.M.T. Florack, B. ter Haar Romeny, J.J Koenderink, and M.A. Viergever. General intensity transformation and differential invariants. *Journal of Mathematical Imaging and Vision*, 4(2):171–187, 1994.
[5] B.V. Funt and G.D. Finlayson. Color constant color indexing. *Transactions on Pattern Analysis and Machine Intelligence*, 17(5):522–529, 1995.

[6] C. Harris and M. Stephens. A combined corner and edge detector. In *Alvey Vision Conference*, pages 147–151, 1988.

[7] P. Havaldar and G. Medioni. Segmented shape descriptions from 3-view stereo. In *International Conference on Computer Vision*, pages 102–108, 1995.

[8] A. Huertas and R. Nevatia. Detecting changes in aerial views of man-made structures. In *International Conference on Computer Vision*, pages 73–80, 1998.

[9] J.J. Koenderink and A.J. van Doorn. Representation of local geometry in the visual system. *Biological Cybernetics*, 55:367–375, 1987.

[10] Y. Lamdan and H.J. Wolfson. Geometric hashing: a general and efficient model-based recognition scheme. In *International Conference on Comuter Vision*, pages 238–249, 1988.

[11] K. Nagao. Recognizing 3D objects using photometric invariant. In *International Conference on Computer Vision*, pages 480–487, 1995.

[12] S.B. Pollard, J.E.W. Mayhew, and J.P. Frisby. PMF: A stereo correspondence algorithm using a disparity gradient constraint. *Perception*, 14:449–470, 1985.

[13] C. Schmid. *Appariement d'images par invariants locaux de niveaux de gris*. Thèse de doctorat, Institut National Polytechnique de Grenoble, 1996.

[14] C. Schmid and R. Mohr. Local grayvalue invariants for image retrieval. *Transactions on Pattern Analysis and Machine Intelligence*, 19(5):530–534, May 1997.

[15] C. Schmid, R. Mohr, and Ch. Bauckhage. Comparing and evaluating interest points. In *International Conference on Computer Vision*, 1998.

[16] C. Schmid and A. Zisserman. Automatic line matching across views. In *Conference on Computer Vision and Pattern Recognition*, pages 666–671, 1997.

[17] C. Schmid and A. Zisserman. The geometry and matching of curves in multiple views. In *European Conference on Computer Vision*, 1998.

[18] M.J. Swain and D.H. Ballard. Color indexing. *International Journal of Computer Vision*, 7(1):11–32, 1991.

[19] P. H. S. Torr and D. W. Murray. Outlier detection and motion segmentation. In *Proc SPIE Sensor Fusion VI*, pages 432–443, Boston, September 1993.

[20] P. H. S. Torr and A. Zisserman. Robust computation and parameterization of multiple view relations. In *International Conference on Computer Vision*, pages 727–732, 1998.

[21] A.P. Witkin. Scale-space filtering. In *International Joint Conference on Artificial Intelligence*, pages 1019–1023, 1983.

[22] G. Xu and Z. Zhang. *Epipolar Geometry in Stereo, Motion and Object Recognition*. Kluwer Academic Press, 1996.

[23] Y. Zhang and J.J. Gerbrands. Method for matching general stereo planar curves. *Image and Vision Computing*, 13(8):645–655, October 1995.

[24] Z. Zhang, R. Deriche, O. Faugeras, and Q.T. Luong. A robust technique for matching two uncalibrated images through the recovery of the unknown epipolar geometry. *Artificial Intelligence*, 78:87–119, 1995.

Towards the Integration of Geometric and Appearance-Based Object Recognition

Joe Mundy and Tushar Saxena

General Electric Corporate
Research and Development
Niskayuna, NY, USA

1   Overview

Progress in object recognition has been relatively slow over the last five years or so. Despite the considerable progress in our understanding due to research in appearance-based methods, invariants and generic models our ability to recognize man-made and natural objects in cluttered scenes with complex illumination has not significantly increased.

A new emphasis will be necessary to gain a substantial increase in recognition performance. There are currently two main themes at work: 1) Theoretical models of object appearance, largely based on geometry and 2) Empirical models derived from image samples, based on direct representations of intensity. Recognition systems based on CAD-derived geometric models[2] is an example of the first approach, and learned models using pattern recognition methods, e.g., SLAM[6], is an example of the second paradigm. Neither approach alone can solve the problem of recognizing an object in a cluttered scene under complex illumination and shadows.

Our current formal models of the world do not account for the full complexity of object appearance due to effects such as inter-reflections, low resolution and complex surface reflectivity functions. At the same, time it is not feasible to collect examples of all the situations in which an object may be viewed. Even a few variables such as viewpoint and illumination direction require tens of thousands of significant empirical sampling conditions. That is, an object's appearance is significantly different at each observation state to warrant including it in the appearance space. When occlusion with other objects is taken into account, the data collection problem becomes intractable.

Access to intensity surface descriptions is much more tractable today with modern image segmentation algorithms which preserve most of the surface topology inherent in the image projection. We need to exploit this topology to define object surfaces and their appearance through physical models rather than through high dimensional nearest-neighbor view spaces. Through rapid advances in projective photogrammetry over the last five years, the geometric properties of image projection are reasonably well-understood. We need a renewed attack on efficient acquisition of surface properties and the exploitation of these properties in the recognition process.

D.A. Forsyth et al. (Eds.): Shape, Contour ..., LNCS 1681, pp. 234–245, 1999.

In the discussion to follow, a preliminary set of experiments are described to illustrate the representation and segmentation approach implied by the integration of geometric and photometric attributes.

2   Edge-Based Regionization

2.1   Regions Derived from Edgel Boundaries

The reflectance properties of a surface are best exploited in terms of regions defined by various low-order models of intensity variation. The segmentation approach is based on the fact that modern edge detectors can achieve nearly perfect detection of intensity discontinuities. The remaining locations in the image are accounted for by relatively slowly varying intensity model. Here we consider linear and quadratic variations, i.e., planar and quadric intensity surface models.

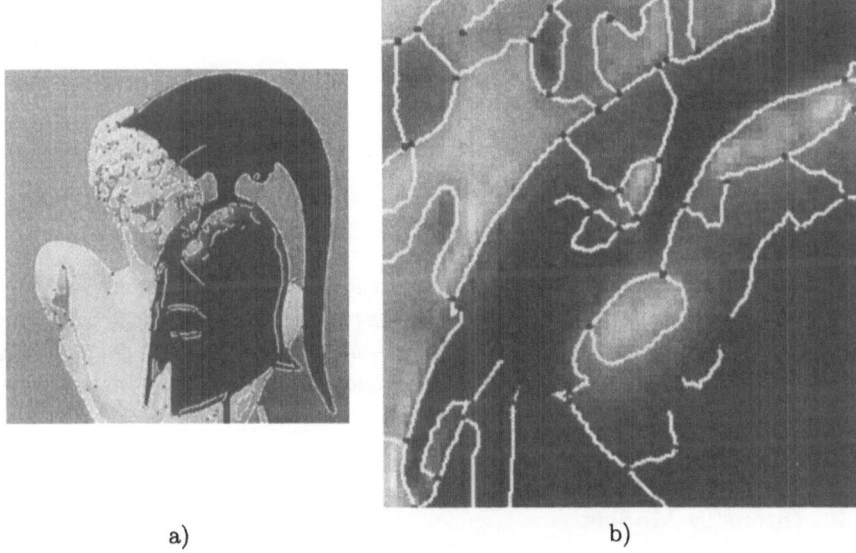

a)   b)

Fig. 1. *a) A traditional edge detection boundary representation of a scene. In b) a close-up shows that most discontinuous intensity events have been captured by the edge detector with good topological performance.*

By this approach we achieve the traditional accuracy and completeness of surface boundaries while producing an effective description of the interior intensity variation of uniform regions. The traditional edge segmentation is shown in Figure 1. In Figure 2, the boundaries in Figure 1 have been polygonized and then regions formed by joining near boundary endpoints using a constrained triangulation[1]. The regions can support a multiply-connected face topology to account for discontinuous intensity variations within a large region. The triangulation edges are retained if there is edgel support.

This edge-based regionization is still quite conservative, as it should be, since further merging of regions should be carried under specific models for intensity surface variation.

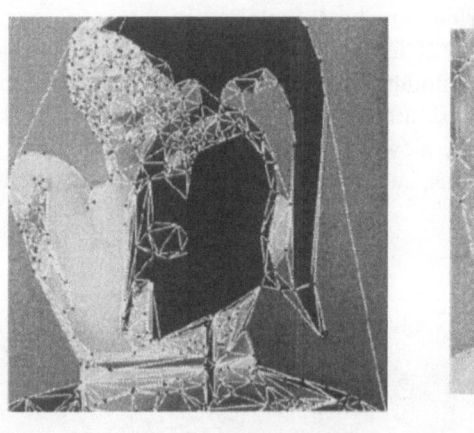
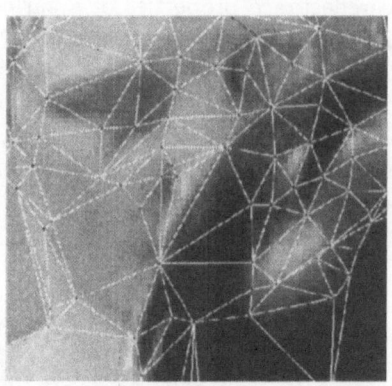

a)   b)

Fig. 2. *a) Regions are formed by closing edgel-derived boundaries using constrained triangulation. The region boundaries are a combination of polygonized edgel chains and Delunay triangle edges. In b) a close-up shows that highlights on the helmet surface have created small regions. Similarly, regions are formed due to shadowing and reflectance variations over Hermes' face.*

2.2   Intensity Models

It is desirable to form larger regions based on a theoretical model for intensity variation. Overall, such models have been largely centered on the Lambertian reflectance function, since it has agreeable mathematical properties and closely links surface geometry with appearance. However, there is considerable scepticism within the vision community that a Lambertian model is realistic.

In this paper, we sidestep the issue for the moment and consider that any robust recovery of intensity region properties will only be practical for low-order models. In this work we consider representing the variation over a region as

---

[1] The authors are grateful to Dani Lischinski of the Hebrew University of Jerusalem for providing the triangulation code.

either linear or quadratic. That is, the intensity surface is modeled as either: $I(x, y) = Io + ax + by$ or $I(x, y) = Io + ax^2 + bxy + cy^2 + dx + ey$. Such models have been previously used in the so-called *facet* edge detection approaches of Beaudet[1] and Haralick [3].

This representation does not make any commitment about the reflectance model, but assumes that a given reflectance model produces slowly varying intensity for smooth surfaces and relatively uniform illumination. It can be seen that violations of this assumption, such as specular highlights, are already captured in terms of the discontinuities of the edgel boundaries as shown in Figure 1 b).

As an example of region extraction based on intensity surface fitting, consider the simple scene shown in Figure 3. In Figure 3 the intensity is not constant

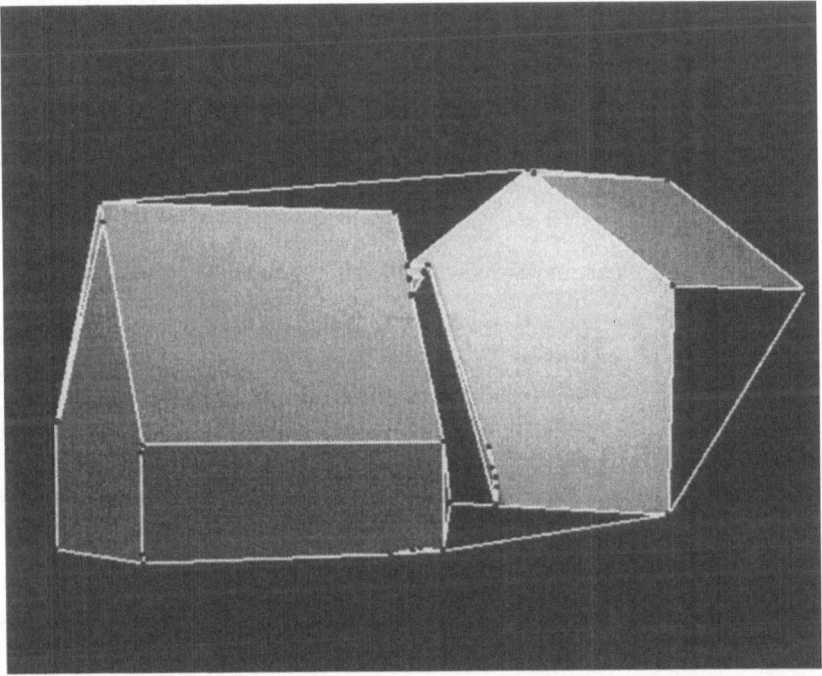

Fig. 3. *The region segmentation of planar surfaces. The regions are defined by intensity discontinuities with merging based on a planar approximation to the intensity surface.*

across each planar face, but varies slowly due to gradual variations in illumination, or abruptly due to shadows. However, a planar model accounts nearly completely for the intensity variations due to illumination. This result is demonstrated in Figure 4 It is not surprising that a low order model can account for most of the region intensity variation of such a simple scene as Figure 3. Also

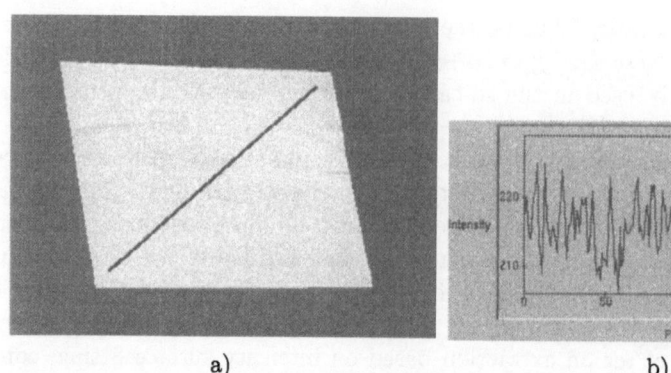

a)   b)

Fig. 4. *a) One of the faces from Figure 3 after subtraction of the planar intensity model. Note that the residual is small, emphasizing subtle saw marks in the wood imposed during the fabrication of the house shapes. The residual intensity variation along the indicated line is shown in b).*

there remains the issue of how this segmentation description would vary with viewpoint.

2.3   Variation of Intensity Models with Viewpoint

A set of views of the Hermes statue, first shown in Figure 1, will be used to illustrate the effect of viewpoint variation on the intensity model. These views are shown in Figure 5. The region shape varies relatively slowly and the residual intensity error is also relatively small. This result demonstrates that the shape interpretation of surface is captured in the higher order terms. However the variation of the underlying low order variation is reasonably continuous with respect to viewpoint, indicating that the major variation is global. This variation is shown in Figure 6.

2.4   Remarks

This result is consistent with the experience in appearance-based systems like SLAM[6]. That is, the main variation in intensity across views is captured in low order functional approximations. In the case of SLAM, these functions are eigenvectors of the covariance matrix of image intensity arrays which bound the object in each view. Here, the approximation is determined from pixels which are interior to a region boundary determined by image discontinuities.

It can be argued that using interior of segment-able regions is a much more salient representation and does not depend on having an easily partition-able background to the object. In this approach, the same boundary which is used to define geometric information about the object is used to derive the intensity distribution. As shown in the next section, the image viewpoint can be derived from

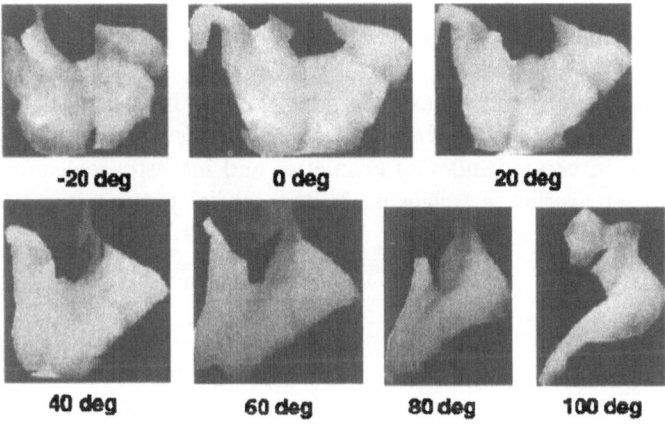

Fig. 5. *A large region extracted from a series of images of the Hermes statue. The illumination was fixed and the statue was rotated on a turntable. The angular positions in degrees are indicated. The intensity of the region in this figure is the residual value after subtraction of a global planar fit.*

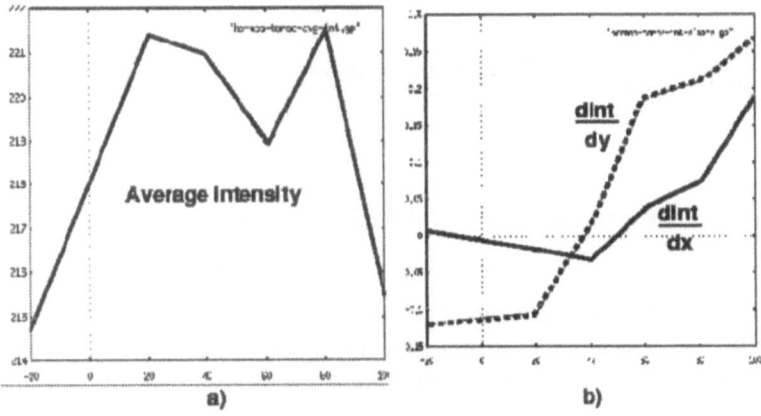

Fig. 6. *The variation of the global fit parameters with respect to viewpoint. In a) the average intensity over the region is derived from the planar fit by integrating within the region boundary. In b) the x,y components of the plane normal are shown.*

the boundary geometry and thus each intensity representation can be indexed in order to participate in verification.

3   Affine Indexing

Given a set of regions which have smoothly varying intensity, the next issue is to define an indexing scheme based on these properties. The ultimate goal is to produce an integrated index of geometric and intensity measurements. One approach to integration is suggested by the special properties of affine image projection.

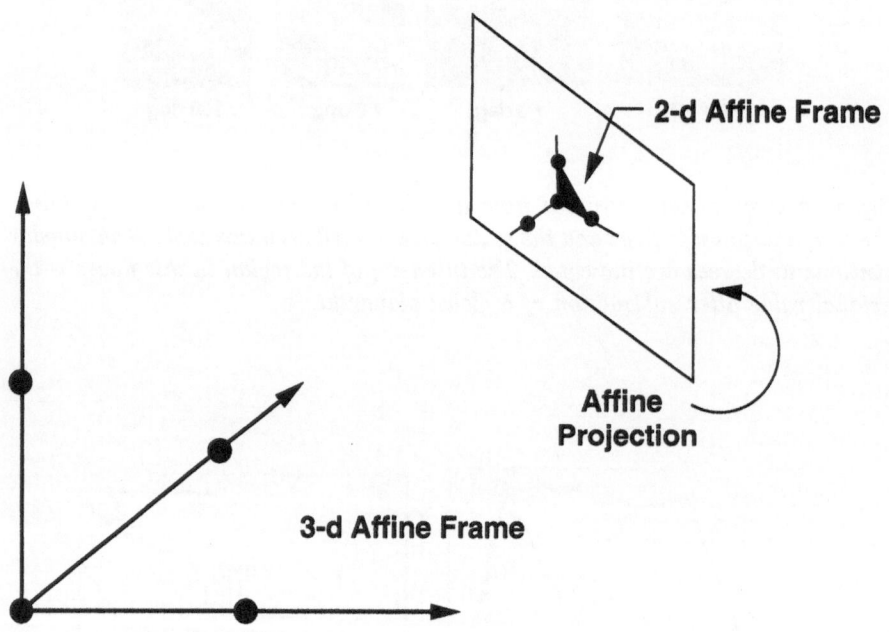

Fig. 7. *The 3-d and 2-d affine coordinate frames.*

Consider Figure 7 which shows the projection of a 3-d affine frame (tetrahedron) onto an image plane. It is assumed that this projection is carried out by an affine camera, where the projection matrix is of the form,

$$T = \begin{bmatrix} t_{11} & t_{12} & t_{13} & t_{14} \\ t_{21} & t_{22} & t_{23} & t_{24} \\ 0 & 0 & 0 & t_{34} \end{bmatrix}$$

Under this projection, all effects of camera calibration can be eliminated by expressing images features in a 2-d affine coordinate frame [5]. Thus, the only variations of object appearance in this representation are due to changes in viewpoint. For the affine camera, the affine coordinates of an image projection vary with the orientation of the view direction. That is, the center of the camera can be considered at infinity where only its position on the view-sphere affects the projected geometric structure. Thus, two degrees of freedom specify the viewing conditions.

On the other hand, any 3-d structure can be placed in a affine canonical frame consisting of four points. Also, the relationship between any 3-d structure and its 2-d affine projection is unaffected by a general affine transformation of space, since everything is expressed in affine coordinates to begin with. It follows that the two unknown parameters of the affine camera can be recovered from the projected image position of the fourth point in the 3-d canonical frame.

The key point is that the affine camera is known *independent of object structure*, however it is necessary to establish four correspondences between as stored object model and its projection. If these correspondences are known, then the entire view of an object can be indexed according to the camera viewpoint as well as the affine coordinates of the projected structure.

This indexing scheme is similar to that of Jacobs[4], except that model indices are directly based on the known camera viewpoint. Jacobs carried out a nearest neighbor search in a set of 1-d decompositions of the index space. By contrast, our approach is similar in flavor to invariant model indexing where the index directly accesses a stored representation of the image features. However, unlike a viewpoint invariant description, it is necessary to acquire a sufficient number of views of the object to account for the variation in object appearance under camera motion.

To evaluate this concept on segmented boundaries a series of views of a Greek helmet were acquired and segmented using the scheme described in Section 2. The segmentations are shown in Figure 8. The two affine orientation parameters are shown in Figure 9. The results are in good agreement up to about 80° where the region used to derive the affine parameters is seen nearly edge on. This experiment shows that there is a functional relationship between the affine frame coordinates and camera viewpoint. One issue to be considered in proceeding is that the affine coordinates, a_0 and a_1 are relatively invariant to viewpoint over the range $-10^o \rightarrow 40^o$. This slow variation is good from an indexing point of view, but bad for inverting the functional relationship to determine Euclidean camera pose. This capability is used in one approach to the integration of intensity attributes in the next section.

4   Initial Thoughts about Intensity Indexing

As described in Section 2.3 it is feasible to characterize the intensity of an edge-segmented region with low order polynomials and further the coefficients of these approximations vary more or less continuously with viewpoint. In the case of the affine index just described, the viewpoint relative to the object 3-d reference frame can be determined from a single image measurement, independent of structure.

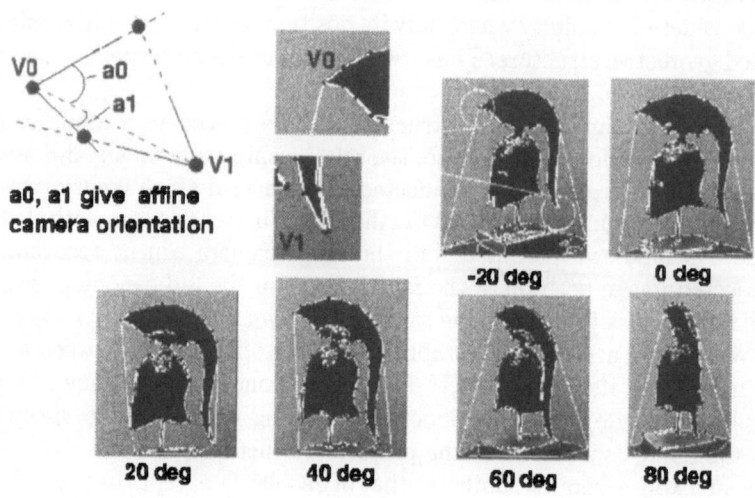

Fig. 8. *A series of boundary segmentations of a Greek helmet. The boundaries are found using the algorithm in Section 2. An affine frame is defined by V_0 and V_1 as defined in the upper left corner of the figure. The two vertices and associated line segments define coordinates from which affine camera orientation can be derived.*

Thus, it is possible to index the intensity fitting coefficients for a given object and illumination direction according to the viewpoint and corresponding region segmentation. In this very preliminary investigation, the intensity attributes are not used as an index directly, but can be used to verify the success of a model retrieved by affine geometric indexing. Ultimately the complete approach would derive invariant surface attributes from the region approximations.

To illustrate this idea, the three parameter model of Oren and Nayar [7] is used to fit the variation of region intensity with object orientation. In the experiments throughout this paper, the object is rotated on a turntable and the relative illumination and camera directions are kept fixed. Thus, the observed region intensity variations are due to both changes in illumination and viewing direction relative to the local surface normal.

The Oren-Nayar theory is derived from a model for surface reflectance based on randomly oriented facets. Using this model, the surface roughness and illumination density was adjusted to give the best fit to the data. The result is shown in Figure 10. The parameters are: ρ, the surface albedo; σ the suface roughness measured as variance of surface slope; and E_0 the incident illumination intensity.

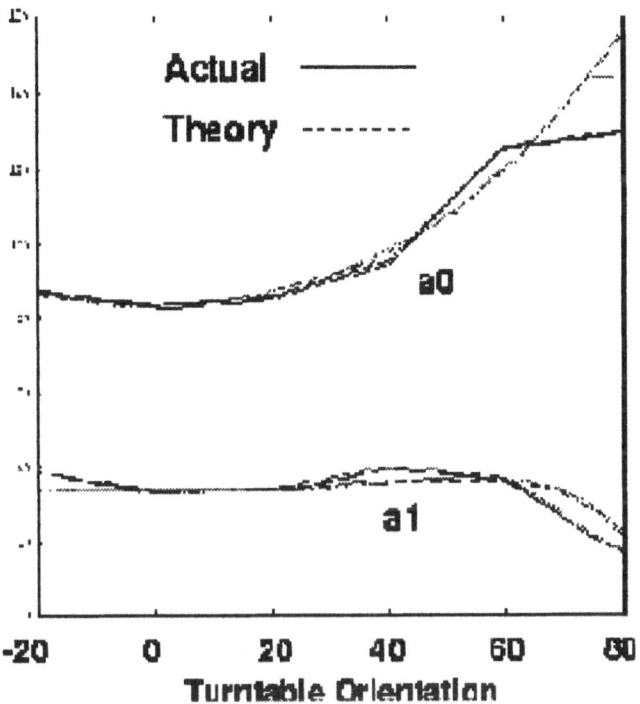

Fig. 9. *The affine orientation parameters derived from the images in Figure 8. The helmet pose about the vertical axis was acquired from the turntable position gauge. This orientation was projected into the camera view plane and used to construct the values of a_0 and a_1, the local affine frame coordinates. The theoretical vs experimental values are shown here.*

The agreement is excellent, however the model has sufficient degrees of freedom, so that a good fit in this simple case is not surprising. Also, a question can be raised about the practicality of assuming a uniform and fixed illumination density. The next step in this line of development is to use adjacent regions to derive more invariant descriptions using the model.

For example, consider three adjacent regions, or more generally, three regions that can be identified during the indexing process each with a general orientation. Let it be assumed that Oren-Nayar reflectance models are available for each region. As just shown, these reflectance models can be derived empirically by fitting observed region intensity data. If it is further assumed that the illumination is constant in both direction and magnitude over the regions, then the illumination intensity and direction can be derived from the observed image region intensities.

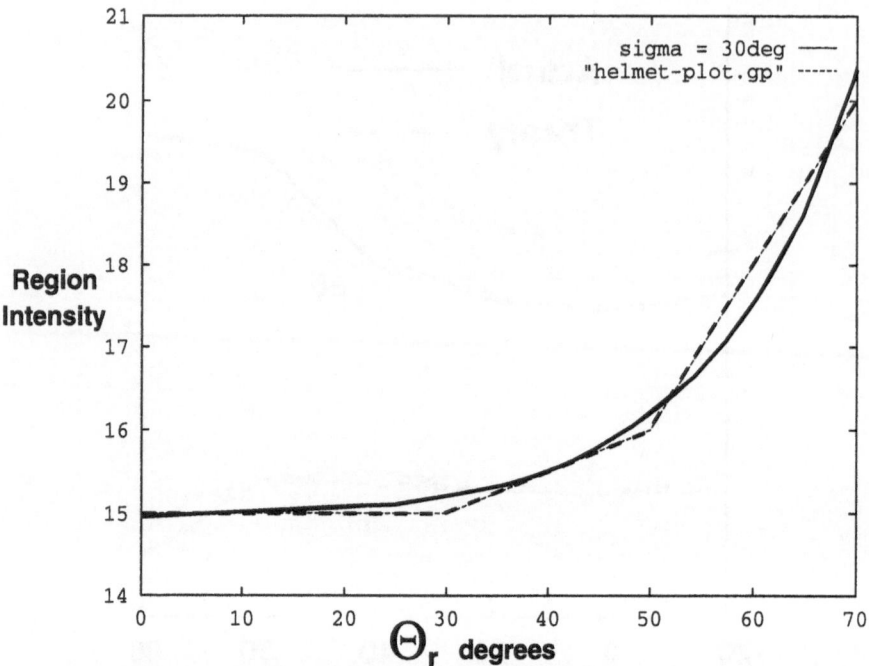

Fig. 10. *A comparison of the Oren-Nayar model with the observed variation of average region intensity. The region intensity is derived from sequence of images shown in Figure 8. The average is derived from a planar approximation to the region intensity of the helmet plume. The Oren-Nayar model parameters for the best fit are $\rho = .9$ and $\sigma = 30°$. The incident illumination intensity, E_0 was set to align the data at $\Theta_r = 0°$*

This process is enabled by the affine indexing process of Section 3 since the orientation of the camera is known in an invariant affine frame relative to the regions. This affine camera orientation can be linked to the actual Euclidean orientation, given a calibrated image acquisition process, such as a turntable. The relative intensity of a fourth region can then be used as a secondary index, or as a validation of purely geometric indexing.

5   Discussion

A few suggestions have been offered as to how one might combine theoretical models of geometry and illumination with the empirical appearance models for recognition. The affine indexing model described above might be considered a form of *geometric appearance* where the object geometry is captured in the variation of affine image invariants over a set of views. These variations can be parametrized with respect to viewpoint in exactly the same manner as the principle components of object image views, i.e. the approach in SLAM.

Further, it is proposed that an image segmentation, based on topologically accurate region boundaries is a better representation for the intensity appearance of a structure than the eigenfunctions of intensity variability over viewpoint. This representation is keyed to the configuration of the object and its internal structure rather than the basis functions derived from principle components. The use of edge detection insures accurate placement of geometric features. Modern edge detectors can place boundaries to sub-pixel accuracy.

These illustrations merely suggest the feasibility of the integration of intensity and geometric representations. The real confirmation of the approach will require the development of a full object recognition system based on such an integration. It will be necessary to show that the addition of intensity-derived indexing and validation attributes produce a significant enhancement to performance.

References

[1] P.R. Beaudet. Rotational invariant image operators. In *International Conference on Pattern Recognition*, pages 579–583, 1978.

[2] W. Eric L. Grimson. *Object Recognition by Computer: The Role of Geometric Constraints*. The MIT Press, Cambridge, Massachusetts, London, England, 1990.

[3] R. M. Haralick and L. G. Shapiro. *Computer and Robot Vision*, volume 1. Addison-Wesley, 1992.

[4] D. Jacobs. Space efficient 3-d model indexing. In *Proceedings of the International Conference on Computer Vision and Pattern Recognition*, pages 439–444, 1992.

[5] Joseph L. Mundy and Andrew Zisserman, editors. *Geometric Invariance in Computer Vision*. MIT Press, 1992.

[6] H. Murase and S. Nayar. Learning and recognition of 3d objects from appearance. *The International Journal of Computer Vision*, 14(1):5–24, 1995.

[7] M. Oren and S. Nayar. Generalization of the lambertian model and implications for machine vision. *The International Journal of Computer Vision*, 14(3):227–253, 1995.

Recognizing Objects Using Color-Annotated Adjacency Graphs

Peter Tu, Tushar Saxena, and Richard Hartley

GE - Corporate Research and Development,
P.O. Box 8, Schenectady, NY, 12301.
T. Saxena : CMA Consulting Services, Schenectady, NY 12309

Abstract. We introduce a new algorithm for identifying objects in cluttered images, based on approximate subgraph matching. This algorithm is robust under moderate variations in the camera viewpoints. In other words, it is expected to recognize an object (whose model is derived from a template image) in a search image, even when the cameras of the template and search images are substantially different. The algorithm represents the objects in the template and search images by weighted adjacency graphs. Then the problem of recognizing the template object in the search image is reduced to the problem of approximately matching the template graph as a subgraph of the search image graph. The matching procedure is somewhat insensitive to minor graph variations, thus leading to a recognition algorithm which is robust with respect to camera variations.

1 Outline

The present paper describes a method for finding objects in images. The typical situation is that one has an image of the object sought – the template image. The task is to find the object in a new image, taken from a somewhat different viewpoint, possibly under different lighting. The method used is based on approximate attributed graph matching. As a first step, the image is segmented into regions of approximately constant color. The geometrical relationship of the segmented colored regions is represented by an attributed graph, in which each segment corresponds to a vertex in the graph, and proximate regions are joined by an edge. Vertices are annotated with the size, shape and color of the corresponding segment. Finding an object in a new image then comes down to an approximate graph-matching problem in which a match is sought in the new image for a subgraph approximating the one corresponding to the sought object. The graph matching can only be approximate, because of the inexactness of the segmentation process, and the changed aspect of the object, due to change of lighting, viewpoint, and possible partial occlusion.

There has been much previous work in the area of recognition from color. An important body of work is concerned with what has been broadly called color constancy [27, 12, 9, 11, 17, 18, 10, 4]. The concern of such papers is to recognize an object based on its color alone. Typically eigenspace or histogram techniques

D.A. Forsyth et al. (Eds.): Shape, Contour ..., LNCS 1681, pp. 246–263, 1999.

or similar approaches are used to characterize an object. These methods rely on the distribution of colors in a usually vaguely defined region of an image. Under different conditions of lighting, the histogram, or eigenspace region or surface will vary. Variously sophisticated models have been proposed for this changeability, ranging from very simple models such as simple intensity variability ([27]) to affine color transformations ([18]) and physical atmospheric illumination models ([19]). Generally such papers are not specifically concerned with locating an object to be recognized in an image, or in finding an object that occupies only a small part of an image. An exception is [19] in which recognition is at the level of individual pixels. In addition, any geometrical information about the relative locations of different colored parts of the image is usually lost (for instance in histogramming techniques).

Similar in concept, a recent popular approach to recognition has been the appearance based learning method of Nayar and Murase, also Lin and Lee ([22, 25, 26, 21]). This approach relies uses surfaces in an eigenspace to represent the views of an object under different poses. The method becomes increasingly complex as the number of degrees of freedom of pose and lighting increase. Once more, such methods are best suited for recognition of an object that constitutes a complete image. Searching for a candidate object in a complex scene is treated as a separate issue.

An alternative line of attack on object recognition has been to use the geometry of the object. Typically, this involves edge detection and grouping, followed by some sort of indexing or template matching based on geometry. Among many possible references we cite one ([32]). The present work seeks to amalgamate the color constancy and geometric approaches to object recognition. Previous work in amalgamating geometry and color includes [23, 5, 24, 7, 30, 6]. Earlier work of Hanson and Riseman ([15, 16]) lays a foundation for this approach. Among this cited work the approach of [5] is related to ours by dealing with blobs, which are ellipsoidal areas of consistent color. Similarly, in our approach, regions of an image segmented obtained from segmentation are represented by their principal moments, effectively treating them as ellipses.

2   Extracting Object Faces from Images

The first step in the algorithm is the division of the image into faces (or regions) of approximately constant color. The face extraction process proceeds in the three basic steps, which will be outlined in subsequent sections.

2.1   Detecting Approximate Region Boundaries

First the boundaries (that is edges) hypothesized to enclose the region are detected. As a first step in this process, the edges in the image are detected using a Canny-style edge detector, and line segments are fitted to the resulting edgels. It is reasonable to assume that the region boundaries pass through the resulting line segments, since under our assumptions, a face boundary will produce

Fig. 1. Left : *The result of edge detection in a template image containing a cup.*
Right : *The result of adjusting lines fitted to the cup edge segmentation.*

a discontinuity in the intensity and color variation of the enclosed region, and
thus show up during edge detection. However, typically, these boundaries are
detected in the form of numerous small broken line segments (see figure 1(left)).
It is difficult to identify the exact geometry of the enclosed faces directly from
these line segments. To improve the boundary geometries, we use some heuristics
to further process the line segments. Some of these heuristics are:

- Merge lines that are nearly collinear and within some proximity threshold of
  each other. This is useful in creating a single edge which may have broken
  up into various smaller (but nearly parallel) segments during edge detection.
- Create T-Junctions from pairs of lines, one of which ends close to the inside
  of, and away from the endpoints of, the other. This is useful in recreating
  intersections of edges on occluding objects. This will help in obtaining well-
  defined faces on both objects.
- Intersect lines whose end-points are close to each other, and the lines are at
  obtuse angles. This recreates the corners of an object which may not have
  been detected during segmentation.

Figure 1(right) shows the result of applying these heuristics on the segmentation
of the image in figure 1(left). In our experience, these heuristics aid significantly
in correcting most of the degenerate boundary segments.

2.2   Estimating Initial Uniform Regions: Constrained Triangulation

Using the boundary line segments from the previous step, we now generate an
initial partition of the image into triangles of uniform intensity and color. This is
accomplished by a *constrained triangulation* of the boundary lines. A constrained
triangulation produces a set of triangles which join nearest points (end-points of
the lines), but respect the constraining boundary lines. That is, each boundary
line segment will be an edge of some triangle.

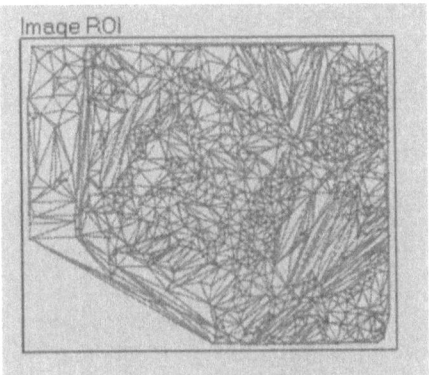 

Fig. 2. *Constrained triangulation on the adjusted cup lines. On the left, the triangles only; on the right the triangles superimposed on the image.*

Since all triangles are formed from the end-points and lines on the boundaries of the faces, each triangle lies completely inside a face. Moreover, since these triangles cover the whole image, each face can be represented by a union of a finite number of these triangles. As an example, see the result of constrained triangulation on an image segmentation in figure 2.

2.3   Extracting Object Faces: Region Merging

In the next step, a region-merging procedure is used to incrementally generate the visible object faces in the image. Starting with the triangular regions from the constrained triangulation, neighboring regions are successively merged if they have at least one of the following properties:

1. **Similar color intensities:** Two adjacent regions are merged if the difference between their average color intensity vectors is less than a threshold. This is a reasonable merging property since neighboring faces in objects are at angles to each other, and are likely to cast images of different intensities. As a refinement of this method, one could merge two regions based on a decision of which of two hypotheses (the two regions are separate; the two regions should form a single region) is preferable based on the color statistics of the regions. In addition, a linear or more complex color gradient over a face could be modeled. These methods have been suggested in [15, 16] but we have not tried them yet.

2. **Unsupported bridge:** Two adjacent regions are merged if the percentage of edges common between them, which are *unsupported*, is larger than a threshold. An edge is said to be supported if a specified percentage of its pixels belong to an edgel detected by the edge detector. Merging based on this property will ensure the inclusion of those boundary segments which were missing from the set of line segments derived from edgels. This is demonstrated by

the fact that a number of non-constraining lines in the triangulation end up being found supported.

After each merge, the properties (size and color) of the new, larger region are recomputed from the properties of the two regions being merged.

Fig. 3. *Faces of the cup (left) and urban scene (right) extracted by our algorithm.*

The merging iterations continue until the color intensities of each pair of neighboring regions are sufficiently different, and most of the edges common between them have support from the segmentation. Under our assumptions about the nature of the objects and the illumination, it is reasonable to assume that the resulting regions are likely to be images of the faces of objects pictured in the image. As an illustration, see figure 3 which shows the faces extracted using our algorithm.

The result of the segmentation and merging algorithm is a set of regions with associated color (RGB) values. Typically, there remain small narrow regions lying along region boundaries. These are removed from consideration, since they do not represent meaningful faces in the image, but are caused by color transition across a boundary. Similarly, any residual very small regions are removed. Thus, small regions less that about 30 square pixels sometimes remain after the region merging, since slight variations of color have prevented them from being merged with adjacent large regions.

3   Deriving Graph Representations of Objects

Once all the object faces in the image have been generated, they are represented as a graph. To capture the relative placements of the objects in the image, and the topology of the scene, an adjacency graph of the faces in the scene is constructed.

Each vertex in the graph represents a region, and is annotated with the shape, position and color attributes of the region. Shape is represented by the moment matrix of the region, from which one may derive the area of the region, along with the orientation and ratio of the principal axes of the region. In effect, the region is being represented as an ellipse. This shape representation is of course an extremely rough representation of the shape of the region. However, it is also quite forgiving of variations of shape along the boundaries, or even a certain degree of fragmentation of the region. Since matching will not be done simply on the basis of a region-to-region match, but rather on matching of region clusters, this level of shape representation has proven to be adequate. More precise shape estimates have been considered, however. Their use must be dictated by the degree of accuracy and repeatability of the segmentation process, however. The color of the region is represented by an RGB color vector. Other representations are of course possible, and have been tried by other authors ([15, 16]).

Because of the possibility of regions being fragmented or regions being improperly merged, it turns out to be inappropriate to use edges in the graph to represent physically adjacent regions. The adjacency graph generated by such a rule is too sensitive to minor variations in the image segmentation. Instead the choice was made of joining each vertex to the vertices representing the N closest regions in the segmented image. A value of $N = 8$ was chosen. Thus, each vertex in the graph has 8 neighbors.

4   The Three-Tier Matching Method

The reduction of the image to an attributed graph represents a significant simplification. The graph corresponding to a typical complicated image (the search image) may contain up to 500 or so vertices, whereas the graph corresponding to an object to be found (the template) may contain 50 vertices or so. Thus a complete one-on-one comparison may be carried out in quite a short time.

The search is carried out in three phases, as follows:

1. **Local comparison.** A one-to-one comparison of each pair of vertices is carried out. Each pair of vertices, one from the *template graph* and one from the *search graph* is assigned a score based on similarity of shape, size and color, within rather liberal bounds.
2. **Neighborhood comparison.** The local neighborhood consisting of a vertex and its neighbors in the template graph is compared with a local neighborhood in the search graph. A score is assigned to each such neighborhood pairing based on compatibility, and the individual vertex-pair scores.
3. **Global matching.** A complete graph-matching algorithm is carried out, in which promising matches identified in the stage-2 matching are pieced together to identify a partial (or optimally a complete) graph match.

Each of these steps will be described in more detail in later sections. The idea behind this multi-stage matching approach is to avoid ruling out possible matches at an early stage, making the matching process robust to differences in the segmentation and viewpoint. This approach is motivated from the scoring method used in tennis matches in which a three-tier scoring system is used – game, set match. At each stage, slight advantages are amplified. A player who wins 55% of points will win 62% of games, 82% of sets and 95.7% of matches. Thus, the better player will (almost) always win despite temporary setbacks. In the same way the three-tier graph matching method provides a robust way of converging to the correct match, despite local fluctuations of region-to-region scoring.

4.1   Local Matching

In local matching, individual vertex pairs are evaluated. Each pair is assigned a score based on shape and color. Recall, that each region is idealized as an ellipse. Shapes are compared on the basis of their size and eccentricity. Up to a factor of 2 difference in size is allowed without significant penalty. This allows for different scales in the two images, within reasonable bounds.

Because of different lighting conditions, colors may differ between two images. The most significant change in color, however is due to a brightness difference. To allow for this, colors are normalized before being compared. The color of a region is represented by a vector, and vectors that differ by a constant multiple are held to represent the same color.

The cost of a local match between two vertices is denoted by C_{local}.

4.2   Neighborhood Matching

Each vertex (here called core) in the graph has eight neighbors representing the eight closest regions. In comparing the local neighborhood of one core vertex v_0 with the local neighborhood of a potential match v_0', an attempt is made to pair the neighbor nodes of v_0 with those of v_0'. In this matching the order of the neighbor vertices must be preserved. Thus, let $v_1, v_2, \ldots, v_n$ be the neighbors of one core vertex, given in cyclic angular order around the core, and let $v_1', \ldots, v_m'$ be the neighbors of a potential match core, similarly ordered. One seeks subsets S of the indices $\{1, \ldots, n\}$ and S' of the indices $\{1, \ldots, m\}$ and a one-to-one mapping $\sigma : S \to S'$ so that the matching $v_i \leftrightarrow v_{\sigma(i)}'$ preserves cyclic order. The total cost of a neighborhood match is equal to

$$C_{\text{nbhd}} = w_0 C_{\text{local}}(v_0, v_0') + \sum_{i \in S} w_i C_{\text{local}}(v_i, v_{\sigma(i)}')$$

where w_i is a weight between 0 and 1 that depends on the ratio of distances between the core vertices and the neighbors v_i and $v_{\sigma(i)}'$. For each pair of core vertices v_0, v_0', the neighborhood matching that maximizes this cost function is speedily and efficiently found by dynamic programming.

4.3   Graph Matching

In previous sections, the template image and the search image were reduced to a graph, and candidate matches between vertices in the two images were found. The goal of this section is to generate a mutually consistent set of vertex matches between the template and the search image. An association graph $\mathbf{G}$ [2, 8] provides a convenient framework for this process. In considering the association graph, it is important not to confuse it with the region adjacency graph that has been considered so far. In the association graph, vertices represent pairs of regions, one from each image. Such a vertex represents a hypothesized matching of a region from the template image with a region from the search image. Weighted edges in the association graph represent compatibilities between the region matchings denoted by the two vertices connected by the edge.

Thus, a vertex in the association graph is given a double index, and denoted v_{ij}, meaning that it represents a match between region R_i in the template image and region R'_j in the search image. This match may be denoted by $R_i \leftrightarrow R'_j$. As an example, if $j_1 \neq j_2$ then v_{ij_1} is not compatible with v_{ij_2}. This is because vertex v_{ij} represents a match $R_i \leftrightarrow R_{j_1}$ and v_{ij_2} represents the match $R_i \leftrightarrow R_{j_2}$, and it is impossible that region R_i should match both R'_{j_1} and R'_{j_2}. Thus, vertices v_{ij_1} and v_{ij_2} are incompatible and there is no edge joining these two vertices in the association graph. There are other cases in which matches are incompatible. For instance, consider a vertex v_{ij} representing a match $R_i \leftrightarrow R'_j$ and a vertex v_{kl} representing a match $R_k \leftrightarrow R'_l$. If regions R_i and R_k are close together in the template image, whereas R'_j and R'_l are far apart in the search image, then the matches $R_i \leftrightarrow R'_j$ and $R_k \leftrightarrow R'_l$ are incompatible, and so there is no edge joining the vertices v_{kl} and v_{ij}. Matches may also be incompatible on the grounds of orientation or color.

Formally, the association graph $\mathbf{G} = \{\mathbf{V}, \mathbf{E}\}$ is composed of a set of vertices $\mathbf{V}$ and a set of weighted edges $\mathbf{E} \subseteq \mathbf{V} \times \mathbf{V}$. Each vertex v represents a possible match between a template region and a search region. If there are N template regions and M search regions then $\mathbf{V}$ would have NM vertices (see figure 4). In order to reduce the complexity of the problem, the graph $\mathbf{G}$ is pruned so that only the top 5 assignments for each template region are included in $\mathbf{V}$. These nodes are labeled v_{ij} which is interpreted at the jth possible assignment for the ith template region. A slack node for each template region is inserted into the graph. The slack node v_{i0} represents the possibility of the NULL assignment for the ith template region, that is, no matching region exists in the other image. If an edge $e = (v_{ij}, v_{kl})$ exists then the assignments between nodes v_{ij} and v_{kl} are considered compatible. The weights for the edges are derived from the compatibility matrix $\mathbf{C}$ which is defined as:

$$
C_{(ij)(kl)} = \begin{cases}
0 & \text{if } j = 0 \text{ or } l = 0 \\
0 & \text{if } i = k \text{ and } j \neq l \\
0 \text{ to } 1 & \text{if } (i, j) = (k, l) \\
0 \text{ to } 1 & \text{if } v_{ij} \text{ and } v_{kl} \text{ are compatible} \\
-N & \text{if vertices } v_{ij} \text{ and } v_{kl} \text{ are not compatible}
\end{cases}
$$

Where N is the number of template regions. The value of $C_{(ij)(ij)}$ represents the score given to the individual assignment defined by node v_{ij}. A subgraph of **G** represents a solution to the matching problem. The choice of weight N for an incompatible match is to discriminate against incompatible matches and make certain that a set of edges with maximum weight represents a clique of compatible matches.

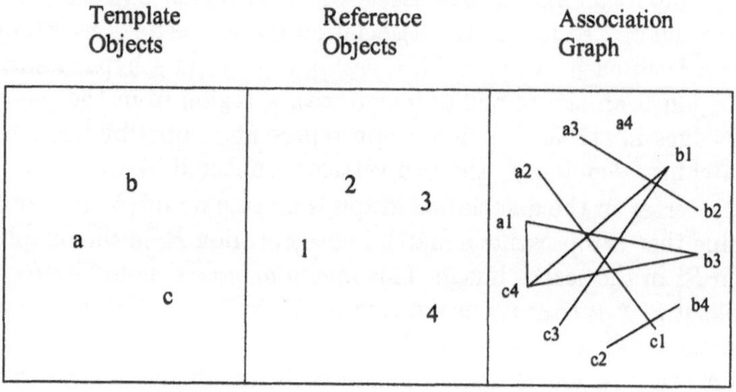

Fig. 4. *The template and search images are reduced to a set of regions. Each possible pair of assignments are assigned to a node in the association graph. Edges in the graph connect compatible assignments.*

The method of determining compatibility and assigning compatibility scores $C_{(ij)(kl)}$ for compatible matches is as follows. Consider a candidate region pair $R_i \leftrightarrow R'_j$. The local neighborhood of region R_i has been matched with neighborhood R'_j during the neighborhood matching stage. In doing this, a set of neighbors of the region R_i have been matched with the neighbors of the region R'_j. This matching may be considered as a correspondence of several regions (a subset of the neighbors of R_i) with an equal number of regions in the other graph. From these correspondences a projective transformation is computed that maps the centroid of R_i to the centroid of R'_j while at the same time as nearly as possible mapping the neighboring regions of R_i to their paired neighbors of R'_j. Thus, the neighborhood correspondence is modeled as closely as possible by a projective transformation of the image. Let H be the projective transformation so computed.

Now let $R_k \leftrightarrow R'_l$ be another candidate region match. To see how well this is compatible with the match $R_i \leftrightarrow R'_i$, the projective transformation H is applied to the region R_k to see how well $H(R_k)$ corresponds with R'_l. As a measure of this correspondence, the vector from $R'_j R'_l$ is compared with the vector $R'_j H(R_k)$. This is illustrated in figure 5. A compatibility score is assigned based on the angle and length difference between these two vectors. The two assignments are deemed incompatible if the angle between the two vectors exceeds 45 degrees, or their length ratio exceeds 2.

A color compatibility score is also defined. The correspondence of a core vertex and its neighbors with the matched configuration in the other image can be used to define an affine transformation of color space from the one image to the other. An affine color transformation is a suitable model for color variability under different lighting conditions ([18]). The affine transformation defined for one matched node pair is used to determine whether another matched node pair is compatible.

The final compatibility score is computed as

$$C_{(ij)(kl)} = C_{\text{nbhd}}(i,j) \times C_{\text{nbhd}}(k,l) \times \text{Angle compatibility score} \times$$
$$\text{length ratio compatibility score} \times \text{color compatibility score}$$

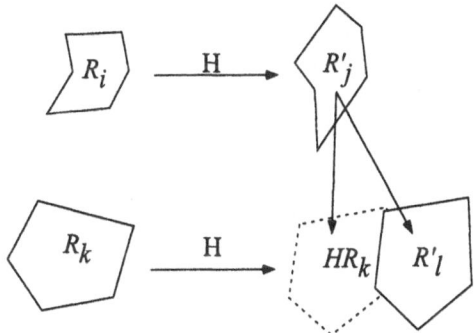

Fig. 5. *Compatibility of two matches is determined by applying the transformation H defined by the neighbors of the first pair (R_i, R'_j) to the region R_k belonging to the second pair. The positions of HR_k and R'_l relative to R'_j are compared.*

4.4 Solution Criteria

The Hough transform or matched filtering approach assumes that a global transformation defined by a relatively small set of parameters can be used to map the template regions onto the search regions. The largest set of nodes in **V** which is consistent with a particular transformation would then constitute a final solution. However just because two nodes are consistent with a particular transformation does not necessarily imply that the two nodes are consistent with each other. For instance, in the association graph of 4, a match $(c, 4)$ is compatible with $(b, 1)$ and $(b, 1)$ is compatible with $(c, 3)$. However $(c, 3)$ is not compatible with $(c, 4)$, since c can not be simultaneously matched with both 3 and 4.

A popular graphical approach which can take advantage of some of the information contained in the edge structure is a node clustering technique where a simple depth first search is used to determine the largest connected subgraph of $\mathbf{G}$. A connected graph is one in which a path of edges exist between every pair of nodes in the graph. This solution represents a certain amount of consistency. However as before, the statement that node a is consistent with node b and node b is consistent with node c does not necessarily imply that node a is consistent with node c. This leads to the conclusion that in order to take full advantage of the mutual constraints embedded in the association graph, the final solution should represent a clique on $\mathbf{G}$.

A subset $\mathbf{R} \subseteq \mathbf{V}$ is a clique on $\mathbf{G}$ if $v_{ij}, v_{kl} \in \mathbf{R}$ implies that $(v_{ij}, v_{kl}) \in \mathbf{E}$. The search for a maximum clique is known to be an NP complete problem [14]. Even after pruning, the computational costs associated with exhaustive techniques such as [1] would be prohibitive. It has been reported [3] that determining a maximum clique is analogous to finding the global maximum of a binary quadratic function. Authors such as [20, 28] have taken advantage of this idea by using relaxation and neural network methods to approximate the global maximum of a quadratic function, where this maximum corresponds to the largest clique in the association graph. Although the largest clique, which is based on the information contained in $\mathbf{E}$, ensures a high level of mutual consistency, the nuances of the compatibility measures in $\mathbf{C}$ are lost. In order to take advantage of the continuous nature of these edge strengths, a quadratic formula is specified where the global maximum corresponds to the clique that has the maximum sum of internal edge strengths. An approach based on Gold and Rangarjans's gradual assignment algorithm (GAA) is used to estimate the optimal solution. The GAA is an iterative optimization algorithm which treats the problem as a continuous process but converges to a discrete solution. Even though the solution might be generated based on a local maximum this solution will be guaranteed to be a maximal clique. A *maximal* clique is one that is not a proper subset of any other clique.

4.5   Binary Quadratic Formulation

A binary solution column vector $\mathbf{m}$ is defined such that if $m_{ij} = 1$ then v_{ij} is part of the final solution and if $m_{ij} = 0$ then v_{ij} is excluded from the final solution. If the slack node v_{i0} is part of the final solution then the template region i has no assignment. The columns and rows corresponding to the slack nodes in the compatibility matrix are filled with 0 entries. From a graph theory point of view, the slack nodes are connected to all other nodes by edges with zero weight.

The binary quadratic formula $F(\mathbf{m})$ is defined as:

$$F(\mathbf{m}) = \mathbf{m}^\top \mathbf{C} \mathbf{m} \tag{1}$$

where $\mathbf{C}$ is the compatibility matrix defined in section 4.3. In order to ensure that each template region can be mapped to at most one search region, the final solution is constrained such that

$$\sum_{j=1}^{6} m_{ij} = 1 \quad \text{for all } i \ . \tag{2}$$

A solution corresponding to a global maximum of $F(\mathbf{m})$ represents a set of assignments with the largest amount of mutual compatibility. Any maximum of $F(\mathbf{m})$ (global or local) represents a maximal clique on G. To show this consider a particular solution $\hat{\mathbf{m}}$ where there exists i, j, k, l such that $\hat{m}_{ij} = 1$ and $\hat{m}_{kl} = 1$ but that the nodes v_{ij} and v_{kl} are incompatible assignments. Clearly this is the only condition necessary for the solution $\hat{\mathbf{m}}$ not to qualify as a clique. A second solution $\bar{\mathbf{m}}$ is introduced, the same as $\hat{\mathbf{m}}$ except that $\bar{m}_{ij} = 0$ and $\bar{m}_{i0} = 1$, which means that region i has no assignment. Using the definition of $\mathbf{C}$ (see section 4.3) and equations 1 and 2 it can be shown that the difference between $F(\bar{\mathbf{m}})$ and $F(\hat{\mathbf{m}})$ is

$$F(\bar{\mathbf{m}}) - F(\hat{\mathbf{m}}) = 0 - 2 \sum_{q=1}^{N} \sum_{r=1}^{6} \hat{m}_{qr} C_{(ij)(qr)} \geq 2(N - (N - 1)) = 2 \qquad (3)$$

Therefore $F(\hat{\mathbf{m}})$ does not represent a maximum which means that only a clique on G can generate a maximum on $F(\mathbf{m})$. The next step is to find a solution which is a maximum of $F(\mathbf{m})$.

4.6 Approximating the Clique with the Largest Degree of Mutual Compatibility

As previously stated the search for global maximum of 0-1 quadratic equations is known to be an NP complete problem so that an approximate solution to the optimum value of $F(\mathbf{m})$ will have to be estimated. The GAA is a recursive routine used to solve a general assignment problem under the constraints that assignments must be one to one. Any binary quadratic cost function can be used to drive the GAA optimization process. When generating the compatibility matrix, two nodes v_{ij} and v_{kl} are considered incompatible if they map template regions i and k to the same search region. Inclusion of v_{ij} and v_{kl} in the final solution would contradict the statement that a final solution is guaranteed to be a maximal clique. This means that the portion of the GAA that prevents a many to one condition from occurring need not be implemented.

Initially $\mathbf{m}$ is treated as a continuous vector. Several constraints are placed on the optimization process:

$$\forall ij \ m_{ij} \geq 0 \qquad (4)$$

$$\forall i \sum_{j=1}^{6} m_{ij} = 1. \qquad (5)$$

During each iteration t the update rule for the GAA is as follows:

$$m_{ij}(t + 1) = \frac{e^{\beta \frac{\delta F(t)}{\delta m_{ij}(t)}}}{\sum_{k}^{6} e^{\beta \frac{\delta F(t)}{\delta m_{ik}(t)}}} \qquad (6)$$

where β is a positive number, and

$$\frac{\delta F(t)}{\delta m_{ij}(t)} = 2 \sum_{p=1}^{N} \sum_{q=1}^{6} m_{pq}(t) C_{(ij)(pq)}. \tag{7}$$

The update equation 6 ensures that conditions 4 and 5 are maintained. Initially β is set to a low value so that multiple solutions can coexist. The value of β is gradually increased. As can be seen from equation 6, as β becomes large the values of m are forced to discrete values of 0 or 1.

Figure 6 shows an example of the optimization process. A sequence of snapshots graphically displays the evolution of the solution vector for a template image of 15 regions. After the first initial iterations, the NULL assignments are favored because of the inconsistencies between rival solutions. Between time 1 and time 3 a dominant solution begins to emerge. The solution is refined during time 4 and time 5. At time 6 the algorithm has converged to a final solution and by time 7 the coefficients have taken on binary values.

5   Results

The algorithm was tried on several sets of color images. The first example was a computer manual, shown in figure 7. The manual was easily found in different images of a cluttered table-top, even when the manual was partially occluded. Note that a second manual shown in the images is not found, since it is actually a different color, though this is not obvious from the grey-scale images shown in the paper. Other examples are shown in figures 10 and 9.

6   Conclusion

The amalgamation of region segmentation algorithms with modern color constancy methods gives the possibility of improved object recognition in color and multi-spectral imagery. The adoption of an inexact graph-matching approach makes recognition independent of moderate lighting and view-point changes. The graph matching approach was able to generate solutions with consistency at multiple levels. The region adjacency graphs were able to highlight image to template correspondences with strong local support. By insisting that the final solution must represent a clique on the association graph, global consistency was achieved. Although the maximum clique problem is NP complete, it was demonstrated that strong maximal cliques can be generated using a variation of the gradual assignment algorithm.

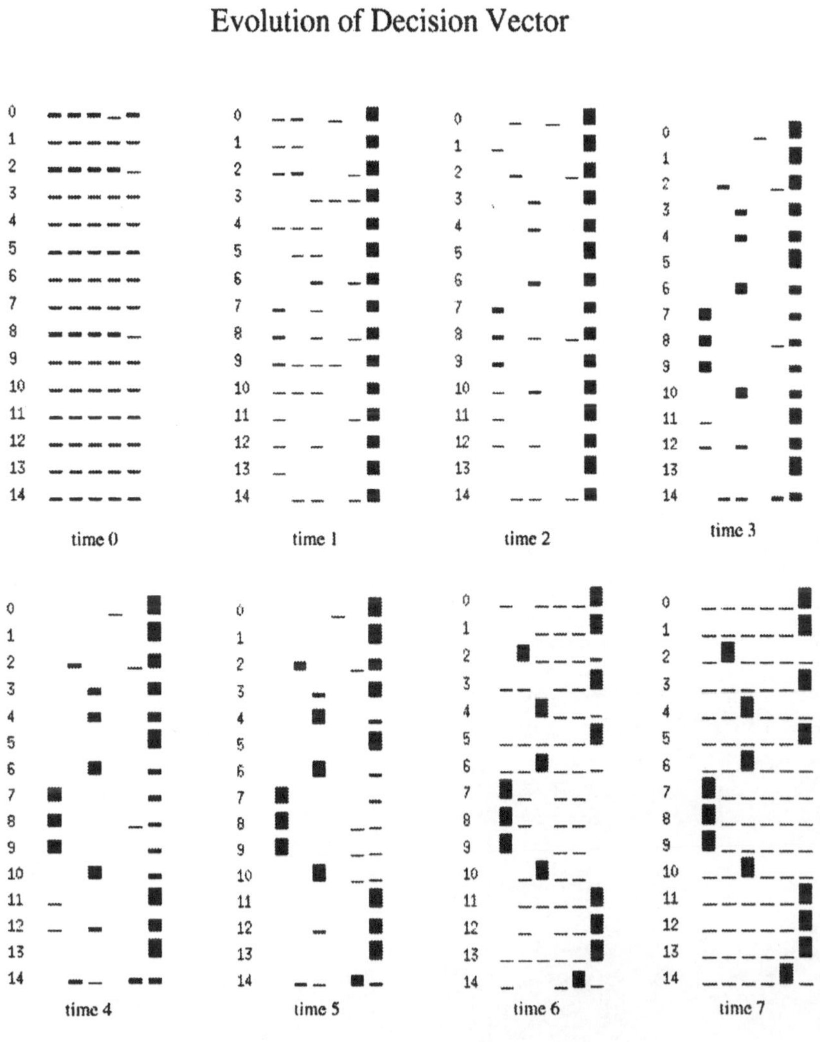

Evolution of Decision Vector

Fig. 6. *Illustration of the GAA optimization process. The coefficients for the solution vector* **m** *are shown at various points in time. Each row represents the coefficients corresponding to a particular template region. The last column at each time represent the coefficients for the NULL assignments. Initially the coefficients take on continuous values between 0 and 1. By the end of the process only binary values exist.*

Fig. 7. *The computer manual used as a template*

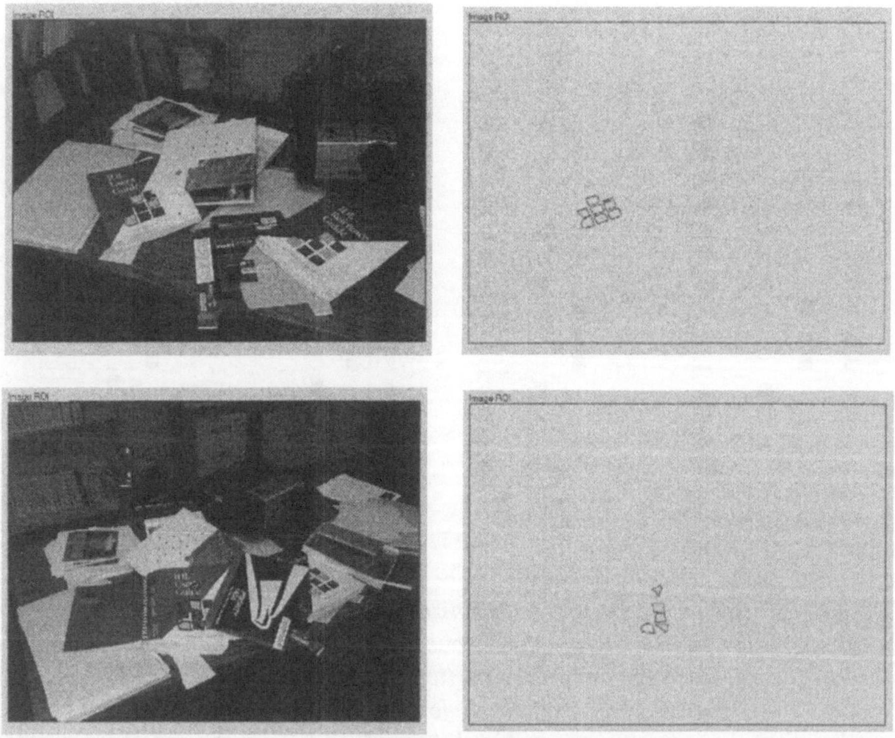

Fig. 8. *Two examples of recognition. On the left the search image, and on the right the outlines of the regions matched against the template.*

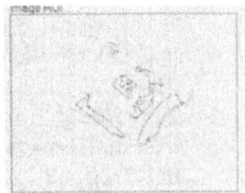

Fig. 9. *Recognition of cup image. On the left is the template, in the center the search image and on the right the identified regions of the located cup. Note that the cup in the search image is seen from a different angle from the template image. The letters REC are visible in the template, but only RE is visible in the search image.*

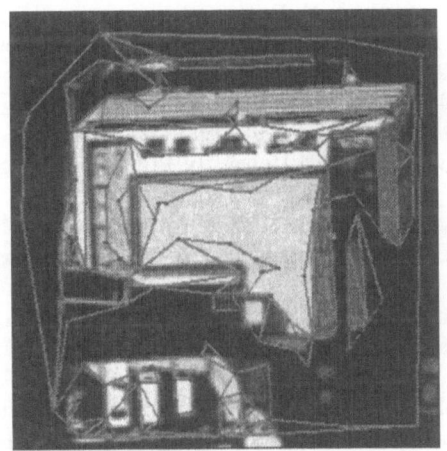

Fig. 10. *Recognizing a building. On the left the template, and on the right the search image showing the recognized building.*

References

[1] Ambler A.P., Barrow H.G., Brown C.M., Burstall R.M., Popplestone R.J., 'A versatile computer-controlled assembly system', IJCAI, pages 298-307, (1973).

[2] Ballard D.H., Brown C.M., 'Computer Vision', Prentice-Hall, Englewood Cliffs, NJ, (1982).

[3] Batahan F., Junger M., Reinelt G., 'Experiments in Quadratic 0-1 programming', Mathematical Programming, vol. 44, pages 127-137, (1989).

[4] David H. Brainard and Brian A. Wandell, 'Analysis of the retinex theory of color vision', Journal of the Optical Society of America, Vol. 3, No 10, pages 1651 – 1661, (1986).

[5] J. Brian Burns and Stanley J. Rosenschein, 'Recognition via Blob Representation and Relational Voting', Proc 27th Asilomar Conference on Signals, Systems and Computer, pages 101 – 105, (1993).

[6] Marie-Pierre Dubuisson and Anil K. Jain, 'Fusing Color and Edge Information for Object Matching', Proceedings, ICIP-94, pages 471 – 476, (1994).

[7] Francois Ennesser and Gerard Medioni, 'Finding Waldo, or Focus of Attention using Local Color Information', IEEE Transactions on PAMI, Vol 17, 8, pages 805–809, (1993).

[8] Faugeras O., 'Three-dimensional computer vision', MIT Press, (1993).

[9] G. D. Finlayson, B. V. Funt and K. Barnard, 'Color Constancy under Varying Illumination', Proceedings of 5th International Conference on Computer Vision, ICCV-95, pages 720 – 725, (1995).

[10] David Forsyth, 'A Novel Approach to Colour Constancy', Proceedings of 2nd International Conference on Computer Vision, ICCV-88, pages 9 – 18, (1988).

[11] Brian V. Funt and Graham D. Finlayson, 'Color Constant Color Indexing', IEEE Transactions on PAMI, Vol. 17, No. 5, pages 522–529, (May 1995).

[12] Graham D. Finlayson, Mark S. Drew and Brian V. Funt, 'Color constancy: generalized diagonal transforms suffice', Journal of the Optical Society of America, Vol. 11, No 11, pages 3011–3019, (1994).

[13] Gold S. and Rangarjan A., 'A gradual assignment algorithm for graph matching', IEEE Transactions on PAMI, Vol. 18 No 4, (April 1996), pages 377 – 387.

[14] Gibson A., 'Algorithmic graph theory', Cambridge University Press, Cambridge (MA), USA, (1985)

[15] Allen R. Hanson and Edward M. Riseman, 'Segmentation of Natural Scenes', in Computer Vision Systems, (edited A. Hanson and E. Riseman), Academic Press, (1978), pages 129 – 164.

[16] Allen R. Hanson and Edward M. Riseman, 'VISIONS : A computer system for interpreting scenes', in Computer Vision Systems, (edited A. Hanson and E. Riseman), Academic Press, (1978), pages 303 – 334.

[17] Glenn Healey and David Slater, 'Global color constancy : recognition of objects by use of illumination-invariant properties of color distributions', Journal of the Optical Society of America, Vol. 11, No 11, pages 3003 – 3010, (1994).

[18] Glenn Healey and David Slater, 'Computing Illumination-Invariant Descriptors of Spatially Filtered Color Image Regions', IEEE Transactions on Image Processing, Vol. 6 No 7, (July 1997), pages 1002 – 1013.

[19] Glenn Healey and David Slater, 'Exploiting an Atmospheric Model for Automated Invariant Material Identification in Hyperspectral Imagery', Preprint report : to appear (Darpa IU Workshop, Monterey, (1998) ?).

[20] Lin, F. 'A parallel computation network for the maximum clique problem', Proceeding 1993 international symposium on circuits and systems, pages 2549-52, vol. 4, IEEE, (May 1993).

[21] Stephen Lin and Sang Wook Lee, 'Using Chromaticity Distributions and Eigenspace Analysis for Pose, Illumination and Specularity Invariant Recognition of 3D objects', Proceedings Computer Vision and Pattern Recognition, CVPR-97, pages 426 – 431, (1997).

[22] Hiroshi Murase and Shree K. Nayar, 'Visual Learning and Recognition of 3-D Objects from Appearance', International Journal of Computer Vision, 14, pages 5–24, (1995)

[23] Adnan A. Y. Mustafa, Linda G. Shapiro and Mark A. Ganter, '3D Object Recognition from Color Intensity Images', Proc. ICPR'96, pages 627 – 631, (1996).

[24] Kenji Nagao, 'Recognizing 3D Objects Using Photogrametric Invariant', Proceedings of 5th International Conference on Computer Vision, ICCV-95, pages 480 – 487, (1995).

[25] Shree K. Nayar, Sameer A. Nene and Hiroshi Murase, 'Real-Time 100 Object Recognition System', Proc. 1996 IEEE Conference on Robotics and Automation, Minneapolis, pages 2321 – 2325, (April 1996).

[26] Sameer A. Nene and Shree K. Nayar, 'A Simple Algorithm for Nearest Neighbor Search in High Dimensions', IEEE Transactions on PAMI, Vol. 19 No 9, pages 989–1003, (Sept, 1997).

[27] Michael J. Swain and Dana H. Ballard, 'Color Indexing', International Journal of Computer Vision, 7:1 pages 11-32, (1991).

[28] Pelillo M., 'Relaxation labeling Networks that solve the maximum clique problem', Fourth international conference on artificial neural networks, pages 166-70, published by IEE (June 1995).

[29] Tushar Saxena, Peter Tu and Richard Hartley, 'Recognizing objects in cluttered images using subgraph isomorphism', to appear in Proceedings of the IU Workshop, Monterey, (1998).

[30] David Slater and Glenn Healey, 'Combining Color and Geometric Information for the Illumination Invariant Recognition of 3D Objects', Proceedings of 5th International Conference on Computer Vision, ICCV-95, pages 563 – 568, (1995).

[31] David Slater and Glenn Healey, 'Exploiting an Atmospheric Model for Automated Invariant Material Identification in Hyperspectral Imagery', Preprint report : to appear (Darpa IU Workshop, Monterey, (1998) ?).

[32] A. Zisserman, D. Forsyth, J. Mundy, C. Rothwell, J. Liu, N. Pillow, '3D Object Recognition Using Invariance', Artificial Intelligence Journal, 78, pages 239–288, (1995).

A Cooperating Strategy for Objects Recognition

Antonio Chella[1], Vito Di Gesù[1], Ignazio Infantino[2], Daniela Intravaia[3], and Cesare Valenti[3]

[1] Centro Interdipart. di Tecnologie della Conoscenza, University of Palermo, Italy
[2] Dipartimento di Ingegneria Elettrica, University of Palermo, Italy
[3] Dipartimento di Matematica ed Applicazioni, University of Palermo, Italy

Abstract. The paper describes an object recognition system, based on the co-operation of several visual modules (*early vision, object detector, and object recognizer*). The system is *active* because the behavior of each module is tuned on the results given by other modules and by the internal models. This solution allows to detect inconsistencies and to generate a feedback process. The proposed strategy has shown good performance especially in case of complex scene analysis, and it has been included in the visual system of the DAISY robotics system. Experimental results on real data are also reported.

1 Introduction

The performance of a perceptual system lies on the ability to focus on areas of interest, by maximizing a given costs/benefit utility criterion [2]. The ability to select salient features is one of the basic questions of intelligence, both in artificial and natural systems. Moreover, visual perceptual systems should be able to adapt their behavior depending on the current goal and the nature of the input data. Such a behavior can be obtained by systems able to dynamically interact with the environment. Information-fusion strategies [4] are an example of a suitable goals-oriented approach [9]. The computation can be driven by complementary information sources, and it may evolve on the basis of adaptive internal models and environment transformations [8].

Here, an object recognition system, based on the co-operation of several visual modules, is described (see Fig.1). The main modules of the system are:

- *Early vision, (DST)*;
- Object detection *(OBD), realized by two co-operating agents (segmentation (Snake) and feature extraction (OST))*;
- *Object recognition*, realized by the classifier *(CL)* and the structural descriptor *(SD)* agents.

The system is also *active* as the behavior of each module is tuned on the results obtained by other modules and by the internal models. The *consistency control* module allows to generate a feedback process whenever inconsistencies are detected.

D.A. Forsyth et al. (Eds.): Shape, Contour ..., LNCS 1681, pp. 264–274, 1999.
© Springer-Verlag Berlin Heidelberg 1999

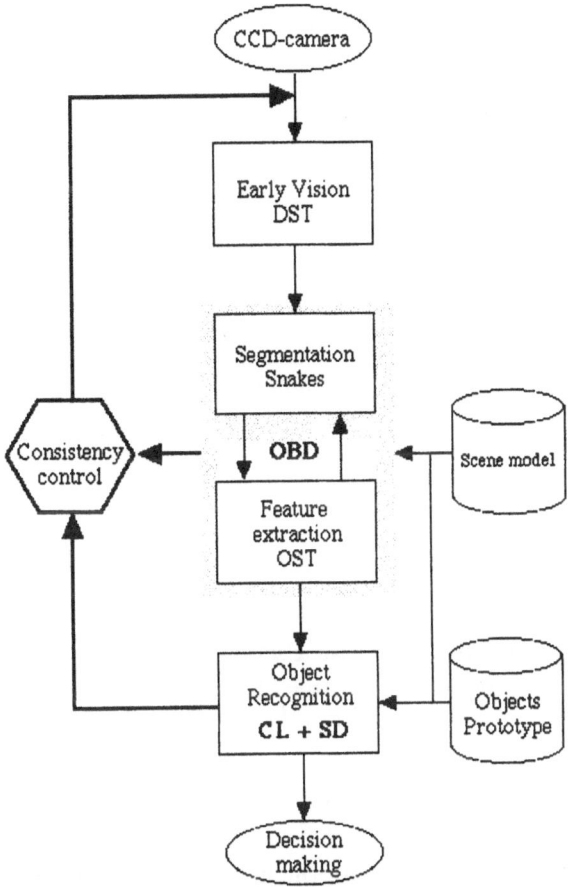

Fig. 1. The schema of the object recognition system.

The proposed strategy has been chosen because the performance of an artificial visual system is strongly influenced by the information processing that is done, during the early vision phase, to *reduce* the huge amount of information collected by the visual system (both natural and artificial) and to avoid the collapse at higher computation levels (see Tsotsos [14]).

Treisman [15] suggested that pre-attentive processing allows to focus pictorial computation on regions of interest. In fact *meaningful* image and shape features (e.g. edges, medial axis, snakes and texture) are selected during this phase. This capability is a fundamental part of an active vision system (Aloimonos [1]). Attention is achieved at different levels of abstraction, starting from early vision. At each level different paradigms of computation can be considered (from local to symbolic) including abstract modeling (Brown [2]).

We are testing our approach on complex scene analysis by including it in the visual system of the DAISY robot system [3]. Fig.2 shows a typical real world scene as detected by the DAISY visual system. It represents a desk with several typical objects. The scene has a crowd of objects and the condition of illumination is natural.

Fig. 2. An example of complex scene with objects on a desk

The paper is organized as follows. Section 2 describes the early vision task. The object detection module is described in Section 3. Section 4 is dedicated to the classifier design. Experimental results and discussion are given in Section 5.

2   The Early Vision Phase

In the following, $D = ||g_{i,j}||$ denotes the input image-frame of size $N \times N$, and $0 \le g_{i,j} \le G - 1$.

An object is said to exhibit symmetry if the application of certain isometries, called symmetry operators, leaves it unchanged while parts are permuted. For instance, the letter A remains unchanged under reflection, the letter H is invariant under both reflection and half-turn, the circle has annular symmetry around its centers.

Symmetry plays a remarkable role in perception problems. For example, peaks of brain activity are measured in correspondence with visual patterns showing *symmetries*. Relevance of symmetry in vision was already noted by psychologists Khöler and Wallach in [11].

Symmetry operators have been included in vision systems to perform different visual tasks. For example, they have been applied to represent and describe object-parts (Kelly [10]), and to perform image segmentation in Gauch [7]. In Reisfeld [13] a measure of symmetry is introduced to detect points of interest in a scene.

The Discrete Symmetry Transform (DST) of D, here described [5], is defined by the product of two local operators:

$$DST_{i,j} = F_{i,j} \times E_{i,j}$$

The first operator is a function of the axial moments computed in a window C_k, of linear size $2k + 1$ and centered in (i, j):

$$T_{i,j}^h = \sum_{r=-k}^{r=+k} \sum_{s=-k}^{s=+k} |r \times sin(\frac{h\pi}{n}) - s \times cos(\frac{h\pi}{n})| \times g_{i-r,j-s}$$

with $h = 0, 1, 2, ..., n - 1$, where n is the number of symmetry axes used. The function F depends on the kind of symmetry to be detected. For example, in case of annular symmetry:

$$F_{i,j} = 1 - \sqrt{\frac{\sum_h (T_{i,j}^h)^2}{n} - \left(\frac{\sum_h (T_{i,j}^h)}{n}\right)^2}$$

The second operator weighs F according to the local smoothness of the image, and it is defined as:

$$E_{i,j} = \sum_{(l,m) \in C_k, (r,s) \in C_{k+1}} |g_{l,m} - g_{r,s}|$$

where pixels (l, m) and (r, s) must be 4-connected $((l - r)^2 + (m - s)^2 = 1)$. It is easy to see that $E_{i,j} = 0$ iff the image is locally flat.

In Fig.3 the DST of the scene in Fig.2 is shown. Bright pixels are center of higher local circular symmetry.

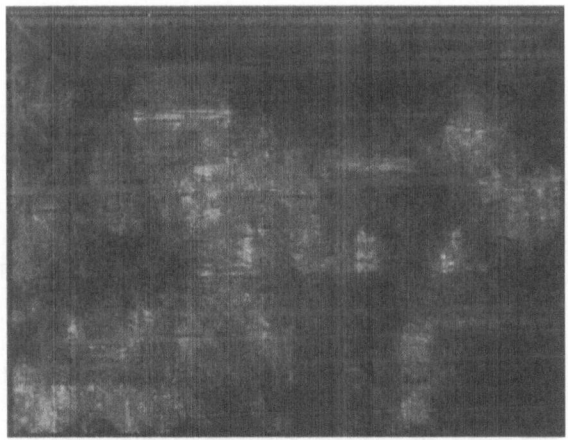

Fig. 3. The DST of the scene in Fig.2.

The DST is applied to the input image, D, to compute the transformed image S. The mean value μ_S and the variance σ_S are also derived by a direct estimation of the image histogram.

The indicators (μ_S and σ_S) are then used to evaluate the selection of the areas of interest by means of the rule:

$$T(DST(D), \mu_S, \sigma)_S, \alpha) = \begin{cases} DST(D) & \text{if } DST(D) > \mu_S + \alpha \times \sigma_S \\ 0 & \text{otherwise} \end{cases}$$

where $\alpha \geq 0$ (in our experiments $\alpha = 3$). Fig.4 shows the result of the selection rule on the transformed image in Fig.3.

Fig. 4. Point of interest selected in the scene in Fig.2.

3   Object Detection

The *OBD* module performs the extraction of the zone containing candidate objects; for example in Fig.5 the Rubik's cube is extracted. The values, in the extracted zone, are then used to compute suitable object descriptors.

The agents, proposed for this task, acquires a sequence of frames images by a robot camera; this sequence represents different views around the object. Each 2D-view of the object is extracted from every frame, by using the snake agent [20].

The *Object Symmetry Transform* (*OST* agent) [6] is then applied on each 2D-view.

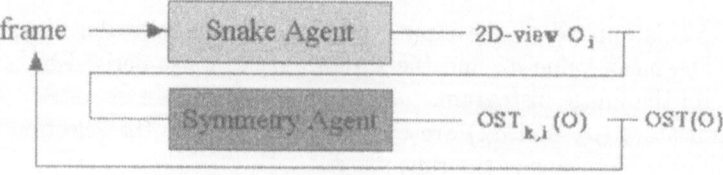

Fig. 5. Object detection module.

It must be pointed out, that during this phase the OBD is driven also by the scene model knowledge base, that is built by taking in account the specific goal (in our case "look at the objects on the desk").

3.1   Snakes and Segmentation

Snake is a deformable curve that moves in the image under the influence of forces related to the local distribution of the gray levels. When the snake reaches an object contour, it is adapted to its shape. In this way it is possible to extract the object shape of the image view. Snake as an open or closed contour is described in a parametric form by

$$v(s)=(x(s),y(s))$$

where x(s),y(s) are x,y co-ordinates along the contour and $s \in [0,1]$ is normalized arc length. The snake model [16] defines the energy of a contour, named the snake energy, E_{snake}, to be

$$E_{snake}(v(s)) = \int_0^1 (E_{int}(v(s)) + E_{image}(v(s)))ds$$

The energy integral is a functional since its independent variable is a function.

The internal energy, E_{int}, is formed from a Tikhonov stabilizer [20] and is defined:

$$E_{int}(v(s)) = a(s)|\frac{dv(s)^2}{ds^2}| + b(s)|\frac{d^2v(s)}{ds^2}|^2$$

where $||$ is the Euclidean norm. The first order continuity term, weighted by a(s), makes the contours behave elastically, whilst the second order curvature term, weighted by b(s), makes it resistant to bending. For example, setting b(s) = 0 at point s, allows the snake to become second-order discontinuous at point and develop a corner.

The image functional determines the features which will have a low image energy and hence the features that attract the contours. In general, [16] [19], this functional made up of three terms:

$$E_{image} = w_{line}E_{line} + w_{edge}E_{edge} + w_{term}E_{term}$$

where w denotes a weighting constant. Each of w and E correspond to lines, edges and termination respectively. The snake used in this framework has only edge functional which attracts the snake to point at high gradient:

$$E_{image} = E_{edge} = -(G_\sigma * \nabla^2 D(x,y))^2$$

This is the image functional proposed by Kass [16].It is a scale based edge operator [18] that increases the locus of attraction of energy minimum. G_σ is a Gaussian of standard deviation sigma which controls the smoothing process prior to edge operator. Minima of E_{edge} lies on zero-crossing of $G_\sigma * \nabla^2 D(x,y)$ which defines edges in Marr-Hildreth theory [17]. Scale space filtering is employed, which allows the snake to come into equilibrium on a heavily filtered image, and then the level of filtering is reduced, increasing the locus of attraction of a minimum.

The implemented snake allows to extract the object shape in a simple way and in short time for every frame of the sequence, this segmentation makes possible to individuate 2D-views of an object (or objects), O, in the image. In our case the views are grabbed, moving around the vertical axis of O. Every 2D-frame, O_i, corresponds to an angle of view given by $\phi_i = i \times \Delta\phi$ for $0 \leq i \leq m-1$ (see Fig.6a). It will be then processed by the agent OST, that compute a symmetry indicator for different axis of symmetry of the object.

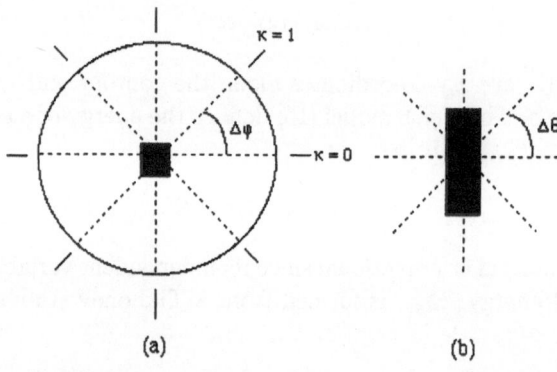

(a)   (b)

Fig. 6. The OST transform: a) 2D-frame views; b) computation of the axial symmetry indicator on a given view.

Fig.7 shows the result of the application of the Snake agent to one view of the Rubik's cube.

3.2   Object Axial Symmetries and Features Extraction

One of the main problem is the computational complexity related to the search of the axes of symmetry in gray levels images; in fact it can be considered an optimization problem. In Kyriati [12] an optimization procedure, based on a genetic algorithm is proposed. In this approach, a Gaussian window is used to select the areas of interest, where to compute the symmetry axes. The time complexity of the algorithm is $O(N \times N)$ for an image, D, of linear size N.

In [6] a new generalized measure of axial symmetry, MS_θ is defined. Its definition in the real plane, is based on the following indicator computed for a given axis r with direction θ, and passing trough the barycenter of the 2D-frame selected by the Snake-agent, O_i:

$$MS_\theta(O_i) = 1 - A_\theta(O_i)$$

Fig. 7. Candidate object extracted by the Snake agent.

where:

$$A_\theta(O_i) = \frac{\int_{C_i} |O_i(\mathbf{p}) - O_i(\mathbf{p_s})| h(\mathbf{p}) d\mathbf{p}}{(G-1) \int_{C_i} h(\mathbf{p}) d\mathbf{p}}$$

where, C_i is the support of O_i. The term $(G-1) \int_{C_s} h(\mathbf{p}) d\mathbf{p}$ normalizes $MS_\theta(O_i)$ in the interval $[0,1]$, while $h > 0$ is a function of the distance, d, of the point, $\mathbf{p}$ from the axis $\mathbf{r}$.

Note that, the chose of h depends on the influence that is given to the distance, d, between the pixels and the given axis. Examples of h-functions are:

a) $h(\mathbf{p}) = d$
b) $h(\mathbf{p}) = 1/d$
c) $h(\mathbf{p}) = e^{-d^2}$
c) $h(\mathbf{p}) = d^2 e^{-d^2}$

The algorithm to find candidates axes of symmetry can be easily implemented in the discrete case. First of all the barycenter $\mathbf{b}$ of the object is determined, then the measure $MS_\theta(O_i)$ is performed for $\theta = \frac{k\pi}{n}$, with $k = 0, 1, ..., n-1$. Maxima of MS_θ are also candidate to be symmetry axes of O_i.

It is easy to see that the computation time of this task is $O(n \times N^2)$.

The OST computation is performed by computing the axial symmetry of different objects views (see Fig.6b). It follows that

$$OST(k,i)(O) = MS_k(O_i)$$

It turns out the OST is an image of dimension $n \times m$, that represents a set of views of a 3D-object. In the following we will refer to it as OST-representation of O.

Fig.8 shows the result of the application of the OST to the Rubik's cube.

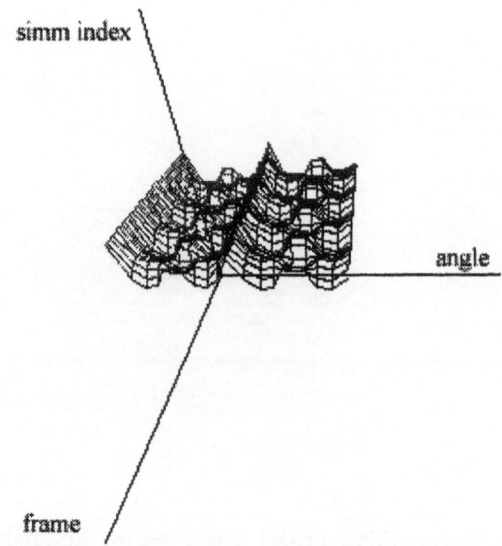

Fig. 8. The *OST* of the Rubik's cube extracted as in Fig.7.

4   The Object Recognizer

In the following the classifier agent is described. In our case a Bayesian classifier has been considered. Let $\{p_1, p_2, ..., p_k, ..., p_L\}$ the set of object prototypes already represented by their *OST*. The classifier assign an unknown object x to that class represented by the closest prototype.

$$x \in Clas_i \rightarrow \rho(x, p_i) = min_{1 \leq k \leq L}\{\rho(x, p_k\}$$

where ρ is a similarity function. The similarities used in our case are: the *normalized correlation* (*NC*) (pseudo-metric), the *Euclidean* (*ED*) and the *Hamming* (*HD*) distances. All of them are defined in the interval $[0, 1]$.

Prototypes are generated by synthetic shapes (parallelogram (PR), cone (CO), cube (CU), cylinder (CY), pyramid (PY), ellipsoid (EL), sphere (SP), torus (TO), and pot-like (PL)) representing sketch of *real* objets on the desk (Rubik's cube (RC), pen-holder (PH), paper-weight (PW), and beer mug (BM)). In Table 2 the correspondence between prototypes and real objects is shown; this corresponds to a simplified world model.

Table 2 shows the classification results for the Rubik's cube. Note that all three similarity functions are brought to a correct classification.

5   Experiments and Discussion

The object-recognition system has been tested on real world scenes. However, in this preliminary experimentation the kind of objects in the scene has been

Object	Model
RC	cube
PH	cylinder, parallelogram, ellipsoid
PW	cone, pyramid, sphere
BM	pot − like

Table 1. Objects-models correspondence.

ρ	PA	CO	CU	CY	EL	PY	SP	PL	TO
NC	0.14	0.40	**0.05**	0.20	0.34	0.25	0.42	0.23	0.30
ED	0.21	0.16	**0.05**	0.07	0.12	0.21	0.17	0.17	0.17
HD	0.16	0.12	**0.03**	0.04	0.16	0.17	0.15	0.12	0.13

Table 2. Classification result for the Rubik's cube.

limited to those included in the object data-base. Table 3 summarizes the classification results obtained using the similarity functions with a *vote* strategy, that computes the mean value of the three distance functions from the prototypes. It is evident that the maximum of similarity has been reached in correspondence with the model. Note that in the reported example on Table 3 the paper-weight is spherical and the pen-holder is cylindrical.

Object	PA	CO	CU	CY	EL	PY	SP	PL	TO
RC	0.17	0.22	**0.04**	0.08	0.13	0.25	0.19	0.17	0.19
PH	0.10	0.18	0.11	**0.03**	0.13	0.21	0.16	0.11	0.19
PW	0.26	0.17	0.15	0.15	0.19	0.22	**0.08**	0.27	0.23
BM	0.13	0.21	0.18	0.14	0.15	0.30	0.19	**0.08**	0.14

Table 3. Object classification.

General experimentation, allowing the presence of any kind of object in the scene, should be performed to test the robustness of our approach. Nevertheless, the examples shown in this paper are quite realistic, and could be a good starting point for a control environment system.

The system has been implemented in the DAISY distributed environment. In case of images of size 256×256 the CPU time to analyze a single 2D-view was of 3 *sec* (from the acquisition of the frame to the computation of the OST), and few *msec.* to perform the classification. The system is able to perform *real time* computation; in fact the acquisition rate is of about 5 *sec.* (this time includes the robot movements around the object).

Further work will be addressed to consider views of the object different from orthogonal ones. Prototype generation should consider more sophisticated object modeling.

References

[1] J.Aloimonos, I.Weiss, and Bandyopadhyay, "Active vision", in *Int. Journal of Computer Vision*, Vol.1, No.4, pp.333-356, 1988.

[2] C.M.Brown, "Issue in Selected Perception", in *Proc.ICPR'92*, (IEEE Computer Soc.), Vol.1, pp.21-30, The Hague,1992.

[3] A.Chella, V.Di Gesù, S.Gaglio, et.al., "DAISY: a Distributed Architecture for Intelligent SYstem", *Proc.CAMP-97*, (IEEE Computer Soc.), Boston, 1997.

[4] V.Di Gesú, G.Gerardi, and D.Tegolo, "M-VIF: a Machine-Vision based on Information Fusion", proceedings of CAMP'93, (ed. M.A.Bayoumi, L.S.Davis, K.P.Valavanis), IEEE Comp.Soc.Press, pp.428-435, New Orleans 1993.

[5] V.Di Gesú, C.Valenti, "Detection of regions of interest via the Pyramid Discrete Symmetry Transform", in Advances in Computer Vision (Solina, Kropatsch, Klette and Bajcsy editors), Springer-Verlag, 1997.

[6] V.Di Gesù, D.Intravaia, "A new approach to face analysis", DMA-IR-05/98, University of Palermo,1998.

[7] J.M.Gauch and S.M.Pizer, "The intensity axis of symmetry application to image segmentation", *IEEE Trans. PAMI*, Vol.15, N.8, pp.753-770, 1993.

[8] E. Gerianotis, Y.A. Chau, Robust data fusion for multisensor detection systems, *IEEE Trans. on Pattern Information Theory* **36(6)**, pp. 1265–1279, 1990.

[9] H.Gomaa, "Configuration of distributed heterogeneous information systems", Proceedings Second International Workshop on Configurable Distributed Systems (Cat. No.94TH0651-0). Pittsburgh, PA, USA; pp. 210. IEEE. Carnegie Mellon Univ. 21-23 March 1994, IEEE Comput. Soc. Press. Los Almitos, CA, USA, 1994.

[10] M.F.Kelly and M.D.Levine, "From symmetry to representation", *Technical Report*, TR-CIM-94-12, Center for Intelligent Machines. McGill University, Montreal, Canada, 1994.

[11] W.Khöler and H.Wallach, "Figural after-effects: an investigation of visual processes", *Proc. Amer. phil. Soc.*, Vol.88, 269-357, 1944.

[12] Kiriati, "Detecting symmetry in gray level images: the global optimization approach", 1996.

[13] D.Reisfeld , H.Wolfson, Y.Yeshurun, "Context Free Attentional Operators: the Generalized Symmetry Transform", *Int. Journal of Computer Vision*, Vol.14, 119-130, 1995.

[14] J.K.Tsotsos, "The complexity of perceptual search tasks", in *Proc., IJCAI*, 1571-1577, 1989.

[15] A.Treisman, "Preattentive processing in vision", *Computer Vision, Graphics, and Image Processing*, Vol.31, 156-177, 1985.

[16] M. Kass, A. Witkin, D. Terzoupolos, "Snakes: Active Contour Models",*International Journal of Computer Vision*, Vol.1, 321-331, 1988.

[17] D. Marr, E. Hildreth, "Theory of Edge Detection", *Proc. R. Soc. Lond. B.*, Vol.207, 187-217, 1980.

[18] V. Torre, A. Poggio, "On Edge Detection", *IEEE Transaction on Pattern Analysis and Machine Intelligence*, Vol.8(2), 147-163, 1986.

[19] K. F. Lai, R. T. Chin, "Deformable Contours - Modelling and Extraction",*IEEE Transaction on Pattern Analysis and Machine Intelligence*, Vol.17(11), 1084-1090, 1995

[20] D. Terzopoulos, "Regularisations of Inverse Visual Problems involving Discontinuites",*IEEE Transaction on Pattern Analysis and Machine Intelligence*, Vol.8(4), 413-424, 1986

Part VI

Statistics, Learning, and Recognition

Model Selection for Two View Geometry:
A Review

Philip H.S. Torr

Microsoft Research, One Microsoft Way, Redmond, WA 98052, USA,
philtorr@microsoft.com,
http://www.research.microsoft.com/research/vision/

Abstract. Computer vision often involves the estimation of models of the world from visual input. Sometimes it is possible to fit several different models or hypotheses to a set of data, the choice of exactly which model is usually left to the vision practitioner. This paper explores ways of automating the model selection process, with specific emphasis on the least squares problem, and the handling of implicit or nuisance parameters (which in this case equate to 3D structure). The statistical literature is reviewed and it will become apparent that although no one method has yet been developed that will be generally useful for all computer vision problems, there do exist some useful partial solutions. This paper is intended as a pragmatic beginner's guide to model selection, highlighting the pertinent problems and illustrating them using two view geometry determination.

1   Introduction

Robotic vision has its basis in geometric modeling of the world, and many vision algorithms attempt to estimate these geometric models from perceived data. Usually only one model is fitted to the data. But what if the data might have arisen from one of several possible models? In this case, the fitting procedure needs to account for all the potential models and select which of these fits the data best. This is the task of robust model selection which, in spite of the many recent developments in the application of robust fitting methods within the field of computer vision, has been, by comparison, quite neglected.

This paper reviews current statistical methods in model selection with respect to determining the two view geometric relations from the point matches between two images of a scene, e.g. the fundamental matrix [13, 19]. These relations can be used to guide matching [52, 60] and thence estimate structure [4] or segmentation [51]. There are several two view relations that could describe an image pair. Hence it is necessary to estimate the type of model as well as the parameters of the model.

The paper is laid out as follows: Section 2 describes four two view motion models as well as their associated degrees of freedom. Section 3 describes the maximum likelihood method for estimation. The use of just maximum likelihood estimation will always lead to the most general model being selected as

D.A. Forsyth et al. (Eds.): Shape, Contour ..., LNCS 1681, pp. 277–301, 1999.
© Springer-Verlag Berlin Heidelberg 1999

most likely. Therefore section 4 introduces the likelihood ratio test for comparing two models. Although not generally useful for comparison amongst multiple models, its exposition will provide insight into the failings of some of the scoring criteria explained later. Section 5 describes the AIC criterion and some variants of it, with specific emphasis on the least squares fitting problem. It is found that the AIC consistently over estimates the number of parameters in the model, the reason for this is explained and some modifications are suggested to compensate. In Section 6 the Bayesian approach is detailed; the main problem with the Bayesian approach is the specification of the priors, and the BIC (Bayesian information criterion) approximation is discussed. In section 7 minimum description length ideas for providing priors are only briefly touched on as they lead to the same sort of algorithms as the Bayesian approach. Finally the benefits of model averaging are outlined in section 8. Results are spread throughout the text and summarized in section 9. The discussion in section 10 covers some commonly asked questions about model selection in computer vision, and in the conclusion it will be seen that this is far from a solved problem.

Notation: A 3D scene point projects to $\mathbf{x}$, and $\mathbf{x}' = \mathbf{x^2}$ in the first and second images, where $\mathbf{x} = (\mathbf{x_1}, \mathbf{x_2}, \mathbf{x_3})^\top$ is a homogeneous three vector. The inhomogeneous coordinate of an image point is $(x, y) = (x_1, x_2)$. The correspondence will also be represented by the vector $\mathbf{m} = (\mathbf{x}, \mathbf{y}, \mathbf{x}', \mathbf{y}')^\top$, the set of all point matches between two views will be denoted by κ. Noise free (true data) will be denoted by an underscore $\underline{x}$, estimates $\hat{x}$, noisy (i.e. measured) data as x. The probability density function (p.d.f.) of x given y is $\Pr(x|y)$. $\mathcal{R}$ is a two view relation, and θ are the parameters of that relation.

2   Putative Motion Models

This section describes the putative motion models which can constrain the rigid motion of points between two views. Each motion model is a *relation* $\mathcal{R}$ described by a set of *parameters* θ which define one or more *implicit functional relationships* $\mathbf{g}(\mathbf{m}, \theta) = \mathbf{0}$ ($\mathbf{0}$ is the zero vector) between the image coordinates i.e. $g_i(x, y, x', y'; \theta) = 0$.

There are four types of relations $\mathcal{R}$ described in this section. Firstly, the relations can be divided between motions for which camera position and structure can be recovered—3D relations; and motions for which it cannot; for instance when all the points lie on a plane, or the camera rotates about its optic centre—2D relations. A second division is between projective and orthographic (affine) viewing conditions (a more complete taxonmy is given in [57]).

Suppose that the viewed features arise from a 3D object which has undergone a rotation and non-zero translation. After the motion, the set of homogeneous image points $\{\mathbf{x_i}\}, i = 1, \ldots n$, is transformed to the set $\{\mathbf{x}'_i\}$. The two sets of features are related by the implicit functional relationship $\mathbf{x_i'}^\top \mathbf{F} \mathbf{x_i} = 0$ where $\mathbf{F}$ is the rank 2, 3×3 [13, 19] fundamental matrix, this is relation $\mathcal{R}_1$. The fundamental matrix encapsulates the epipolar geometry. It contains all the information on camera motion and internal camera parameters available from image feature correspondences alone.

When there is degeneracy in the data such that a unique solution for $\mathbf{F}$ cannot be attained it is desirable to use a simpler motion model. For instance when the camera is only rotating about its optic centre. Three other models are considered: $\mathcal{R}_2$, which is the affine camera model of Mundy & Zisserman [38] with linear fundamental matrix $\mathbf{F_A}$. The affine camera is applicable when the data is viewed under orthographic conditions and gives rise to a fundamental matrix with zeroes in the upper 2 by 2 submatrix [1]. The homography $\mathbf{x}' = \mathbf{Hx}$ is relation $\mathcal{R}_3$, and affinity $\mathbf{x}' = \mathbf{H_A x}$ is relation $\mathcal{R}_4$ which arise when the viewed points all lie on a plane or the camera is rotating about its optic centre between images, the homography being in the projective case, the affinity in the orthographic.

Relation, $\mathcal{R}$	c	k	d	Constraint	Parameters
General	7	7	3	$\mathbf{x}'^{\top}\mathbf{Fx} = 0$	$\mathbf{F} = \begin{bmatrix} f_1 & f_2 & f_3 \\ f_4 & f_5 & f_6 \\ f_7 & f_8 & f_9 \end{bmatrix}$
Affine $\mathbf{F_A}$	4	4	3	$\mathbf{x}'^{\top}\mathbf{F_A x} = 0$	$\mathbf{F_A} = \begin{bmatrix} 0 & 0 & g_1 \\ 0 & 0 & g_2 \\ g_3 & g_4 & g_5 \end{bmatrix}$
Homography	4	8	2	$\mathbf{x}' = \mathbf{Hx}$	$\mathbf{H} = \begin{bmatrix} h_1 & h_2 & h_3 \\ h_4 & h_5 & h_6 \\ h_7 & h_8 & h_9 \end{bmatrix}$
Affinity	3	6	2	$\mathbf{x}' = \mathbf{H_A x}$	$\mathbf{H_A} = \begin{bmatrix} a_1 & a_2 & a_3 \\ a_4 & a_5 & a_6 \\ 0 & 0 & a_7 \end{bmatrix}$

Table 1. *A description of the reduced models that are fitted to degenerate sets of correspondences. c is the minimum number of correspondences needed in a sample to estimate the constraint. k is the number of parameters in the relation; d is the dimension of the constraint.*

Model Complexity: Following the maxim of Occam "Entities are not to be multiplied without necessity" [2] model selection typically scores models by a cost function that penalizes models with more parameters. It is convenient

---

[1]   Actually $\mathbf{F_A}$ occurs in the non-orthographic case when the optical planes of the two cameras coincide [50]. Triggs claims (personal communication) that affine reconstruction in this case gives projectively correct results.

[2]   In fact Occam did not actually say this, but said something which has much the same effect, namely: 'It is vain to do with more what can be done with fewer'. That is to say, if everything in some science (here computer vision) can be interpreted without assuming this or that entity, there is no ground for assuming it [44].

at this point to introduce the number of explicit degrees of freedom for the parameters of each model. The fundamental matrix has 7 degrees of freedom, the homography has 8, and yet the fundamental matrix is more general. The affine fundamental matrix has 4 degrees of freedom, affinity 6, again the affine fundamental matrix is more general; this seeming paradox can be resolved by considering the dimension of the model.

In addition to the degrees of freedom in the parameters we shall see that the complexity of a model is also determined by its dimension, which is defined now. Each pair of corresponding points $\mathbf{x}, \mathbf{x}'$ defines a single point $\mathbf{m}$ in a measurement space $\mathcal{R}^\Delta$, formed by joining the coordinates in each image. These image correspondences, which are induced by a rigid motion, have an associated algebraic variety V in $\mathcal{R}^\Delta$. The fundamental matrix, and affine fundamental matrix for two images are dimension 3 varieties of degree 4 (quartic) and 1 (linear) respectively. The homography and affinity between two images are dimension 2 varieties of degree 2 (quadratic) and 1 (linear) respectively. The properties of the relations $\mathcal{R}$ are summarized in table 1. This loosely speaking means that the fundamental matrix describes a three dimensional surface in $\mathcal{R}^\Delta$ and the homography a two dimensional surface. Each point on this fundamental matrix surface (affine or general) is simply a match between two of the images, and it has three degrees of freedom equivalent to the fact that it maps to a three dimensional point in the scene. Similarly each point on a homography (or affinity) surface represents a match with two degrees of freedom.

3   Maximum Likelihood Estimation

Within this section the maximum likelihood estimate of the parameters θ of a given relation $\mathcal{R}$ is non-rigorously derived. Although this is a standard result the derivation will reveal that there are more parameters to be considered in the model formulation than just the explicit parameters of θ given in the last section and Table 1. These additional parameters are sometimes referred to as nuisance parameters [47]. This is important as later it will be seen that the prior distribution of $\mathcal{R}$ is related to the number of parameters that need to be estimated. Furthermore deriving the maximum likelihood error from first principles is a useful exercise as there is a long history of researchers using *ad hoc* error measures to estimate multiple view relations which are sub optimal.

Let $\mathbf{m}$ be a vector of the observed x, y coordinates $\mathbf{m} = (\mathbf{x}, \mathbf{y}, \mathbf{x}'\mathbf{y}')^\top$. It is assumed that the noise on $\mathbf{m}$ is Gaussian: $\mathbf{m} = \underline{\mathbf{m}} + \boldsymbol{\epsilon}$. with covariance matrix Λ. The covariance matrix for a set of correspondences, represented by a stacked vector $\kappa = (\mathbf{m}_1^\top, \dots \mathbf{m}_n^\top)^\top$, is $\Lambda_\kappa = \mathrm{diag}\,(\Lambda, \dots \Lambda)$. In this paper it is assumed that the noise in the location of features in all the images is Gaussian on each image coordinate with zero mean and uniform standard deviation σ, thus $\Lambda = \mathbf{I}\sigma^2$ (extension to the more general case is not difficult and is described by Kanatani [26]). Recall that the true value $\underline{\mathbf{m}}$ of $\mathbf{m}$ satisfies the q implicit functional relationships (e.g. algebraic polynomials $q = 1$ for dimension 3 varieties, and $q = 2$ for dimension 2 varieties in two images)

$$g_i(\mathbf{m}; \mathcal{R}) = 0 \qquad i = 1 \ldots q \ . \tag{1}$$

Given $\theta, \mathcal{R}, \hat{\kappa}, \hat{\sigma}^2$ (the last being the estimated variance of the noise, which typically can be independently derived from the properties of the feature matcher) the probability density function of a set of observed correspondences κ is:

$$\Pr(\kappa | \hat{\theta}, \mathcal{R}, \hat{\kappa}, \hat{\sigma}^2) = \left(\frac{1}{\sqrt{2\pi}\hat{\sigma}}\right)^{4n} e^{-((\kappa - \hat{\kappa})^\top \Lambda_\kappa^{-1}(\kappa - \hat{\kappa}))/(2\hat{\sigma}^2)} \ , \tag{2}$$

where $\mathbf{g}(\kappa; \hat{\theta}) = \mathbf{0}$. To find the maximum likelihood solution, the negative log-likelihood

$$-L = -\log \Pr(\kappa | \hat{\theta}, \mathcal{R}, \hat{\kappa}, \hat{\sigma}^2) \tag{3}$$

is minimized subject to the restrictions of $\mathbf{g}$. To accomplish this Lagrange multipliers are used, the derivatives of

$$-L = 2n \log \hat{\sigma}^2 + \frac{1}{2\hat{\sigma}^2}(\kappa - \hat{\kappa})^\top \Lambda_\kappa^{-1}(\kappa - \hat{\kappa}) + \lambda^\top \mathbf{g}(\hat{\kappa}; \hat{\theta}) \tag{4}$$

with respect to[3] $\hat{\theta}, \hat{\kappa}, \hat{\sigma}^2$ [28] are equated to zero. These equations are [47]

$$\frac{\partial L}{\partial \hat{\sigma}^2} = \frac{nI}{\hat{\sigma}^2} - \frac{1}{2\hat{\sigma}^4}(\kappa - \hat{\kappa})^\top \Lambda_\kappa^{-1}(\kappa - \hat{\kappa}) = 0$$

$$\frac{\partial L}{\partial \hat{\kappa}} = \frac{1}{\hat{\sigma}^2}\Lambda_\kappa^{-1}(\kappa - \hat{\kappa}) + \mathbf{S}^\top \lambda = 0$$

$$\frac{\partial L}{\partial \hat{\theta}^2} = \mathbf{T}^\top \lambda = 0$$

$$\mathbf{g}(\hat{\kappa}; \hat{\theta}) = 0$$

where $\mathbf{S}$ and $\mathbf{T}$ are the Jacobians of the implicit functional relationships $\mathbf{g}(\kappa; \hat{\theta})$ with respect to κ and $\hat{\theta}$ respectively $\mathbf{S} = \left[\left(\frac{\partial g_i(\kappa; \hat{\theta})}{\partial \kappa_k}\right)\right]$, $\mathbf{T} = \left[\left(\frac{\partial g_i(\kappa; \hat{\theta})}{\partial \theta_k}\right)\right]$. The solution of this set of equations are the maximum likelihood estimates of the noise $\hat{\sigma}$, the parameters θ for the relation, and the best fitting correspondences κ. Assuming $\hat{\sigma}$ is given, the number of free parameters in this system is the number of degrees of freedom k in $\hat{\theta}$ given in Table 1, plus number of degrees of freedom in $\hat{\kappa}$. Each correspondence $\hat{\mathbf{m}}$ obeys the constraints given by $\mathbf{g}$ and hence lies in the variety defined by $\mathcal{R}$; such that it is the least squares distance in $\mathcal{R}^\triangle$ away from the observed match $\mathbf{m}$, thus each correspondence $\hat{\mathbf{m}}$ has d degrees of freedom as given by Table 1; thus the number of degrees of freedom in $\hat{\kappa}$ is nd (the extra number of nuisance parameters—although in this problem these parameters are far from being a nuisance as they implicitly define the estimated structure of the scene). *The total number of parameters to be estimated (excluding $\hat{\sigma}$) is $p = k + nd$, and the total number of observations is $N = 4n$, both of which are important for the derivation of confidence intervals in the next section.*

---

[3] At this juncture the selection of the functional form of the data—the most appropriate motion model $\mathcal{R}$ is assumed known.

Given that $\Lambda = \mathbf{I}\sigma^2$, then the negative log likelihood (3) of all the correspondences $\mathbf{m_i}$, $i = 1..n$ where n is the number of correspondences, is:

$$- 2L(\kappa, \mathcal{R}) = \sum_{ij} \left(\frac{\hat{x}_i^j - x_i^j}{\hat{\sigma}}\right)^2 = \left|\frac{\kappa - \hat{\kappa}}{\hat{\sigma}}\right|^2 = \sum_i \left|\frac{\mathbf{m} - \hat{\mathbf{m}}}{\hat{\sigma}}\right|^2 = \sum_i \left(\frac{\mathbf{e_i}}{\hat{\sigma}}\right)^2 \quad (5)$$

where the log likelihood of a given match is $l(\mathbf{m}, \mathcal{R}) = \left(\frac{\mathbf{e_i}}{\hat{\sigma}}\right)^2$, discounting the constant terms (which is equivalent to the reprojection error of Hartley and Sturm [20]). If the type of relation $\mathcal{R}$ is known then, observing the data, we can estimate the parameters of $\mathcal{R}$ to minimize this log likelihood. This inference is called 'Maximum Likelihood Estimation' (Fisher 1936 [14]). Numerical methods for finding these two view relations are given in [5, 53, 56]. To enforce the constraints on the parameters such as $|\mathbf{F}| = \mathbf{0}$ sequential quadratic programming (SQP) [16] is used, a state of the art method for solving constrained minimization problems, which has been found to out perform many other methods in terms of efficiency, accuracy, and percentage of successful solutions, over a large number of test problems [45].

Robust Estimation The above derivation assumes that the errors are Gaussian, often however features are mismatched and the error on $\mathbf{m}$ is not Gaussian. Thus the error is modeled as a mixture model of Gaussian and uniform distribution:-

$$\Pr(e) = \left(\gamma \frac{1}{\sqrt{2\pi\sigma^2}} \exp(-\frac{e^2}{2\sigma^2}) + (1 - \gamma)\frac{1}{v}\right) \quad (6)$$

where γ is the mixing parameter and v is just a constant, σ is the standard deviation of the error on each coordinate. To correctly determine γ and v entails some knowledge of the outlier distribution; here it is assumed–without a *priori* knowledge–that the outlier distribution is uniform, with $-v.. + v$ being the pixel range within which outliers are expected to fall (for feature matching this is dictated by the size of the search window for matches). Usually the model selection methods are derived under Gaussian assumptions, but this assumption is not necessary, and the methods are equally valid using the robust function for probability given above (e.g. see Ronchetti in [17], or [41]). Thus in all that follows the robust likelihood is used. Rather than minimize (6), it is often computationally more simple to minimize a robust function [23] of the form:

$$\rho(e) = \begin{cases} e^2 & \text{if } e^2 < \lambda_3 d \\ \lambda_3 d & \text{if } e^2 \geq \lambda_3 d, \end{cases} \quad (7)$$

where d is the number of degrees of freedom in e (2 for $\mathbf{H}$, 1 for $\mathbf{F}$), and $\lambda_3 = 4$. The threshold $\lambda_3 = 4$ corresponds to the 95% confidence level. This means that an inlier will only be incorrectly rejected 5% of the time.

This form of the function has several advantages. Firstly it provides a clear dichotomy between inliers and outliers. Secondly outliers to a given model are given a fixed cost, reflecting that they probably arise from a diffuse or uniform distribution, the log likelihood of which is a constant, whereas inliers conform to a Gaussian model. Furthermore if the outliers follow a sufficiently diffuse uniform distribution then they will only be incorrectly flagged as inliers a small percentage of the time (false positives).

The robust cost function (7) allows the minimization to be conducted on all correspondences whether they are outliers or inliers. Use of the robust function limits the effects of outliers on the minimization. Typically, as the minimization progresses many outliers are redesignated inliers.

Problems with MLE: If the type of relation $\mathcal{R}$ is unknown then maximum likelihood estimation cannot be used to decide the form of $\mathcal{R}$ as the most general model will always be most likely i.e. have lowest $-L$. In Table 2 the average sum of square of this error (SSE) are shown for 100 sets of 100 synthetic matches. The matches were generated to be consistent with random $\mathbf{F}$, $\mathbf{F_A}$, $\mathbf{H}$ or $\mathbf{H_A}$ constraints, i.e. with a general motion, orthographic projection, camera rotation, or orthographic plane with Gaussian noise $\sigma = 1$ added to the projected match coordinates. Each model is estimated for each data set and the mean of the SSE recorded. It can be seen that just picking the model with lowest SSE will in general always lead to choosing the most general model—$\mathbf{F}$, thus the need for a more sophisticated model selection method. Fisher was aware of the limitations of maximum likelihood estimation and admits the possibility of a wider form of inductive argument that would determine the functional form of the data (Fisher 1936 p. 250 [14]); but then goes on to state 'At present it is only important to make clear that no such theory has been established'.

Estimated		Point Motion		
	General $\mathbf{F}$	Orthographic $\mathbf{F_A}$	Rotation $\mathbf{H}$	Affinity $\mathbf{F_A}$
Fundamental $\hat{\mathbf{F}}$	93.074 (93)	87.037	80.6162	78.378
Affine $\hat{\mathbf{F}}_A$	978.350	96.448 (96)	806.389	85.875
Homography $\hat{\mathbf{H}}$	4986.881	4834.735	193.964 (192)	189.132
Affinity $\hat{\mathbf{F}}_A$	4993.045	4967.894	1023.118	191.643 (194)

Table 2. *Mean SSE for 100 matches over 100 trials. Variance of noise on the coordinates: $\sigma^2 = 1$. Bracketted values are the expected value if the model is correct.*

4   Model Selection—Hypothesis Testing

One way of model comparison is via hypothesis testing, this procedure tests the null hypothesis that one relation $\mathcal{R}_1$ describes the data by comparing it to an alternate hypothesis that the relation $\mathcal{R}_2$ describes the data. The relations must be *nested* so that the parameters of the more general model θ_1 include all the parameters of the less general model θ_2 in addition to some extra ones. A common way to do this is by the likelihood ratio test (e.g. see [31, 35]). To do this the MLE of the parameters $\hat{\theta}_1$ and $\hat{\theta}_2$ for both relations must be recovered. Then the test statistic

$$\lambda(\kappa) = 2\log\left(\frac{\Pr(\kappa|\mathcal{R}_1, \hat{\theta}_1))}{\Pr(\kappa|\mathcal{R}_2, \hat{\theta}_2))}\right) = 2(L_1 - L_2) \tag{8}$$

is examined, where $\mathcal{R}_1$ has more parameters than $\mathcal{R}_2$, which asymptotically [4] follows a χ^2 distribution with $p_1 - p_2$ degrees of freedom, where p_i is the total number of parameters in model i. If $\lambda(\kappa)$ is less than some threshold (determined by a level of significance α) then model 2 is accepted otherwise model 2 is rejected, i.e. the test is

$$\lambda(\kappa) = 2(L_1 - L_2) < \chi^2(\alpha, p_1 - p_2) \ . \tag{9}$$

If $\mathcal{R}_2$ holds then the chance of overfitting is the user specified α. If $\mathcal{R}_1$ holds then the chance of underfitting is an unknown β, and the quantity $1 - \beta$ referred to as the *power* of the test. The power of the test is obviously related to the choice of α and the distribution of the data. For instance if all the matches have small disparities then the power of the test for given α is likely to be much lower than if the disparities are higher. Ideally α should be chosen so that the chance of overfitting (α) and underfitting (β) are small (i.e. the power of the test is high).

In the Neyman-Pearson theory of statistical hypothesis testing only the probabilities of rejecting and accepting the correct and incorrect hypotheses, respectively, are considered to define the cost of a decision. The problem with this approach is that it is difficult to adapt to a situation where several models might be appropriate, as the test procedure for a multiple-decision problem involves a difficult choice of a number of dependent significance levels. This suggests a different approach in which a scoring mechanism is used to rank each model. As seen, maximum likelihood methods will always lead to the most general model being selected; hence the need for a more general method of inductive inference that takes into account the complexity of the model. This has lead to the development of various *information criteria* (see the special issue of Psychometrika on information criteria, Vol 52, No 3). Foremost amongst these is 'an information criterion' (AIC) (Akaike 1974), described next.

5   AIC for Model Selection

Akaike's information criterion is a useful statistic for model identification and evaluation. Akaike (1974) was perhaps the first to lay the foundations of information theoretic model evaluation. He developed a model selection procedure–for use in auto-regressive modeling of time series–that chose the model with minimum expected prediction error for future observations as the best fitting. The

---

[4] meaning as the number of observations tends to infinity

procedure selects the model that minimizes expected error of new observations with the same distribution as the ones used for fitting [5]. It has the form

$$AIC = -2L + 2p \ , \qquad (10)$$

where p is the number of parameters in the chosen model, and L is the log likelihood. It can be seen that AIC has two terms, the first corresponding to the badness of fit, the second a penalty on the complexity of the model. When there are several competing models, the parameters within the models are estimated by maximum likelihood and the AIC scores compared to find the model with the minimum value of AIC. This procedure is called the minimum AIC procedure, and the model with the minimum AIC is called the minimum AIC estimate (MAICE) which is chosen as the best model. Therefore the best model is the one with highest information content but least complexity. An advantage of the AIC is its simplicity, as it does not require reference to look up tables, it is very easy to calculate AIC once the maximum likelihood estimate of the model parameters is made. Furthermore, Akaike claims that there is no problem of specifying an arbitrary significance level at which models should be acceptable, and comparison between two models need not be nested or ordered.

The AIC is developed from the idea that the best model is that which minimizes the expected SSE for future data. Consider the case of fitting a variety of dimension d to r dimensional points (recall our definition of relations in terms of varieties in section 2), in this case the codimension is $r - d$. Kanatani [26] points out that the AIC in this case is

$$AIC = -2L + 2(dn + k) \ . \qquad (11)$$

Kanatani's derivation of the AIC for least squares is rather drawn out, and the interested reader is referred to his book [26]. In fact Akaike [3] gave a similar form for the AIC in the case of factor analysis when fitting models of differing dimensions. Rather than present it here an intuitive interpretation is presented in the next section; in the two dimensional case $r = 2$, fitting a line model $d = 1$ and point model $d = 0$.

Intuitive Interpretation Consider equation (11), the first term is the usual sum of squares of residuals, divided by their variances, representing the goodness of fit. The next two terms represent the parsimony of the model. The second being a penalty term for the dimensionality of the model, the greater the dimension for the model the greater the penalty. The last term is the usual AIC criterion of adding the number of parameters of the model, to penalize models with more parameters.

This is now illustrated by a simple example, consider the two dimensional example shown in figure 1. Suppose points are generated from a fixed location

---

[5] He later demonstrated that AIC was an estimate of the expected entropy (Kullback-Leibler information) of the fitted distribution for the observed sample against their true one, showing that the model with the minimum AIC score also minimized the expected entropy, thus providing one way of generalizing MLE.

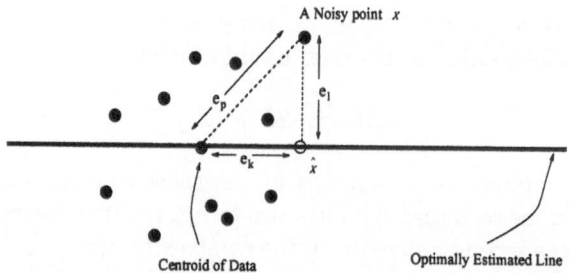

Fig. 1. *Showing the relationship between the noisy points, the optimally estimated line and the centroid of the noisy points. For Gaussian noise the optimally estimated line is that which minimizes the sum of squares of perpendicular distances, and consequently it passes through the centroid of the data. For each point the distance to the centroid may be broken up into two components one parallel and one perpendicular to the line.*

with added mean zero, unit standard deviation, Gaussian noise in both the x and y coordinates. If a point and a line are fitted separately by minimizing the sum of squared Euclidean distances, the optimally fitted point (the centroid) will lie on the optimally fitted line [40]. Let the sum of squared distances of the points to the line model be $\sum e_l^2$ and the sum of squared distances of the points to the point model be $\sum e_p^2$, then $\sum e_p^2 = \sum e_l^2 + \sum e_k^2$, where $\sum e_k^2$ is the 'parallel' sum of squared distances as shown for one point in Figure 1. It can be seen that unless the data all lie exactly on a point then $\sum e_l^2$ is always less than $\sum e_p^2$. The AIC for the line model compensates for this bias by the penalty term, which is twice the expectation of the 'parallel' sum of squares $(\sum e_k^2)$. If the model estimated is a line then the AIC has the form

$$\text{AIC(line)} = \sum e_l^2 + 2n + 4 \ , \tag{12}$$

as the model has dimension one, codimension one and two degrees of freedom in the parameters. If the number of the data is large the degree of freedom of the model (i.e., the number of the parameters) has little effect because it is a simple constant. What matters is twice the dimension of the model, which is multiplied by the number of the data. The dimension equals the 'internal' degree of freedom of the data, which in turn equals the expectation of the 'parallel' (or in a direction on the manifold) sum of squares per datum. Returning to the example the GIC for a point is

$$\text{AIC(point)} = \sum e_l^2 + \sum e_k^2 + 4 \ , \tag{13}$$

thus a point is favoured if AIC(point) $\leq$ AIC(line) i.e. $\sum e_k^2 \leq 2n$. Hence the algorithm is equivalent to a test of spread along the line.

Test results using AIC. Consider the average SSE given in table 2 for 100 data points. These can be turned into AIC by the addition of 614, 608, 416, and

412—$2(nd+k)$—for $\mathbf{F}$, $\mathbf{F_A}$, $\mathbf{H}$ and $\mathbf{H_A}$ respectively, tabulated in Table 5. It can be seen that on average the lowest AIC equates to the correct model, although it behaves less well for distinguishing $\mathbf{F}$ from $\mathbf{F_A}$, than $\mathbf{F}$ from $\mathbf{H}$. Generally the AIC tends to underestimate the dimension of the data and overestimate the number of motion model parameters. The reason for this can be seen in the context of the likelihood test explained in the last section. Consider using AIC to compare two models $\mathcal{R}_1$ and $\mathcal{R}_2$ such that the model with lowest AIC is accepted i.e. model 2 is accepted if $\text{AIC}_2 - \text{AIC}_1 < 0$ or if

$$2(L_1 - L_2) < 2(p_1 - p_2) \tag{14}$$

which can be seen to be directly equivalent to (9). Following this line of thought the significance level of the AIC criterion is given by the significance level of the χ^2 distribution with $|p_1 - p_2|$ degrees of freedom and critical value $2|p_1 - p_2|$. For

$|p_1 - p_2|$	1	2	3	4	5	6	8	10	12	14	20
α	0.156	0.135	0.111	0.091	0.074	0.061	0.042	0.029	0.020	0.014	0.005

Table 3. *Calculates values for significance level α given a χ^2 with $|p_1 - p_2|$ degrees of freedom and critical value/threshold $2|p_1 - p_2|$.*

$|p_1 - p_2| = 2$, the difference in the number of parameters between $\mathbf{H}$ and $\mathbf{H_A}$, this leads to $\alpha = 0.135$ or a 13.5 percent chance of overfitting, for $(p_1 - p_2) = 3$, the difference in number of parameters between $\mathbf{F}$ and $\mathbf{F_A}$, this leads to $\alpha = 0.11$ or a 11 percent chance of overfitting, some typically values are given in table 3. It can be seen that this borne out experimentally be scrutinizing Table 5. As $(p_1 - p_2)$ increases the value of α becomes smaller (less than 0.005 for $(p_1 - p_2) = 20$).

Model Selected		General	Orthographic	Rotation	Affinity
		$\mathbf{F}$	$\mathbf{F_A}$	$\mathbf{H}$	$\mathbf{F}$
Fundamental	$\hat{\mathbf{F}}$	707.074	701.037	694.6162	692.378
Affine	$\hat{\mathbf{F}}_A$	1586.350	704.448	1414.389	683.875
Homography	$\hat{\mathbf{H}}$	5402.881	5240.735	609.964	605.132
Affinity	$\hat{\mathbf{F}}_A$	5405.045	5379.894	1435.118	603.643

Table 4. *Mean AIC for 100 matches over 100 trials. It can be seen that the chance of overfitting dimension is small relative to the chance of overfitting the degree; i.e. average AIC for $\mathbf{F}$ lower than for $\mathbf{F_A}$.*

Recall that the number of parameters within each model has two components $p = k + nd$, the first k is the number of parameters in the relation, the second nd

Estimated	Point Motion			
	General	Orthographic	Rotation	Affinity
	F	F_A	H	F_A
Fundamental $\hat{F}$	99	11	0	0
Affine $\hat{F}_A$	1	88	0	0
Homography $\hat{H}$	0	0	98	15
Affinity $\hat{F}_A$	0	0	2	85

Table 5. *Number of times each model selected over 100 trials, using AIC for each of the four motion types. It can be seen that AIC tends to overfit the degree of the model.*

is a number of parameters proportional to the quantity of data. This suggests that a more general form, the geometric robust information criteria GRIC:

$$GRIC = -2L + \lambda_1 dn + \lambda_2 k \qquad (15)$$

might be appropriate, with λ_1 and λ_2 chosen to reduce misfits. Issues in determining values for these parameters, and suggested values for them are now discussed. Higher values of λ_1 and λ_2 decrease α but increase β, decreasing the *power* of the test; thus the two parameters should be chosen with an eye to minimizing α and β. For the estimation of two view geometry from feature matches $\lambda_1 = 2$ and $\lambda_2 = 4$ have provided good results, over a wide range of conditions. The first parameter λ_1 influences the decision as to whether the the relation should be dimension 3 or 2, for $n \geq 20$, $\alpha < 0.005$ which may be considered acceptably low. Thus there is little chance of over fitting the dimension as this adds a number of parameters equal to the number of matches, usually sufficiently high to guarantee low α. Now consider decomposing a general motion into plane plus parallax motions [24], the size of β depends on the amount of parallax. Setting $\lambda_1 = 2$ means that the amount of parallax needs to be on average be greater than $2.0\hat{\sigma}$ pixels to identify a none homography relation.

Recall that there is a high probability of overfitting the degree of the relation for two models of the same dimension. For the second parameter $\lambda_2 = 4.0$ ensures that for $(p_1 - p_2) = 1$ $\alpha = 0.0456$ which prevents the tendency to overfit the degree of the relation whilst not significantly effecting the power of the test (which is dominated by the choice of λ_1 for large data sets). The average GRIC is given in Table 6 and the models selected in Table 7, it can be seen that the GRIC outperforms the standard AIC.

AIC Variants: The fact that the AIC tends to overfit is generally recognized in the literature. Bozdogan [7] attempts to derive measures that are asymptotically consistent

$$CAIC = -2L + \frac{p}{2}(\log(N) + 1)$$

$$CAICF = -2L + \frac{p}{2}(\log(N) + 2) + \log|\mathbf{J}|$$

Model Selected		Point Motion			
		General	Orthographic	Rotation	Affinity
		$\mathbf{F}$	$\mathbf{F_A}$	$\mathbf{H}$	$\mathbf{F}$
Fundamental	$\hat{\mathbf{F}}$	721.074	715.037	708.6162	706.378
Affine	$\hat{\mathbf{F}}_A$	1592.350	712.448	1422.389	691.875
Homography	$\hat{\mathbf{H}}$	5410.881	5248.735	617.964	613.132
Affinity	$\hat{\mathbf{F}}_A$	5411.045	5385.894	1441.118	609.643

Table 6. *Mean GRIC for 100 matches over 100 trials.*

Estimated		Point Motion			
		General	Orthographic	Rotation	Affinity
		$\mathbf{F}$	$\mathbf{F_A}$	$\mathbf{H}$	$\mathbf{F_A}$
Fundamental	$\hat{\mathbf{F}}$	99	1	0	0
Affine	$\hat{\mathbf{F}}_A$	1	98	0	0
Homography	$\hat{\mathbf{H}}$	0	0	98	3
Affinity	$\hat{\mathbf{F}}_A$	0	1	2	97

Table 7. *Number of times each model selected over 100 trials, using GRIC for each of the four motion types.*

where $\mathbf{J}$ is the information matrix of the estimated parameters. Unfortunately both of these measures tend to chronically underfit, they have an exact similarity to the BIC approximation to the Bayes factors discussed in the next section.

6 Bayes Factors

Within this section the Bayesian approach to model comparison is introduced. Suppose that the set of matches κ is to be used to determine between K competing motion models with relations $\mathcal{R}_1 \ldots \mathcal{R}_K$ with parameter vectors $\theta_1 \ldots \theta_K$. Then by Bayes' theorem, the posterior probability that $\mathcal{R}_k$ is the correct relation is

$$\Pr(\mathcal{R}_k | \kappa) = \frac{\Pr(\kappa | \mathcal{R}_\mathbf{k}) \Pr(\mathcal{R}_\mathbf{k})}{\sum_{i=1}^{i=K} \Pr(\kappa | \mathcal{R}_\mathbf{i}) \Pr(\mathcal{R}_\mathbf{i})} \quad (16)$$

note that by construction $\sum_{i=1}^{i=K} \Pr(\mathcal{R}_i | \kappa) = 1$. All the probabilities are implicitly conditional on the set of relations $\{\mathcal{R}_1, \ldots \mathcal{R}_K\}$ being considered. In the case of image matching the models $\mathbf{F}$, $\mathbf{F_A}$, $\mathbf{H}$, $\mathbf{H_A}$ should suffice to completely describe most situation. The marginal probability $\Pr(\kappa | \mathcal{R}_\mathbf{k})$ is obtained by integrating out θ_k,

$$\Pr(\kappa | \mathcal{R}_\mathbf{k}) = \int \Pr(\kappa | \mathcal{R}_\mathbf{k}, \theta_\mathbf{k}) \Pr(\theta_\mathbf{k} | \mathcal{R}_\mathbf{k}) d\theta_\mathbf{k} \quad (17)$$

$$= \int \text{likelihood} \times \text{prior} \, d\theta_k \quad . \quad (18)$$

The extent to which the data supports $\mathcal{R}_i$ over $\mathcal{R}_j$ is measured by the *posterior odds*,

$$B_{ij} = \frac{\Pr(\mathcal{R}_i|\kappa)}{\Pr(\mathcal{R}_j|\kappa)} = \frac{\Pr(\kappa|\mathcal{R}_i)}{\Pr(\kappa|\mathcal{R}_j)} \frac{\Pr(\mathcal{R}_i)}{\Pr(\mathcal{R}_j)} \tag{19}$$

$\frac{\Pr(\mathcal{R}_i|\kappa)}{\Pr(\mathcal{R}_j|\kappa)}$ is called a Bayes Factor, the term originated by Good, the method attributed by Good to Turing and Jeffreys [25]. It is similar to the likelihood ratio for model comparison but involves integration of the probability distributions rather than comparing their maxima. The first term on the right hand side of (19) is the ratio of two integrals given in (18). The second factor is the prior odds, which is here set to 1, representing the absence of any prior preference between the two relations, i.e. $\Pr(\mathcal{R}_i) = \Pr(\mathcal{R}_j)$. Thus (19) can be rewritten

$$\text{posterior odds} = \text{Bayes Factor} \times \text{prior odds}. \tag{20}$$

6.1 Calculating Bayes Factors

In order to compute the Bayes factor, the prior distributions $\Pr(\theta_k|\mathcal{R}_k)$ of each model must be specified. This is both good and bad, good as it allows the incorporation of prior information (such as the estimate of the relation from previous frames), bad because these prior densities are hard to obtain when there is no such information.

The easiest approach is to use the **BIC** approximation which assumes that $\Pr(\theta_k)$ is approximately normal with mean $\hat{\theta}_k$ and covariance matrix $\mathbf{H}$; the derivation is given in appendix 11. The BIC approximation for the kth model is

$$\text{BIC}_k = -L_k + \frac{p}{2} \log N \tag{21}$$

the model with lowest BIC being most likely. Assuming that the prior on the models $\Pr(\mathcal{R}_k)$ is uniform the probability of each model may be calculated as

$$\Pr(\mathcal{R}_k|\kappa) = \frac{\exp(\text{BIC}_k)}{\sum_{i=1}^{i=K} \exp(\text{BIC}_i)} \tag{22}$$

Given two views, simpler models will be favoured over more complex ones as the $\frac{p}{2} \log N$ term will dominate, but as the number of images increases the likelihood function $\log(\kappa|\hat{\theta}_k)$ will take precedence.

Test results using BIC. The BIC is attractive because of its simple form which makes it easy to compute. Unfortunately the BIC approximation consistently underfits the model favouring models of too low a dimension. This is due to the poor approximation to equation (29). Consider 100 matches then $N = 400$, the number of observation, and the number of parameters to be estimated is $p = 307$ for the fundamental matrix and 208 for a homography. Which leads to a BIC penalty term of $307 \ln 400$ for $\mathbf{F}$ and $208 \ln 400$ for $\mathbf{H}$ a difference of 593.15, generally a homography would have to be an exceptionally poor fit between two views before its BIC would be that much larger than for a fundamental matrix. This would only occur with a very large baseline and very large perspective effects. The problem comes by the approximation of $\frac{1}{2}|A_L^{-1}|$ by $-\frac{p}{2}\log n$, see appendix 11 which is generally a bad approximation if $N < 5p$ [27] but also a bad approximation for the Hessian of the nuisance parameters.

Other Ways to Approximate Bayes Factors The crux of the problem with Bayes factors is the choice of prior $\Pr(\theta_k|\mathcal{R}_k)$ as this may influence the result. The BIC approximation finesses this detail by assuming the prior is very diffuse, whereas ideally the Bayes factors should be evaluated over a range of priors to check their stability. Aitkin [1] suggests using the posterior PDF of θ to compute what he calls posterior Bayes factors. However as Akaike points out "the repeated use of one and the same sample in the posterior mean of the likelihood function for the definition and evaluation of a posterior density certainly introduces a particular type of bias that invalidates the use of the mean as the likelihood of the model". Another variation is to divide the data into two, using one part to estimate a prior and another perform the model selection. In data contaminated with outliers this procedure is fraught with peril, e.g. all the outliers lie in one of the sets. One can use uniform or diffuse priors but great care must be taken when doing this or Lindley's paradox may occur [10] in which one model is arbitrarily favoured over another. The problem is that flat priors are specified only up to an undefined multiplicative constant.

6.2 Modified BIC for Least Squares Problems

It is apparent that the penalty term for the number of nuisance parameters due to the dimension of the relation, and the number of parameters due to degree of the relation should be weighted differently. In the appendix it is explained how the BIC is obtained by approximating the determinant of the log Hessian— the information matrix or inverse covariance matrix A_L^{-1}—by $\frac{p}{2}\log n$. Should the estimation of the parameters be influenced by all the data then this is a reasonable first order approximation. However for the least squares problem this is not the case. The estimation of each optimal match $\hat{m}_i$ (the estimation of the nuisance or internal parameters parameters with d degrees of freedom, where d is the dimension of the two view relation) is only effected by the 4 noisy coordinates of the match m under the assumption that the matches are independent. This is characterized by a block diagonal covariance matrix among matches This suggests the geometric Bayesian information criterion GBIC:

$$\text{GBIC} = -2L + \log(4)nd + \log(N)k \tag{23}$$

might be appropriate, with $N = 4n$ (recall n is the number of matches). This gives very similar performance to GRIC.

7   The Quest for the Universal Prior: MDL

Within this section the minimum description length principle is outlined, based upon the idea of parsimony. That the model that requires least coding is best, this principal has been one of the main rules of science since its inception: "We are to admit no more causes of natural things than such as are both true and sufficient to explain their appearances. To this purpose the philosophers say that Nature does nothing in vain, and more is in vain when less will serve; for Nature is pleased with simplicity; and affects not the pomp of superfluous causes." (Newton *Principia* 1726,vol. II,p.398) The key intuitive idea is that the simplest description of the a process will asymptotically (as the number of observations of that process becomes infinite) be functionally equivalent to the true one.

Rissanen [42] (1978) developed a criterion with a similar form to the BIC from a totally different standpoint. He derived the minimum-bit representation of the data, termed SSD—shortest description length, and MDL—minimum description length—an approach suggested by the idea of Algorithmic Complexity (Solomonoff [48] and Kolmogorov [29]). Wallace and Boulton [58] developed a very similar idea to MDL called the minimum message length (MML) approach. The criteria MDL and MML are based on minimum code lengths—given the data represented up to a finite precision, one picks the parameters so that the model they define permits the shortest possible code length. The code length being the sum of the code length for the model, and the code length for the data given the model i.e. the error (the two are directly analogous to the log prior and log likelihood). Given that it takes approximately $\log_2 X$ bits to encode a number X then it becomes clear that the most frequently occurring observations should be given smallest code lengths, hence MDL methods are integrally linked with Bayesian methods. Bayesian attempts at model selection can be stymied by the need for prior distributions, which are the Bayesian's philosopher's stone; MDL appears to promise such a universal prior for the complexity/parsimony of the model. However the term derived

$$\text{MDL} = -2L - \frac{p}{2} \log N \qquad (24)$$

has the same form and deficiencies as the BIC. Yet this is only a first order approximation to the optimal code length. Wallace & Freeman [59] (1987) further develop/expand MML leading to a very similar criterion to Bozdogan's CAICF.

Test results using MDL: Generally MDL criteria are the same as Bayesian and produce similar results.

8   Bayesian Model Selection and Model Averaging

A criterion not considered for model selection here is Inductive reasoning dates back at least to the Greek philosopher Epicurus (342?-270? B.C.), who proposed the following approach: "**Principle of Multiple Explanations**. If more than one theory is consistent with the observations, keep all theories" [32]. Thus as pointed out by his follower Lucretius (95-55 B.C.) if there are several explanations as to why a man died, but one does not definitively know which one is true, then Lucretius (and later Solomonoff [32]) advocates maintaining them all *for the purpose of prediction* (somewhat the opposite of Ockham's point of view).

So far I have described methods in which all the potential models are fitted and a model selection procedure is used to select which is best and it is adopted rather than from other defensible models. This is somewhat arbitrary ("a quiet scandal" [8]), first admitting that there is model uncertainty by searching for a "best" model and then ignoring this uncertainty by making inferences and forecasts as if it were certain that his chosen model is actually correct. Selection of just one model means that the uncertainty on some parameters is underestimated [21, 36] as will now be demonstrated. Hjorth distinguishes between *global* parameters which are defined for all models and *local* parameters which are not. Consider figure 2 depicting a two dimensional slice of parameter space for two global parameters. As the 2 parameters are altered (fixing for a moment all other parameters) the model selection criterion (e.g. AIC) will lead to different models being selected, given fixed data. This will not (significantly) effect the uncertainty of a parameter estimate at point X in figure 2 as it is away from a boundary; but point Y will have its uncertainty incorrectly estimated unless the fact that multiple models are being considered is taken into account, as the model parameterization will change over the boundary between model 1 and model 2. Furthermore as there is no chance for model 1 to take values of the parameters within the regions that AIC allocates to model 2 or 3 for this data set; *even if that is the correct answer.*

Hjorth [21] gives a rather neglected bias theorem which is intuitively obvious: that the expected value of the MAIC will be less than the minimum of the expected value of the AIC for all the models under consideration. Thus if model i were the true model the overall expectation of the MAIC would be less than AIC_i (as occasionally the wrong model is selected because is has lower AIC). Which in turn means that the residuals and covariance are slightly lower than would be expected.

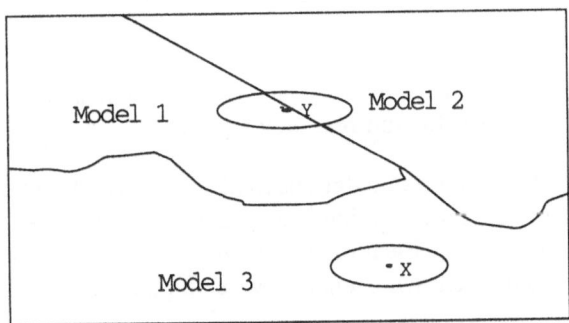

Fig. 2. *Two cases, X where the uncertainty in the model is unimportant, Y where the uncertainty in the model becomes important*

Bayesian model averaging takes into account explicitly model uncertainty by representing the data—each set of matches by a combination of models [11, 22,

27, 30, 37]. Rather than using one motion model a standard Bayesian formalism is adopted which averages the posterior distributions of the prediction under each model, weighted by their posterior model probabilities.

One of the main advantages of model averaging comes in prediction: if a new match is observed then its likelihood is computed as a weighted average over all the models. Indeed it has been shown that model averaging can produce superior results in predictive performance than commitment to a single model [34]. Suppose that there are K competing motion models with relations $\mathcal{R}_1 \ldots \mathcal{R}_K$ with parameter vectors $\theta_1 \ldots \theta_K$, that could describe C_j. Then Bayesian inference about $\mathbf{m}_i$ is based its posterior distribution, which is

$$\Pr(\mathbf{m}_i|\kappa) = \sum_{i=1}^{i=K} \Pr(\mathbf{m}_i|\mathcal{R}_k, \kappa) \Pr(\mathcal{R}_k|\kappa) \tag{25}$$

by the law of total probability [30]. Thus the full posterior probability of $\mathbf{m}_i$ is a weighted average of its posterior distribution under each of the models, where the weights are the posterior model probabilities, $\Pr(\mathcal{R}_k|\kappa)$ derived in (22). Equation (25) provides inference about $\mathbf{m}_i$ that takes into full account the uncertainty between models, and is particularly useful when two of the models describe the data equally well.

Test results using model averaging. As there is no model selection procedure a slightly different test criterion had to be used. The results for model averaging were assessed by examining how points were correctly classified as inlying or outlying, using the combination of models for the classification (elsewhere model averaging is assessed for segmentation [55]). Overall the results were disappointing with there being very little difference between the model averaging approach and using the model suggested by model selection procedure used to generate the posterior distribution over the models (AIC and BIC were tried).

9   Results

All of the model selection procedures have been implemented and compared on a large test bed of synthetic and real image pairs.

Synthetic Data. Three synthetic databases of one hundred sets of 100 synthetic matches, with $10-30\%$ outliers added, are generated to be consistent with either random $\mathbf{F}$, $\mathbf{F_A}$, $\mathbf{H}$ or $\mathbf{H_A}$. Each of the model selection algorithms was run on each set and the model chosen compared with the known ground truth.

Real Data. The algorithms have been tested on many images, here two typical image pairs are shown. In all the examples tested for this paper, the corners are obtained by using the detector described in [18], the matching procedure uses cross correlation in a square search window. The standard deviation of the error of the point correspondences σ was estimated robustly [57]. For model comparison testing is somewhat easier than in the general case of estimation, as

Fig. 3. *Left images, Indoor sequence, camera translating and rotating to fixate on the house; Right Images, two views of a buggy rotating on a table. With disparity vectors for features superimposed.*

all that needs to be known of the ground truth are some qualitative aspects in order to determine which model is the true one; i.e. if the motion is general and there are discernible perspective effects then $\mathbf{F}$ is the true model, if the camera rotates about its optic centre then $\mathbf{H}$ is the true model, if the scene is distant so as to be near orthographic then $\mathbf{F_A}$ is the true model, and if all the points lie on a distant plane then $\mathbf{H_A}$ is the true model, also if the focal length is long and the camera rotates $\mathbf{H_A}$ is appropriate. Two typical image pairs from the database are the Buggy and Model house:

Buggy. The left two images Figures 3 two views of a buggy rotating on a turn table, good orthographic but not perspective structure can be generated for this scene Hence the correct (or ground truth model) should be $\mathbf{F_A}$.

Model house data. The right two images Figure 3 show a scene in which a camera rotates and translates whilst fixating on a model house. The scene is a general motion, this is because the translational and rotational components of the camera motion were both significant, and full perspective structure can be recovered.

Summary of Results

1. Likelihood ratio test, only really appropriate for comparison of two nested models.

2. AIC tends to correctly reveal the dimension but overfits the degree of the relation.
3. BIC and MDL tend to greatly underfit the dimension and degree.
4. The geometric robust information criterion GRIC (15) with $\lambda_1 = 2.0$, $\lambda_2 = 4.0$ and $\lambda_3 = 4.0$ produced the most consistently good results, so far.
5. Model averaging produced little improvement together with increasing the amount of computation necessary to estimate likelihoods.

Results of using the robust model selector GRIC on the real images are given in Table 8.

Estimated	n	Motion of Points			
		General	Orthographic	Homography	Affinity
Model House	80	<u>596</u>	618	652	755
Buggy	167	1221	<u>1190</u>	1240	1450

Table 8. GRIC *values for the images. The model with lowest* **GRIC** *is underlined.*

10   Discussion

Another popular class of methods for model selection include cross validation, jackknifing, bootstrap, and data splitting [12, 21] in which the data is divided into two parts one is used to fit the relation and the other is used to evaluate the goodness of fit. However such procedures are very computationally intensive and highly sensitive to outliers, and results on real images are poor. In the asymptotic case Stone [49] demonstrates that AIC and cross validation are equivalent. The results are somewhat better in the outlier free case, but removal of the outliers presupposes knowledge of the correct relation for the data.

It has been observed that the construction of a prior distribution for each relation is the crux of determining the Bayes factors, and yet we are not without prior information about the distributions of such things as **F**. It is possible to construct this prior by introducing *our* subjective prior knowledge (like a true Bayesian) of camera calibration and the range of possible camera motions; e.g. it might be known that the principle point is roughly in the centre of the image, that the aspect ratio is roughly unity and the focal length lies within a certain range it might also be known that the camera was a hand held cameras moving roughly walking pace. By assigning Gaussians probability distributions to these with meaningful parameters monte carlo sampling methods [15] can be used to generate the prior for each $\mathcal{R}$, and hence the Bayes factor. It is then possible to use (29) directly to calculate the Bayes factor. Kass and Raftery [27] review a large number of such Monte Carlo style techniques for estimating Bayes factors.

Another interesting question is whether it is necessary to calculate all the models prior to model selection? All the approaches advocated involve estimation of all putative models which is costly in computation time. I have experimented with the use of covariance matrices (non-robust and robust [43]) in the hope that by fitting the most general model the covariance matrix might reveal if there are degeneracies. This works reasonably well if there are few outliers in the data but poorly otherwise. The alternative approach is to fit the least general model and assess its goodness of fit, only progressing to a more general model if the fit is bad. However again this is problematic in the case where there are outliers in the data it is hard to distinguish a set of outliers to a low order model from a set of inliers to the high order model without fitting both models. To quote from William Blake "The road of excess leads to the palace of wisdom; You never know what is enough unless you know what is more than enough" (*Proverbs of Hell*).

Now a warning: After model selection estimates of model parameters and of the residual variances are likely to be biased. Generally model selection biases are hard to quantify, but are characterized by deflation of covariance estimates. The type of bias will very much depend on the algorithm used to perform the model selection (as well as the criterion of model selection). To quote Pearl [39] "It would, therefore, be more appropriate to connect credibility with the nature of the selection procedure rather than the properties of the final product. When the former is not explicitly known...simplicity merely serves as a rough indicator for the type of processing that took place prior to the discovery". The quantification of these biases is an on going topic for research.

11   Conclusion

Generally there are two problem areas in computer vision; the first is of finding the correct representation of the data, and the second is manipulating that representation to make decisions and form hypotheses about the world. Model selection lies within both areas and it is critical to the design of computer vision algorithms, and yet often neglected. This can lead to bias in estimation. For instance there are a large number of papers about the uncertainty of the fundamental matrix (e.g.[9, 54, 60]) but that ignore the fact that there is uncertainty in the choice of model itself.

Several methods for model selection in the least squares regression problem have been reviewed and it has been shown that (a) care must be taken to count the degrees of freedom in the model (b) that careful distinction must be made between internal (nuisance) and external parameters.

Finally, it can be seen that there are several different model selection methodologies discussed in this paper. It is apparent that although the model selection paradigms arose in different areas they have great similarities as if they are shadows of some greater theory to come, the discovery of this theory is a line for future thought. Meanwhile only by incorporating and understanding model selection algorithms (which are merely mechanisms for making inference) into computer vision algorithms can progress be made to fully automated systems.

Acknowledgments I gratefully acknowledge W. Triggs, A. Fitzgibbon, D. Murray, and A. Zisserman for conversations that contributed to this paper.

Appendix: The BIC Approximation

The easiest approach to calculating Bayes Factors is to use the **BIC** approximation in which it is assumed that $\Pr(\theta_k|\mathcal{R}_k)$ is approximately normal with mean $\hat{\theta}_k$ and covariance matrix Λ^{-1}. The mean and covariance can be estimated as follows, let

$$\log(\Pr(\kappa|\mathcal{R}_\mathbf{k})) = \phi(\theta_k) = \log\left(\Pr(\kappa|\mathcal{R}_\mathbf{k},\theta_\mathbf{k})\Pr(\theta_\mathbf{k}|\mathcal{R}_\mathbf{k})\right) \tag{26}$$

then $\hat{\theta}_k$ is the MAP estimate of θ_k, such that $\phi(\theta_k)$ is minimized at $\hat{\theta}$, with the Hessian equal to Λ^{-1}, and covariance estimated as inverse Hessian, Λ. Performing a Taylor expansion around $\hat{\theta}$ gives

$$\Pr(\kappa|\mathcal{R}_\mathbf{k}) = \int \exp -\phi(\theta_k)d\theta_k$$
$$\approx \exp -\phi(\hat{\theta}_k)\int \exp\left(-\frac{1}{2}(\hat{\theta}_k - \theta_k)^\top \Lambda^{-1}(\hat{\theta}_k - \theta_k)\right)d\theta_k$$
$$= \exp -\phi(\hat{\theta}_k)(2\pi)^{p/2}|\Lambda|^{1/2}.$$

The last step in the equation above is a standard result for the integration of multi-variate Gaussians. Thus

$$\log(\Pr(\kappa|\mathcal{R}_\mathbf{k}) \approx \mathbf{L} + \frac{\mathbf{p}}{2}\log 2\pi + \frac{1}{2}\log|\mathbf{\Lambda}| + \log(\Pr(\hat{\theta}_\mathbf{k})|\mathcal{R}_\mathbf{k}) \tag{27}$$

which is Laplace's approximation [6, 33], from this various approximations can be made leading to calculable model selection criteria. Perhaps the simplest is given by Schwarz who approximates the prior by a normal distribution with mean θ_{prior} and covariance Λ_{prior} leading to

$$\Pr(\hat{\theta}_k|\mathcal{R}_k) = (2\pi)^{-p/2}|\hat{\Lambda}^{-\frac{1}{2}}|\exp(\frac{1}{2}(\theta_{\text{prior}} - \hat{\theta}_k)^\top \Lambda_{\text{prior}}^{-1}(\theta_{\text{prior}} - \hat{\theta}_k)) \tag{28}$$

thus

$$\log(\Pr(\mathcal{R}_k|\kappa)) \approx L - \frac{1}{2}(\hat{\theta}_k - \theta_{\text{prior}})^\top \Lambda_{\text{prior}}^{-1}(\hat{\theta}_k - \theta_{\text{prior}}) + \frac{1}{2}\log|\frac{\Lambda}{\Lambda_{\text{prior}}}|.$$

Now $\Lambda = \Lambda_{\text{prior}}\Lambda_L$, where Λ_L is the inverse of the Hessian of the log-likelihood at $\hat{\theta}_k$, leading to

$$\log(\Pr(\mathcal{R}_k|\kappa)) \approx \mathbf{L} - \frac{1}{2}(\hat{\theta}_\mathbf{k} - \theta_{\text{prior}})^\top \mathbf{\Lambda}_{\text{prior}}^{-1}(\hat{\theta}_\mathbf{k} - \theta_{\text{prior}}) - \frac{1}{2}\log|\mathbf{\Lambda_L^{-1}}|. \tag{29}$$

If the prior is assumed to be very diffuse then Schwarz [46] suggests discounting the second term and approximating the Hessian by $\frac{1}{2}\log|A_L^{-1}| \approx \frac{p}{2}\log n$ to get

$$\log(\mathcal{R}_k|\kappa) \approx \log(\kappa|\hat{\theta}_k) - \frac{\mathbf{p}}{\mathbf{2}}\log\mathbf{N} = \mathbf{L} - \frac{\mathbf{p}}{\mathbf{2}}\log\mathbf{N} \tag{30}$$

where $p = dn + k$ is the total number of parameters in the system, and $N = 4n$ is the total number of observations, n the number of matches, and d the dimension of R. Twice the negative of this, $-L + p\log N$, is referred to as the Bayesian Information Criterion or BIC and can be used to compare the likelihood of competing models.

General Comments: The BIC diverges from the full Bayesian viewpoint by discounting the prior term in (30). The determinant of the log Hessian $\frac{1}{2}\log|A_L^{-1}$ encodes the uncertainty in the parameter estimates (the smaller this value the greater the precision in the estimate). If available the Hessian itself should be calculated and used.

References

[1] M.A. Aitkin. Posterior Bayes Factors. *J.R. Statist. Soc. B*, 53(1):111–142, 1991.
[2] H. Akaike. A new look at the statistical model identification. *IEEE Trans. on Automatic Control*, Vol. AC-19(6):716–723, 1974.
[3] H. Akaike. Factor analysis and AIC. *Psychometrika*, 52(3):317–332, 1987.
[4] P. Beardsley, P. H. S. Torr, and A. Zisserman. 3D model aquisition from extended image sequences. In B. Buxton and Cipolla R., editors, *Proc. 4th European Conference on Computer Vision, LNCS 1065, Cambridge*, pages 683–695. Springer–Verlag, 1996.
[5] P. Beardsley, P. H. S. Torr, and A. Zisserman. 3D model aquisition from extended image sequences. In B. Buxton and Cipolla R., editors, *Proc. 4th European Conference on Computer Vision, LNCS 1065, Cambridge*, pages 683–695. Springer–Verlag, 1996.
[6] C. M. Bishop. *Neural Networks for Pattern Recognition*. Clarendon Press, Oxford, 1995.
[7] H. Bozdogan. Model selection and Akaike's information criterion (AIC): The general theory and its analytical extensions. *Psychometrika*, 52(3):345–370, 1987.
[8] C. Chatfield. Model uncertainty, data mining and statistical inference. *J. R. Statist Soc A.*, 158:419–466, 1995.
[9] G. Csurka, C. Zeller, Z. Zhang, and O. Faugeras. Characterizing the uncertainty of the fundamental matrix. *CVIU*, 68(1):18–36, 1996.
[10] M. DeGroot. *Optimal Statistical Decisions*. McGraw-Hill, 1970.
[11] D. Draper. Assessment and propagation of model uncertainty (with discussion). *Journal of the Royal Statistical Society series B*, 57:45–97, 1995.
[12] B. Efron and R.J. Tibshirani. *An Introduction to the Bootstrap*. Chapman and Hall, London, UK, 1993.
[13] O.D. Faugeras. What can be seen in three dimensions with an uncalibrated stereo rig? In G. Sandini, editor, *Proc. 2nd European Conference on Computer Vision, LNCS 588, Santa Margherita Ligure*, pages 563–578. Springer–Verlag, 1992.
[14] R. A. Fisher. Uncertain inference. *Proc. Amer. Acad. Arts and Sciences*, 71:245–258, 1936.

[15] A. Gelman, J. B. Carlin, H. S. Stern, and D. B. Rubin. *Bayesian Data Analysis.* Chapman & Hall, New York, 1995.

[16] P. E. Gill, W. Murray, and M. H. Wright. *Practical Optimization.* Academic Press, 1981.

[17] J. P. Hampel, E. M. Ronchetti, P. J. Rousseeuw, and W. A. Stahel. *Robust Statistics: An Approach Based on Influence Functions.* Wiley, New York, 1986.

[18] C. Harris. Structure-from-motion under orthographic projection. In O. Faugeras, editor, *Proc. 1st European Conference on Computer Vision, LNCS 427,* pages 118–128. Springer–Verlag, 1990.

[19] R. I. Hartley. Estimation of relative camera positions for uncalibrated cameras. In G. Sandini, editor, *Proc. 2nd European Conference on Computer Vision, LNCS 588, Santa Margherita Ligure,* pages 579–87. Springer–Verlag, 1992.

[20] R. I. Hartley and P. Sturm. Triangulation. In *American Image Understanding Workshop,* pages 957–966, 1994.

[21] U. Hjorth. On model selection in the computer age. *J. Statist Planng Inf,* 23:101–115, 1989.

[22] J. S. Hodges. Uncertainty, policy analysis and statistics (with discussion). *Statistical Science,* 2:259–291, 1987.

[23] P. J. Huber. *Robust Statistics.* John Wiley and Sons, 1981.

[24] M. Irani, P. Anandan, and D. Weinshall. From reference frames to reference planes: Multi-view parallax geometry and its applications. In H. Burkhardt and B. Neumann, editors, *Proc. 5th European Conference on Computer Vision, LNCS 1406, Freiburg,* pages 829–846. Springer-Verlag, 1998.

[25] H. Jeffreys. *Theory of Probability.* Clarendon Press, Oxford, third edition, 1961.

[26] K. Kanatani. *Statistical Optimization for Geometric Computation: Theory and Practice.* Elsevier Science, Amsterdam, 1996.

[27] R. E. Kass and A. E. Raftery. Bayes factors. *Journal of the American Statistical Association,* 90:733–795, 1995.

[28] M. Kendall and A. Stuart. *The Advanced Theory of Statistics.* Charles Griffin and Company, London, 1983.

[29] A.N. Kolmogorov. Three approaches to the quantitative definition of information. *Problems of Information Transmission,* 1:4–7, 1965.

[30] E. E. Leamer. *Specification searches: ad hoc inference with nonexperimental data.* Wiley, New York, 1978.

[31] I. J. Leontaritis and S. A. Billings. Model selection and validation methods for non-linear systems. *INT J CONTROL,* 45(1):311–341, 1987.

[32] M. Li and P. Vitányi. *An introduction to Kolmogorov complexity and its applications.* Springer-Verlag, 1997.

[33] D. V. Lindley. Approximate Bayesian methods. In J. M. Bernardo, M. H. De-Groot, D. V. Lindley, and A. F. M. Smith, editors, *Bayesian Statistics,* pages 223–237, Valencia, 1980. Valencia University Press.

[34] D. Madigan and A. E. Raftery. Model selection and accounting for model uncertainty in graphical models using Occam's window. *Journal of the American Statistical Association,* 89:1535–1546, 1994.

[35] G.I. McLachlan and K. Basford. *Mixture models: inference and applications to clustering.* Marcel Dekker. New York, 1988.

[36] A. J. Miller. Selection of subsets of regression variables (with discussion). *Journal of the Royal Statistical Society (Series A),* 147:389–425, 1984.

[37] B. R. Moulton. A Bayesian-approach to regression selection and estimation with application to a price-index for radio services. *Journal of Econometrics,* 49:169–193, 1991.

[38] J. Mundy and A. Zisserman. *Geometric Invariance in Computer Vision*. MIT press, 1992.

[39] J. Pearl. On the connection between the complexity and credibility of inferred models. *Int. J. General Systems*, 4:255–264, 1978.

[40] K. Pearson. On lines and planes of closest fit to systems of points in space. *Philos. Mag. Ser. 6*, 2:559, 1901.

[41] B. D. Ripley. *Pattern recognition and neural networks*. Cambridge University Press, Cambridge, 1996.

[42] J. Rissanen. Modeling by shortest data description. *Automatica*, 14:465–471, 1978.

[43] P. J. Rousseeuw. *Robust Regression and Outlier Detection*. Wiley, New York, 1987.

[44] B. Russell. *History of Western Philosophy*. Routledge, 1961.

[45] K. Schittowski. NLQPL: A FORTRAN-subroutine solving constrained nonlinear programming problems. *Annals of Operations Research*, 5:485–500, 1985.

[46] G. Schwarz. Estimating dimension of a model. *Ann. Stat.*, 6:461–464, 1978.

[47] G.A.F. Wild C. J. Seber. *Non-Linear Regression*. Wiley, New York, 1989.

[48] R. Solomonoff. A formal theory of inductive inference i. *Information and Control*, 7:1–22, 1964.

[49] M. Stone. An asymptotic equivalence of choice of model by cross-validation and Akaike's criterion. *J. Roy. Statist. Soc. B*, 39:44–47, 1977.

[50] P. H. S. Torr. *Outlier Detection and Motion Segmentation*. PhD thesis, Dept. of Engineering Science, University of Oxford, 1995.

[51] P. H. S. Torr. Geometric motion segmentation and model selection. In J. Lasenby, A. Zisserman, R. Cipolla, and H. Longuet-Higgins, editors, *Philosophical Transactions of the Royal Society A*, pages 1321–1340. Roy Soc, 1998.

[52] P. H. S. Torr, A. FitzGibbon, and A. Zisserman. Maintaining multiple motion model hypotheses through many views to recover matching and structure. In U Desai, editor, *ICCV6*, pages 485–492. Narosa Publishing House, 1998.

[53] P. H. S. Torr and D. W. Murray. The development and comparison of robust methods for estimating the fundamental matrix. *Int Journal of Computer Vision*, 24(3):271–300, 1997.

[54] P. H. S. Torr and D. W. Murray. The development and comparison of robust methods for estimating the fundamental matrix. *IJCV*, 24(3):271–300, 1997.

[55] P. H. S. Torr and A. Zisserman. Concerning bayesian motion segmentation, model averaging, matching and the trifocal tensor. In H. Burkhardt and B. Neumann, editors, *ECCV98 Vol 1*, pages 511–528. Springer, 1998.

[56] P. H. S. Torr and A. Zisserman. Robust computation and parametrization of multiple view relations. In U Desai, editor, *ICCV6*, pages 727–732. Narosa Publishing House, 1998.

[57] P. H. S. Torr, A Zisserman, and S. Maybank. Robust detection of degenerate configurations for the fundamental matrix. *CVIU*, 71(3):312–333, 1998.

[58] C.S. Wallace and D.M. Boulton. An information measure for classification. *Computer Journal*, 11(2):195–209, 1968.

[59] C.S. Wallace and P.R. Freeman. Estimation and inference by compact coding. *J. R. Statist. Soc B*, 49(3):240–265, 1987.

[60] Z. Zhang. Determining the epipolar geometry and its uncertainty: A review. *IJCV*, 27(2):161–195, 1997.

Finding Objects by Grouping Primitives

David Forsyth, John Haddon, and Sergey Ioffe

Computer Science Division, U.C. Berkeley, Berkeley, CA 94720, USA
daf,ioffe,haddon@cs.berkeley.edu,
http://www.cs.berkeley.edu/~daf,ioffe,haddon

Abstract. Digital library applications require very general object recognition techniques. We describe an object recognition strategy that operates by grouping together image primitives in increasingly distinctive collections. Once a sufficiently large group has been found, we declare that an object is present. We demonstrate this method on applications such as finding unclothed people in general images and finding horses in general images. Finding clothed people is difficult, because the variation in colour and texture on the surface of clothing means that it is hard to find regions of clothing in the image. We show that our strategy can be used to find clothing by marking the distinctive shading patterns associated with folds in clothing, and then grouping these patterns.

1 Background

Several typical collections containing over ten million images are listed in [6]. There is an extensive literature on obtaining images from large collections using features computed from the whole image, including colour histograms, texture measures and shape measures; significant papers include [9, 13, 16, 21, 24, 25, 27, 30, 31, 36, 37, 38, 39, 42].

However, in the most comprehensive field study of usage practices (a paper by Enser [6] surveying the use of the Hulton Deutsch collection), there is a clear user preference for searching these collections on image semantics; typical queries observed are overwhelmingly oriented toward object classes ("dinosaurs", p. 40, "chimpanzee tea party, early", p. 41) or instances ("Harry Secombe", p. 44, "Edward Heath gesticulating", p. 45). An ideal search tool would be a quite general recognition system that could be adapted quickly and easily to the types of objects sought by a user. Building such a tool requires a much more sophisticated understanding of the process of recognition than currently exists.

Object recognition will not be comprehensively solved in the foreseeable future. Solutions that are good enough to be useful for some cases in applications are likely, however. Querying image collections is a particularly good application, because in many cases no other query mechanism is available — there is no prospect of searching all the photographs by hand. Furthermore, users are typically happy with low recall queries - in fact, the output of a high-recall search for "The President" of a large news collection would be unusable for most application purposes. This proposal focuses on areas that form a significant subset of these queries where useful tools can reasonably be expected.

D.A. Forsyth et al. (Eds.): Shape, Contour ..., LNCS 1681, pp. 302–318, 1999.

Discussing recognition requires respecting a distinction between two important and subtly different problems: *finding*, where the image components that result from a single object are collected together; and *naming*, where the particular name of a single isolated object is determined. Finding is not well defined, because objects are not well defined — for example, would one regard the image components corresponding to an ear or an eye as separate objects that comprise a face, or do these components belong together as part of a single indissoluble object?

2 Primitives, Segmentation, and Implicit Representations

Writings on object recognition have tended to concentrate on naming problems. For some types of object or scene finding can be avoided by quite simple techniques. For example, for small numbers of geometrically exact object models search is effective [7, 14, 18, 22, 26, 28, 29, 34, 40]; and for isolated objects, finding is irrelevant.

However, in many applications finding is an important component of the problem; often, the name of an object is required only at a very limited level of detail ("person", "big cat", etc.). While naming is not an easy problem, quite good solutions appear possible with extensions of current pose-based techniques. There are several reasons finding is very difficult and poorly understood. Finding is essentially segmentation writ large, using generic cues — like coherence in colour and texture, used by current work on segmentation — initially and high-level knowledge later to obtain *regions that should be recognised together*. However, deciding which bits of the image belong together and should be recognised together requires knowledge of object properties. As a result, finding involves deploying object knowledge to direct and guide segmentation — but how is the right piece of knowledge to be used in the right place? One wishes to recognize objects at a class level independent of geometric detail, so that finding algorithms should be capable of **abstraction**. For example, most quadrupeds have roughly the same body segments in roughly the same place — good finding algorithms would exploit this fact before, say, measuring the distribution of musculature on each segment or the number of hairs on an ear. Finally, a sensible approach to finding should use representations that are robust to the effects of **pose**, and of **internal degrees of freedom**, such as joints.

If we use the word primitive more loosely, to mean a feature or assembly of features that has a constrained, stylised appearance, then a representation based around primitives at many levels has the great advantage that, at each stage of finding, a program can know what it is looking for. For example, horses can be represented (crudely!) as assemblies of hide-coloured cylinders — this results in a finding process that first looks for hide-like regions; then finds edge points, and uses geometrical constraints to assemble sets of edge points that could have come from cylinders; and finally reasons about the configuration of the cylinders. At each stage there are few alternatives to choose from, which means the search is efficient; and, while each individual test is weak, the collective of tests in sequence can be quite powerful. The choice of primitives and the order and nature of assembly routines together form an *implicit representation* — a representation of an object as a finding process which functions as a source of top-down knowledge.

We now have some insight into what should be a primitive. Primitives should have **stereotyped appearance**. The most useful form of primitive is one where it is possible to test an assembly of image features and say whether it is likely to have come from a primitive or not. For example, it is known that such tests are easy for surfaces of revolution, straight homogeneous generalised cylinders, canal surfaces, and cylinders [32, 33, 43]. As a result, it is possible to segment image regions that are likely to correspond to such surfaces *without knowing to what object they belong*[1]. A second feature of a useful primitive is that it is **significant**. For example, a cylinder is a significant property, because many objects are - at a crude level - made of cylinders. A third useful property is **robustness**; cylindrical primitives are quite easy to find even in the presence of some deformations. These properties mean that finding objects that are assemblies of primitives essentially involves finding the primitives, and then reasoning about their assembly. As we have indicated, previous work has typically concentrated on parsing activities (which assume that finding has already occurred); this proposal concentrates on finding.

2.1   Body Plans - Interim Results on Implicit Representations

A natural implicit representation to use for people and many animals is a *body plan* — a sequence of grouping stages, constructed to mirror the layout of body segments. These grouping stages assemble image components that could correspond to appropriate body segments or other components (as in figure 1, which shows the plan used as an implicit representation of a horse). Having a sequence of stages means the process is efficient: the process can start with checking individual segments and move to checking multi-segment groups, so that not all groups of four (or however many for the relevant body plan) segments are presented to the final classifier. We have done extensive experiments with two separate systems that use the same structure:

- Images are masked for regions of appropriate colour and texture.
- Roughly cylindrical regions of appropriate colour and texture are identified.
- Assemblies of regions are formed and tested against a sequence of predicates.

The first example identifies pictures containing people wearing little or no clothing, to finesse the issue of variations of appearance of clothing. This program has been tested on an usually large and unusually diverse set of images; on a test collection of 565 images known to contain lightly clad people and 4289 control

---

[1] While current techniques for finding generalised cylinders are fragile, because they winnow large collections of edges to find subsets with particular geometric properties and so are overwhelmed by images of textured objects, the principle remains. We indicate an attack on this difficulty below.

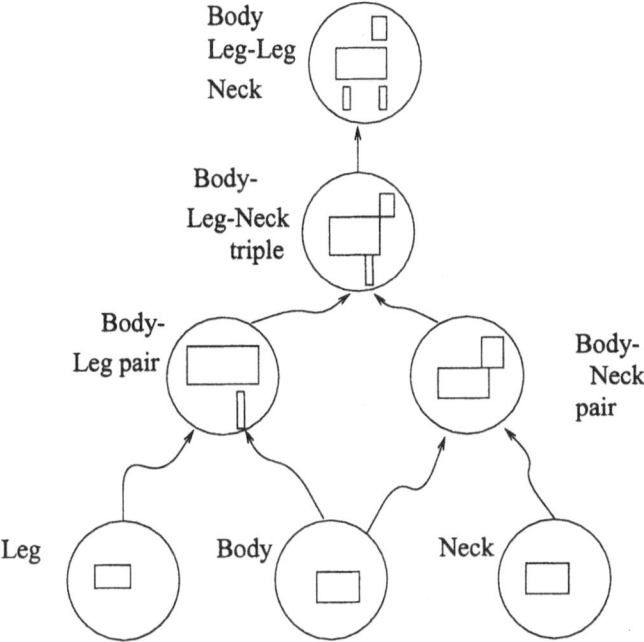

Fig. 1. *The body plan used for horses. Each circle represents a classifier, with an icon indicating the appearance of the assembly. An arrow indicates that the classifier at the arrowhead uses segments passed by the classifier at the tail. The topology was given in advance. The classifiers were then trained using image data from a total of 38 images of horses.*

images with widely varying content, one tuning of the program marked 241 test images and 182 control images (the performance of various different tunings is indicated in figure 3; more detailed information appears in [12, 10]). The recall is comparable with full-text document recall [3, 4, 35] (which is surprisingly good for so abstract an object recognition query) and the rate of false positives is satisfactorily low. In this case, the representation was entirely built by hand.

The second example used a representation whose combinatorial structure — the order in which tests were applied — was built by hand, but where the tests were learned from data. This program identified pictures containing horses, and is described in greater detail in [11]. Tests used 100 images containing horses, and 1086 control images with widely varying content. The geometric process makes a significant different, as figure 2 illustrates. The performance of various different configurations is shown in figure 3. For version "F", if one estimates performance omitting images used in training and images for which the segment finding process fails, the recall is 15% — i.e. about 15% of the images containing horses are marked — and control images are marked at the rate of approximately

Fig. 2. *Typical images with large quantities of hide-like pixels (white pixels are not hide-like; others are hide-like) that are classified as not containing horses, because there is no geometric configuration present. While the test of colour and texture is helpful, the geometric test is important, too, as the results in figure 3 suggest. In particular, the fact that a horse is brown is not nearly as distinctive as the fact that it is brown, made of cylinders, and these cylinders have a particular set of possible arrangements.*

0.65%. In our test collection, this translates to 11 images of horses marked and 4 control images marked[2].

Finding using body plans has been shown to be quite effective for special cases in quite general scenes. It is relatively insensitive to changes in aspect [11]. It is quite robust to the relatively poor segmentations that our criteria offer, because it is quite effective in dealing with nuisance segments — in the horse tests, the average number of four segment groups was $2,500,000$, which is an average of forty segments per image. Nonetheless, the process described above is crude: it is too dependent on colour and texture criteria for early segmentation; the learning process is absent (humans) or extremely simple (horses); and there is one recogniser per class.

3   Learning Assembly Processes from Data

We have been studying processes for learning to assemble primitives. The recognition processes described above have a strong component of correspondence; in

---

[2] These figures are *not* 15 and 7, because of the omission of training images and images where the segment finder failed in estimating performance.

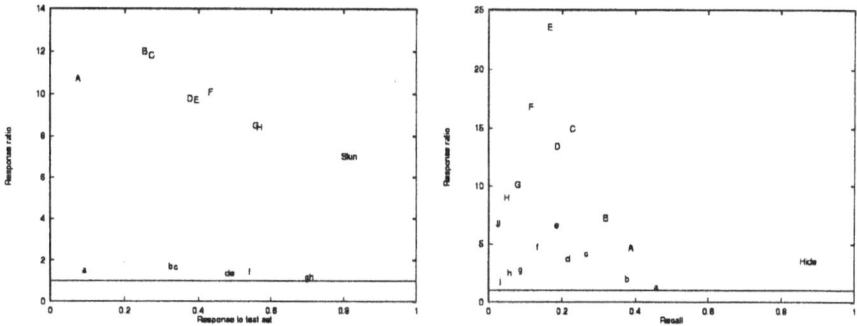

Fig. 3. *The response ratio, (percent incoming test images marked/percent incoming control images marked), plotted against the percentage of test images marked, for various configurations of the two finding programs. Data for the nude human finder appears on the top, for the horse finder on the right. Capital letters indicate the performance of the complete system of skin/hide filter and geometrical grouper, and lower case letters indicate the performance of the geometrical grouper alone. The label "skin" (resp "hide") indicates the selectivity of using skin (resp hide) alone as a criterion. For the human finder, the parameter varied is the type of group required to declare a human is present — the trend is that more complex groups display higher selectivity and lower recall. For the horse finder, the parameter being varied is the maximum number of that will be considered.*

particular, we are pruning a set of correspondences between image segments and body segment labels by testing for kinematic plausibility.

The search for acceptable correspondences can be made efficient by using *projected classifiers*, which prune labelings using the properties of smaller sub-labelings (as in [18], who use manually determined bounds and do not learn the tests). Given a classifier C which is a function of a set of features whose values depend on segments with labels in the set $L = \{l_1 \ldots l_m\}$, the projected classifier $C_{l_1 \ldots l_k}$ is a function of of all those features that depend only on the segments with labels $L' = \{l_1 \ldots l_k\}$. In particular, $C_{l_1 \ldots l_k}(L') > 0$ if there is some extension L of L' such that $C(L) > 0$. This criterion corresponds to insisting that groups should pass intermediate classifiers if, *with appropriate segments attached*, they pass a final classifier.

The converse need not be true: the feature values required to bring a projected point inside the positive volume of C may not be realized with any labeling of the current set of segments $1, \ldots, N$. For a projected classifier to be useful, it must be easy to compute the projection, and it must be effective in rejecting labelings at an early stage. These are strong requirements which are not satisfied by most good classifiers; for example, in our experience a support vector machine with a positive definite quadratic kernel projects easily but typically yields unrestrictive projected classifiers.

We have been using an axis-aligned bounding box, with bounds learned from a collection of positive labellings, for a good first separation, and then using a boosted version of a weak classifier that splits the feature space on a single feature value (as in [15]). This yields a classifier that projects particularly well, and allows clean and efficient algorithms for computing projected classifiers and expanding sets of labels (see [23]).

The segment finder may find either 1 or 2 segments for each limb, depending on whether it is bent or straight; because the pruning is so effective, we can allow segments to be broken into two equal halves lengthwise, both of which are tested.

3.1 Results

The training set included 79 images without people, selected randomly from the COREL database, and 274 images each with a single person on uniform background. The images with people have been scanned from books of human models [41]. All segments in the test images were reported; in the control images, only segments whose interior corresponded to human skin in colour and texture were reported. Control images, both for the training and for the test set, were chosen so that all had at least 30% of their pixels similar to human skin in colour and texture. This gives a more realistic test of the system performance by excluding regions that are obviously not human, and reduces the number of segments in the control images to the same order of magnitude as those in the test images.

The models are all wearing either swim suits or no clothes, otherwise segment finding fails; it is an open problem to segment people wearing loose clothing. There is a wide variation in the poses of the training examples, although all body segments are visible. The sets of segments corresponding to people were then hand-labeled. Of the 274 images with people, segments for each body part were found in 193 images. The remaining 81 resulted in incomplete configurations, which could still be used for computing the bounding box used to obtain a first separation. Since we assume that if a configuration looks like a person then its mirror image would too, we double the number of body configurations by flipping each one about a vertical axis. The bounding box is then computed from the resulting 548 points in the feature space, without looking at the images without people.

The boosted classifier was trained to separate two classes: the $193 \times 2 = 386$ points corresponding to body configurations, and 60727 points that did not correspond to people but lay in the bounding box, obtained by using the bounding box classifier to incrementally build labelings for the images with no people. We added 1178 synthetic positive configurations obtained by randomly selecting each limb and the torso from one of the 386 real images of body configurations (which were rotated and scaled so the torso positions were the same in all of them) to give an effect of joining limbs and torsos from different images rather like childrens' flip-books. Remarkably, the boosted classifier classified each of the

Features	# test images	# control images	False negatives	False positives
367	120	28	37%	4%
567	120	86	49%	10 %

Table 1. *Number of images of people and without people processed by the classifiers with 367 and 567 features, compared with false negative (images with a person where no body configuration was found) and false positive (images with no people where a person was detected) rates.*

real data points correctly but misclassified 976 out of the 1178 synthetic configurations as negative; the synthetic examples were unexpectedly more similar to the negative examples than the real examples were.

The test dataset was separate from the training set and included 120 images with a person on a uniform background, and varying numbers of control images, reported in table 1. We report results for two classifiers, one using 567 features and the other using a subset of 367 of those features. Table 1 shows the false positive and false negative rates achieved for each of the two classifiers. By marking 51% of test images and only 10% of control images, the classifier using 567 features compares extremely favourably with that of [8], which marked 54% of test images and 38% of control images using hand-tuned tests to form groups of four segments. In 55 of the 59 images where there was a false negative, a segment corresponding to a body part was missed by the segment finder, meaning that the overall system performance significantly understates the classifier performance. There are few signs of overfitting, probably because the features are highly redundant. Using the larger set of features makes labelling faster (by a factor of about five), because more configurations are rejected earlier.

4   Shading Primitives, Shape Representations, and Clothing

Finding clothed people is a far more subtle problem than finding naked people, because the variation in colour, texture and pattern of clothing defeats a colour segmentation strategy. Clothing does have distinctive properties: the patterns formed by folds on clothing appear to offer cues to the configuration of the person underneath (as any textbook on figure drawing will illustrate). These folds have quite distinctive shading patterns [19], which are a dominant feature of the shading field of a person clad in a loose garment, because, although they are geometrically small, the surface normal changes significantly at a fold. Folds are best analysed using the theory of buckling, and arise from a variety of causes including excess material, as in the case of a full skirt, and stresses on a garment caused by body configurations. Folds appear to be the single most distinctive, reliable and general visual cue to the configuration of a person dressed in a cotton garment.

4.1   Grouping Folds Using a Simple Buckling Model

Garments can be modelled as elastic shells, allowing rather simple predictions of the pattern of folds using the Von Karman-Donnell equation or a linearised version of that equation. This is known to be a dubious source of predictions of buckling force, but the frequencies of the eigenfunctions — which give the buckled solutions — are accepted as fair predictions of the buckling mode for the cases described (this is the topic of a huge literature, introduced in [5]). The eigenfunctions allow us to predict that garments buckling in compression or torsion will display long, nearly straight folds that are nearly parallel and nearly evenly spaced. These folds will be approximately perpendicular to the direction of compression and will indicate the direction of the torsion. The number of folds depends on tension in the garment, and is hard to predict.[3] For torsion, reasonable estimates of a garment's size yield on the order of five visible folds. As figures 4 and 5 indicate, these predictions are accurate enough to drive a segmentation process.

We apply the simple fold finder described in [20] to the image at twelve different orientations. Using these twelve response maps, we use non-maximum supression to find the centre of the fold, and follow this maximum along the direction of maximum response to link all points corresponding to a single fold. The linking process breaks sharp corners, by considering the primary direction of the preceding points along the fold.

After finding all of the folds in the image, the next step is to find pairs which are approximately parallel, and in the same part of the image. If the projections of the two folds onto their average direction are disjoint, they are considered to belong to different parts of the image.

From the theory, we expect that multiple folds will be at regularly spaced intervals. Thus, we look for pairs which have one common fold, and consistent separations. (The separations should either be the same, or one should be double the other—if a single fold gets dropped, we do not want to ignore the entire pattern.) The separation between folds is required to be less than the maximum length of the folds. Finally, some of these groups can be further combined, if the groups have almost the same set of folds.

The program typically extracts 10–25 groups of folds from an image. Figure 4 shows one image with three typical groups. The group in 4(b) clearly corresponds to the major folds across the torso in the image. This is in fact a segmentation of the image into coherent regions consisting of possible pieces of cloth. The region covered by the folds in (b) is most of the torso of the figure, and suggests a likely candidate for consideration as a torso. There are other groups as well, such as (c), the venetian blinds, and (d), an aliased version of (d), but these extra segments are easily dealt with by higher level processes.

Any image of man-made scenes will have a number of straight parallel lines which may have similar shading to folds (see, for example, figure 6). While this

---

[3] This can be demonstrated with a simple experiment. Wearing a loose but tucked-in T-shirt, bend forward at the waist; the shirt hangs in a single fold. Now pull the T-shirt taut against your abdomen and bend forward; many narrow folds form.

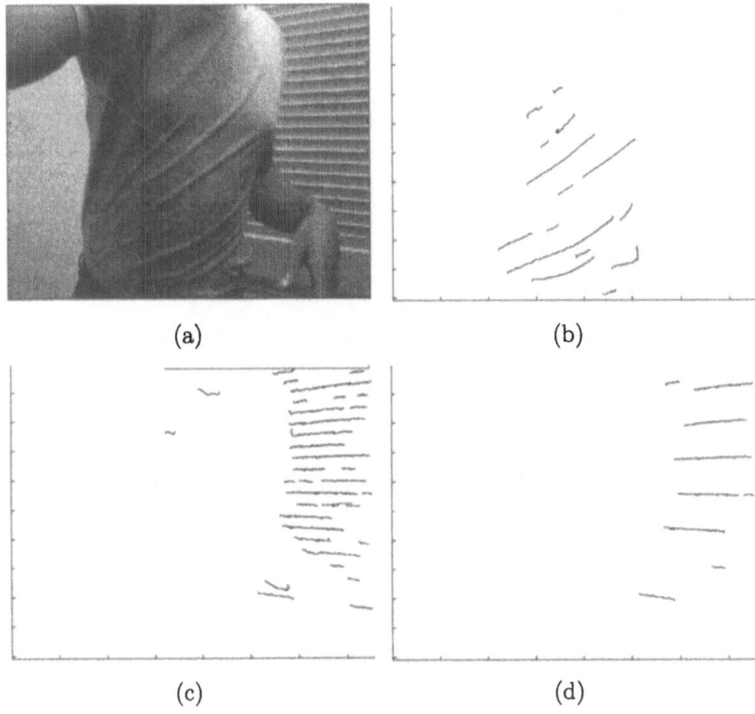

(a)

(b)

(c)

(d)

Fig. 4. *Results of a segmenter that obtains regions by grouping folds that satisfy the qualitative predictions of the linear buckling theory. (a) An image showing folds corresponding to torsional buckling. (b,c,d) Three groups of folds found by our program. The group in (b) is, in essence the torso; it contains the major folds across the torso, and can be used to represent the torso. An edge detector could not extract the outline points of the torso from this image, since the venetian blinds would result in a mess of edges. The group of fold responses in (c) is due to the venetian blinds in the background. Such a large set of parallel lines is unlikely to come from a picture of a torso, since it would require the torso to be unrealistically long. (d) A group that is an aliased version of the group in (c). Each group has quite high level semantics for segmenter output; in particular, groups represent image regions that could be clothing.*

may be initially interpreted as groups of folds—hence as clothing—higher-level reasoning should enable us to reject these groups as coming from something other than folds in cloth.

4.2   Grouping Folds by Sampling

An alternative approach is to obtain groups which are samples from a posterior on groups given image data. This approach has the virtue that we do not need

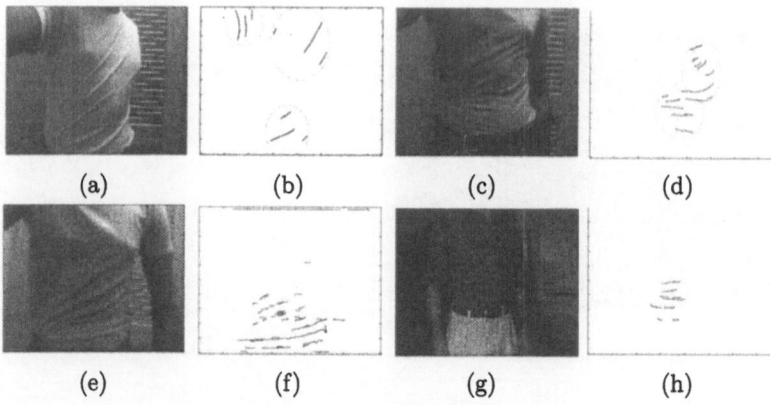

(a)   (b)   (c)   (d)

(e)   (f)   (g)   (h)

Fig. 5. *Further examples of segmentations produced by our grouping process. The figures show groups of fold responses, for the torsional (b,f) and axial (d,h) cases. In some cases, more than one group should be fused to get the final extent of the torso — these groups are separated by circles in the image. In each case, there are a series of between 10 and 25 other groups, representing either aliasing effects, the venetian blinds, or other accidental events. Each group could be a region of clothing; more high-level information is required to tell which is and which is not.*

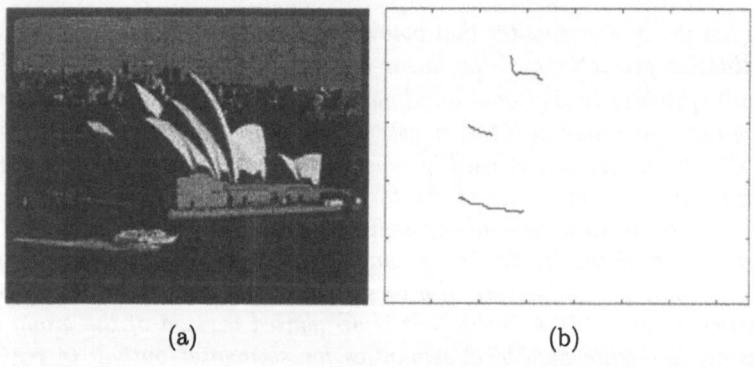

(a)   (b)

Fig. 6. *There are parallel folds that appear without clothing, too; (a) An image of an architectural curiosity. (b) One of four groups of folds found in the image. It is certainly expected that in images of man-made scenes, there will be a large number of nearly-parallel lines, which may be interpreted as groups of folds. Other cues should allow us to determine that this is not in fact clothing.*

to come up with a detailed physical model of garment buckling — a process complicated by cloth anisotropy, etc. A simple likelihood model can be fitted to groups in real images, instead.

We describe each group of folds by a coordinate system and a series of variables which describe the scale of the folds, their angle, and their location with respect to a coordinate system. We also include the change in angle between adjacent folds (this enables us to describe star-shaped folds). By examining a number of groups in real images, we estimate a probability distribution on the parameters of the coordinate system. This allows us to describe how likely a group with those parameters is. We also estimate the probability distribution for individual folds within a group.

The folds are grouped by running a reversible-jump Markov Chain Monte Carlo algorithm (as in [17]. If a fold has a high likelihood of belonging to a particular group, an assignment of the fold to that group should be fairly stable. In other words, it will have a high probability in the stationary distribution. The assignments which appear most frequently over a large number of iterations are taken to be the correct grouping. Proposal moves for this MCMC grouper are:

1. Add a new group. Two folds which have not previously been assigned to another group are combined to form a new group.
2. Delete a two-fold group.
3. Change the parameters of a group.
4. Add a fold to a group. An unassigned fold is assigned to an existing group.
5. Remove a fold from a group
6. Change the group of a fold. Change the group assignment of a fold.

After several thousand iterations, we observe that the MCMC spends a relatively high proportion of its time in certain states. We take the grouping in the most popular state to be the best grouping of folds for the images. Figure 7 shows an image, and the most popular grouping of folds. (The lower-level fold finder is not yet robust enough to generate reliable folds, so the putative folds here were marked by hand.) Parallel groups are taken to be a unit, and the edge of the figure is largely ignored, as desired.

4.3 Choosing Primitives and Building Representations

Clothing is an interesting case because it is not obvious that folds are the right primitive to use. This raises the standard, difficult question that any theory based on primitives must address — how do we determine what is to be a primitive? As a possible alternative to our current fold-finder, we have been studying a mechanism for determining what should be a primitive following the ideas of [1, 2]. We obtain a large set of images of regions showing regions of folds, at the same orientation and scale. There is a comparison set, containing non folds that are not easy to distinguish from the folds using crude methods (e.g. a linear classifier on principal components). As measurements, we use spatial relations between filter outputs, for a reasonable set of filters at a variety of scales. We take uniform samples of subimages from each set.

The task is now to explore the structure of the clothing set with respect to the non-clothing set. We do this by setting up a decision tree; each decision

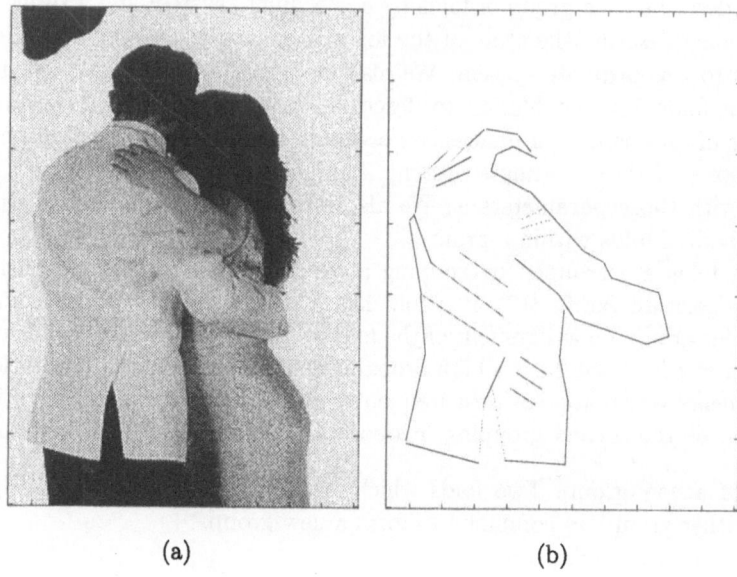

(a)   (b)

Fig. 7. *The Markov Chain Monte Carlo method can be used to group folds together. (a) The original image. (b) Folds marked by hand, but grouped automatically. This is the most popular grouping of the image, after 10,000 iterations. Note that parallel folds are grouped together, and that the outline of the figure is largely ignored.*

attempts to split the set at the leaf using an entropy criterion. The measurement used is the value of the output of one filter at one point — the choice of filter and point is given by the entropy criterion. The approach can be thought of as supervised learning of segmentation — we are training a decision tree to separate windows associated with objects to from those that are not. We split to several levels — a total of twelve leaves in the current experiments – and then use the representation at each leaf as a primitive. In particular, a leaf is defined by a series of filter outputs at a series of points; at each leaf we have an estimate of the frequency of observation of this pattern given clothing, and given no clothing. The remaining task is to postprocess the set of primitives to remove translational redundancies.

5   Conclusions

For recognition systems to be practically useful, we need a system of representation that can handle a reasonable level of abstraction and that can support segmentation from quite general backgrounds. These requirements strongly suggest representations in terms of relations between primitives. We have shown that, using a simple primitive that is obviously convenient and useful, it is possible to

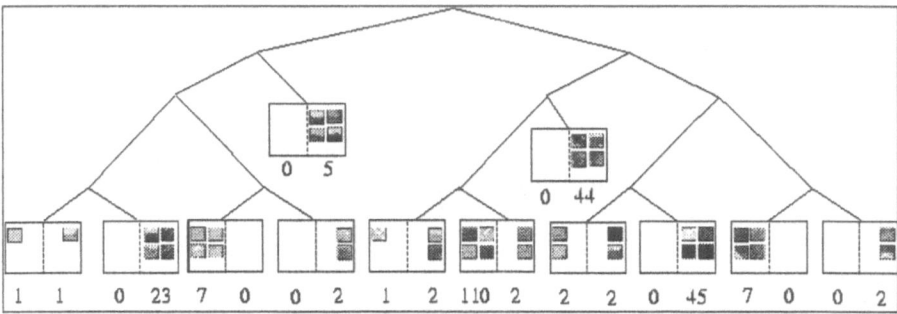

Fig. 8. *A representation of the decision tree used to find fold primitives. Each leaf contains a few windows representative of image windows classified at that level; on the left, clothing, and on the right, non-clothing. Below each leaf is the number of clothing and non-clothing windows that arrived at that leaf, out of a total of 128 in each category. 110 clothing and 2 non-clothing windows arrive at one leaf, strongly suggesting this combination of filter outputs is an appropriate clothing primitive.*

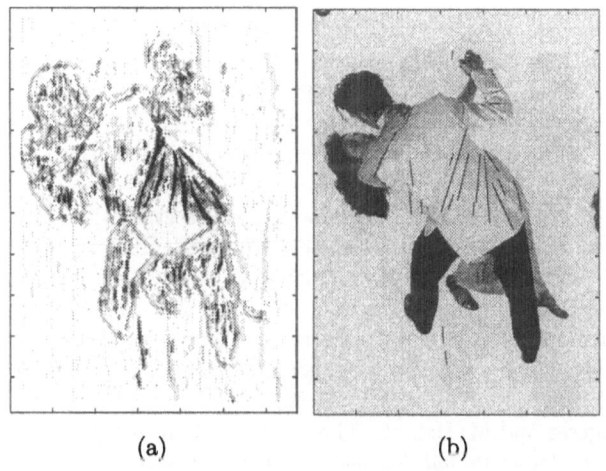

(a)   (b)

Fig. 9. *Folds in clothing result from buckling and have quite characteristic shading and spatial properties, which are linked to the configuration of the person. (a) shows the probability that an image window centered at each point contains a clothing primitive, using automatically defined primitives sketched in figure 8; (b) shows lines of primitives linked together using an extremisation criterion. Note that edges are in general not marked, and that the process is insensitive to changes in albedo; these properties are a result of the learning process.*

build relational representations that are quite effective at finding naked people and horses. Furthermore, we have shown that a grouping process that finds such assemblies can be learned from data. These representations are crucially limited by the crude primitives used.

Primitives need not just be stylised shapes. The stylised appearance of folds in clothing means that we can study the appearance of clothing in a reasonably effective way. These are shading primitives. Although it is currently difficult to know how to choose primitives, the problem appears to be statistical on its face. Statistical criteria appear to be able to suggest promising choices of shading primitives from image data.

Acknowledgements

Thanks to Stuart Russell for focussing our attention on the attractions of MCMC as an inference method. The discussion of body plans is based on joint work with Margaret Fleck. Various components of this research were carried out with the support of an NSF Digital Library Grant (IRI 94-11334) and an NSF Graduate Fellowship to S.I.

References

[1] Y. Amit and D. Geman. Shape quantization and recognition with randomized trees. *Neural computation*, 9:1545–1588, 1997.

[2] Y. Amit, D. Geman, and K. Wilder. Joint induction of shape features and tree classifiers. *IEEE T. Pattern Analysis and Machine Intelligence*, 19(11):1300–1305, 1997.

[3] D.C. Blair. Stairs redux: thoughts on the stairs evaluation, ten years after. *J. American Soc. for Information Science*, 47(1):4–22, 1996.

[4] D.C. Blair and M.E. Maron. An evaluation of retrieval effectiveness for a full text document retrieval system. *Comm. ACM*, 28(3):289–299, 1985.

[5] C.R. Calladine. *Theory of shell structures*. Cambridge University Press, 1983.

[6] P.G.B. Enser. Query analysis in a visual information retrieval context. *J. Document and Text Management*, 1(1):25–52, 1993.

[7] O.D. Faugeras and M. Hebert. The representation, recognition, and locating of 3-D objects. *International Journal of Robotics Research*, 5(3):27–52, Fall 1986.

[8] M. M. Fleck, D. A. Forsyth, and C. Bregler. Finding naked people. In *European Conference on Computer Vision 1996, Vol. II*, pages 592–602, 1996.

[9] M. Flickner, H. Sawhney, W. Niblack, and J. Ashley. Query by image and video content: the qbic system. *Computer*, 28(9):23–32, 1995.

[10] D. A. Forsyth and M. M. Fleck. Identifying nude pictures. In *IEEE Workshop on Applications of Computer Vision 1996*, pages 103–108, 1996.

[11] D.A. Forsyth and M.M. Fleck. Body plans. In *IEEE Conf. on Computer Vision and Pattern Recognition*, 1997.

[12] D.A. Forsyth, M.M. Fleck, and C. Bregler. Finding naked people. In *European Conference on Computer Vision*, 1996.

[13] D.A. Forsyth, J. Malik, M.M. Fleck, H. Greenspan, T. Leung, S. Belongie, C. Carson, and C. Bregler. Finding pictures of objects in large collections of images. In *Proc. 2'nd International Workshop on Object Representation in Computer Vision*, 1996.

[14] D.A. Forsyth, J.L. Mundy, A.P. Zisserman, C. Coelho, A. Heller, and C.A. Rothwell. Invariant descriptors for 3d object recognition and pose. *PAMI*, 13(10):971–991, 1991.

[15] Y. Freund and R.E. Schapire. Experiments with a new boosting algorithm. In *Machine Learning - 13*, 1996.

[16] M.M. Gorkani and R.W. Picard. Texture orientation for sorting photos "at a glance". In *Proceedings IAPR International Conference on Pattern Recognition*, pages 459–64, 1994.

[17] P.J. Green. Reversible jump markov chain monte carlo computation and bayesian model determination. *Biometrika*, 82(4):711–732, 1995.

[18] W.E.L. Grimson and T. Lozano-Pérez. Localizing overlapping parts by searching the interpretation tree. *IEEE Trans. Patt. Anal. Mach. Intell.*, 9(4):469–482, 1987.

[19] J. Haddon and D.A. Forsyth. Shading primitives. In *Int. Conf. on Computer Vision*, 1997.

[20] J. Haddon and D.A. Forsyth. Shape descriptions from shading primitives. In *European Conference on Computer Vision*, 1998.

[21] A. Hampapur, A. Gupta, B. Horowitz, and Chiao-Fe Shu. Virage video engine. In *Storage and Retrieval for Image and Video Databases V – Proceedings of the SPIE*, volume 3022, pages 188–98, 1997.

[22] D.P. Huttenlocher and S. Ullman. Object recognition using alignment. In *Proc. Int. Conf. Comp. Vision*, pages 102–111, London, U.K., June 1987.

[23] S. Ioffe and D.A. Forsyth. Learning to find pictures of people. In *In review — NIPS*, 1998.

[24] P. Lipson, W.E. L. Grimson, and P. Sinha. Configuration based scene classification and image indexing. In *IEEE Conf. on Computer Vision and Pattern Recognition*, pages 1007–13, 1997.

[25] F. Liu and R.W. Picard. Periodicity, directionality, and randomness: Wold features for image modeling and retrieval. *IEEE T. Pattern Analysis and Machine Intelligence*, 18:722–33, 1996.

[26] D. Lowe. Three-dimensional object recognition from single two-dimensional images. *Artificial Intelligence*, 31(3):355–395, 1987.

[27] T.P. Minka and R.W. Picard. Interactive learning with a "society of models". *Pattern Recognition*, 30:465–481, 1997.

[28] J.L. Mundy and A. Zisserman. *Geometric Invariance in Computer Vision*. MIT Press, Cambridge, Mass., 1992.

[29] J.L. Mundy, A. Zisserman, and D. Forsyth. *Applications of Invariance in Computer Vision*, volume 825 of *Lecture Notes in Computer Science*. Springer-Verlag, 1994.

[30] V.E. Ogle and M. Stonebraker. Chabot: retrieval from a relational database of images. *Computer*, 28:40–8, 1995.

[31] R.W. Picard, T. Kabir, and F. Liu. Real-time recognition with the entire brodatz texture database. In *IEEE Conf. on Computer Vision and Pattern Recognition*, pages 638–9, 1993.

[32] J. Ponce. Straight homogeneous generalized cylinders: differential geometry and uniqueness results. *Int. J. of Comp. Vision*, 4(1):79–100, 1990.

[33] J. Ponce, D. Chelberg, and W. Mann. Invariant properties of straight homogeneous generalized cylinders and their contours. *IEEE Trans. Patt. Anal. Mach. Intell.*, 11(9):951–966, September 1989.

[34] L.G. Roberts. Machine perception of three-dimensional solids. In J.T. Tippett et al., editor, *Optical and Electro-Optical Information Processing*, pages 159–197. MIT Press, Cambridge, 1965.

[35] G. Salton. Another look at automatic text retrieval systems. *Comm. ACM*, 29(7):n649–657, 1986.

[36] S. Santini and R. Jain. Similarity queries in image databases. In *IEEE Conf. on Computer Vision and Pattern Recognition*, pages 646–651, 1996.

[37] M. Stricker and M.J. Swain. The capacity of color histogram indexing. In *IEEE Conf. on Computer Vision and Pattern Recognition*, pages 704–8, 1994.

[38] M.J. Swain. Interactive indexing into image databases. In *Storage and Retrieval for Image and Video Databases – Proceedings of the SPIE*, volume 1908, pages 95–103, 1993.

[39] M.J. Swain and D.H. Ballard. Color indexing. *Int. J. Computer Vision*, 7(1):11–32, 1991.

[40] D.W. Thompson and J.L. Mundy. Three-dimensional model matching from an unconstrained viewpoint. In *IEEE Int. Conf. on Robotics and Automation*, pages 208–220, Raleigh, NC, April 1987.

[41] unknown. *Pose file*, volume 1-7. Books Nippan, 1993-1996. A collection of photographs of human models, annotated in Japanese.

[42] D.A. White and R. Jain. Imagegrep: fast visual pattern matching in image databases. In *Storage and Retrieval for Image and Video Databases V – Proceedings of the SPIE*, volume 3022, pages 96–107, 1997.

[43] A. Zisserman, J.L. Mundy, D.A. Forsyth, J.S. Liu, N. Pillow, C.A. Rothwell, and S. Utcke. Class-based grouping in perspective images. In *Int. Conf. on Computer Vision*, 1995.

Object Recognition with Gradient-Based Learning

Yann LeCun, Patrick Haffner, Léon Bottou, and Yoshua Bengio

AT&T Shannon Lab, 100 Schulz Drive, Red Bank NJ 07701, USA,
yann@research.att.com
http://www.research.att.com/~yann

Abstract. Finding an appropriate set of features is an essential problem in the design of shape recognition systems. This paper attempts to show that for recognizing simple objects with high shape variability such as handwritten characters, it is possible, and even advantageous, to feed the system directly with minimally processed images and to rely on learning to extract the right set of features. Convolutional Neural Networks are shown to be particularly well suited to this task. We also show that these networks can be used to recognize multiple objects without requiring explicit segmentation of the objects from their surrounding. The second part of the paper presents the Graph Transformer Network model which extends the applicability of gradient-based learning to systems that use graphs to represents features, objects, and their combinations.

1 Learning the Right Features

The most commonly accepted model of pattern recognition, is composed of a *segmenter* whose role is to extract objects of interest from their background, a hand-crafted *feature extractor* that gathers relevant information from the input and eliminates irrelevant variabilities, and a *classifier* which categorizes the resulting feature representations (generally vectors or strings of symbols) into categories. There are three major methods for classification: *template matching* matches the feature representation to a set of class templates; *generative methods* use a probability density model for each class, and pick the class with the highest likelihood of generating the feature representation; *discriminative models* compute a discriminant function that directly produces a score for each class. Generative and discriminative models are often estimated (learned) from training samples. In all of these approaches, the overall performance of the system is largely determined by the quality of the segmenter and the feature extractor.

Because they are hand-crafted, the segmenter and feature extractor often rely on simplifying assumptions about the input data and can rarely take into account all the variability of the real world. An ideal solution to this problem is to feed the entire system with minimally processed inputs (e.g. "raw" pixel images), and train it from data so as to minimize an overall loss function (which maximizes a given performance measure). Keeping the preprocessing to a minimum ensures that no unrealistic assumption is made about the data. Unfortunately, that also

D.A. Forsyth et al. (Eds.): Shape, Contour ..., LNCS 1681, pp. 319–345, 1999.
© Springer-Verlag Berlin Heidelberg 1999

requires to come up with a suitable learning architecture that can handle the high dimension of the input (number of pixels), the high degree of variability due to pose variations or geometric distortions among other things, and the necessarily complex non-linear relation between the input and the output.

Gradient-Based Learning provides a framework in which to build such a system. The learning machine computes a function $Y^p = F(Z^p, W)$ where Z^p is the p-th input pattern, and W represents the collection of adjustable parameters in the system. The output Y^p contains scores or probabilities for each category. A loss function $E^p = \mathcal{D}(D^p, F(W, Z^p))$, measures the discrepancy between D^p, the "correct" output for pattern Z^p, and the output produced by the system. The average loss function $E_{train}(W)$ is the average of the errors E^p over a set of labeled examples called the training set $\{(Z^1, D^1), ...(Z^P, D^P)\}$. In the simplest setting, the learning problem consists in finding the value of W that minimizes $E_{train}(W)$.

Making the loss function *differentiable* with respect to W ensures that efficient, gradient-based non-linear optimization methods can be used to find a minimum. To ensure global differentiability, the system is built as a feed-forward network of modules. In the simplest case, each module computes a function $X_n = F_n(W_n, X_{n-1})$, where X_n is an object (a vector in the simplest case) representing the output of the module, W_n is the vector of tunable (trainable) parameters in the module (a subset of W), and X_{n-1} is the module's input (as well as the previous module's output). The input X_0 to the first module is the system's input pattern Z^p.

The main idea of Gradient-Based Learning, which is a simple extension of the well-known back-propagation neural network learning algorithm, is that the objective function can be efficiently minimized through gradient descent (or other more sophisticated non-linear optimization methods) because the gradient of E with respect to W can be efficiently computed with a backward recurrence through the network of modules. If the partial derivative of E^p with respect to X_n is known, then the partial derivatives of E^p with respect to W_n and X_{n-1} can be computed using the following backward recurrence:

$$\frac{\partial E^p}{\partial W_n} = \frac{\partial F_n}{\partial W}(W_n, X_{n-1})\frac{\partial E^p}{\partial X_n}$$
$$\frac{\partial E^p}{\partial X_{n-1}} = \frac{\partial F_n}{\partial X}(W_n, X_{n-1})\frac{\partial E^p}{\partial X_n} \tag{1}$$

where $\frac{\partial F_n}{\partial W}(W_n, X_{n-1})$ is the Jacobian of F_n with respect to W evaluated at the point (W_n, X_{n-1}), and $\frac{\partial F_n}{\partial X}(W_n, X_{n-1})$ is the Jacobian of F_n with respect to X. The first equation computes some terms of the gradient of $E^p(W)$, while the second equation propagates the partial gradients backward. The idea can be trivially extended to any network of functional modules. A completely rigorous derivation of the gradient propagation procedure in the general case can be done using Lagrange functions [14, 15, 2].

2 Shape Recognition with Convolutional Neural Networks

Traditional multi-layer neural networks are a special case of the above where the states X_n are fixed-sized vectors, and where the modules are alternated layers of matrix multiplications (the weights) and component-wise sigmoid functions (the units). Traditional multilayer neural nets where all the units in a layer are connected to all the units in the next layer can be used to recognize raw (roughly size-normalized and centered) images, but there are problems.

Firstly, typical images are large, often with several hundred variables (pixels). A fully-connected network with, say 100 units in the first layer, would already contain several 10,000 weights. Such a large number of parameters increases the capacity of the system and therefore requires a larger training set. But the main deficiency of unstructured nets is that they have no built-in invariance with respect to translations, scale, or geometric distortions of the inputs. Images of objects can be approximately size-normalized and centered, but no such preprocessing can be perfect. This, combined with intrinsic within-class variability, will cause variations in the position of distinctive features in input objects. In principle, a fully-connected network of sufficient size could learn to produce outputs that are invariant with respect to such variations. However, learning such a task would probably result in multiple units with similar weight patterns positioned at various locations in the input so as to detect distinctive features wherever they appear on the input. Learning these weight configurations requires a very large number of training instances to cover the space of possible variations. In convolutional networks, described below, the robustness to geometric distortions is automatically obtained by forcing the replication of weight configurations across space.

Secondly, a deficiency of fully-connected architectures is that the topology of the input is entirely ignored. The input variables can be presented in any (fixed) order without affecting the outcome of the training. On the contrary, images have a strong 2D local structure: variables (pixels) that are spatially nearby are highly correlated. Local correlations are the reasons for the well-known advantages of extracting and combining *local* features before recognizing spatial or temporal objects, because configurations of neighboring variables can be classified into a small number of relevant categories (e.g. edges, corners...). *Convolutional Networks* force the extraction of local features by restricting the receptive fields of hidden units to be local.

2.1 Convolutional Networks

Convolutional Networks combine three architectural ideas to ensure some degree of shift, scale, and distortion invariance: *local receptive fields*, *shared weights* (or weight replication), and spatial *sub-sampling*. A typical convolutional network for recognizing shapes, dubbed LeNet-5, is shown in figure 1. The input plane receives images of objects that are approximately size-normalized and centered.

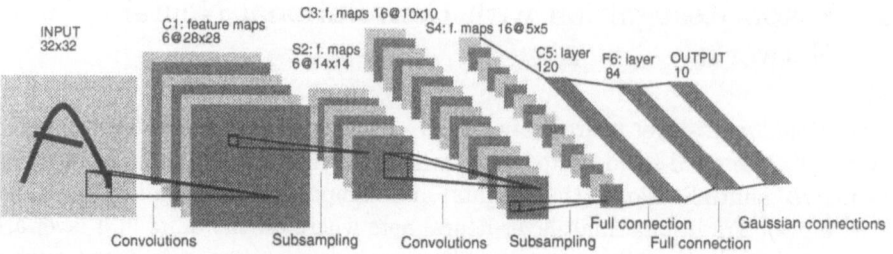

Fig. 1. Architecture of LeNet-5, a Convolutional Neural Network, here for digits recognition. Each plane is a feature map, i.e. a set of units whose weights are constrained to be identical.

Each unit in a layer receives inputs from a set of units located in a small neighborhood in the previous layer. The idea of connecting units to local receptive fields on the input goes back to the early 60s, and was largely inspired by Hubel and Wiesel's discovery of locally-sensitive, orientation-selective neurons in the cat's visual system [9]. Local connections have been used many times in neural models of visual learning [7, 13, 16, 23]. With local receptive fields, neurons can learn to extract elementary visual features such as oriented edges, end-points, corners (or similar features in other signals such as speech spectrograms). These features are then combined by the subsequent layers in order to detect higher-order features. As stated earlier, distortions or shifts of the input can cause the position of salient features to vary. In addition, elementary feature detectors that are useful on one part of the image are likely to be useful across the entire image. This knowledge can be applied by forcing a set of units, whose receptive fields are located at different places on the image, to have identical weight vectors [8], [28],
[16]. Units in a layer are organized in planes within which all the units share the same set of weights. The set of outputs of the units in such a plane is called a *feature map*. Units in a feature map are all constrained to perform the same operation on different parts of the image. A complete convolutional layer is composed of several feature maps (with different weight vectors), so that multiple features can be extracted at each location. A concrete example of this is the first layer of LeNet-5 shown in Figure 1. Units in the first hidden layer of LeNet-5 are organized in 6 planes, each of which is a feature map. A unit in a feature map has 25 inputs connected to a 5 by 5 area in the input, called the *receptive field* of the unit. Each unit has 25 inputs, and therefore 25 trainable coefficients plus a trainable bias. The receptive fields of contiguous units in a feature map are centered on correspondingly contiguous units in the previous layer. Therefore receptive fields of neighboring units overlap. For example, in the first hidden layer of LeNet-5, the receptive fields of horizontally contiguous units overlap by 4 columns and 5 rows. As stated earlier, all the units in a feature map share the same set of 25 weights and the same bias so they detect the same feature at all possible locations on the input. The other feature maps in the layer use different

sets of weights and biases, thereby extracting different types of local features. In the case of LeNet-5, at each input location six different types of features are extracted by six units in identical locations in the six feature maps. A sequential implementation of a feature map would scan the input image with a single unit that has a local receptive field, and store the states of this unit at corresponding locations in the feature map. This operation is equivalent to a convolution, followed by an additive bias and squashing function, hence the name *convolutional network*. The kernel of the convolution is the set of connection weights used by the units in the feature map. An interesting property of convolutional layers is that if the input image is shifted, the feature map output will be shifted by the same amount, but will be left unchanged otherwise. This property is at the basis of the robustness of convolutional networks to shifts and distortions of the input.

Once a feature has been detected, its exact location becomes less important. Only its approximate position relative to other features is relevant. Using handwritten digits as an example, once we know that the input image contains the endpoint of a roughly horizontal segment in the upper left area, a corner in the upper right area, and the endpoint of a roughly vertical segment in the lower portion of the image, we can tell the input image is a 7. Not only is the precise position of each of those features irrelevant for identifying the pattern, it is potentially harmful because the positions are likely to vary for different instances of the shape. A simple way to reduce the precision with which the position of distinctive features are encoded in a feature map is to reduce the spatial resolution of the feature map. This can be achieved with a so-called *sub-sampling layers* which performs a local averaging and a sub-sampling, reducing the resolution of the feature map, and reducing the sensitivity of the output to shifts and distortions. The second hidden layer of LeNet-5 is a sub-sampling layer. This layer comprises six feature maps, one for each feature map in the previous layer. The receptive field of each unit is a 2 by 2 area in the previous layer's corresponding feature map. Each unit computes the *average* of its four inputs, multiplies it by a trainable coefficient, adds a trainable bias, and passes the result though a sigmoid function. Contiguous units have non-overlapping contiguous receptive fields. Consequently, a sub-sampling layer feature map has half the number of rows and columns as the feature maps in the previous layer. The trainable coefficient and bias control the effect of the sigmoid non-linearity. If the coefficient is small, then the unit operates in a quasi-linear mode, and the sub-sampling layer merely blurs the input. If the coefficient is large, sub-sampling units can be seen as performing a "noisy OR" or a "noisy AND" function depending on the value of the bias. Successive layers of convolutions and sub-sampling are typically alternated, resulting in a "bi-pyramid": at each layer, the number of feature maps is increased as the spatial resolution is decreased. Each unit in the third hidden layer in figure 1 may have input connections from several feature maps in the previous layer. The convolution/sub-sampling combination, inspired by Hubel and Wiesel's notions of "simple" and "complex" cells, was implemented in Fukushima's Neocognitron [8], though no globally supervised learning procedure such as back-propagation was available then. A large degree of invariance to geometric transformations of the input can be achieved with this progressive reduction of spatial resolution compensated by a progressive increase of the richness of the representation (the number of feature maps).

Since all the weights are learned with back-propagation, convolutional networks can be seen as synthesizing their own feature extractors, and tuning them to the task at hand. The weight sharing technique has the interesting side effect of reducing the number of free parameters, thereby reducing the "capacity" of the machine and reducing the gap between test error and training error [16]. The network in figure 1 contains 345,308 connections, but only 60,000 trainable free parameters because of the weight sharing.

Fixed-size Convolutional Networks have been applied to many applications, among others: handwriting recognition [18, 21], as well as machine-printed character recognition [32], on-line handwriting recognition [1], and face recognition [12]. Fixed-size convolutional networks that share weights along a single temporal dimension are known as Time-Delay Neural Networks (TDNNs) and applied widely in speech processing and time-series prediction. Variable-size convolutional networks, which have applications in object detection and location are described in section 3.

2.2   LeNet-5

This section describes in more detail the architecture of LeNet-5, the Convolutional Neural Network used in the experiments. LeNet-5 comprises 7 layers, not counting the output, all of which contain trainable parameters (weights). The input is a 32x32 pixel image. Input shapes should be significantly smaller than that (e.g. on the order of 20x20 pixels). The reason is that it is desirable that potential distinctive features such as end-points or corner can appear *in the center* of the receptive field of the highest-level feature detectors. In LeNet-5 the set of centers of the receptive fields of the last convolutional layer (C3, see below) form a 20x20 area in the center of the 32x32 input. The values of the input pixels are normalized so that the background level (white) corresponds to a value of -0.1 and the foreground (black) corresponds to 1.175. This makes the mean input roughly 0, and the variance roughly 1 which accelerates learning [20]. In the following, convolutional layers are labeled Cx, sub-sampling layers are labeled Sx, and fully-connected layers are labeled Fx, where x is the layer index.

Layer C1 is a convolutional layer with 6 feature maps. Each unit in each feature map is connected to a 5x5 neighborhood in the input. The size of the feature maps is 28x28 which prevents connection from the input from falling off the boundary. C1 contains 156 trainable parameters, and 122,304 connections.

Layer S2 is a sub-sampling layer with 6 feature maps of size 14x14. Each unit in each feature map is connected to a 2x2 neighborhood in the corresponding feature map in C1. The four inputs to a unit in S2 are added, then multiplied by a trainable coefficient, and added to a trainable bias. The result is passed through a sigmoidal function. The 2x2 receptive fields are non-overlapping, therefore feature maps in S2 have half the number of rows and column as feature maps in C1. Layer S2 has 12 trainable parameters and 5,880 connections.

Layer C3 is a convolutional layer with 16 feature maps. Each unit in each feature map is connected to several 5x5 neighborhoods at identical locations in a subset of S2's feature maps. Why not connect every S2 feature map to every C3 feature map? The reason is twofold. First, a non-complete connection scheme keeps the number of connections within reasonable bounds. More importantly, it forces a break of symmetry in the network. Different feature maps are forced to extract different (hopefully complementary) features because they get different sets of inputs. The rationale behind the connection scheme is the following. The first six C3 feature maps take inputs from every contiguous subsets of three feature maps in S2. The next six take input from every contiguous subset of four. The next three take input from some discontinuous subsets of four. Finally the last one takes input from all S2 feature maps. The full connection table is given in [19], Layer C3 has 1,516 trainable parameters and 156,000 connections.

Layer S4 is a sub-sampling layer with 16 feature maps of size 5x5. Each unit in each feature map is connected to a 2x2 neighborhood in the corresponding feature map in C3, in a similar way as C1 and S4. Layer S4 has 32 trainable parameters and 2,000 connections.

Layer C5 is a convolutional layer with 120 feature maps. Each unit is connected to a 5x5 neighborhood on all 16 of S4's feature maps. Here, because the size of S4 is also 5x5, the size of C5's feature maps is 1x1: this amounts to a full connection between S4 and C5. C5 is labeled as a convolutional layer, instead of a fully-connected layer, because if LeNet-5 input were made bigger with everything else kept constant, the feature map dimension would be larger than 1x1. This process of dynamically increasing the size of a convolutional network is described in the section Section 3. Layer C5 has 48,120 trainable connections.

Layer F6, contains 84 units (the reason for this number comes from the design of the output layer, explained later) and is fully connected to C5. It has 10,164 trainable parameters.

As in classical neural networks, units in layers up to F6 compute a dot product between their input vector and their weight vector, to which a bias is added. This weighted sum is then passed through a scaled hyperbolic tangent function to produce the state of the unit.

Finally, the output layer is composed of Euclidean Radial Basis Function units (RBF), one for each class, with 84 inputs each. Each output RBF unit computes the Euclidean distance between its input vector and its parameter vector. The output of a particular RBF can be interpreted as a penalty term measuring the fit between the input pattern and a model of the class associated with the RBF. Given an input pattern, the loss function should be designed so as to get the configuration of F6 as close as possible to the parameter vector of the RBF that corresponds to the pattern's desired class. The parameter vectors of these units were chosen by hand and kept fixed (at least initially). The components of those parameters vectors were set to -1 or +1 to predetermined values. The parameter vectors of the RBFs play the role of target vectors for layer F6.

The simplest output loss function that can be used with the above network is:

$$E(W) = \frac{1}{P} \sum_{p=1}^{P} y_{D^p}(Z^p, W) \tag{2}$$

where y_{D^p} is the output of the D_p-th RBF unit, i.e. the one that corresponds to the correct class of input pattern Z^p. The actual loss function used in our experiments has additional term to make it more discriminative. More details are available in [19]. Computing the gradient of the loss function with respect to all the weights in all the layers of the convolutional network is done with back-propagation. The standard algorithm must be slightly modified to take account of the weight sharing. An easy way to implement it is to first compute the partial derivatives of the loss function with respect to each *connection*, as if the network were a conventional multi-layer network without weight sharing. Then the partial derivatives of all the connections that share a same parameter are added to form the derivative with respect to that parameter.

2.3   An Example: Recognizing Handwritten Digits

Recognizing individual digits is an excellent benchmark for comparing shape recognition methods. This comparative study concentrates on adaptive methods that operate directly on size-normalized images. Handwritten digit recognition may seem a little simplistic when one's interest is Computer Vision, but the simplicity is only apparent, and the problems to solve are essentially the same as with any 2D shape recognition, only there is abundant training data available, and the intra-class shape variability is considerably larger than with any rigid object recognition problem.

The database used to train and test the systems described in this paper was constructed from the NIST's Special Database 3 and 1 containing binary images of handwritten digits. From these, we built a database called MNIST which contains 60,000 training samples (half from SD1, half from SD3), and 10,000 test images (half from SD1 and half from SD3). The original black and white (bilevel) images were size normalized to fit in a 20x20 pixel box while preserving their aspect ratio. The resulting images contain grey levels as result of anti-aliased resampling. Three versions of the database were used. In the first version, the images were centered in a 28x28 image by computing the center of mass of the pixels, and translating the image so as to position this point at the center of the 28x28 field. In some instances, this 28x28 field was extended to 32x32 with background pixels. This version of the database will be referred to as the *regular* database. In the second version of the database, (referred to as the *deslanted* version) the character images were deslanted using the moments of inertia of the black pixels and cropped down to 20x20 pixels images. In the third version of the database, used in some early experiments, the images were reduced to 16x16 pixels. The regular database is available at http://www.research.att.com/~yann.

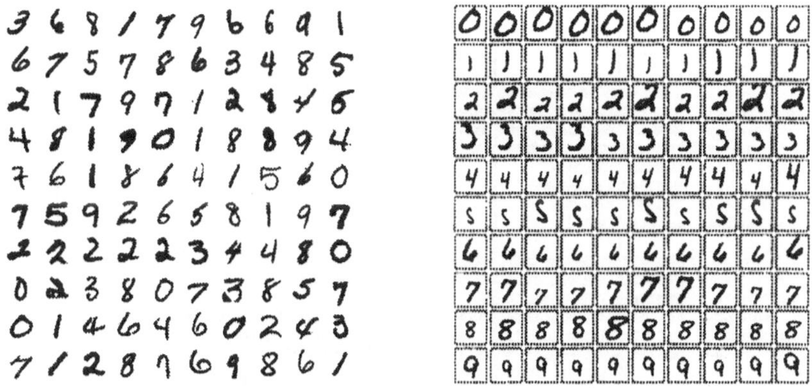

Fig. 2. Examples from the test set (left), and examples of distortions of ten training patterns (right).

2.4   Results and Comparison with Other Classifiers

Several versions of LeNet-5 were trained on the regular database, with typically 20 iterations through the entire training data. The test error rate stabilizes after around 10 passes through the training set at 0.95%. The error rate on the training set reaches 0.35% after 19 passes. The influence of the training set size was measured by training the network with 15,000, 30,000, and 60,000 examples. The results made it clear that additional training data would be beneficial. In another set of experiments, we artificially generated more training examples by randomly distorting the original training images. The increased training set was composed of the 60,000 original patterns plus 540,000 instances of distorted patterns with randomly picked distortion parameters. The distortions were combinations of the following planar affine transformations: horizontal and vertical translations, scaling, squeezing (simultaneous horizontal compression and vertical elongation, or the reverse), and horizontal shearing. Figure 2 shows examples of distorted patterns used for training. When distorted data was used for training, the test error rate dropped to 0.8% (from 0.95% without deformation). Some of the misclassified examples are genuinely ambiguous, but several are perfectly identifiable by humans, although they are written in an under-represented style. This shows that further improvements are to be expected with more training data.

For the sake of comparison, a variety of other trainable classifiers was trained and tested on the same database. The error rates on the test set for the various methods are shown in figure 3. The experiments included the following methods: *linear classification* with 10 two-way classifiers trained to classify one class from the other nine; *pairwise linear classifier* with 45 two-way classifiers trained to classify one class versus one other followed by a voting mechanism; *K-Nearest Neighbor classifiers* with a simple Euclidean distance on pixel images; *40-dimension principal component analysis followed by degree 2 polynomial classifier; radial basis function network* with 1000 Gaussian RBF trained with K-

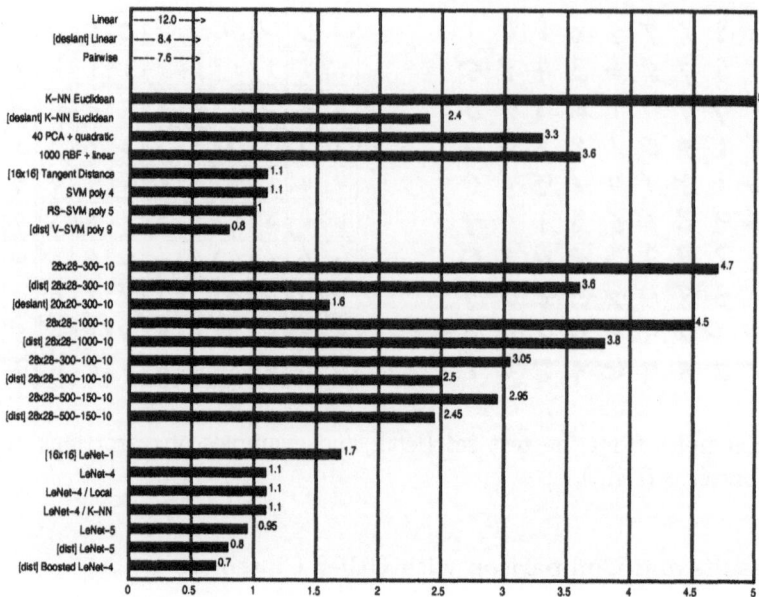

Fig. 3. Error rate on the test set (%) for various classification methods. [deslant] indicates that the classifier was trained and tested on the deslanted version of the database. [dist] indicates that the training set was augmented with artificially distorted examples. [16x16] indicates that the system used the 16x16 pixel images. The uncertainty in the quoted error rates is about 0.1%.

means per class, and followed by a linear classifier; *Tangent Distance classifier*, a nearest-neighbor classifier where the distance is made invariant to small geometric distortions by projecting the pattern onto linear approximations of the manifolds generated by distorting the prototypes; *Support Vector Machines* of various types (regular SVM, reduced-set SVM, virtual SVM) using polynomial kernels; *fully connected neural nets* with one or two hidden layers and various numbers of hidden units; *LeNet-1*, a small convolutional neural net with only 2600 free parameters and 100,000 connections; *LeNet-4*, a convolutional neural net with 17,000 free parameters and 260,000 connection similar to but slightly different from LeNet-5; *Boosted LeNet4*, a classifier obtained by voting three instances of LeNet-4 trained on different subsets of the database; and finally *LeNet-5*.

Concerning fully-connected neural networks, it remains somewhat of a mystery that unstructured neural nets with such a large number of free parameters manage to achieve reasonable performance. We conjecture that the dynamics of gradient descent learning in multilayer nets has a "self-regularization" effect. Because the origin of weight space is a saddle point that is attractive in almost every direction, the weights invariably shrink during the first few epochs. Small weights cause the sigmoids to operate in the quasi-linear region, making the network essentially equivalent to a low-capacity, single-layer network. As the learning proceeds, the weights grow, which progressively increases the effective capacity of the network. This seems to be an almost perfect, if fortuitous, implementation of Vapnik's "Structural Risk Minimization" principle [31].

The Support Vector Machine [31] has excellent accuracy, which is most remarkable, because unlike the other high performance classifiers, it does not include *a priori* knowledge about the problem [4]. In fact, this classifier would do just as well if the image pixels were permuted with a fixed mapping and lost their pictorial structure. However, reaching levels of performance comparable to the Convolutional Neural Networks can only be done at considerable expense in memory and computational requirements. The computational requirements of Burges's reduced-set SVM are within a factor of two of LeNet-5, and the error rate is very close. Improvements of those results are expected, as the technique is relatively new.

Boosted LeNet-4 performed best, achieving a score of 0.7%, closely followed by LeNet-5 at 0.8%. Boosted LeNet-4 [6] is based on theoretical work by R. Schapire [29]. Three LeNet-4s are combined: the first one is trained the usual way. the second one is trained on patterns that are filtered by the first net so that the second machine sees a mix of patterns, 50% of which the first net got right, and 50% of which it got wrong. Finally, the third net is trained on new patterns on which the first and the second nets disagree. During testing, the outputs of the three nets are simply added.

When plenty of data is available, many methods can attain respectable accuracy. Compared to other methods, convolutional neural nets offer not only the best accuracy, but also good speed, low memory requirements, and excellent robustness as discussed below.

2.5   Invariance and Noise Resistance

While fully invariant recognition of complex shapes is still an elusive goal, it seems that convolutional networks, because of their architecture, offer a partial answer to the problem of invariance or robustness with respect to distortions, varying position, scale and orientation, as well as intrinsic class variability. Figure 4 shows several examples of unusual and distorted characters that are correctly recognized by LeNet-5. For these experiments, the training samples were artificially distorted using random planar affine transformations, and the pixels in the training images were randomly flipped with probability 0.1 to increase the noise resistance. The top row in the figure shows the robustness to size and orientation variations. It is estimated that accurate recognition occurs for scale variations up to about a factor of 2, vertical shift variations of plus or minus about half the height of the character, and rotations up to plus or minus 30 degrees. While the characters are distorted during training, it seems that the robustness of the network subsists for distortions that are significantly larger than the ones used during training. Figure 4 includes examples of characters written in very unusual styles. Needless to say, there are no such examples in the training set. Nevertheless, the network classifies them correctly, which seems to suggest

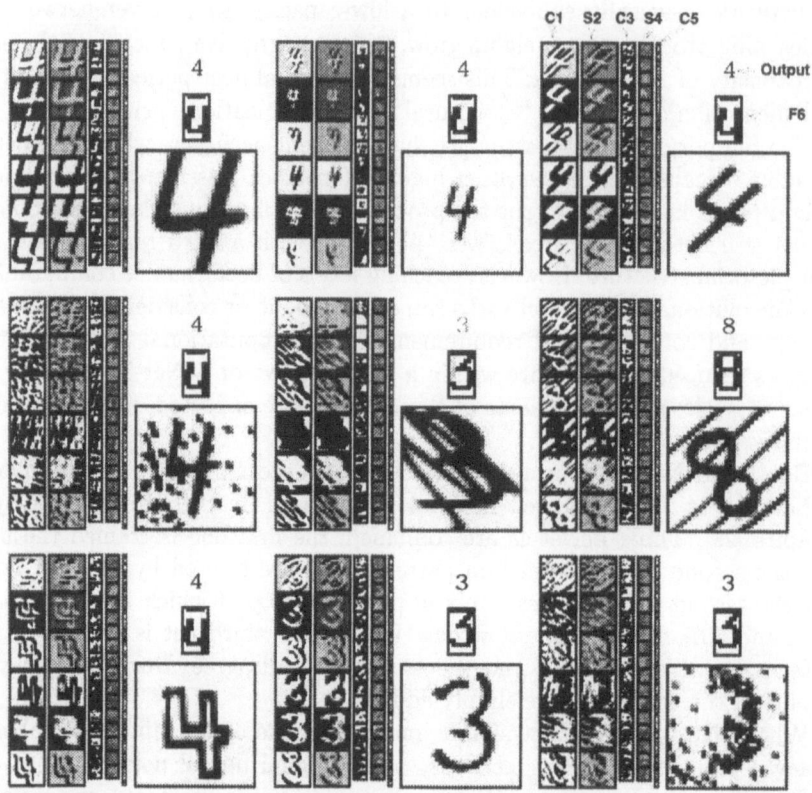

Fig. 4. Examples of unusual, distorted, and noisy characters correctly recognized by LeNet-5. The grey-level of the output label represents the penalty (lighter for higher penalties).

that the features that have been learned have some degree of generality. Lastly, figure 4 includes examples that demonstrates LeNet-5's robustness to extremely high levels of structured noise. Handling these images with traditional segmentation and feature extraction techniques would pose insurmountable problems. Even though the only noise used during training was random pixel flipping, it seems that the network can eliminate the adverse effects of non-sensical but structured marks from images such as the 3 and the 8 in the second row. This demonstrates a somewhat puzzling ability of such networks to perform (if implicitly) a kind of elementary *feature binding* solely through feed-forward linear combinations and sigmoid functions.

Animated examples of LeNet-5 in action are available on the Internet at http://www.research.att.com/~yann.

3 Multiple Object Recognition with Space Displacement Neural Networks

A major conceptual problem in vision and pattern recognition is how to recognize individual objects when those objects cannot be easily segmented out of their surrounding. In general, this poses the problem of feature binding: how to identify and bind together features that belong to a single object, while suppressing features that belong to the background or to other objects. The common wisdom is that, except in the simplest case, one cannot identify and bind together the features of an object unless one knows what object to look for.

In handwriting recognition, the problem is to separate a character from its neighbors, given that the neighbors can touch it or overlap with it. The most common solution is called "heuristic over-segmentation". It consists in generating a large number of potential cuts between characters using heuristic image analysis techniques. Candidate characters are formed by combining contiguous segments in multiple ways. The candidate characters are then sent to the recognizer for classification and scoring. A simple graph-search technique then finds the consistent sequence of character candidates with the best overall score.

There is a simple alternative to explicitly segmenting images of character strings using heuristics. The idea is to sweep a recognizer across all possible locations on an image of the entire word or string whose height has been normalized. With this technique, no segmentation heuristics is required. However, there are problems with this approach. First, the method is in general quite expensive. The recognizer must be applied at every possible location on the input, or at least at a large enough subset of locations so that misalignments of characters in the field of view of the recognizers are small enough to have no effect on the error rate. Second, when the recognizer is centered on a character to be recognized, the neighbors of the center character will be present in the field of view of the recognizer, possibly touching the center character. Therefore the recognizer must be able to correctly recognize the character in the center of its input field, even if neighboring characters are very close to, or touching the central character. Third, a word or character string cannot be perfectly size normalized. Individual characters within a string may have widely varying sizes and baseline positions. Therefore the recognizer must be very robust to shifts and size variations.

These three problems are elegantly circumvented if a convolutional network is replicated over the input field. First of all, as shown in the previous section, convolutional neural networks are very robust to shifts and scale variations of the input image, as well as to noise and extraneous marks in the input. These properties take care of the latter two problems mentioned in the previous paragraph. Second, convolutional networks provide a drastic saving in computational requirement when replicated over large input fields. A replicated convolutional network, also called a *Space Displacement Neural Network* or SDNN [22], is shown in Figure 5. While scanning a recognizer can be prohibitively expensive in general, convolutional networks can be scanned or replicated very efficiently over large, variable-size input fields. Consider one instance of a convolutional

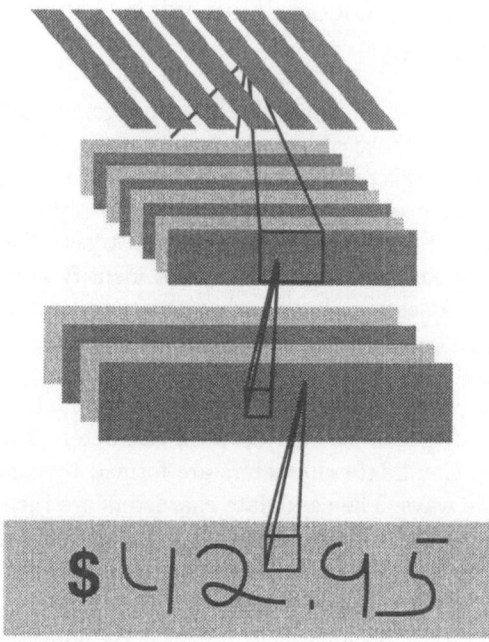

Fig. 5. A Space Displacement Neural Network is a convolutional network that has been replicated over a wide input field.

net and its *alter ego* at a nearby location. Because of the convolutional nature of the network, units in the two instances that look at identical locations on the input have identical outputs, therefore their states do not need to be computed twice. Only a thin "slice" of new states that are not shared by the two network instances needs to be recomputed. When all the slices are put together, the result is simply a larger convolutional network whose structure is identical to the original network, except that the feature maps are larger in the horizontal dimension. In other words, replicating a convolutional network can be done simply by increasing the size of the fields over which the convolutions are performed, and by replicating the output layer accordingly. The output layer effectively becomes a convolutional layer. An output whose receptive field is centered on an elementary object will produce the class of this object, while an in-between output may indicate no character or contain rubbish. The outputs can be interpreted as evidences for the presence of objects at all possible positions in the input field.

The SDNN architecture seems particularly attractive for recognizing cursive handwriting where no obvious segmentation heuristics exist. Although the idea of SDNN is quite old [10, 22], and very attractive by its simplicity, it has not generated wide interest until recently because of the enormous demands it puts on the recognizer.

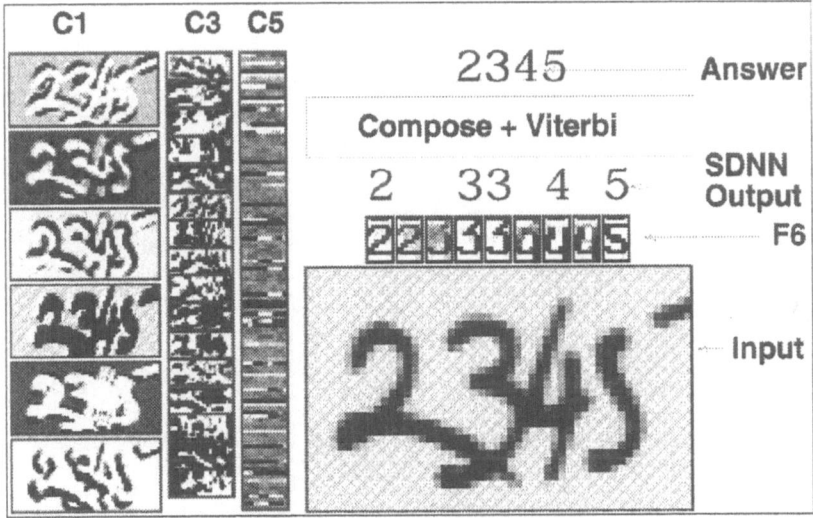

Fig. 6. An example of multiple character recognition with SDNN. With SDNN, no explicit segmentation is performed.

3.1   Interpreting the Output of an SDNN

The output of a horizontally replicated SDNN is a sequence of vectors which encode the likelihoods, penalties, or scores of finding character of a particular class label at the corresponding location in the input. A post-processor is required to pull out the best possible label sequence from this vector sequence. An example of SDNN output is shown in Figure 6. Very often, individual characters are spotted by several neighboring instances of the recognizer, a consequence of the robustness of the recognizer to horizontal translations. Also quite often, characters are erroneously detected by recognizer instances that see only a piece of a character. For example a recognizer instance that only sees the right third of a "4" might output the label 1. How can we eliminate those extraneous characters from the output sequence and pull-out the best interpretation? This can be done with a simple weighted finite state machine. The sequence of vectors produced by the SDNN is first turned into a linear graph constructed as follows. Each vector in the output sequence is transformed into a bundle of arcs with a common source node and target node. Each arc contains one of the possible character labels, together with its corresponding penalty. Each bundle contains an additional arc bearing the "none of the above"label with a penalty. These bundles are concatenated in the order of the vector sequence (the target node of a bundle becomes the source node of the next bundle). Each path in this graph is a possible interpretation of the input. A grammar is then constructed as a weighted finite-state machine that contains a model for each character. The grammar ensures for example that neighboring characters must be separated by a "none of the above" label (white space), and that successive occurrences of the same label

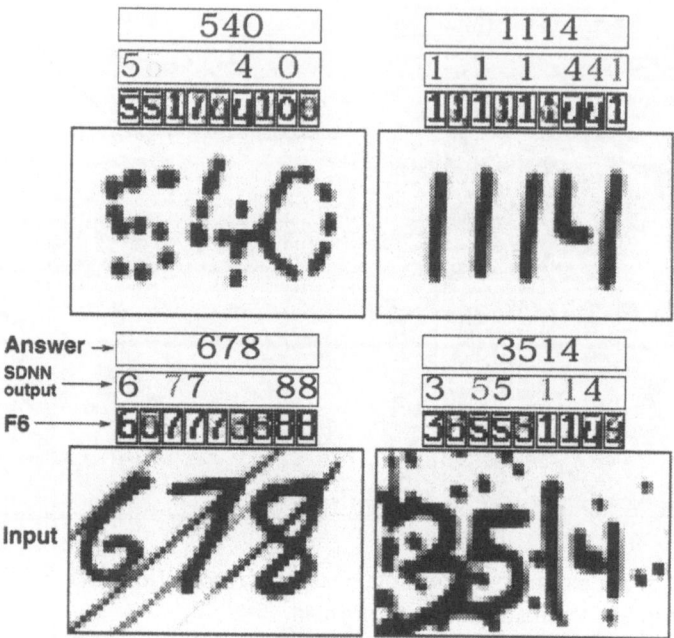

Fig. 7. An SDNN applied to a noisy image of digit string. The digits shown in the SDNN output represent the winning class labels, with a lighter grey level for high-penalty answers.

are probably produced by a single input character. The grammar and the linear graph are then *composed* (a graph operation similar to a tensor product). The composed graph contains all the paths of the linear graph that happen to be grammatically correct. A Viterbi algorithm can then be used to find the path with the smallest overall penalty.

3.2   Experiments with SDNN

In a series of experiments, LeNet-5 was trained with the goal of being replicated into an SDNN so as to recognize multiple characters without segmentations. The data was generated from the previously described MNIST set as follows. Training images were composed of a central character, flanked by two side characters picked at random in the training set. The separation between the bounding boxes of the characters were chosen at random between -1 and 4 pixels. In other instances, no central character was present, in which case the desired output of the network was the blank space class. In addition, training images were degraded by randomly flipping the pixels with probability 0.1.

Figures 6 and 7 show a few examples of successful recognitions of multiple characters by the LeNet-5 SDNN. Standard techniques based on Heuristic Over-Segmentation would likely fail on most of those examples. The robustness of the network to scale and vertical position variations allows it to recognize characters in such strings. More importantly, it seems that the network is able to individually recognize the characters even when there is a significant overlap with the neighbors. It is also able to correctly group disconnected pieces of ink that form characters, as exemplified in the upper half of the figure. In the top left example, the 4 and the 0 are more connected to each other than they are connected with themselves, yet the system correctly identifies the 4 and the 0 as separate objects. The top right example is interesting for several reasons. First the system correctly identifies the three individual "1". Second, the left half and right half of the disconnected 4 are correctly grouped, even though no simple proximity criterion could decide to associate the left half of the 4 to the vertical bar on its left or on its right. The right half of the 4 does cause the appearance of an erroneous "1" on the SDNN output, but this "1" is removed by the grammar which prevents different non-blank characters from appearing on contiguous outputs. The bottom left example demonstrates that extraneous marks that do not belong to identifiable characters are suppressed even though they may connect genuine characters to each other. The lower right example shows the combined robustness to character overlaps, vertical shifts, size variations, and noise.

Several authors have argued that invariance and feature binding for multiple object recognition requires specific mechanisms involving feedback, explicit switching devices (3-way multiplicative connections) [11], object-centered representations, graph matching mechanisms, or generative models that attempt to simultaneously extract the pose and the category of the objects. It is somewhat disconcerting to observe that the above SDNN seems to "solve" the feature binding problem, albeit partially and in a restricted context, even though it possesses no built in machinery to do it explicitly. If nothing else, these experiments show that purely feed-forward "numerical" multi-layer systems with a fixed architecture can emulate functions that appear combinatorial, and are qualitatively much more complex than anticipated by most (including the authors).

Several short animations of the LeNet-5 SDNN, including some with characters that move on top of each other, can be viewed at
http://www.research.att.com/ yann.

3.3   Face Detection and Spotting with SDNN

An interesting application of SDNNs is object detection and spotting. The invariance properties of Convolutional Networks, combined with the efficiency with which they can be replicated over large fields suggest that they can be used for "brute force" object spotting and detection in large images. The main idea is to train a single Convolutional Network to distinguish images of the object of interest from images present in the background. Once trained, the network is replicated so as to cover the entire image to be analyzed, thereby forming a two-dimensional Space Displacement Neural Network. The output of the SDNN is a two-dimensional plane in which the most activate units indicate the presence of the object of interest in the corresponding receptive field. Since the size of the objects to be detected within the image are unknown, the image can be presented to the network at multiple resolutions, and the results at multiple resolutions combined. The idea has been applied to face location, [30], address block location on envelopes [33], and hand tracking in video [24].

To illustrate the method, we will consider the case of face detection in images as described in [30]. First, images containing faces at various scales are collected. Those images are filtered through a zero-mean Laplacian filter so as to remove variations in global illumination and large-scale illumination gradients. Then, training samples of faces and non-faces are manually extracted from these images. The face sub-images are then size normalized so that the height of the entire face is approximately 20 pixels while keeping fairly large variations (within a factor of two). The scale of background sub-images are picked at random. A single convolutional network is trained on those samples to classify face sub-images from non-face sub-images. When a scene image is to be analyzed, it is first filtered through the Laplacian filter, and sub-sampled by ratios that are successive powers of the square root of 2. The network is replicated over each of the images at each resolution. A simple voting technique is used to combine the results from multiple resolutions.

More recently, some authors have used Neural Networks, or other classifiers such as Support Vector Machines for face detection with great success [27, 25]. Their systems are somewhat similar to the one described above, including the idea of presenting the image to the network at multiple scales. But since those systems do not use Convolutional Networks, they cannot take advantage of the speedup described here, and have to rely on other techniques, such as pre-filtering and real-time tracking, to keep the computational requirement within reasonable limits. In addition, because those classifiers are much less invariant to scale variations than Convolutional Networks, it is necessary to use a large number multiscale images with finely-spaced scales.

4   Graph Transformer Networks

Despite the apparent ability of the systems described in the previous sections to solve combinatorial problems with non-combinatorial means, there are situations where the need for *compositionality* and combinatorial searches is inescapable. A good example is language modeling and more generally, models that involve finite-state grammars, weighted finite-state machines, or other graph-based knowledge representations such as finite-state transducers. The main point of this section is to show that gradient-based learning techniques can be extended to situations where those models are used.

It is easy to show that the modular gradient-based learning model presented in section 1 can be applied to networks of modules whose state variables X_n are graphs with numerical information attached to the arcs (scalars, vectors, etc), rather than fixed-size vectors. There are two main conditions for this. First, the modules must produce the values on the output graphs from the values on the input graphs through differentiable functions. Second, the overall loss function should be continuous and differentiable *almost everywhere* with respect to the parameters. Networks of graph-manipulating modules are called *Graph Transformer Networks* [3, 19].

4.1   Word Recognition with a Graph Transformer Network

Though the Space Displacement Neural Net method presented in the previous section is very promising for word recognition applications, the more traditional method (and so far still the most developed) is called heuristic over-segmentation. With this methods, the word is segmented into candidate characters using heuristic image analysis techniques. Unfortunately, it is almost impossible to devise techniques that will infallibly segment naturally written words into well formed characters. This section and the next describe in detail a simple example of GTN for reading words. The method can rely on gradient-based learning to avoids the expensive and unreliable task of manually segmenting and hand-truthing a database so as to train the recognizer on individual characters.

Segmentation. Given a word, a number of candidate cuts are generated with heuristic methods. The cut generation heuristic is designed so as to generate more cuts than necessary, in the hope that the "correct" set of cuts will be included. Once the cuts have been generated, alternative segmentations are best represented by a graph, called the *segmentation graph*. The segmentation graph is a *Directed Acyclic Graph* (DAG) with a start node and an end node. Each internal node is associated with a candidate cut produced by the segmentation algorithm. Each arc between a source node and a destination node is associated with an image that contains all the ink between the cut associated with the source node and the cut associated with the destination node. An arc is created between two nodes if the segmenter decided that the piece(s) of ink between the corresponding cuts could form a candidate character. Typically, each individual piece of ink would be associated with an arc. Pairs of successive pieces of ink would also be included, unless they are separated by a wide gap, which is a clear indication that they belong to different characters. Each complete path through the graph contains each piece of ink once and only once. Each path corresponds to a different way of associating pieces of ink together so as to form characters.

Recognition Transformer and Viterbi Transformer. A simple GTN to recognize character strings is shown in Figure 8. Only the right branch of the top half is used for recognition. The left branch is used for the training procedure described in the next sub-section. The GTN is composed of two main graph transformers called the *recognition transformer* T_{rec}, and the *Viterbi transformer* T_{vit}. The goal of the recognition transformer is to generate a graph, called the *interpretation graph* or *recognition graph* G_{int}, that contains all the possible interpretations for all the possible segmentations of the input. Each path in G_{int} represents one possible interpretation of one particular segmentation of the input. The role of the Viterbi transformer is to extract the best interpretation from the interpretation graph.

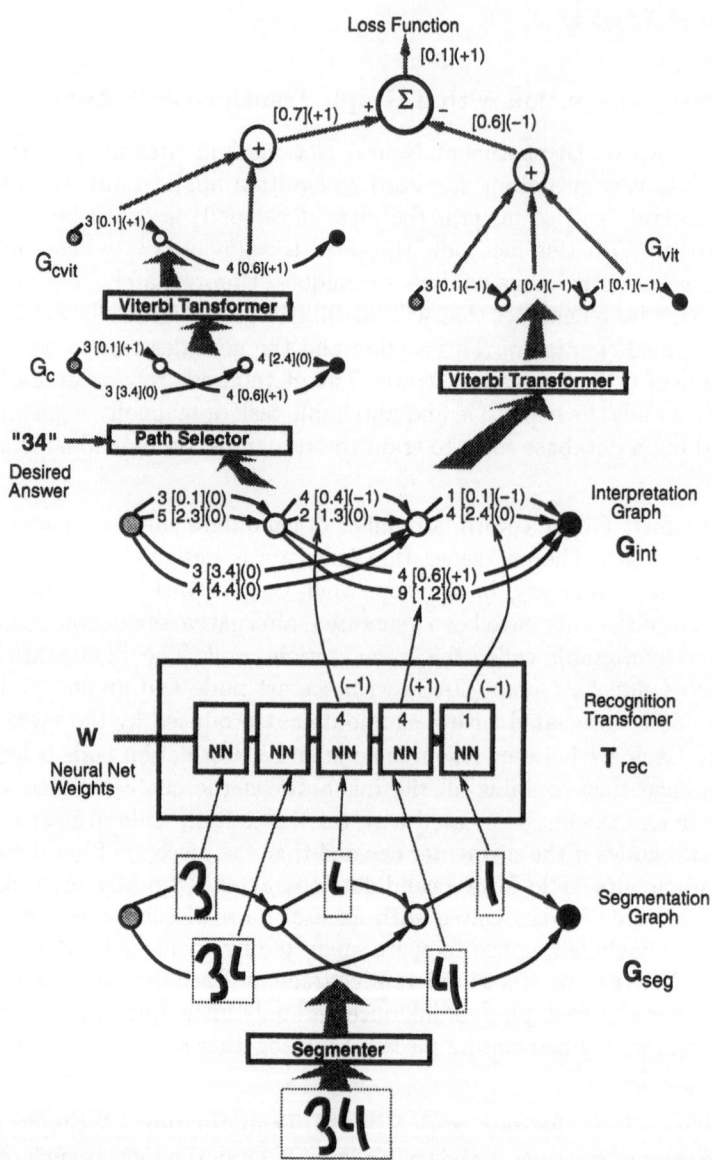

Fig. 8. A GTN Architecture for word recognition based on Heuristic Over-Segmentation. During recognition, only the right-hand path of the top part is used. For training with Viterbi training, only the left-hand path is used. For discriminative Viterbi training, both paths are used. Quantities in square brackets are penalties computed during the forward propagation. Quantities in parentheses are partial derivatives computed during the backward propagation.

The recognition transformer T_{rec} takes the segmentation graph G_{seg} as input, and applies the recognizer for single characters to the images associated with each of the arcs in the segmentation graph. The interpretation graph G_{int} has almost the same structure as the segmentation graph, except that each arc is replaced by a set of arcs from and to the same node. In this set of arcs, there is one arc for each possible class for the image associated with the corresponding arc in G_{seg}. To each arc is attached a class label, and the penalty that the image belongs to this class as produced by the recognizer. If the segmenter has computed penalties for the candidate segments, these penalties are combined with the penalties computed by the character recognizer, to obtain the penalties on the arcs of the interpretation graph. Although combining penalties of different nature seems highly heuristic, the GTN training procedure will tune the penalties and take advantage of this combination anyway. Each path in the interpretation graph corresponds to a possible interpretation of the input word. The penalty of a particular interpretation for a particular segmentation is given by the sum of the arc penalties along the corresponding path in the interpretation graph. Computing the penalty of an interpretation independently of the segmentation requires to combine the penalties of all the paths with that interpretation. This can be done using the "forward" algorithm widely used in Hidden Markov Models.

The Viterbi transformer produces a graph G_{vit} with a single path. This path is the path of least cumulated penalty in the interpretation graph. The result of the recognition can be produced by reading off the labels of the arcs along the graph G_{vit} extracted by the Viterbi transformer. The Viterbi transformer owes its name to the famous *Viterbi algorithm* to find the shortest path in a graph.

4.2   Gradient-Based Training of a GTN

The previous section describes the process of recognizing a string using Heuristic Over-Segmentation, assuming that the recognizer is trained so as to assign low penalties to the correct class label of correctly segmented characters, high penalties to erroneous categories of correctly segmented characters, and high penalties to all categories for badly formed characters. This section explains how to train the system at the string level to do the above without requiring manual labeling of character segments.

In many applications, there is enough a priori knowledge about what is expected from each of the modules in order to train them separately. For example, with Heuristic Over-Segmentation one could individually label single-character images and train a character recognizer on them, but it might be difficult to obtain an appropriate set of non-character images to train the model to reject wrongly segmented candidates. Although separate training is simple, it requires additional supervision information that is often lacking or incomplete (the correct segmentation and the labels of incorrect candidate segments). The following section describes two of the many gradient-based methods for training GTN-based handwriting recognizers at the string level: Viterbi training and discriminative Viterbi training. Unlike similar approaches in the context of speech recognition, we make no recourse to a probabilistic interpretation, but show that, within the Gradient-Based Learning approach, discriminative training is a simple instance of the pervasive principle of error correcting learning.

Viterbi Training. During recognition, we select the path in the Interpretation Graph that has the lowest penalty with the Viterbi algorithm. Ideally, we would like this path of lowest penalty to be associated with the correct label sequence as often as possible. An obvious loss function to minimize is therefore the average over the training set of the penalty of the path *associated with the correct label sequence* that has the lowest penalty. The goal of training will be to find the set of recognizer parameters (the weights, if the recognizer is a neural network) that minimize the average penalty of this "correct" lowest penalty path. The gradient of this loss function can be computed by back-propagation through the GTN architecture shown in figure 8, using only the left-hand path of the top part, and ignoring the right half. This training architecture contains a graph transformer called a *path selector*, inserted between the Interpretation Graph and the Viterbi Transformer. This transformer takes the interpretation graph and the desired label sequence as input. It extracts from the interpretation graph those paths that contain the correct (desired) label sequence. Its output graph G_c is called the *constrained interpretation graph*, and contains all the paths that correspond to the correct label sequence. The constrained interpretation graph is then sent to the Viterbi transformer which produces a graph G_{cvit} with a single path. This path is the "correct" path with the lowest penalty. Finally, a path scorer transformer takes G_{cvit}, and simply computes its cumulated penalty C_{cvit} by adding up the penalties along the path. The output of this GTN is the loss function for the current pattern:

$$E_{vit} = C_{cvit} \qquad (3)$$

The only label information that is required by the above system is the sequence of desired character labels. No knowledge of the correct segmentation is required on the part of the supervisor, since the system chooses among the segmentations in the interpretation graph the one that yields the lowest penalty.

The process of back-propagating gradients through the Viterbi training GTN is now described. As explained in section 1, the gradients must be propagated backwards through all modules of the GTN, in order to compute gradients in preceding modules and thereafter tune their parameters. Back-propagating gradients through the path scorer is quite straightforward. The partial derivatives of the loss function with respect to the individual penalties on the constrained Viterbi path G_{cvit} are equal to 1, since the loss function is simply the sum of those penalties. Back-propagating through the Viterbi Transformer is equally simple. The partial derivatives of E_{vit} with respect to the penalties on the arcs of the constrained graph G_c are 1 for those arcs that appear in the constrained Viterbi path G_{cvit}, and 0 for those that do not. Why is it legitimate to back-propagate through an essentially discrete function such as the Viterbi Transformer? The answer is that the Viterbi Transformer is nothing more than a collection of min functions and adders put together. It can be shown easily that gradients can be back-propagated through min functions without adverse effects. Back-propagation through the path selector transformer is similar to back-propagation through the Viterbi transformer. Arcs in G_{int} that appear in G_{c} have the same gradient as the corresponding arc in G_{c}, i.e. 1 or 0, depending on whether the arc appear in G_{cvit}. The other arcs, i.e. those that do not have an *alter ego* in G_{c} because they do not contain the right label have a gradient of 0. During the forward propagation through the recognition transformer, one instance of the recognizer for single character was created for each arc in the segmentation graph. The state of recognizer instances was stored. Since each arc penalty in G_{int} is produced by an individual output of a recognizer instance, we now have a gradient (1 or 0) for each output of each instance of the recognizer. Recognizer outputs that have a non zero gradient are part of the correct answer, and will therefore have their value pushed down. The gradients present on the recognizer outputs can be back-propagated through each recognizer instance. For each recognizer instance, we obtain a vector of partial derivatives of the loss function with respect to the recognizer instance parameters. All the recognizer instances share the same parameter vector, since they are merely clones of each other, therefore the full gradient of the loss function with respect to the recognizer's parameter vector is simply the sum of the gradient vectors produced by each recognizer instance. Viterbi training, though formulated differently, is often use in HMM-based speech recognition systems [26].

While it seems simple and satisfying, this training architecture has a flaw that can potentially be fatal. If the recognizer is a simple neural network with sigmoid output units, the minimum of the loss function is attained, not when the recognizer always gives the right answer, but when it ignores the input, and sets its output to a constant vector with small values for all the components. This is known as *the collapse problem*. The collapse only occurs if the recognizer outputs can simultaneously take their minimum value. If on the other hand the recognizer's output layer contains RBF units with fixed parameters, then there is no such trivial solution. This is due to the fact that a set of RBF with fixed distinct parameter vectors cannot simultaneously take their minimum value. In this case, the complete collapse described above does not occur. However, this does not totally prevent the occurrence of a milder collapse because the loss function still has a "flat spot" for a trivial solution with constant recognizer output. This flat spot is a saddle point, but it is attractive in almost all directions and is very difficult to get out of using gradient-based minimization procedures. If the parameters of the RBFs are allowed to adapt, then the collapse problems reappears because the RBF centers can all converge to a single vector, and the underlying neural network can learn to produce that vector, and ignore the input. A different kind of collapse occurs if the width of the RBFs are also allowed to adapt. The collapse only occurs if a trainable module such as a neural network feeds the RBFs. Another problem with Viterbi training is that the penalty of the answer cannot be used reliably as a measure of confidence because it does not take low-penalty (or high-scoring) competing answers into account. A simple way to address this problem and to avoid the collapse is to train the whole system with a discriminative loss function as described in the next section.

Discriminative Viterbi Training. The idea of discriminative Viterbi training is to not only minimize the cumulated penalty of the lowest penalty path with the correct interpretation, but also to somehow increase the penalty of competing and possibly incorrect paths that have a dangerously low penalty. This type of criterion is called *discriminative*, because it plays the good answers against the bad ones. Discriminative training procedures can be seen as attempting to build appropriate separating surfaces between classes rather than to model individual classes independently of each other.

One example of discriminative criterion is the difference between the penalty of the Viterbi path in the constrained graph, and the penalty of the Viterbi path in the (unconstrained) interpretation graph, i.e. the difference between the penalty of the best correct path, and the penalty of the best path (correct or incorrect). The corresponding GTN training architecture is shown in figure 8. The left side of the diagram is identical to the GTN used for non-discriminative Viterbi training. This loss function reduces the risk of collapse because it forces the recognizer to *increases* the penalty of wrongly recognized objects. Discriminative training can also be seen as another example of *error correction procedure*, which tends to minimize the difference between the desired output computed in the left half of the GTN in figure 8 and the actual output computed in the right half of figure 8.

Let the discriminative Viterbi loss function be denoted E_{dvit}, and let us call C_{cvit} the penalty of the Viterbi path in the constrained graph, and C_{vit} the penalty of the Viterbi path in the unconstrained interpretation graph:

$$E_{\text{dvit}} = C_{\text{cvit}} - C_{\text{vit}} \tag{4}$$

E_{dvit} is always positive since the constrained graph is a subset of the paths in the interpretation graph, and the Viterbi algorithm selects the path with the lowest total penalty. In the ideal case, the two paths C_{cvit} and C_{vit} coincide, and E_{dvit} is zero.

Back-propagating gradients through the discriminative Viterbi GTN adds some "negative" training to the previously described non-discriminative training. Figure 8 shows how the gradients are back-propagated. The left half is identical to the non-discriminative Viterbi training GTN, therefore the back-propagation is identical. The gradients back-propagated through the right half of the GTN are multiplied by -1, since C_{vit} contributes to the loss with a negative sign. Otherwise the process is similar to the left half. The gradients on arcs of G_{int} get positive contributions from the left half and negative contributions from the right half. The two contributions must be added, since the penalties on G_{int} arcs are sent to the two halves through a "Y" connection in the forward pass. Arcs in G_{int} that appear neither in G_{vit} nor in G_{cvit} have a gradient of zero. They do not contribute to the cost. Arcs that appear in both G_{vit} and G_{cvit} also have zero gradient. The -1 contribution from the right half cancels the the +1 contribution from the left half. In other words, when an arc is rightfully part of the answer, there is no gradient. If an arc appears in G_{cvit} but not in G_{vit}, the gradient is +1. The arc should have had a lower penalty to make it to G_{vit}. If an arc is in G_{vit} but not in G_{cvit}, the gradient is -1. The arc had a low penalty, but should have had a higher penalty since it is not part of the desired answer. Variations of this technique have been used for the speech recognition. Driancourt and Bottou [5] used a version of it where the loss function is saturated to a fixed value.

An important advantage of global and discriminative training is that learning focuses on the most important errors, and the system learns to integrate the ambiguities from the segmentation algorithm with the ambiguities of the character recognizer. There are other training procedures than the ones described here, some of which are described in [19]. Complex Graph Transformer modules that combine interpretation graphs with language models can be used to take linguistic constraints into account [19].

5   Conclusion

The methods described in this paper confirms what the history of Pattern Recognition has already shown repeatedly: finding ways to increase the role of learning and statistical estimation almost invariably improves the performance of recognition systems. For 2D shape recognition, Convolutional Neural Networks have been shown to eliminate the need for hand-crafted feature extractors. Replicated Convolutional Networks have been shown to handle fairly complex instances of the feature binding problem with a completely feed-forward, trained architecture instead of the more traditional combinatorial hypothesis testing methods. In situation where multiple hypothesis testing is unavoidable, trainable Graph Transformer Networks have been shown to reduce the need for hand-crafted heuristics, manual labeling, and manual parameter tuning in document recognition systems.

Globally-trained Graph Transformer Networks have been applied successfully to on-line handwriting recognition and check recognition [19]. The check recognition system based on this concept is used commercially in several banks across the US and reads millions of checks per day. The concepts and results in this paper help establish the usefulness and relevance of gradient-based minimization methods as a general organizing principle for learning in large systems. It is clear that Graph Transformer Networks can be applied to many situations where the domain knowledge or the state information can be represented by graphs. This is the case in many visual tasks where graphs can represent alternative interpretations of a scene, multiple instances of an object, or relationship between objects.

References

[1] Bengio, Y., LeCun, Y., Nohl, C., and Burges, C. (1995). LeRec: A NN/HMM Hybrid for On-Line Handwriting Recognition. *Neural Computation*, 7(5).

[2] Bottou, L. and Gallinari, P. (1991). A Framework for the Cooperation of Learning Algorithms. In Touretzky, D. and Lippmann, R., editors, *Advances in Neural Information Processing Systems*, volume 3, Denver. Morgan Kaufmann.

[3] Bottou, L., LeCun, Y., and Bengio, Y. (1997). Global Training of Document Processing Systems using Graph Transformer Networks. In *Proc. of Computer Vision and Pattern Recognition*, Puerto-Rico. IEEE.

[4] Burges, C. J. C. and Schoelkopf, B. (1997). Improving the accuracy and speed of support vector machines. In M. Mozer, M. J. and Petsche, T., editors, *Advances in Neural Information Processing Systems 9*. The MIT Press, Cambridge.

[5] Driancourt, X. and Bottou, L. (1991). MLP, LVQ and DP: Comparison & Cooperation. In *Proceedings of the International Joint Conference on Neural Networks*, Seattle.

[6] Drucker, H., Schapire, R., and Simard, P. (1993). Improving performance in neural networks using a boosting algorithm. In Hanson, S. J., Cowan, J. D., and Giles, C. L., editors, *Advances in Neural Information Processing Systems 5*, pages 42–49, San Mateo, CA. Morgan Kaufmann.

[7] Fukushima, K. (1975). Cognitron: A Self-Organizing Multilayered Neural Network. *Biological Cybernetics*, 20:121–136.

[8] Fukushima, K. and Miyake, S. (1982). Neocognitron: A new algorithm for pattern recognition tolerant of deformations and shifts in position. *Pattern Recognition*, 15:455–469.

[9] Hubel, D. H. and Wiesel, T. N. (1962). Receptive Fields, Binocular Interaction, and Functional Architecture in the Cat's Visual Cortex. *Journal of Physiology (London)*, 160:106–154.

[10] Keeler, J., Rumelhart, D., and Leow, W. K. (1991). Integrated segmentation and recognition of hand-printed numerals. In Lippmann, R. P., Moody, J. M., and Touretzky, D. S., editors, *Neural Information Processing Systems*, volume 3, pages 557–563. Morgan Kaufmann Publishers, San Mateo, CA.

[11] Lades, M., Vorbrüggen, J. C., Buhmann, J., and von der Malsburg, C. (1993). Distortion Invariant Object Recognition in the Dynamic Link Architecture. *IEEE Trans. Comp.*, 42(3):300–311.

[12] Lawrence, S., Giles, C. L., Tsoi, A. C., and Back, A. D. (1997). Face Recognition: A Convolutional Neural Network Approach. *IEEE Transactions on Neural Networks*, 8(1):98–113.

[13] LeCun, Y. (1986). Learning Processes in an Asymmetric Threshold Network. In Bienenstock, E., Fogelman-Soulié, F., and Weisbuch, G., editors, *Disordered systems and biological organization*, pages 233–240, Les Houches, France. Springer-Verlag.

[14] LeCun, Y. (1987). *Modeles connexionnistes de l'apprentissage (connectionist learning models)*. PhD thesis, Université P. et M. Curie (Paris 6).

[15] LeCun, Y. (1988). A theoretical framework for Back-Propagation. In Touretzky, D., Hinton, G., and Sejnowski, T., editors, *Proceedings of the 1988 Connectionist Models Summer School*, pages 21–28, CMU, Pittsburgh, Pa. Morgan Kaufmann.

[16] LeCun, Y. (1989). Generalization and Network Design Strategies. In Pfeifer, R., Schreter, Z., Fogelman, F., and Steels, L., editors, *Connectionism in Perspective*, Zurich, Switzerland. Elsevier.

[17] LeCun, Y., Boser, B., Denker, J. S., Henderson, D., Howard, R. E., Hubbard, W., and Jackel, L. D. (1989). Backpropagation Applied to Handwritten Zip Code Recognition. *Neural Computation*, 1(4):541–551.

[18] LeCun, Y., Boser, B., Denker, J. S., Henderson, D., Howard, R. E., Hubbard, W., and Jackel, L. D. (1990). Handwritten digit recognition with a back-propagation net-

work. In Touretzky, D., editor, *Advances in Neural Information Processing Systems 2 (NIPS*89)*, Denver, CO. Morgan Kaufman.

[19] LeCun, Y., Bottou, L., Bengio, Y., and Haffner, P. (1998). Gradient-Based Learning Applied to Document Recognition. *Proceedings of the IEEE*, (86)11:2278–2324.

[20] LeCun, Y., Kanter, I., and Solla, S. (1991). Eigenvalues of covariance matrices: application to neural-network learning. *Physical Review Letters*, 66(18):2396–2399.

[21] Martin, G. L. (1993). Centered-object integrated segmentation and recognition of overlapping hand-printed characters. *Neural Computation*, 5:419–429.

[22] Matan, O., Burges, C. J. C., LeCun, Y., and Denker, J. S. (1992). Multi-Digit Recognition Using a Space Displacement Neural Network. In Moody, J. M., Hanson, S. J., and Lippman, R. P., editors, *Neural Information Processing Systems*, volume 4. Morgan Kaufmann Publishers, San Mateo, CA.

[23] Mozer, M. C. (1991). *The perception of multiple objects: A connectionist approach.* MIT Press-Bradford Books, Cambridge, MA.

[24] Nowlan, S. and Platt, J. (1995). A Convolutional Neural Network Hand Tracker. In Tesauro, G., Touretzky, D., and Leen, T., editors, *Advances in Neural Information Processing Systems 7*, pages 901–908, San Mateo, CA. Morgan Kaufmann.

[25] Osuna, E., Freund, R., and Girosi, F. (1997). Training Support Vector Machines: an Application to Face Detection. In *Proceedings of CVPR'96*, pages 130–136. IEEE Computer Society Press.

[26] Rabiner, L. R. (1989). A Tutorial On Hidden Markov Models and Selected Applications in Speech Recognition. *Proceedings of the IEEE*, 77(2):257–286.

[27] Rowley, H. A., Baluja, S., and Kanade, T. (1996). Neural Network-Based Face Detection. In *Proceedings of CVPR'96*, pages 203–208. IEEE Computer Society Press.

[28] Rumelhart, D. E., Hinton, G. E., and Williams, R. J. (1986). Learning internal representations by error propagation. In *Parallel distributed processing: Explorations in the microstructure of cognition*, volume I, pages 318–362. Bradford Books, Cambridge, MA.

[29] Schapire, R. E. (1990). The strength of weak learnability. *Machine Learning*, 5(2):197–227.

[30] Vaillant, R., Monrocq, C., and LeCun, Y. (1994). Original approach for the localisation of objects in images. *IEE Proc on Vision, Image, and Signal Processing*, 141(4):245–250.

[31] Vapnik, V. N. (1995). *The Nature of Statistical Learning Theory.* Springer, New-York.

[32] Wang, J. and Jean, J. (1993). Multi-resolution neural networks for omnifont character recognition. In *Proceedings of International Conference on Neural Networks*, volume III, pages 1588–1593.

[33] Wolf, R. and Platt, J. (1994). Postal address block location using a convolutional locator network. In Cowan, J. D., Tesauro, G., and Alspector, J., editors, *Advances in Neural Information Processing Systems 6*, pages 745–752.

Author Index

Lecture Notes in Computer Science

For information about Vols. 1–1650
please contact your bookseller or Springer-Verlag

Vol. 1689: F. Solina, A. Leonardis (Eds.), Computer Analysis of Images and Patterns. Proceedings, 1999. XIV, 650 pages. 1999.

Vol. 1690: Y. Bertot, G. Dowek, A. Hirschowitz, C. Paulin, L. Théry (Eds.), Theorem Proving in Higher Order Logics. Proceedings, 1999. VIII, 359 pages. 1999.

Vol. 1691: J. Eder, I. Rozman, T. Welzer (Eds.), Advances in Databases and Information Systems. Proceedings, 1999. XIII, 383 pages. 1999.

Vol. 1692: V. Matoušek, P. Mautner, J. Ocelíková, P. Sojka (Eds.), Text, Speech and Dialogue. Proceedings, 1999. XI, 396 pages. 1999. (Subseries LNAI).

Vol. 1693: P. Jayanti (Ed.), Distributed Computing. Proceedings, 1999. X, 357 pages. 1999.

Vol. 1694: A. Cortesi, G. Filé (Eds.), Static Analysis. Proceedings, 1999. VIII, 357 pages. 1999.

Vol. 1695: P. Barahona, J.J. Alferes (Eds.), Progress in Artificial Intelligence. Proceedings, 1999. XI, 385 pages. 1999. (Subseries LNAI).

Vol. 1696: S. Abiteboul, A.-M. Vercoustre (Eds.), Research and Advanced Technology for Digital Libraries. Proceedings, 1999. XII, 497 pages. 1999.

Vol. 1697: J. Dongarra, E. Luque, T. Margalef (Eds.), Recent Advances in Parallel Virtual Machine and Message Passing Interface. Proceedings, 1999. XVII, 551 pages. 1999.

Vol. 1698: M. Felici, K. Kanoun, A. Pasquini (Eds.), Computer Safety, Reliability and Security. Proceedings, 1999. XVIII, 482 pages. 1999.

Vol. 1699: S. Albayrak (Ed.), Intelligent Agents for Telecommunication Applications. Proceedings, 1999. IX, 191 pages. 1999. (Subseries LNAI).

Vol. 1700: R. Stadler, B. Stiller (Eds.), Active Technologies for Network and Service Management. Proceedings, 1999. XII, 299 pages. 1999.

Vol. 1701: W. Burgard, T. Christaller, A.B. Cremers (Eds.), KI-99: Advances in Artificial Intelligence. Proceedings, 1999. XI, 311 pages. 1999. (Subseries LNAI).

Vol. 1702: G. Nadathur (Ed.), Principles and Practice of Declarative Programming. Proceedings, 1999. X, 434 pages. 1999.

Vol. 1703: L. Pierre, T. Kropf (Eds.), Correct Hardware Design and Verification Methods. Proceedings, 1999. XI, 366 pages. 1999.

Vol. 1704: Jan M. Żytkow, J. Rauch (Eds.), Principles of Data Mining and Knowledge Discovery. Proceedings, 1999. XIV, 593 pages. 1999. (Subseries LNAI).

Vol. 1705: H. Ganzinger, D. McAllester, A. Voronkov (Eds.), Logic for Programming and Automated Reasoning. Proceedings, 1999. XII, 397 pages. 1999. (Subseries LNAI).

Vol. 1706: J. Hatcliff, T. Æ. Mogensen, P. Thiemann (Eds.), Lectures on Partial Evaluation. Proceedings, 1998. IX, 433 pages. 1999. (Subseries LNAI).

Vol. 1707: H.-W. Gellersen (Ed.), Handheld and Ubiquitous Computing. Proceedings, 1999. XII, 390 pages. 1999.

Vol. 1708: J.M. Wing, J. Woodcock, J. Davies (Eds.), FM'99 – Formal Methods. Proceedings Vol. I, 1999. XVIII, 937 pages. 1999.

Vol. 1709: J.M. Wing, J. Woodcock, J. Davies (Eds.), FM'99 – Formal Methods. Proceedings Vol. II, 1999. XVIII, 937 pages. 1999.

Vol. 1710: E.-R. Olderog, B. Steffen (Eds.), Correct System Design. XIV, 417 pages. 1999.

Vol. 1711: N. Zhong, A. Skowron, S. Ohsuga (Eds.), New Directions in Rough Sets, Data Mining, and Granular-Soft Computing. Proceedings, 1999. XIV, 558 pages. 1999. (Subseries LNAI).

Vol. 1712: H. Boley, A Tight, Practical Integration of Relations and Functions. XI, 169 pages. 1999. (Subseries LNAI).

Vol. 1713: J. Jaffar (Ed.), Principles and Practice of Constraint Programming – CP'99. Proceedings, 1999. XII, 493 pages. 1999.

Vol. 1714: M.T. Pazienza (Eds.), Information Extraction. IX, 165 pages. 1999. (Subseries LNAI).

Vol. 1715: P. Perner, M. Petrou (Eds.), Machine Learning and Data Mining in Pattern Recognition. Proceedings, 1999. VIII, 217 pages. 1999. (Subseries LNAI).

Vol. 1716: K.Y. Lam, E. Okamoto, C. Xing (Eds.), Advances in Cryptology – ASIACRYPT'99. Proceedings, 1999. XI, 414 pages. 1999.

Vol. 1717: Ç. K. Koç, C. Paar (Eds.), Cryptographic Hardware and Embedded Systems. Proceedings, 1999. XI, 353 pages. 1999.

Vol. 1718: M. Diaz, P. Owezarski, P. Sénac (Eds.), Interactive Distributed Multimedia Systems and Telecommunication Services. Proceedings, 1999. XI, 386 pages. 1999.

Vol. 1719: M. Fossorier, H. Imai, S. Lin, A. Poli (Eds.), Applied Algebra, Algebraic Algorithms and Error-Correcting Codes. Proceedings. 1999. XIII, 510 pages. 1999.

Vol. 1721: S. Arikawa, K. Furukawa (Eds.), Discovery Science. Proceedings, 1999. XI, 374 pages. 1999. (Subseries LNAI).

Vol. 1722: A. Middeldorp, T. Sato (Eds.), Functional and Logic Programming. Proceedings, 1999. X, 369 pages. 1999.

Vol. 1723: R. France, B. Rumpe (Eds.), UML'99 – The Unified Modeling Language99. XVII, 724 pages. 1999.

Vol. 1726: V. Varadharajan, Y. Mu (Eds.), Information and Communication Security. Proceedings, 1999. XI, 325 pages. 1999.

Vol. 1727: P.P. Chen, D.W. Embley, J. Kouloumdjian, S.W. Liddle, J.F. Roddick (Eds.), Advances in Conceptual Modeling. Proceedings, 1999. XI, 389 pages. 1999.

Vol. 1728: J. Akoka, M. Bouzeghoub, I. Comyn-Wattiau, E. Métais (Eds.), Conceptual Modeling – ER '99. Proceedings, 1999. XIV, 540 pages. 1999.

Vol. 1729: M. Mambo, Y. Zheng (Eds.), Information Security. Proceedings, 1999. IX, 277 pages. 1999.

Vol. 1734: H. Hellwagner, A. Reinefeld (Eds.), SCI: Scalable Coherent Interface. XXI, 490 pages. 1999.

Vol. 1564: M. Vazirgiannis, Interactive Multimedia Documents. XIII, 161 pages. 1999.

Vol. 1591: D.J. Duke, I. Herman, S. Marshall, PREMO: A Framework for Multimedia Middleware. XII, 254 pages. 1999.